The H
of Crim

The Harms of Crime Media

Essays on the Perpetuation of Racism, Sexism and Class Stereotypes

Edited by
DENISE L. BISSLER *and*
JOAN L. CONNERS

McFarland & Company, Inc., Publishers
Jefferson, North Carolina, and London

LIBRARY OF CONGRESS CATALOGUING-IN-PUBLICATION DATA

The harms of crime media : essays on the perpetuation of racism,
    sexism and class stereotypes / edited by Denise L. Bissler and
Joan L. Conners.
        p.   cm.
    Includes bibliographical references and index.

    ISBN 978-0-7864-6380-0
    softcover : acid free paper ∞

    1. Mass media and crime — United States.   2. Crime in mass
media.   3. Racism in mass media.   4. Sexism in mass media.
5. Social classes in mass media.   6. Victims of crimes in mass
media.   7. Detective and mystery television programs — United
States.   8. Television broadcasting of news — Objectivity — United
States.   9. Mass media and criminal justice — United States.
I. Bissler, Denise L., 1971–   II. Conners, Joan L.
P96.C742U638   2012
364.2'54 — dc23   2012005684

BRITISH LIBRARY CATALOGUING DATA ARE AVAILABLE

Front cover images © 2012 Shutterstock

Manufactured in the United States of America

McFarland & Company, Inc., Publishers
    Box 611, Jefferson, North Carolina 28640
    www.mcfarlandpub.com

Table of Contents

Preface.. 1

Introduction: Media, Crime and Hegemony.—GARY W. POTTER and
VICTOR E. KAPPELER... 3

Constructing and Reconstructing Female Sexual Assault Victims
Within the Media.—VENESSA GARCIA 18

The Social Construction of Serial Murder Victims: A Multivariate
Level Analysis.—JANELLE M. ELIASSON-NANNINI and DEIRDRE
SOMMERLAD-ROGERS 38

"These kids are killing each other": Gender-Neutral vs. Gender-
Specific Framing in the School Shooting Media Discourse.
—BRIAN KNOP 53

The Social Construction of Methamphetamine in the Print Media.
—TERESA ROACH 64

Media vs. Reality: Who Is the Real Female Sex Offender?—BRIDGET
A. HEPNER-WILLIAMSON 78

Monstrous, Demonic and Evil: Media Constructs of Women Who
Kill.—KATE WHITELEY.. 91

Gangs, Politics and Media: Lessons from the New York Chapter of
the Almighty Latin King and Queen Nation.—LOUIS KONTOS......... 111

Inequalities in *CSI: Crime Scene Investigation*: Stereotypes in the
CSI Investigators.—DENISE L. BISSLER and JOAN L. CONNERS......... 127

"Who are you?" Shared Responsibility and the Victims of *CSI:
Crime Scene Investigation*.—KATHERINE FOSS 151

Macho Cops, Corner Boys and Soldiers: The Construction of Race
and Masculinity on HBO's *The Wire*.—LINDA WALDRON and
CHERYL CHAMBERS.. 171

Fictionalized Women in Trouble: An Exploration of the Television
Crime Drama *CSI: Miami*.—SARAH RIZUN 190

v

Ripped from the Headlines: The Depiction of Sexual Orientation–Based Hate Crimes in Television Crime Dramas.— NICHOLAS GUITTAR 208

Crime News Sources and Crime Views: The Relationship Between News Media Exposure Patterns and Whites' Opinions about Criminal Justice Issues.—ALICIA D. SIMMONS. 224

Conclusion: Cultivating Bias in the Media.— JACK LEVIN and ERIC MADFIS 239

About the Contributors. 249
Index. 253

Preface

It's impossible to scan headlines, in print or online or watch prime-time television without encountering numerous media reports, factual and fictional, discussing some aspect of crime. Headlines announce missing children, suspects arrested or tried in court, victims reacting to developments in a case, as well as crime statistics. Television dramas rely heavily on crime stories, often those "ripped from the headlines" or inspired by real-life cases, as the basis for their plots; in many such programs, a crime is committed, and a suspect is identified, apprehended and brought to justice in just one hour. This is just one "unreality" portrayed in television crime drama.

What is more concerning, and less obvious in mediated portrayals, is the unreality seen in news coverage and fictional interpretation of crime stories with respect to the gender, race, and class of those involved. This work does not offer a direct comparison of U.S. demographics to mediated portrayals of crime, but rather discusses particular examples of inequalities and stereotypes in crime media and considers their implications. Even though some of these portrayals are fictional, they may influence the public's expectations about crime in reality and their beliefs about real-world crime. For example, we know from decades of cultivation research that those who have higher rates of television viewing have a greater fear of being victimized. If we look at this further in terms of representations of individuals with respect to gender, race, and/or class, those perceptions of society may be even more disconnected from reality.

Much of the criminological literature on crime media focuses on the mis-representations of crime and criminals, the perpetuation of crime myths, and comparisons between media portrayals and reality. Criminologists have shown that the media portrayal of crime distorts reality to make people worry about the least common crime and increases fear of crime. Media literature often analyzes portrayals of race, class and gender inequality but not necessarily in crime media. The media literature has shown that stereotypes of race, class and gender are still present in much media today even in this time of "political cor-rectness." This work focuses on inequality issues and race, class and gender stereotypes as specifically portrayed in crime media. Crime media is widely popular, widely viewed, and, as stated above, may affect one's view of criminals, crime, and crime fighters.

This collection includes original analyses of race, class, and gender inequality in crime and media representations from the perspective of crime news as well as crime dramas. News stories are crafted and revised before publication and broadcast; headlines and leads are written to capture readers' attention. The process of agenda setting in newsroom decision making relies on particular formulas of coverage, many which emphasize crime news in local communities (hence the phrase "If it bleeds, it leads"). How an individual news story is framed will focus on particular aspects of the crime, and reinforce themes about crime, which will also reinforce beliefs about crime in news audiences. We see in this collection of essays that even though news organizations strive for objectivity and representativeness, the social construction of different individuals related to crime stories reinforces stereotypes, especially those related to gender and race.

The popularity of crime dramas such as *Law and Order* and *CSI: Crime Scene Investigation* is evident by the number of years these programs have remained on the air, as well as by the number of spin-offs they have inspired. In the representations of crime, the perpetrators, the victims, the investigators and even those involved in the criminal justice process, we find stereotypes being reinforced.

We are honored to have edited this collection of such varied research on these topics. We are also honored to have the introduction and conclusion of this collection authored by leading scholars on topics of crime and mass media. Gary W. Potter and Victor E. Kappeler offer the introduction with a focus on issues of hegemony and the reinforcement of stereotypes in crime media content. Jack Levin and Eric Madfis conclude our collection with a discussion of the cultivation effect and how perceptions of crime may be influenced by news and fictional representations.

Introduction: Media, Crime and Hegemony

GARY W. POTTER AND
VICTOR E. KAPPELER

This collection of scholarly essays confronts two immense institutionalized orders of social life today: the media and crime. Individually these institutions present an immense challenge to confronting and understanding the order they reproduce; collectively they are nearly insurmountable. At the least the interplay of these two institutions and their social realities creates a dangerous world, full of risk, with stereotyped "others" to both fear and at the same time perversely entertain us through a flood of mediated images emanating from our televisions, computers, books, newspapers and magazines, movies and even popular music. These mediated images instruct us on the seemingly natural order of the social world. It is through an incessant institutionalized attack on our senses that we come to understand what Jock Young calls the vertigo of modern society. But the irony of all this is that our fears, prejudices, stereotypes, and pervasive impulses toward meanness and retribution are something less than real. They are created, mediated images offered to us as news and entertainments by a handful of immense and very motivated global corporations bound to state power.

The Media and Crime

The research literature leaves no doubt that media representations of crime, whether for news or entertainment purposes, or both, has exaggerated public fears about crime and generated ever-increasing support for repressive and punitive crime control policies (Gerbner 1995; Brown 2003; Jewkes 2004; Greer 2003; Wykes 2001). The fact that these representations are presented to us as merely "news" (some unbiased presentation of information) or "entertainment" (a harmless collection of images for enjoyment) makes them even more effective at directing social thought and policy. The confluence of these institutionalized products makes their claims on reality even more convincing.

3

These mediated representations creep into our very conception of criminality and the appropriate social response to it.

The distinction between fact and fiction is becoming increasingly tenuous in media presentations about crime with the advent of infotainment or what is euphemistically referred to as "reality television" (Beckett and Sasson 2000, 111–116; Fishman and Cavender 1998; Leishman and Mason 2002; Surette 1998). Quasi-documentaries, like *Cops*, have increasingly shown us highly selective video images of "actual" incidents, creating an ever more distorted view of crime and policing (Kooistra, Mahoney, and Westervelt 1998). In this version of reality policing is one continuous high-speed chase of criminals; judges hand down snap decisions of justice from the bench; and prisons are filled with only the most violent of offenders. The justice system has used this blurring of fact and fiction to build support for their initiatives and to highlight their own version of serious criminality (Mawby 2001, 2002, 2003). Today the media and the criminal justice system have become symbiotic partners thereby blurring fact and fiction to the point at which discerning one from the other is impossible (Manning 1998; Ferrell 1998; Brown 2003).

Crime as News

There are two indisputable facts related to the mass media's portrayal of crime in both news and entertainment formats. First, crime sells. It attracts viewers and readers, advertising revenue, and consumer subscriptions to newspapers, magazine, satellite and cable services, as well as purchasers of movie tickets. Second, the mediated knowledge produced through mass media entertainment and infotainment bears virtually no relationship to the reality of crime itself or the functioning of the criminal justice system.

There is little question that crime is the most popular subject for both print and broadcast news outlets. While crime is covered more heavily in broadcast mediums than in print outlets, the research clearly shows that crime news is the most common topic in all mediums, in all markets, and on all media platforms (Cumberbatch, Woods, and Maguire 1995). Graber found that crime made up between 22 and 28 percent of the newspaper stories, 20 percent of the stories covered on all local news programs, and 12 to 13 percent of the stories on network evening news program (Graber 1980). A meta-analysis of research on news coverage of crime found overall coverage from all sources to be about 33.5 percent (Marsh 1991).

More recent studies find a remarkable persistence for crime domination of news stories. In research tracking crime stories in the evening news presentation of 100 local television stations it was found that 72 of those stations led their news programming with a crime story and that 33 percent of all stories covered on the evening news were crime-related (Klite, Bardwell, and Salzman 1997).

The coverage of crime in news formats also exhibits a consistent pattern of misinformation, sensationalism and exaggeration. For example, there is an over-emphasis on violent crime and an under-emphasis on property crimes. In the United States there is a 9 to 1 ratio of property to violent crimes, but a 4 to 1 ratio of violent to property crimes in news reports (Marsh 1991). Other research studies confirm this massive over-representation of violent and sex crimes (Chiricos, Eschholz, and Gertz 1997; Beckett and Sasson 2000; Greer 2003).

Crime coverage in newspapers and local news shows overwhelmingly focus on ethnic minority perpetrators and suspects from the lowest socio-economic groups (Beckett and Sasson 2000). "Reality" television shows dealing with crime and law enforcement have even a greater emphasis on stories with young, underclass, ethnic minority suspects (Beckett and Sasson 2000; Fishman and Cavender 1998; Kooistra et al. 1998; Oliver and Armstrong 1998).

News coverage dramatically exaggerates the crime risks faced by economically privileged white people, as well as greatly over representing women, children, or older people as victims (Chermak 1995; Chiricos, et al. 1997; Beckett and Sasson 2000; Greer 2003; Reiner, Livingstone, and Allen 2003; Peelo et al. 2004).

There has been a considerable body of scholarly research related to the relationship between fear of crime and media influences (Barzagan 1994; Heath and Gilbert 1996). By far the most methodologically sound and rigorous research on the subject involved a survey of Florida media consumers in which the effect of media crime images on fear of crime was isolated, with the research controlling for respondents' prior victimization experience and perceptions of levels of safety in their communities (Chiricos, Padgett, and Gertz 2000). That research found that exposure to news media coverage of crime significantly increased the subjects' fear of crime. In addition, that research showed that media effects were twice as powerful as personal victimization experiences in raising respondents' fear of crime (Chiricos et al. 2000). In a similar vein, Beckett's (1997) research found that public concern about crime was totally unrelated to crime rates. Instead, the public's apprehension was directly related to media portrayals of crime and drug use. In addition, the public's perception of a serious crime problem was found to be directly related to "the number of speeches, statements, policy initiatives, or summaries pertaining to crime ... made by federal officials and reported in the mass media" (Beckett 1997, 116). The conclusion is simple. The fear of crime and much of their support for punitive crime policies among U.S. citizens is largely a result of a crime spectacle, a carnival of crime, paraded before them by the mass media. In essence, media representations of crime are detached from the empirical reality of crime.

Because news reports concern isolated incidents presented without context there is virtually no reporting in the media on crime patterns or the possible causes of crime (Barlow 1998; Beckett and Sasson 2000; Greer 2003). The prime example of this "out of context" reporting is found in stories dealing with rape and sexual assault. Dramatic events, a focus on personalities, and demonization of the perpetrator, the victim or both shield the consumer from considerations of power and gender relations reproduced in society (Gregory and Lees 1999; Greer 2003).

Of course, the exception to all of this is in the media's handling of stories related to corporate or white-collar crime. Crimes of the powerful are rarely mentioned and the little coverage that does exist is in specialist print or broad cost sources, usually dealing with financial issues. Even when the stories are reported they are handled in a manner that makes these crimes seems different from other crime (Levi 2001; Stephenson-Burton 1995; Tombs and Whyte 2001). Outside of the specialized financial and media outlets corporate and white-collar crimes are rarely mentioned unless there is a salacious personal scandal attendant to the actual story. About two million people are killed each year simply because they went to work, a far higher number than the 16,000–17,000 deaths resulting from homicide. But with the exception of major catastrophes like the Bhopal gas leak which killed thousands in 1984, crimes resulting in death from corporate negligence are of little interest to the corporate media (Tombs and Whyte 2001).

The media treat crime news with a double-standard that is astonishing. They are loath to report on corporate wrongdoing and crime, but they actively create crime waves on the streets which simply do not exist. The media play a key role in creating a narrow social definition of crime. To the media, crime is simply a pathological malady of improperly socialized individuals. Corporate crime is too complex to be reported in simple terms with compelling visuals. In fact, the media are loath to report corporate "wrongdoing" as crime. Instead of crime and negligence, words like disaster and accident are used in the rare cases that corporate malfeasance is addressed at all. Sometimes corporate killing and maiming is just dismissed as an "act of God" (Punch 1996). It need not be pointed out that the media is in fact a child of corporatization and the media's profits from advertising emanate from corporate coffers. But, in the end the media do much more than ignore corporate crime; they actually manage and control damaging information about the corporate world (Herman and Chomsky 1988).

Crime as Fiction

It seems questionable to contrast news coverage of crime-related topics to fictional crime stories in entertainment media. As Jewkes notes about crime news, "We have to conclude that media images are not reality; they are a version of reality that is culturally determined" (Jewkes 2004, 37). But as we shall see, the images of crime in fictional accounts intended to entertain differ very little from the "fictions" of the news media. Casting crime fictions, whether emanating from the media or the literary world, as "culture" masks another important aspect of the production of crime. Crime representations are not merely some mindlessly selected aspect of a "naturally" occurring culture; they are artifacts of the political economy.

There is no way to know exactly how many pot-boiling paperback books with crime as their central theme have been sold. The best estimate is that between 1945 and 1984 about 10 million such books were sold (Mandel 1984). Prime-time television offers viewers a program menu in which about 25 percent of all entertainment programming is delivered in the form of a crime show (Reiner, Livingstone, and Allen 2001). In addition, a significant portion of the storylines in shows that are strictly crime shows have crimes as a central plotline. Movies show a similar distribution. On average about 20 percent of all movies released annually are in the crime genre, but about half of all films have significant crime content in their plots (Rafter 2000). As is the case with crime news, crime films feature murder and other violent crimes in the overwhelming majority of films (Reiner et al. 2001). Violent crime is presented as an ever-present, if not inevitable, threat, rather than a relatively rare occurrence. Crime is also presented as a horrifying and dramatic event which will be dealt with by police heroes, almost always frustrated in the quest for justice by excessive concerns over human and civil rights (Reiner 2003; Rafter 2000; Wilson 2000; Leishman and Mason 2002).

The research shows that about two-thirds of crimes portrayed on prime-time television dramas are murders, aggravated assaults, or armed robberies (Lichter, Lichter, and Rothman 1994; Beckett and Sasson 2000). According to the FBI's UCR the actual victimization rate for violent crimes is about 3 out every 1,000 people. The TV violent crime victimization rate is 114 out of every 1,000 characters (Lichter et al. 1994). Most actual murders result from masculinity contests between young men or as the outcome of domestic violence (Dorling 2004). Real murder involves alcohol, rage or fear and no element of premeditation or rational calculation. Murder in fiction is almost always premeditated and carefully planned and motivated by pure, wanton greed (Lichter et al. 1994; Allen, Livingstone, and Reiner 1998).

Rape and sexual assault are also presented in media fiction in a manner totally at odds with reality. In the "real world" the vast majority of rapes are perpetrated by intimates or acquaintance but in television and movie fiction rape invariably is committed by psychopathic strangers and usually includes torture or murder (Greer 2003; Jewkes 2004).

While property crime is grossly underestimated in fictional media accounts, when it is involved in a plot line the crime bears no relationship to real property crimes. The typical property crime involves no perpetrator-victim interaction, results in minimal financial losses and is an unplanned, opportunistic event. In crime fiction almost all property crimes are elaborately plotted, well-planned events involving highly skilled offenders (Lichter et al. 1994). In reality, offenders are overwhelmingly young males of lower socio-economic status. In fiction property criminals are invariably middle-aged, white males with significant economic resources (Lichter et al. 1994; Reiner et al. 2001).

In addition, film and television accounts of crime offer intense, graphic and emotionally charged images of victimization. The suffering of the victim is, of course, ameliorated by functionaries of the criminal justice system who are both supportive and retributive (Allen et al. 1998; Reiner et al. 2000, 2001).

The Media and Stereotyping

The media tendency to portray crime as a series of shocking, dramatic, and visually graphic events diverts public attention from politics, policies, and social structures which are at the heart of those stories (Barak 1994; Manning 2001). Despite the introduction of many new media outlets and the use of newer communication platforms, the many outlets for media representation have not resulted in a diversity of content (Barak 1994). The media continue to deliver a mediated, homogenized version of reality that reifies the status quo and avoids controversy. The audience remains uninformed and ignorant about the reality of crime and preconceived racist, sexist and classist stereotypes are reinforced, building support for the criminalization of groups along the lines of race, class and gender.

As Croteau and Hoynes (2005) point out, this spectacle is not created by accident. Several distinct elements go into the selection of topics and the production process of these mediated images designed to produce a saleable, profitable product. First, the media do not select representative crimes for infotainment; rather they select the most dramatic, shocking and scandalous stories to hold the audience's attention and provoke an emotional reaction. Even the handling of post–9/11 topics was dramatized and sensationalized:

> However, claims that nothing was the same after the attack proved to be vastly overstated.... Indeed, some critics argue that the subsequent "war on terror" itself became just another sensationalized media story [Croteau and Hoynes 2005, 227].

News coverage of 9/11 was full of drama and compelling video images. But there was little or no discussion of the causes of terrorism and no discussion of U.S. foreign policy decisions that may have led terrorists to target the United States.

The media-selected crime stories also are those stories that have a "negative tone" (Croteau and Hoynes 2005, 218). Shocking and outrageous stories take precedence over the mundane day-to-day facts of crime and criminal justice. Dramatic and sensationalistic crime stories are image driven. Compelling pictures make the story. But those shocking images and often equally shocking words actually disengage the audience from any thoughtful consideration of the issue being presented.

The mass media, whether for entertainment or as news items, present crime as a series of isolated but seemingly pervasive events. Crime stories are parsimonious, dramatic and without context. Violence as an issue is seldom if ever addressed. But a violent crime as a spectacle is repeated incessantly (Croteau and Hoynes 2005).

In addition to portraying crime as a series of dramatic and horrendous isolated incidents, the media tend to place a heavy emphasis on personalities, focusing on the deviance of perpetrators and the tragedies of victims. "Human" profiles and dramatic events substitute for substantive examinations of crime as a public issue or a social problem (Croteau and Hoynes 2005).

The portrayal of crime, whether in fictional or nonfictional media presentations, is superficial at best. Isolated events are quickly replaced by another dose of isolated events. The dramatic and disturbing images of crime and criminals come to us at such a fast pace and in such immense quantity that it is impossible to make sense of them. Because crime events are presented in brief and isolated portrayals, context is nonexistent (Croteau and Hoynes 2005).

The end result of these media portrayals is a reinforcement of ethnic, gender, and class stereotypes, cobbled together in brief, dramatic, and disturbing images and words. Rather than understanding crime or criminal justice, the public reacts with the same emotion which has driven the media portrayals. Those prejudices, stereotypes and almost cartoon-like images are made clear by the research presented in this volume. This collection first presents discussions of such issues from crime news, then other arguments from crime fiction.

The stereotypes that develop from crime news sources focus on victims of crime, as well as on the alleged perpetrators. For example, Venessa Garcia's research presented in "Constructing and Reconstructing Female Sexual Assault Victims within the Media" illustrates how female sexual assault victims are subjected to both the personalization and negativity of media images related to crime. Unless victims of rape and sexual assault are attacked by strangers while engaged in "respectable" undertakings, the same stereotyped images of the victim as both promiscuous and disingenuous are pervasive in the coverage of sexual assaults.

The media process of stereotyping, personalizing and demonizing some crime victims while at the same time selecting others for sympathetic portrayals is well represented in Janelle M. Eliasson-Nannini and Deirdre Sommerlad-Rogers' essay, "The Social Construction of Serial Murder Victims: A Multivariate Level Analysis." They explore the idea of noteworthy victims, pointing out that women, whites, the elderly and children get far more coverage of their victimization than men, the poor or minority group members. Their analysis shows that coverage of victims of serial murderers is directly related to the victims' personal characteristics.

Certainly gender representations by the media reinforce the gender stereotypes so familiar in a hyper-masculine, patriarchal society. As Brian Knop proves in "'These kids are killing each other': Gender-Neutral vs. Gender-Specific Framing in the School Shooting Media Discourse," 81 percent of references made to shooters use gender-neutral language. That representation obscures, perhaps quite deliberately, the fact that this form of violence is clearly gendered. It also obscures the victimization of girls and women at the hands of men.

The ability of the media to set the public agenda by highlighting, exaggerating and sensationalizing a crime theme is explored in Teresa Roach's "The Social Construction of Methamphetamine in the Print Media." While amphetamine use is not widespread in the U.S. it is heavily covered by the news media. The news media focuses on perceived harms related to the drug, and links amphetamine use to a litany of other social problems. As Roach shows the media creates an emotional reaction to a socially constructed danger, which allows them to exploit amphetamine use as a scapegoat for other problems, allowing structural causes to be safely ignored.

Bridget A. Hepner-Williamson's research presented in "Media vs. Reality: Who Is the Real Female Sex Offender?" looks at the media stereotyping prevalent in the coverage of female offenders. The striking differences in media coverage of two female sex offenders presented by Hepner show the impact of gender, but also of class and social position on media depictions of women.

When women are the perpetrators of dramatic and sensational crimes, stereotyped gender roles are even more evident, as Kate Whiteley shows in "Monstrous, Demonic and Evil: Media Constructs of Women Who Kill." As Whiteley points out when women step outside of their socially constructed roles as loving, nurturing mothers and wife, they are often vilified in the media as "mad" or "bad." In the case of female perpetrators gendered stereotypes are compounded by racial stereotypes. Black female offenders are not only mad or bad, but also hostile, dirty, aggressive and hyper sexed.

The role of racial stereotyping and the media's promotion of moral panics are explored in Louis Kontos' "Gangs, Politics and Media: Lessons from the New York Chapter of the Almighty Latin King and Queen Nation." The media's imprecision in the use of the term "gang" and its reluctance to explore broader social issues related to that concept are highlighted by Kontos' essay. The inability of news reports to explore the meaning of race, cultural symbols, and community folklore also plays a key role in stereotyping both "gangs" and minorities.

Gender representations in the fictional television series *CSI* were the subject of several compelling pieces of research. Bissler and Conners in "Inequalities in *CSI: Crime Scene Investigation:* Stereotypes in the series *CSI* Investigators" find that male characters on the show are consistently portrayed as detached and strong, while female characters are consistently nurturing, concerned with minor issues, and almost prudish. The women are frequently confronted with inappropriate language and suggestive conversations and actions. But as attractive, career-driven functionaries they simply ignore sexual harassment. Personal and family problems of female characters are trivialized. Rather than using logic, the women in the show react to situations emotionally. Male characters are competitive and driven to achieve success. They often find the work performed by their female co-workers to be unimportant and find the commitment to details of the investigation by women agents to be tiresome and an unneeded burden.

Katherine Foss's examination of victim portrayal on *CSI* in "'Who are you?' Shared Responsibility and the Victims of *CSI: Crime Scene Investigation*" also demonstrates the prevalence of gender stereotypes. She found that myths about victim precipitation are common. The stories suggest that women need to change their lifestyles rather than that society needs to understand male violence. "Deviant" victim lifestyles are portrayed in curious spectacles with humanity stripped from the victim. In the media world of crime even victims are reduced to an iconic order-reproducing representation.

Race and gender also play a complex role in Linda Waldron and Cheryl Chambers's "Macho Cops, Corner Boys and Soldiers: The Construction of Race and Masculinity on HBO's *The Wire*." The authors point to the differences in depictions of white and black masculinity in the plots. White masculinity is related to control over people and black masculinity is depicted as resistance to control. Masculinity is also depicted in terms of respect, loyalty, revenge and violence. A particularly interesting finding of the research was the role of guns as symbols of power and therefore means of control, and means of resistance.

And as Sarah Rizun's research tells us in her essay, "Fictionalized Women in Trouble: An Exploration of the Television Crime Drama *CSI: Miami*," criminalized women are also presented in a way that is directly contradictory to both the social status of women and the facts of female criminality. Female offenders on *CSI* are economically well-off, attractive, libertines whose violent acts are unreasonable and totally at odds with the gendered view of women and their roles.

In those relatively rare storylines in television crime dramas involving portrayals of LGB individuals as victims, Nicholas Guittar ("Ripped from the Headlines: The Depiction of Sexual Orientation–Based Hate Crimes in Television Crime Dramas") finds the same kind of stereotyping in both character development and storylines. Typical storylines revolve around either "coming out"; AIDS/HIV infections; or repressed sexuality. Characters are often depicted as overly sexual gay males, men-hating lesbians, or closeted, sexually repressed persons striking out as a means of dealing with their confused overall sexual identity. Guittar's research demonstrates the media's promotion of conservative values in relation to sexual orientation by depicting homosexuality as a strictly moral choice and extolling the virtues of heterosexism.

The media's ability to set the crime agenda and its impact is explored by Alicia D. Simmons in "Crime News Sources and Crime Views: The Relationship between News Media Exposure Patterns and Whites' Opinions about Criminal Justice Issues." Simmons' research makes several important points about public beliefs related to crime and the criminal justice system. First, she finds that exposure to newspaper and local television station coverage is associated with perception that the crime rate is continually rising and the crime problem is getting worse. Watching greater amounts of local television newscasts is also associated with increased spending on crime issues and police. Watching local television is also related to support for the death penalty. Simmons suggests that heavy doses of crime news covered by local television and the episodic reporting style, which provides no context for understanding crime or criminal justice policies, are keys to explaining these relationships.

Furthermore, as Jack Levin and Eric Madfis point out in the "Conclusion: Cultivating Bias in the Media," in the "infotainment" era, the lines between reality and fiction are blurred as both news and dramas have to compete for ratings. Media depictions of crime often misinform the viewer which affects perceptions of the amount of crime, likelihood of victimization, and fear of certain types of perpetrators and types of crime. Levin and Madfis emphasize the importance of focusing on race, class, and gender stereotypes in crime media because it reinforces bias toward certain groups for example by overstating their participation in crime and ignoring victimization rates (young, African-American males). Both crime and media depictions of crime are complex entities and are steeped in social, historical, and political tradition. Levin and Madfis conclude that simply changing depictions will not change the structural benefit of these stereotypes nor the cultural support for such views. Changes must come in the structural, cultural, and political realms.

The Process and Politics of Crime News

The majority of newspapers certainly exhibit a conservative political ideology. Individual reporters, no matter what their own political leaning, operate within this context. As a result the press inculcates values which are not offensive to those with economic and political power and not at odds with the consensus views of their reader. Stuart Hall referred to this as a "world at one with itself" (Hall 1970, 1056).

Reporters, whether dealing in print or broadcast media, face tight schedules for news production which leads to a focus on the specific details of individual acts and little or no consideration of structural issues or enforcement policies (Lawrence 2000). As a result, the police and other criminal justice system functionaries control almost all of the information relied on by crime reporters, giving the police immense power in shaping crime stories. Reporters quickly develop symbiotic relationships with the social control agencies they are supposed to be covering (Chibnall 1977). The net effect of all of this is that official agencies of social control become the actual definers of what is crime news and how it is reported (Hall et al. 1978; Lawrence 2000). "Journalists are not necessarily biased towards the powerful — but their bureaucratic organization and cultural assumptions make them conduits of that power" (McNair 1993, 48).

Media representations vastly exaggerate the danger of crime and offer intensive policing and harsh punishment as the solution to the problem. Both ideology and the shape of news organizations themselves lead the media to present crime in terms of the "official story." "Law and order" is the cure and other perspectives are either marginalized or entirely omitted in crime reporting (Altheide 2002; Cavender 2004).

Ultimately, "the news media are as much an agency of policing as the law enforcement agencies whose activities and classifications are reported on" (Ericson, Baranek, and Chan 1991). The media both represent and reproduce the official version of social order.

Globalization and the Media

For decades scholars have warned us about the dangers of the corporatization of and concentration of ownership of the media (Bagdikian 1983; McChesney & Schiller 2003; McChesney 2008). But even amidst these warnings, it is fair to say that the situation has become more dire in recent years. The media industry has undergone dramatic changes in the last 30 years (Croteau and Hoynes, 2005). First, a series of mergers, takeovers and buyouts has created huge, globalized media corporations. Second, these enormous multinational corporations have integrated all five major media platforms (TV/Satellite; Radio/Music; Film; Print; Internet) into their holdings. Third, these major media giants have gone global, marketing their mediated images of reality worldwide. Fourth, the ownership of the media on all five platforms has become increasingly concentrated (Croteau and Hoynes 2005).

As Arsenault and Castells (2008) have shown in their meticulous research, seven corporate empires dominate the media industry: Time Warner, Disney, News Corp., Bertelsmann, CBS, NBC, and Viacom. The cultural, social, political and economic power of these seven corporations across the entire globe is enormous.

Three factors have made this immense concentration of power possible. First, polices of privatization and deregulation dramatically changed the rules by which media corporations operate and market their wares. Second, deregulation led directly to the corporatization of all five media platforms. This process of corporatization has produced one of the most stunning ironies of the globalized economy. While there are far more media outlets than ever before, there has been a corresponding reduction in the diversity of media content. In other words, the same mediated realities are being reproduced through more and more outlets. Third, the corporatization of the media has occurred concurrently with the digitization of information. This produces yet another irony. While there is a vast increase in the number of media networks and modes of communication, there is a concomitant consolidation what is actually being communicated (Arsenault and Castells 2008).

Crime, the Media and Hegemony

The mass media are in fact corporate entities in a profit-seeking capitalist economy. Media corporations seek to improve profitability, try to mollify corporate advertisers, and are governed by boards of directors composed of corporate leaders from all sectors of the economy. Likewise, there is an exclusive, persistent exchange of actors and monies that move reciprocally between the corporate world and positions of political power. It is therefore not surprising that mass media presentations related to crime discourage investigations of society's political and economic structures, while at the same time reifying the cultural, economic and political views of the corporate world. Nor is it surprising that with a proliferation of media outlets there still is little or no room in media reports for oppositional views. Simply put, media corporations form a key industry in the capitalist economy, and they have immense power to reinforce values that legitimate a stratified society and its tactics of governance.

The mass media are key players in what Gramsci referred to hegemony. Hegemony is simply a social process by which the values and actions of those with power are made to seem reasonable, necessary and the only real alternatives in dealing with social problems. Hegemony creates the basis for mass approval of those values and actions thereby reducing the need for a reliance on overt coercion. Hegemony is the process whereby the values and beliefs of the powerful become defined as "common sense." The media, the educational system, religion, the family, and the law all play important roles in reproducing meanings that make the interests of the powerful seem inevitable, and rejection of those interests that seem to be irrational if not treasonous. The media, and to a large degree its coverage of crime and war, are crucial in gaining public consent and approval for the present social system. And the mass media can accomplish this in the most subtle way by appearing to cover a wide spectrum of opinion, while in reality marginalizing any criticism.

Of course, it is the state which has the power to define criminals and arrest and prosecute them. Acts are defined as crime only because it is in the interests of those with power to define them as such. But the state has a powerful ally in the media which is able to direct public attention away from a myriad of serious issues by directing that attention to moral panics and crime waves.

The primary conclusion that can be drawn from research on the media's representation of crime is that it reproduces a dominant ideology and allows no dissenting points of view. It is not an overstatement to suggest that mass media quite deliberately engages in a "dumbing down" of American culture, which stifles serious political thought and limits the possibilities of dissent (Herman and Chomsky, 1988). Exoo, in his superb discussion of hegemony and the wars in Iraq and Afghanistan, concludes:

> Herbert Marcuse put the point this way: In our society, "speech moves in synonyms and tautologies" (1964, p. 88). Words that should begin debates, end them. Words whose meanings should be argued over are instead invariably defined by the status quo, where the "haves" have and the ruling class rules. The "free press" is our press, never mind that it is bound wrist and ankles by commercial imperatives, while news editors in other countries have no commercial overseers, leaving our press behind that of 30 other countries in the "Second World Press Freedom Ranking" (Reporters Without Borders 2003). "Success" is commercial success. "The American way" is the capitalists' way. "The good life" is their life. Good words, words whose only limits should be limitless imagination, are, for the moment, bound to the service of one idea, one class [Exoo 2010, 10].

REFERENCES

Allen, Jessica, Sonia Livingstone, and Robert Reiner. 1998. "True Lies: Changing Images of Crime in British Postwar Cinema." *European Journal of Communication* 13(1): 53–75.

Altheide, David. 2002. *Creating Fear: News and the Construction of Crisis*. New York: Aldine de Gruyter.

Arsenault, Amelia H., and Manuel Castells. 2008. "The Structure and Dynamics of Global Multi-Media Business Networks." *International Journal of Communication* 2: 707–748.

Bagdikian, Ben. 1983. *The Media Monopoly*. Boston: Beacon Press.

Barak, Greg (ed.). 1994. *Media, Process, and the Social Construction of Crime*. New York: Garland Press.

Barlow, Melissa H. 1998. "Race and the Problem of Crime in Time and Newsweek Cover Stories, 1946–1995." *Social Justice* 25: 149–83.

Barzagan, Mark. 1994. "'The Effects of Health, Environmental and Socio-psychological Variables on Fear of Crime and Its Consequences Among Urban Black Elderly Individuals." *International Journal of Aging and Human Development* 38: 99–115.

Beckett, Katherine. 1997. *Making Crime Pay*. New York: Oxford University Press.

Beckett, Katherine and Theodore Sasson. 2000. *The Politics of Injustice*. Thousand Oaks, CA: Pine Forge Press.

Brown, Sheila. 2003. *Crime and Law in Media Culture*. Buckingham, UK: Open University Press.

Cavender, Gray. 2004. "Media and Crime Policy." *Punishment and Society* 6(3): 335–348.

Chermak, Steven M. 1995. *Victims in the News: Crime in American News Media*. Boulder, CO: Westview.

Chibnall, Steve. 1977. *Law-and-Order News*. London: Tavistock.

Chiricos, Ted, Sarah Eschholz, and Marc Gertz. 1997. "Crime, News and Fear of Crime." *Social Problems* 44(3): 342–57.

Chiricos, Ted, Kathy Padgett, and Marc Gertz. 2000. "Fear, TV News and the Reality of Crime." *Criminology* 38: 755–785.

Croteau, David, and William Hoynes. 2005. *The Business of Media*. Thousand Oaks, CA: Pine Forge Press.

Cumberbatch, Guy, Samantha Woods, and Andrea Maguire. 1995. *Crime in the News: Television, Radio and Newspapers: A Report for BBC Broadcasting Research*. Birmingham, UK: Aston University, Communications Research Group.

Dorling, Daniel. 2004. "Prime Suspect: Murder in Britain." In Paddy Hillyard, Christina Pantazis, Steve Tombs and Daniel Dorling (eds.), *Beyond Criminology*. London: Pluto Press.

Ericson, Richard, Patricia Baranek, and Janet Chan. 1991. *Representing Order*. London: Open University Press.

Ericson, Richard V. 1991. "Mass Media, Crime, Law, and Justice." *British Journal of Criminology* 31(3): 219–49.

Exoo, Calvin F. 2010. *The Pen and the Sword*. London: Sage.

Ferrell, Jeff. 1998. "Criminalizing Popular Culture." In Franke Bailey and Donna Hale (eds.), *Popular Culture, Crime and Justice*: 71–84. Belmont, CA: Wadsworth.

Fishman, Mark, and Gray Cavender (eds.). 1998. *Entertaining Crime: Television Reality Programs*. New York: Aldine De Gruyter.

Gerbner, George. 1995. "Television Violence: The Power and the Peril." In Gail Dines and Jean Humez (eds.), *Gender, Race and Class in the Media*: 547–57. Thousand Oaks, CA: Sage.

Graber, Doris. 1980. *Crime News and the Public*. New York: Praeger.

Greer, Chris. 2003. *Sex, Crime and the Media*. Cullompton, Devon: Willan.

Gregory, Jeanne, and Sue Lees. 1999. *Policing Sexual Assault*. London: Routledge.

Hall, Stuart. 1970. "A World at One with Itself." *New Society* 18: 1056–8.

Hall, Stuart, Chas Critcher, Tony Jefferson, John Clarke, and Brian Adams. 1978. *Policing the Crisis*. London: Palgrave.

Heath, Linda, and Kevin Gilbert. 1996. "Mass Media and Fear of Crime." *American Behavioral Scientist* 39(4): 379–386.

Herman, Edward, and Noam Chomsky. 1988. *Manufacturing Consent*. New York: Pantheon.

Jewkes, Yvonne. 2004. *Media and Crime*. London: Sage.

Klite, Paul, Robert A. Bardwell, and Jason Salzman. 1997. "Local TV News: Getting Away with Murder." *Press/Politics* 2(2): 102–112.

Kooistra, Paul G., John S. Mahoney, and Saundra D. Westervelt. 1998. "The World of Crime According to 'Cops.'" In Mark Fishman and Gray Cavender (eds.), *Entertaining Crime*: 141–58. New York: Aldine De Gruyter.

Lawrence, Regina. G. 2000. *The Politics of Force: Media and the Construction of Police Brutality*. Berkeley: University of California Press.

Leishman, Frank, and Paul Mason. 2002. *Policing and the Media: Facts, Fictions and Factions*. Cullompton, Devon: Willan.

Levi, Mark. 2001. "White-Collar Crime in the News." *Criminal Justice Matters* 43: 24–5.

Lichter, S. Robert, Linda S. Lichter, and Stanley Rothman. 1994. *Prime Time: How TV Portrays American Culture*. Washington, DC: Regnery.

Mandel, Ernest. 1984. *Delightful Murder: A Social History of the Crime Story*. London: Pluto.

Manning, Peter K. 1998. "Media Loops." In Frankie Bailey and Donna Hale (eds.), *Popular Culture, Crime and Justice*: 25–39. Belmont, CA: Wadsworth.

_____. 2001. "Review of Cop Knowledge: Police Power and Cultural Narrative in Twentieth Century America." *Journal of Criminal Justice and Popular Culture* 8(1): 58–60.

Marsh, Harry L. 1991. "A Comparative Analysis of Crime Coverage in Newspapers in the United States and Other Countries from 1960–1989: A Review of the Literature." *Journal of Criminal Justice* 19(1): 67–80.

Mawby, Rob C. 2001. "Promoting the Police? The Rise of Police Image Work." *Criminal Justice Matters* 43: 44–5.

_____. 2002. *Policing Images: Policing, Communication and Legitimacy*. Cullompton, Devon: Willan.

_____. 2003. "Completing the 'Half-formed Picture'? Media Images of Policing." In Paul Mason (ed.), *Criminal Visions*: 214–37. Cullompton, Devon: Willan.

McChesney, Robert W. 2008. *The Political Economy of Media: Enduring Issues, Emerging Dilemmas*. New York: Monthly Review Press.

McChesney, Robert W., and Dan Schiller. 2003. *The Political Economy of International Communications: Foundations for the Emerging Global Debate about Media Ownership and Regulation*. Geneva: United Nations Research Institute for Social Development.

McNair, Brian. 1993. *News and Journalism in the UK*. London: Routledge.

Oliver, Mary Beth, and G. Blake Armstrong. 1998. "The Color of Crime: Perceptions of Caucasians' and African Americans' Involvement in Crime." In Mark Fishman and Gray Cavender (eds.), *Entertaining Crime*: 19–36. New York: Aldine De Gruyter.

Peelo, Moira, Brian Francis, Keith Soothill, Jayn Pearson, and Elizabeth Ackerly. 2004. "Newspaper Reporting and the Public Construction of Homicide." *British Journal of Criminology* 44(2): 256–75.

Punch, Maurice. 1996. "Dirty Business: Exploring Corporate Misconduct." *Crime, Law and Social Change* 29(1): 81–83.

Rafter, Nicole. 2000. *Shots in the Mirror: Crime Films and Society*. New York: Oxford University Press.

Reiner, Robert. 2003. "Policing and the Media." In Tim Newburn (ed.), *Handbook of Policing*: 259–82. Cullompton, Devon: Willan.

Reiner, Robert, Sonia Livingstone, and Jessica Allen. 2000. "No More Happy Endings? The Media and Popular Concern About Crime Since the Second World War." In Tim Hope and Richard Sparks (eds.), *Crime, Risk and Insecurity*: 107–25. London: Routledge.

Reiner, Robert, Sonia Livingstone, and Jessica Allen. 2001. "Casino Culture: Media and Crime in a Winner-Loser Society." In Kevin Stenson and Robert Sullivan (eds.), *Crime, Risk and Justice*: 175–93. Cullompton, Devon: Willan.

Reiner, Robert, Sonia Livingstone, and Jessica Allen. 2003. "From Law and Order to Lynch Mobs: Crime News Since the Second World War." In Paul Mason (ed.), *Criminal Visions*. Cullompton: Willian.

Stephenson-Burton, A.E. 1995. "Through the Looking-Glass: Public Images of White Collar Crime." In David Kidd-Hewitt and Richard Osborne (eds.), *Crime and the Media*: 131–63. London: Pluto.

Surette, Ray. 1998. *Media, Crime and Criminal Justice: Images and Realities*. Belmont, CA: Wadsworth.

Tombs, Steve, and Dave Whyte. 2001. "Reporting Corporate Crime Out of Existence." *Criminal Justice Matters* 43: 22–23.

Wilson, Christopher P. 2000. *Cop Knowledge: Police Power and Cultural Narrative in Twentieth-Century America*. Chicago: University of Chicago Press.

Wykes, Maggie. 2001. *News, Crime and Culture*. London: Pluto.

Constructing and Reconstructing Female Sexual Assault Victims Within the Media

Venessa Garcia

Media coverage of rape and sexual assault of women has taken various angles. This coverage includes the criminal justice response (including laws, police, prosecutors and judges), the community response (including services and public attitudes and prejudices), and the media response (including media responsibility in naming victims, and in reporting the criminal events). Prior to the 1970s, rape was not a crime typically reported in the media. If rape was covered in the media, it usually focused on stranger rape. U.S. crime news typically focused on murder trials and political issues rather than rape (Surette 1998).

News stories that covered victimization of women often reflected violent crimes. Early coverage of rape often covered criminal trials or rape-murder cases; the idea of acquaintance rape such as date rape and marital rape did not exist. Thus, a historical review of rape tends to be somewhat limited until one enters the mid– to late–twentieth century when the country experienced a rape law reform. Rape law reform of the 1970s, widely covered by the media, came out of the women's movement when women began to demand protection from the state. Reformation of rape laws meant redefining the power structure of men and women in intimate relationships, such as with marital rape laws. In the public sphere, reformation meant redefining gender roles and definitions of the "good girl," such as with corroboration and statutory rape laws. News coverage of rape law reform shows the media struggle with this cultural shift.

Since justice officials, specifically the police, are the gatekeepers of crime news (Surette 1998) newspapers tend to endorse the "knowledge" shared by these authorities. Further, crime news writers tend to take a forensic journalistic approach by utilizing a fact-only method to maintain objectivity, gaining "evidence" from gatekeepers, without providing the writers' interpretations. The presentation of crime is based on organizational factors, such as newsworthiness; however, the "negotiated process" between the media and the gatekeepers reproduces cultural ideologies of power and sexual relations of men and women.

While many media scholars are engulfed in a discourse that tries to determine how much influence the media have on culture, the focus here is that this process of *doing* is intertwined. The media industry is a reflection of the larger society and, as a result, reproduces the norms of society. However, the intertwining nature also allows the media to influence social change. Hence, the purpose of this chapter is to explore newspaper coverage of rape and sexual assault against women through an examination of *The Historical New York Times* database. First, literature on the social construction of female victims of rape and sexual assault will be examined. These constructs are reinforced within media and are important to discuss. Second, newspaper presentation of rape law reform in the 1970s will be examined. Finally, the chapter will present six miniseries of two types of sexual victimizations, stranger rape and acquaintance rape, to demonstrate how rape law reform has influenced media coverage of rape.

Social Construction of Sexual Victimization

Mythology in Social Attitudes

The social construction of sexual assault victims tends to revolve around victim-blaming more than most other types of crime victims. Promiscuous behaviors and clothing, drug or alcohol use, and sexual relations with the attacker are said to have provoked or precipitated the assault (for discussion see Belknap 2007; Spencer 1987). Gelles (1979) found that society tends to presume that rape victims have asked for it, deserved it, or enjoyed rough sex. In these cases, society gives credibility to the rapist, minimizing his behavior and blaming the victim. Amir (1971) found that rapists placed blame on 19 percent of rape victims in Philadelphia for inciting the male to rape them. More recent research has uncovered the continued persistence of rape myths within society as well as within the criminal justice system (Muehlenhard et al. 1992; Peterson and Muehlenhard 2004; Melton 2010). While the above does not determine the sex offender's behaviors victims may engage in behaviors that are deemed to be subtle invitations to sexual assault. Known as victim facilitation, this includes such behaviors as living alone, walking alone at night, or not locking their doors (Burt and Albin 1981; Burt 1997). Among date rape victims, society tends to apply cultural dating scripts presuming that she owes him sex since he paid for the date (Belknap 2007; Sutherland 1995). Additionally, victims who consume alcohol before their attack are deemed reckless and careless, thus facilitating the attack (Scronce and Corcoran 1995). The victim-offender relationship is a strong factor in victim blaming (LeDoux and Hazelwood 1985; Muehlenard et al. 1992); however, Whatley (1996) found that in many cases, the victim's dress and reputation are stronger determinants to victim blaming than the victim-offender relationship. A major consequence of victim blaming is that the police and legal systems tend to hold the same victim-blaming ideology (Field 1978; Gordon and Riger 1980).

Social constructs of sexual assault victims are guided by the institutionalization of victimhood and social ideologies of doing gender. Victimhood is a concept that becomes so ingrained within the ideologies of society that it is addressed as an institution (Berger and Luckmann 1966; Altheide 2002; Garcia and McManimon 2010). Social understanding of victimhood tells us who victims are, what the circumstances of the crimes are, and what roles the victims played in their victimizations. The woman who does not fit definitions of the "ideal victim," meaning she does not engage in risky behavior, may be perceived as sharing responsibility or blame for the attack.

In addition to fitting an image of an ideal victim, sexual assault victims must fit into an image of the ideal woman.[1] Historical and contemporary examinations of womanhood have identified that a "good" woman must be family oriented, chaste, and passive (Mason 1994; Garcia 2003; Pascale 2001). She does not use alcohol or drugs, does not date too often, is not promiscuous, and socializes only with decent people. The good woman must consistently follow these gender role expectations. This is referred to as *doing gender* (Acker 1992; West and Fenstermaker 1993). A good woman does gender on a continual basis, looking, thinking and behaving like a good woman. Thus, a woman who is not properly doing gender is unable to convince society that she had no intention of engaging in a sexual relationship with the offender. The institutionalization of the ideal victim has been found to be an ingrained criminal justice practice, and most often in cases of sexual assault (Garcia and Schweikert 2010).

Researchers have identified a second victimization that female victims of sexual assault experience from the criminal justice system, the community, and the media. This second victimization is heightened for women who step out of gender role expectations (Belknap 2007). Women who do not do gender, not behaving as a good women would, are more likely to have their victimizations unfounded by the police. This "unfounding" identifies the victim's claims to be false or exaggerated and leaves her no legal recourse or protection from her attacker. As a result, it is the character or conduct of the victim that is brought into question and not the behavior of the rapist (LaFree, Reskin, and Visher 1985). LaFree et al. (1985) found that police question conduct including hitchhiking, sex outside of marriage, frequenting bars without a male, going to the home of the accused, and being an uncooperative witness. LeDoux and Hazelwood (1985) found that police are more likely to unfound or blame a sexual assault victim who has had previous consensual sexual relations with the accused. Muehlenhard et al. (1992) found that any prior victim-offender relationship, especially when considering class and race and ethnicity, strongly influenced unfounding and victim blaming.

Courts have also been found to hold strongly to rape myths (Garcia and Schweikert 2010; LaFree 1989; Postmus 2007). Judges and prosecutors hold similar attitudes toward rape as do police. Research has revealed that police and prosecutors are 40 percent more likely to agree on sexual assault charges when attackers were strangers than when they were intimates (Holleran, Beichner, and Spohn 2010). In 2004, less than one percent of all felony defendants were charged with rape (Cohen and Kyckelhahn 2008). In that same year, 94,635 forcible rapes were reported with 42 percent being cleared (Federal Bureau of Investigation 2004). Rape represented almost 2 percent of all arrests in the United States. In the latest court statistics available when this chapter was written, less than 50 percent of all rape defendants were convicted of the charges against them, while 72 percent of non-rape felony defendants were convicted of the charges against them (Cohen and Kyckelhahn 2010). Researchers report that there is a greater likelihood that consent is believed to have been given in rape cases where female victims are divorced, racial/ethnic minorities or travel alone at night (Burt and Albin 1981), which falls in line with past and current rape myths.

Rape Myths and Rape Law Reform

The above discussion points to various rape myths that have been identified within the research (Belknap 2007; Fry 2010; Los and Chamard 1997). Some of these rape myths are as follows:

- Rape is motivated by sexual need.
- Women provoke or are partially responsible for rape.
- Rape is mainly committed by those unknown to the victim.
- Rapists are psychologically abnormal.
- Only respectable girls can be raped.
- "No" really means "yes."
- Women enjoy violence in sexual relations.
- Women lie, especially when scorned.
- Rape is a crime of lust and passion in which the man loses control when confronted by a sexually provocative woman.

These myths raise many questions. Are these rape myths the product of women stepping out of prescribed gender roles? Or are rape myths the product of political ideologies of power relations between men and women? These rape myths are not simply personal or social beliefs regarding rape victims, but they are also implied in the law and practiced in justice. An examination of rape law reform in the United States presents a power struggle between legislatures and some civil libertarians claiming to protect the reputations of respectable men and feminist activists who claim that "protection" is a guise to further victimize women and hold them as the property of men.

Often rape myths are presented within media coverage of rape law reform. In their examination of media depictions of the 1983 Great Britain rape law reform, Los and Chamard (1997) found that before the 1983 rape law reform, feminists were depicted in a positive light. However, after the legislated reform, media depictions presented the fight as having been won through legislation and feminists who voiced dissatisfaction with the reform were depicted in a negative light. Furthermore, their analysis found that rape trial media coverage maintained constructs of rape victims as undeserving of justice and partly responsible for their victimizations.

Rape law reform in the United States began in the mid–1970s with the focus of marital rape and legal requirements of corroboration. The reform covered four primary areas: redefinition of the offense, evidentiary rules, statutory age offenses, and penalty structure (Berger, Searles, and Neuman 1988). The most drastic reformation of the offense redefined rape as sexual assault to include all sexual misconduct on a continuum of typology and seriousness. The reforms recognized that women are often raped by people they know and that these spouses and intimate partners are often "average" citizens we would define as normal.

Reform in the evidentiary rules worked to abolish rules of corroboration and proof of resistance (which made prosecution nearly impossible). These reforms limited jury instructions that lead jurors to believe that women often lie and imposed rape shield laws that limit the admissibility of the victim's prior sexual history. These reforms attempted to challenge myths that stated that (1) women provoke or are partially responsible for their rape, (2) only respectable girls can be raped, and (3) "no" really means "yes." The reform recognized that every woman no matter her past or reputation has a right to say "no" and that their victimizations must be taken seriously.[2] Finally, penalty reformation involved imposing mandatory minimum sentences versus minimizing sentencing in order to ensure a conviction.

Methodology

Data collection for the analysis was twofold. First, I examine media depictions of rape law reform of the 1970s as it was depicted by the *New York Times*. Only articles that covered rape laws addressing adult sexual victimization were examined. Using the ProQuest, ABI database, I searched the *Historical New York Times* database for all coverage of rape law reform from January 1, 1970, through December 31, 1979. Key terms used to search for all newspaper coverage included "rape law" or "sexual assault." There were many articles that covered commentaries, social services and community responses; however, only articles that covered rape laws were analyzed. While rape law reform involved extensive legal and ideological change, a search for such coverage in the *New York Times* resulted in only 25 articles.[3] Secondly, I examined how changing ideologies affected the reporting of rape cases. In order to observe application of rape myths and changing constructs it is important to examine stories that are given in-depth coverage. As a result, the study examines the media miniseries of rape trials.

The most notable method of socially constructing sexual victimization and justice has been through media trials, or miniseries. The miniseries, as defined by Surette (1998), is a media trial presented as a soap opera in which the media take a real crime case and, 'give it a life' through dramatization and entertainment. Often the choice of the case is based on celebrity status of the offender, as with O.J. Simpson or Robert Blake; however, it is common for the media to take a crime involving unknowns and transform the victim and/or the offender into celebrities— as either heroes or villains. Through the miniseries, the media present and reinforce constructs to the audience who often do not have direct experience with the crime. Furthermore, although the miniseries cover one crime event, the continual presentation often creates an image of an epidemic or a crisis. With each presentation of the miniseries cultural myths of rape are reinforced.

It must be stressed that the social construction of crime and victimization is not the primary goal of these miniseries. As stated by Surette (1998), organizational considerations tend to drive the miniseries presentation, specifically serialization, personification and commodification. Serialization is the progressive and dramatic presentation of a crime in order to build an audience. Personification is the human focus of the crime which trivializes the social impact and places the focus on individual peculiarities. Commodification involves the packaging of the crime into a commercialized structure of crime and justice. In essence, through a highly dramatized progressive presentation of the crime in which the human interest story is presented, via the emotions of the police, lawyers, judges, victims, friends and family, but mostly the defendant, the crime is trivialized to individual problems that can be avoided by the average person.

Los and Chamard (1997) examined miniseries of rape trials in two British newspapers using Surette's (1998) definition. They examined rape trial coverage in order to understand the social construction of rape victims. They found that media depictions of rape victims frequently fell in line with cultural images of victim blaming.

I examine popular rape trials presented as miniseries in the print news media. While the media presentation of legal reform may take an extremist or more subtle tone, media trials tend to be filled with cultural myths and victim blaming. I examine three of the most popular acquaintance rapes since the 1970s rape law reform: the Rideout Rape (representing society's reactions to new marital rape laws); the William Kennedy Smith date rape trial (representing images of sexual promiscuity and mental instability against a politically popular family), and the Kobe Bryant case (representing sexual promiscuity pitted against a sports star and society's response to rape shield laws). This study then examined coverage of three stranger rape cases. While the media often present acquaintance rapes as miniseries (they make for more interesting reading when the prior relationship can present some controversial issues), there have been a number of stranger rapes that garnered sufficient attention to become media miniseries. The New Bedford Rape Case, the most sensationalized rape case of its time, represented the extreme in victim blaming when the female steps out of her prescribed gender role. The Condom Rape Case, though not as widely covered, represented conflicting ideas of consent. This case was particularly interesting because it questioned a woman's integrity even in the case of a knife-wielding stranger who has broken into her house. The Central Park Jogger, perhaps the most widely covered sex crime, represents the stereotypical image of rapist and the "ideal victim."

Findings

Media Construction of Rape Law Reform

On January 1, 1972, the *New York Times* released a story covering judicial opinions concerning the leniency of rape laws. Family Court Judge Millard L. Midonick argued that the rape laws were archaic especially those requiring corroboration of the victim's charges in order for a rape conviction to be secured (Wagoner 1972). Corroboration meant that more than just the victim's word was required; a witness or a confession must corroborate the victim's claim. Judge Midonick cited the fact that the law for other crimes, such as robbery, allows for the victim's testimony solely to convict the defendant and that the corroboration requirements diminish the value of women.

The coverage of this story gives the reader a sense of satisfaction that government officials saw a pressing need for change. However, the first story on rape law reform published by the *New York Times* in the 1970s does not reveal the serious nature of the need for reform. In an article published on March 26, 1971, Thomas P. Ronan reported on "Rape Law Modified." The three-paragraph, 123-word section of a larger article reporting on the meeting of the State Assembly begins with the approval to relax stiff requirements of corroboration in rape cases. This is a good beginning to introducing a serious problem in the law regarding a serious crime predominantly committed against women. However, the story ends with a discussion in which a politician associated the reform with the Women's Liberation Movement which was followed by laughter and a joke that feminist advocates were "horrible-looking bags" who were not attractive enough to be raped.

The depiction in the article is that rape is a crime of passion and lust. More importantly, the description of the laughter by the Assembly diminishes the seriousness of the crime and the need for reform. Furthermore, the media focuses the story on the image of human actors involved in lobbying for change with no focus on the wrongfulness of the Assemblymen's comments. While these first two articles reveal an extreme in the controversy of how rape law should be reformed, most other news coverage did not reveal such societal controversy. For the most part, the stories presented subtle reinforcement of rape myths in their failure to debunk these myths.

Rape Law Reform in Context

In presenting these legal conversations, media depictions often presented the social, legal, and historical contexts of rape laws. Historical context presented past ideologies of marriage and the power relations between men and women by defining women as male property. Holding such an ideology, rape would not be possible. Sex in marriage was not the privilege of the husband, it was his right. Such historical depictions were presented in such statements as

> ...New York's law dated from a time "when women were considered second-class citizens in the eyes of the law..." [Montgomery November 16, 1973, 45].

and

> All states were bound by the 17th-century view that "a husband cannot be guilty of rape upon his wife for by their mutual matrimonial consent and contract the wife hath given up herself in this kind to her husband" [*The New York Times* December 29, 1978, A22].

In such instances, how could she have been raped? The wife provided consent upon marriage which cannot be reneged. However, the media consistently presented the historical context as living in the past: "As a result, most women (as well as men who were sexually assaulted) suffered in silence" (Lichtenstein June 4, 1975, 21). Even in the face of presentations of current social constructs, the historical context presented the idea that the fight was over.

The social context was very frequently presented within these articles. Specifically, media stories presented cultural beliefs regarding rape and women's credibility. The stories often presented the problems with the legal system depending on these unfounded rape myths. Such media depictions were presented in such statement as

> Even doctors are warned to be careful: "It must be remembered that it is easy for a woman, whether for spite or revenge, to make a physician believe rape has occurred" [Taylor June 15, 1971, 52].

and

> In the ghetto, a man doesn't have to commit rape to get a woman.... Around here, it's mostly love, boy and girl stuff [Taylor June 15, 1971, 52].

In this myth, rape is romanticized. Especially among the poor, women are *unrapeable* (Los and Chamard 1997). Other myths depicted within the social context included that women are spiteful. Doctors are warned, as in the quote

above, legislators are weary as demonstrated in the prolonged reform movement, and jurors are cautioned, as with the "Lord Hale instructions":

> Judges in some state were, and still are, required to give juries the 17th century "Lord
> Hale instructions" about rape being the easiest charge to make and the most difficult
> to prove (Lichtenstein June 4, 1975, 21).

The "Lord Hale instructions" referred to Judge Matthew Hale who was well
known for ordering the hanging of witches in seventeenth-century England. Juries
were instructed to be careful in their deliberations. The instructions warned jurors
that women are spiteful and lie and that these lies can ruin a man's life, who has
no defense other than his word. As a result of this ideology and connecting this
to the legal context, corroboration laws required that the victim provide evidence
such as eyewitness testimony or medical evidence of resistance in order to prove
that she did not consent. While this requirement placed the burden on the prosecution and eliminated any requirement for the defendant to provide witness
against himself, it was the only crime that required victim corroboration:

> For the crimes of robbery and assault and fraud and countless more, the victim's
> word is enough — enough for the prosecutor to make out a *prima facie* case, enough
> to take to a jury. But with the crime of rape, it is not enough at all (Oelsner May 14,
> 1972, E5).

However, in presenting the historical, social and legal context of rape law
reform, the common and persistent problem was the media's failure to discuss
the myths. The failure to discuss rape myths leads to a reinforcement of the
myths which perpetuates the ideas that her "no" means "yes," that she really is
spiteful, that she asked for it, and that she does lie.

The most common theme within the coverage of the rape law reform within
the 1970s was the belief that women lie about rape in an act of spite. Several articles present the common legal practice of presenting women as liars and hence
the need for corroboration laws. Angela Taylor's June 15, 1971, article "The Rape
Victim: Is She Also the Unintended Victim of the Law?" seemingly attempts to
debunk these common myths, however, it gives no real substance to the dangers
and inaccuracies of these myths. Lesley Oelsner's May 14, 1972, article "Law of
Rape: Because Ladies Lie" attempts to show the harm that this rape myth provides; however, other coverage suggests that criminal justice official opinions
tend to reinforce the myth. As discussed by Campbell, "the storytelling traditions
of the news industry tend to subtly sustain dominant political ideologies" (2003,
50) in telling the story and then supplementing the story with cultural myths.

> **The Story:** The 1970s media coverage of rape law reform tells us that while we
> have traditionally held women as property of men and have held to various rape
> myths which blame the victim; this is a thing of the past because now we have
> improved rape laws that do not blame the victim.
>
> **The Addendum to the Story:** Legislators and criminal justice officials, including
> prosecutors, understand the complexities of the legal system and the true nature of
> the crime of rape as well as the true nature of women: "women lie."

So how does this addendum to the story fair in a society undergoing rape law reform and cultural changes in gender role expectations? How does the addendum play itself out in media depictions of rape and rape victims? As discussed earlier, media rape trial miniseries provide society with contemporary social constructs of rape. If the addendum operates to reinforce existing myths then these should be evident to the reader. The follow six miniseries demonstrate that media depictions of rape victims fall in line with cultural images of victim blaming and illustrate which women "deserve" to claim the victim status and which do not.

Newspaper Constructions of Acquaintance Rape Victims

Miniseries 1: *The Rideout Saga* (1978) [15 news stories]. On October 18, 1978, Greta Rideout was raped and beaten by her husband John Rideout, while their 2½-year-old daughter watched and cried. "The Rideout Saga" (name taken from media headline, Haberman and Krebs August 20, 1979), was the first crime under the 1977 Oregon law in which a husband was charged with a rape of his wife while cohabitating. The only two other states that had marital rape laws at this time were Iowa and Delaware. It was also the first marital rape case to go to trial. Starting on December 20, 1978, the day after the case finally went to trial the *New York Times* ran 13 stories in this miniseries.[4]

The main concern for the defense was whether a man had a right to have sex with his wife regardless of her consent. The defense attorney made the case that "the only questions are whether 'forcible compulsion' was involved and whether marriage is 'common law' evidence of consent" (Special to *The New York Times*, December 20, 1978a, A16). From the onset of the trial, judicial decisions presented implicit support for the rape myth that the husband has a right to sex and that the wife does not have a right to say "no." The judge refused to rule on whether or not common law defenses would be allowed although the Oregon marital rape law made the defense obsolete. Media depictions moved from the presentation of the crime to the unconventional behavior of the victim. For example, in the second day of the miniseries the focus was placed on the defense's negative presentation of Greta Rideout's "longtime 'serious sexual problem'" and that "she did not mention rape but said, 'My husband just got through beating me' (Around the Nation, December 21, 1978, A20). At the same time, the media reflected the innocence of the defendant's frame of mind: "The defendant honestly believed if you are married to a woman, you have a right to sex" (Around the Nation, December 21, 1978).

With the exception of a brief presentation of the historical context of the justice system's response to the husband's right to sex in referencing Lord Hale (Ledbitter December 26, 1978), the primary focus was on the deviance of Greta Rideout. The headline "Rape-Case Wife Quoted About Becoming Rich" (Special to *The New York Times*, December 20, 1978b) began the presentation of Greta

Rideout as planning the charge before the rape occurred in order to sell her story. On December 28, the jury acquitted John Rideout of the rape, claiming: "We didn't know who to trust" (Ledbitter December 28, 1978, A14).

This represents the workings of the rape myth that women lie, as the jury finally decided after a six-day trial and three-hour deliberation. It was also quoted in two articles after the acquittal that the couple should have been more "adult." Late news coverage presented the couple as in a honeymoon phase without mention of the violence that was testified to by both the husband and wife with the following two headlines: HUSBAND SAYS WIFE'S RAPE CHARGE SAVED MARRIAGE (January 11, 1979) and A HAPPY ENDING (January 14, 1979, E7).

These media depictions presented the couple as living in bliss, although Greta Rideout did not withdraw her divorce petition. The stories also blatantly accused Greta Rideout of lying: "If nothing else will save a marriage, try shouting 'Rape!' in a crowded courtroom" (Headliners, January 14, 1979, E7). By August 30, 1979, the *New York Times* released a brief update on the "Rideout Saga." Greta did divorce John and he was being charged with criminal trespassing for breaking into her home. There was no mention that perhaps Greta Rideout was telling the truth the entire time.

Miniseries 2: *The William Kennedy Smith Date Rape* (1991) [73 news stories]. In 1991, Patricia Brown met William Kennedy Smith, the young, wealthy nephew of the late President John F. Kennedy, at a bar in Palm Beach, Florida. After conversation and a few drinks, Patricia Bowman was escorted by William Kennedy Smith to his family's Palm Beach estate (Suros April 3, 1991). It was here that William Kennedy Smith was accused of raping Patricia Bowman. The Kennedy Smith case was referenced in 150 *The New York Times* stories; however, the actual case was covered in only 73 articles. The initial reporting of the Kennedy Smith date rape focused on the importance of the family and the reluctance of the police to provide any detail. As *New York Times* writer Roberto Suros described, the police claimed to be withholding information from the public in an attempt to gather all of the facts without playing favorites toward an affluent family. The media, however, argued that the police were attempting to protect a wealthy family in refusing to release the information and unsuccessfully sued for access to the police reports (Suros April 6, 1991). Again, the use of rape myths creeps into the stories. One reporter describes the bar in which Kennedy Smith and Bowman met as a place where one would find "young single women" and "older moneyed men" (Madigan April 7, 1991, A20). In this instance, we start to see the myth that young women are fishing for wealthy men to take care of them.

Five days after the media uncovered the story we find media suggestions that this is a deviant woman who claimed to be raped but who stole from the estate (Suros April 8, 1991). Within this story the writer is trying to release "facts" of the case without official investigative evidence and even admits to gaining information from hearsay. While the media's goal is to release the news to the public, we see the case going through a media trial without evidence. More importantly, this comes at the heel of rape myths such as women lie, women are money grubbers, and women are malicious. While media stories may appear to be engaging in "forensic journalism" (see Surette 1998), the facts are not yet proven and they are not interpreted within the social context of common cultural stereotypes and myths. Another writer even goes so far as citing other news accounts as evidence (Butterfield April 11, 1991).

Within the Kennedy Smith case, we see that there are inconsistencies within Bowman's case that should certainly require further investigation that a crime has been committed. However, as the story unravels we quickly see a shift in focus from the favoritism toward a rich family to the deviance of a woman crying rape and the friend who came to her aid. We find, in these depictions, that deviant individuals are not deserving victims (i.e., victims who deserve to claim the victim status and who deserve justice). We also find that Bowman's friend, Ann Mercer, has a father who was convicted of fraud and perjury (Butterfield April 11, 1991). Mercer's statement that she took an urn from the Kennedy estate was used in the media and in the trial as evidence that Bowman and Mercer were smearing the good Kennedy name in order to make money.

As the case progressed, *The New York Times* published various Op-Ed pieces that described the social context of rape, date and acquaintance rape, and releasing the identities of rape victims within the media (Estrich April 18, 1991; Gross May 28, 1991; Lewin May 27, 1991). These stories helped to shed light on social and legal use of rape myths and how damaging they can be:

> The publicity surrounding the Palm Beach incident, and the stories about the woman who complained, make all too painfully clear the extent to which acquaintance rape is still not considered to be a real rape [Estrich April 18, 1991, A25].

However, these few stories were overshadowed by the more frequent coverage that presented the trial via forensic journalism. Accordingly, the trial was presented in the media, as if the arguments presented were fact and not mere defense tactics, and without explaining the social context. As the trial progressed, Bowman was portrayed as an unstable, promiscuous, single mother, crying rape in an attempt to damage the promising life of a vulnerable famous figure. The jury deliberation took roughly two hours. Margolick provided an overview of the tactics used by the prosecution and the defense (Margolick December 12, 1991). Unfortunately, with no discussion of the social, legal, and historical context of date rape, while Kennedy Smith's innocence may be questionable, the prevalence of rape myths make it unlikely that the public would see anything but a conniving woman and a good boy.

Miniseries 3: *The Kobe Case* (2003) [29 news stories]. In June of 2003, basketball star Kobe Bryant was accused of rape. A 19-year-old hotel employee filed rape charges claiming that Bryant restrained her neck and wrists and then raped her. Similar to the Kennedy Smith defense tactics, Bryant's defense counsel and the media painted images of the victim as sexually promiscuous (Garcia and Schweikert 2010). Headlines of various newspapers provided such negative images of the accuser as "nutty or slutty" and sexually promiscuous. *The New York Times* was much more tactful with its 29 article coverage of the case. The use of forensic journalism was found among the stories of the court case and courtroom strategies.

As with the Kennedy Smith case, *The New York Times* did print several articles that provided the social context of date rape. In one such story, Benedict described how athletes are more likely to be charged with violent crimes and are more likely to be acquitted (August 5, 2003). Benedict pointed to a system of protection and support afforded an athlete that gives them an upper hand over their accusers. This support system, though not identified by Benedict, often includes the media:

> Unlike most accused rapists, an accused athlete typically asserts his claims through a press conference, putting his accuser on the defensive and touching off pretrial press coverage where the accuser is vilified as an opportunist out to seek fame or money by filing a false rape complaint [Benedict August 5, 2003, 15].

Unfortunately, these attempts to unravel the realities of crime and justice remain overshadowed by the forensic journalism that provides the details without context. For example, one article reported that the prosecution presented evidence that was inconsistent with consensual sex but that "defense lawyers elicited evidence that the underwear the woman wore to her sexual assault examination bore traces of semen and pubic hair that did not belong to Mr. Bryant" (Liptak October 21, 2003, A13).

News coverage went on to discuss the "purple 'G-string' she wore when she met Mr. Bryant" as opposed to the yellow underwear she wore to her rape examination (Liptak August 4, 2004, A13). Without providing the context that many victims wait a period of time before reporting their victimization, the reader is to assume that she made a false accusation. Further, the evidence of sexual intercourse with another man within a 12-hour period of the Bryant incident leads the reader to believe that she was sexually reckless.

In light of rape myths, without providing social context, the writer is reinforcing the myth that sexually promiscuous girls cannot be raped. In this case, the defense was claiming that she had sex with more than one man that same day, so how can we believe that she did not consent. The public reacted strongly to the victim's accusations of a famous basketball star; she received death threats (Johnson July 24, 2004). Ultimately, the victim withdrew her rape charge.

Newspaper Constructions of Stranger Rape Victims

Miniseries 4: *New Bedford Rape* (1983) [40 news stories]. On March 6, 1983, 21-year-old Cheryl Ann Araujo (named by the prosecutor and released by the media) entered Big Dan's Tavern in New Bedford, Massachusetts with a female friend to buy a pack of cigarettes and to have a drink. Cheryl stayed at the tavern though her friend had left. However, when Cheryl attempted to leave she was dragged back by her coat collar to the pool table where she was gang raped while the rest of the bar patrons laughed and cheered the rapists on. The New Bedford case initially represented the shock and shame of a community that could not believe that these men would not care:

> Women, and the Portuguese in particular, have been offended. On Monday night, a silent candle-lit protest march by 2,500 people drew support from women's groups throughout the Northeast. "Rape is not a Spectator Sport" proclaimed one banner, as the face of city hall glowed from the massed candlelight [Clendinen March 17, 1983, A16].

Much of the initial focus was on the ethnic history and pride of New Bedford with several briefs on the initial court proceedings and the defendants. In these stories, Cheryl Ann Araujo (known as Sarah Tobias in the acclaimed movie *The Accused*, starring Jodie Foster) was portrayed as an innocent young woman who had recently moved into a crime-ridden community. However, once the trial began the miniseries moved away from the rape as the focus and toward the personification of a deviant woman who got what she asked for and an angered community who protested the convictions. In order words, the seriousness of the rape was diminished by the image of a woman who was not *doing gender* properly.

When describing police records and Araujo's testimony, the news focused on the victim's reported exaggerations instead of the psychological trauma that may have influenced her to exaggerate to the police and in court testimony (Special to *The New York Times*, February 28, 1984). Cheryl Araujo was required to testify for hours at a time over a period of several days. Further, the stories alluded to prior psychiatric issues. This supports the myth that mentally unstable women cry rape. News also mentions that Araujo was having problems with her live-in boyfriend — and father of her two children. Without the social context of the modern women, this coverage supports the myth that sexually promiscuous women don't say "no" so cannot be raped.

In further coverage of Araujo's testimony, the article describes the victim as a criminal: "she admitted she had cheated the State Welfare Department by collecting welfare payments for three years even though she was living with Mr. Lagasse, a machinist" (Special to *The New York Times*, February 28, 1984, A18). The unnamed writer also includes the defense's suggestion that the victim would be filing a $10 million lawsuit and was offered a book contract. While all of these were explained in the victim's testimony, *The New York Times* only covers the negative images presented by the defense that also support rape myths and does not include any testimony of the actual crime.

On March 18 and 23, four of the six defendants were convicted of rape. However, the stigma that the Portuguese community had been feeling ultimately moved the focus onto the victim as a bad person. Between 7,000 and 10,000 people protested the convictions as an act of prejudice against the Portuguese-American community. Accusations that the victim "should have been home in the first place" and "they should hang her" were made during the protests (Clendinen March 17, 1983, A16).

Miniseries 5: *The Condom Rape Case* (1992) [6 news stories]. On October 24, 1992, Xan Wilson, publicly self-identified, woke up to find a strange man, Joel Rene Valdez, in her home holding a knife. Wilson ran to the bathroom and tried to call the police. After breaking down her bathroom door and knocking the telephone out of her hand, he ordered Wilson to take off her pants. In a decision of self-preservation considering the concern about AIDS, Wilson asked the rapist to wear a condom. This demonstrates images of consent and images of "real" rape. The first grand jury acquitted Valdez deciding that "the woman's handing Mr. Valdez a condom, which she described as an act of self-protection against AIDS, might have implied her consent" (*The New York Times*, October 28, 1992, A15).

This case was a stranger rape where no injury, other than the rape, was incurred (also known as a coercive rape). However, a condom in the possession of a young single woman living alone and returning from a party does not present the image of the ideal victim. While the District Attorney did seek a second grand jury indictment and the rapist was ultimately sentenced to 40 years in prison, the case represents the rape myth that "'no' really means 'yes'" and "only good girls (who don't carry condoms) get raped." Wilson commented on her portrayal as a victim:

> I'm not beaten up or maimed or even infected with the AIDS virus or pregnant. I find it sickening that in a very aware city with very aware people, the fact that I took extreme measures to protect my life means that I deserve to get raped [Milloy October 25, 1992, A30].

As a result, victim blaming was a factor in the first grand jury's failure to indict, though not enough to allow a second grand jury to let the rapist to go uncharged.

Miniseries 6: *The Central Park Jogger* (1989) [233 news stories]. On April 19, 1989, 28-year-old Trisha Meili was brutally attacked and raped while jogging in Central Park in New York City. The media quickly labeled her the "Central Park Jogger." National media images of Trisha Meili presented a woman who was health conscious, young, white and attacked by a gang of young violent Black and Hispanic teenagers (Facts on File World News Digest August 31, 1990); though *The New York Times* specifically did not characterize the youth as a gang (Wolff April 21, 1989). As media coverage of the case turned into a frenzy, the case quickly became symbolic of racial tensions in New York City (Cose May 7, 1989). The media and criminal justice system brought forth an alarmist image of innocent, young, white women facing senseless violence at the hands of young, racial and ethnic minority males.

Trisha Meili, whose name was not released by *The New York Times*,[5] was said to be health conscious, "an avid runner and cyclist" and a hard working investment banker who "worked at Salomon Brothers for three years" (Wolff April 21, 1989, B1). Trisha remained in a coma for two weeks. As she went through a difficult recovery, it was described that she suffered brain, eye and other injuries that would make it difficult to serve as an effective witness in court. Nevertheless, the media's positive attitude toward the victim attended to the human side of rape victims: "'She's got a great attitude,' said one friend. 'It's inspiring — better than going to church'" (Sullivan November 30, 1989, A1).

Unlike most other rape miniseries, Meili's life after the crime was described in detail and coverage remained favorable. While many people wondered why a woman would jog by herself at night in Central Park, the media remained sympathetic toward the victim. However, many more stories remained focused on the racial tensions surrounding this case, once again detracting from the seriousness of the rape.

It is unfortunate that the Central Park Jogger case ultimately gave more focus to race relations in New York City. However, history has proven that race is often a determining factor in investigation, arrest, convictions, and sentencing (Garcia and Schweikert 2010). Six young teenagers, Black and Hispanic, were prosecuted, convicted, and incarcerated. Fifteen years after the attack they were exonerated based on DNA evidence and the confession of the actual perpetrator.

Conclusion

Rape law reform saw its most prominent change in the 1970s. Although reform continued into the 1980s and 1990s, the reform of the 1970s changed our definitions of rape and sexual assault. There was an expansion of sexual assault crimes under the penal code and an admission by justice officials to holding to antiquated ideologies of gender power structures and sexual assault. However, while the 1970s experienced major legal reform, *The New York Times* gave little attention to these changes and instead maintained rape myths.

News coverage of corroboration laws initially appear to be helpful in revealing socially reconstructed images of ideal victims and the use of rape myths. However, further analysis reveals that the coverage presented a tone that belittles and diminishes the seriousness of sexual assault, equating it with passion and lust. While this news reporting occurred in the 1970s with a culture that held strongly to rape myths and traditional ideals of doing gender, we can still see strong evidence of an unspoken corroboration rule. As discussed previously, research through the decades reveals the persistence of rape myths that blame the victim and presume that women lie (Fry 2010; Muehlenhard et al. 1992; Garcia and Schweikert 2010). We saw the power of rape myths in police and prosecutorial decision making (Holleran, Beichner, and Spohn 2010; Cohen and Kyckelhahn 2010; Federal Bureau of Investigation 2004; Cohen and Kyckelhahn 2008) and in judicial sentencing decisions (Cohen and Kyckelhahn 2008, 2010).

As seen in various news stories of the rape law reform, legislators and news writers struggled to maintain rape myths when discussing these issues. Unfortunately, in this analysis of the effects of these legal reforms on media rape trial miniseries, we see continued reliance by the media on rape myths. Among the acquaintance rape miniseries examined, we saw evidence of the practiced rape myth that only good girls get raped and that she wanted it. However, even when the victim was attacked by a stranger and no prior victim-offender relationship existed, we saw that it is very difficult for a rape victim to claim innocence. The only miniseries in which the victim was presumed to be innocent was the Central Park Jogger. A review of the crime reveals that this was the only case discussed above that fit the ideal rape construct. Trisha Meili was raped by strangers at night in a deserted area and brutally attacked. She was a hard-working young woman who was health conscious and had no way to defend herself against her attackers. A quick search of the many rape cases detailed by the media reveals that this type of case is rarely covered.

With the advent of rape law reform in the 1970s, cultural acceptance of the "modern woman" opened the doors for women to live less restrictive lives. Reconstructions of womanhood accepted women living alone, frequently dating and perhaps never marrying, drinking in social settings, even joining male dominant occupations; however, examination of media rape trial miniseries revealed that women are still given shared responsibility for the rapes committed against them. These presumptions are founded within rape myths of promiscuous and lying women (the William Kennedy Smith, New Bedford, and Kobe Bryant cases), money-grubbing women (the William Kennedy Smith, Kobe Bryant, and Rideout Saga cases), or the mentally unstable woman (as was presented in the William Kennedy Smith Case). Presenting the continued belief that rape is not violent but a case of intimate passion, the William Kennedy Smith and Kobe Bryant cases successfully argued that the victim wanted it.

These findings, though an examination of only one media outlet, tell us that rape myths are still alive and well. This chapter examined *The New York Times*, a widely respected newspaper that prides itself on reporting the news via forensic journalism and not gossip. Though we found evidence in the Kennedy Smith case of citing unfounded hearsay and other news stories, the news articles were found to be much more kind to victims than other widely read newspapers, such as the *Daily News* and *Newsday*. Taken together, while *The New York Times* engaged in a milder form of rape myth promulgation, most other media outlets tended to reproduce victim blaming and rape myths.

NOTES

1. It should be noted that male sexual assault victims are often denied victim status.

2. Reformation of statutory age offenses, not a focus of this chapter though a very controversial area of reform, sought to limit the exploitation of children while simultaneously eliminating the moral focus that placed double standards on girls.

3. The search only included articles specifically covering rape law reform, excluding statutory rape. It did not include stories that only mention rape law reform within the coverage of a specific rape case. Further, the search yielded articles that typically included mere mentions of rape law reform, though many other media forms and organizations also covered this topic. Themes explored included corroboration, consent, victim credibility, and ideal rapes.

4. The case gained such notoriety that the entertainment media created a made-for-television movie about the case. In 1980, CBS released the drama *Rage and Marriage: The Rideout Case* starring Mickey Rourke, at which time two more stories were released by the paper.

5. Trisha Meili announced her own identity. She came forward in an effort to share her trauma with the public and in order to make people aware of the horrific nature of rape.

REFERENCES

Acker, Joan. 1992. "Gender Institutions: From Sex Roles to Gendered Institutions." *Contemporary Sociology* 21(5): 565–569.

Altheide, David L. 2002. *Creating Fear: News and the Construction of Crisis*. New York: Aldine De Gruyter.

Amir, Menachem. 1971. *Patterns in Forcible Rape*. Chicago: University of Chicago Press.

Around the Nation. December 21, 1978. "Opening Arguments Heard in Husband-Wife Rape Case." *New York Times*, A20.

Belknap, Joanne. 2007. *The Invisible Woman: Gender, Crime, and Justice*, 3d ed. Belmont, CA: Thomson Wadsworth.

Benedict, Jeff. August 5, 2003. "Athletes and Accusations." *The New York Times*, 15.

Berger, Peter L., and Thomas Luckmann. 1966. *The Social Construction of Reality: A Treatise in the Sociology of Knowledge*. New York: Anchor Books.

Berger, Ronald J., Patricia Searles, and W. Lawrence Neuman. 1988. "The Dimensions of Rape Reform Legislation." *Law and Society Review* 22: 329–358.

Burt, M.R. 1997. "Rape Myths." In M.E. Odom and J. Clay-Warner (eds.), *Confronting Rape and Sexual Assault*, 129–144. Lanham, MD: Rowman & Littlefield.

Burt, Martha R., and R.S. Albin. 1981. "Rape Myths, Rape Definitions, and Probability of Conviction." *Journal of Applied Social Psychology* 11: 212–230.

Butterfield, Fox. April 11, 1991. "New Detail, and New Questions, in Kennedy Case." *The New York Times*, A18.

Campbell, Christopher P. 2003. "Commodifying September 11: Advertising, Myth, and Hegemony." In S. Chermack, F.Y. Bailey and M. Brown (eds.), *Media Representation of September 11*: 47–65. Westport, CT: Praeger.

Clendinen, Dudley. March 17, 1983. "Barroom Rape Shames Town of Proud Heritage." *New York Times*, A16.

Cohen, Thomas H., and Tracey Kyckelhahn. 2008. "Felony Defendants in Large Urban Counties, 2004." Washington, DC: U.S. Department of Justice.

_____. 2010. "Felony Defendants in Large Urban Counties, 2006." Washington, DC: U.S. Department of Justice.

Cose, Ellis. May 7, 1989. "Rape in the News Mainly about Whites." *The New York Times*, 27.

Estrich, Susan. April 18, 1991. "The Real Palm Beach Story: The Right Question: Not What She Did, But What He Did." *The New York Times*, A25.

Facts on File World News Digest. 2004. *Crime: Convictions in New York City Jogger Attack*. Facts.com. August 31, 1990 Available from http://www.2facts.com.

Federal Bureau of Investigation. 2004. "Uniform Crime Reports: Crime in the United States, 2004." Washington, DC: U.S. Department of Justice.

Feild, Hubert. S. 1978. "Attitudes Toward Rape: A Comparative Analysis of Police, Rapists, Crisis Counselors, and Citizens." *Journal of Personality and Social Psychology* 36: 156–179.

Fry, Melissa S. 2010. "Becoming Victims, Becoming Citizens: A Brief History of Gender-Motivated Violence in U.S. Law." In V. Garcia and J.E. Clifford (eds.), *Female Victims of Crime: Reality Reconsidered*. Upper River Saddle, NJ: Prentice Hall.

Garcia, Venessa. 2003. "Difference in the Police Department: Women, Policing and Doing Gender." *Journal of Contemporary Criminal Justice* 19(3): 330–344.

Garcia, Venessa, and Patrick McManimon. 2010. *Gendered Justice: Intimate Partner Violence and the Criminal Justice System.* Lanham, MD: Rowman & Littlefield.

Garcia, Venessa, and Erica J. Schweikert. 2010. "Cultural Images—Media Images: 'Doing Culture' and Victim Blaming of Female Crime Victims." In V. Garcia and J.E. Clifford (eds.), *Female Victims of Crime: Reality Reconsidered*: 3–19. Upper Saddle River, NJ: Pearson Education.

Gelles, Richard J. 1979. *Family Violence.* Beverly Hills: Sage.

Gordon, Margaret T., and Stephanie Riger. 1980. *The Female Fear.* New York: Free Press.

Gross, Jane. May 28, 1991. "Even the Victim Can Be Slow to Recognize Rape." *The New York Times,* A14.

Haberman, Clyde, and Albin Krebs. August 20, 1979. "Notes on People: The Rideout Saga." *New York Times,* B4.

Headliners. January 11, 1979. "Husband Says Wife's Rape Charge Saved Marriage." *New York Times,* A17.

_____. January 14, 1979. "A Happy Ending." *New York Times,* E7.

Holleran, David, Dawn Beichner, and Cassia Spohn. 2010. "Examining Charging Agreement Between Police and Prosecutors in Rape Cases." *Crime & Delinquency* 56: 385–413.

Johnson, Kirk. July 24, 2004. "Judge Limiting Sex-Life Shield at Bryant Trial." *The New York Times,* 1A.

LaFree, Gary D. 1989. *Rape and Criminal Justice: The Social Construction of Sexual Assault.* Belmont, CA: Wadsworth.

LaFree, Gary D., Barbara F. Reskin, and Christy A. Visher. 1985. "Jurors' Responses to Victims' Behavior and Legal Issues in Sexual Assault Trials." *Social Problems* 32: 389–407.

Ledbitter, Les. December 26, 1978. "Oregon Wife Due to Testify in Spouse-Rape Case." *New York Times,* A14.

_____. December 28, 1978. "Oregon Man Found Not Guilty on a Charge of Raping His Wife." *New York Times,* A1.

LeDoux, J.C., and R.R. Hazelwood. 1985. "Police Attitudes and Beliefs Toward Rape: A Comparative Analysis of Police, Rapists, Crisis Counselors, and Citizens." *Journal of Police Science and Administration* 13: 211–230.

Lewin, Tamar. May 27, 1991. "Tougher Laws Mean More Cases Are Called Rape." *The New York Times,* A8.

Lichtenstein, Grace. June 4, 1975. "Rape Laws Undergoing Changes to Aid Victims." *New York Times,* 1, 21.

Liptak, Adam. August 4, 2004. Papers Reveal New Details in Kobe Bryant Rape Case." *The New York Times,* A13.

_____. October 21, 2003. "Bryant Is Ordered to Stand Trial in Rape Case." *The New York Times,* A16.

Los, Maria, and Sharon E. Chamard. 1997. "Selling Newspapers or Educating the Public? Sexual Violence in the Media." *Social Problems* 32: 293–328.

Madigan, Nick. April 7, 1991. A Refuge of the Rich Is a Trove of Scandal." *New York Times,* A20.

Margolick, David. December 12, 1991. "Smith Acquitted of Rape Charge After Brief Deliberation by Jury." *The New York Times,* A1.

Mason, Mary Ann. 1994. *From Father's Property to Children's Rights: The History of Child Custody in the United States.* New York: Columbia University Press.

Melton, Heather C. 2010. "Rape Myths: Impacts on Victims of Rape." In V. Garcia and J.E. Clifford (eds.), *Female Victims of Crime: Reality Reconsidered*: 113–127. Upper Saddle River, NJ: Prentice Hall.

Milloy, Ross E. October 25, 1992. Furor Over a Decision Not to Indict in a Rape Case." *New York Times,* A30.

Montgomery, Paul L. November 16, 1973. "Legislators Say Changes in Rape Law Are Likely." *New York Times,* 45.

Muehlenard, Charlene, Irene G. Powch, Joi L. Phelps, and Laura M. Giusti. 1992. "Definitions of Rape: Scientific and Political Implications." *Journal of Social Issues* 48(1): 23–44.

The New York Times. December 29, 1978. "Marriage, Rape and the Law." *The New York Times,* A22.

_____. October 28, 1992. "2d Jury Charges Man in Condom-Rape." *The New York Times,* A15.

Oelsner, Lesley. May 14, 1972. "Law of Rape: 'Because Ladies Lie.'" *New York Times,* E5.

Pascale, Celine-Marie. 2001. "All in a Day's Work: A Feminist Analysis of Class Formation and Social Identity." *Race, Gender & Class* 8(2): 34.

Peterson, Zoe D., and Charlene L. Muehlenhard. 2004. "Was it Rape? The Function of Women's

Rape Myth Acceptance and Definition of Sex in Labeling Their Own Experiences." *Sex Roles* 51: 129–144.

Postmus, Judy L. 2007. "Challenging the Negative Assumptions Surrounding Civil Protection Orders: A Guide for Advocates." *Affilia: Journal of Women and Social Work* 22: 347–356.

Scronce, Christine A., and Kevin J. Corcoran. 1995. "The Influence of Victim's Consumption of Alcohol on Perceptions of Stranger and Acquaintance Rape." *Violence Against Women* 1: 241–253.

Special to *The New York Times*. December 20, 1978a. "Jury Selection Starts in Oregon Trial of Man Accused of Raping Wife." *The New York Times*, A16.

_____. December 20, 1978b. "Rape-Case Wife Quoted About Becoming Rich." *The New York Times*, A18.

_____. February 28, 1984. "Reports to Police Questioned in New Bedford Rape Trials." *The New York Times*, A18.

Spencer, Cassis C. 1987. "Sexual Assault: The Second Victimization." In Laura L. Crites and Winifred L. Hepperle (eds.) *Women, Courts, and Equality*: 54–73. Newbury Park, CA: Sage.

Sullivan, Ronald. November 30, 1989. "Jogger Returns to Limited Work at Salomon." *The New York Times*, A1.

Surette, Ray. 1998. *Media, Crime, and Criminal Justice: Images and Realities*, 2d ed. Belmont, CA: Wadsworth.

Suros, Roberto. April 3, 1991. "Woman Says She Was Raped at Kennedy Estate." *The New York Times*, A12.

_____. April 6, 1991. "Kenney Nephew Refusing Questions in Rape Inquiry." *The New York Times*, A7.

_____. April 8, 1991. "Kennedy Nephew Gives Blood to Police." *The New York Times*, A8.

Sutherland, Mittie D. 1995. "Assaultive Sex: The Victim's Perspective." In A.V. Merlo and J.M. Pollock (eds.), *Women, Law and Social Control*: 179–201. Boston: Allyn & Bacon.

Taylor, Angela. June 15, 1971. "The Rape Victim: Is She Also the Unintended Victim of the Law?" *The New York Times*, 52.

Waggoner, Walter H. 1972. "Judge Call Law on Rape Lenient." *The New York Times*, 37.

West, Candace, and Sarah Fenstermaker. 1993. "Power, Inequality, and the Accomplishment of Gender: An Ethnomethodological View." In Paula England (ed.), *Theory on Gender/Feminism on Theory*: 151–174. New York: Aldine.

Whatley, Mark A. 1996. "Victim Characteristics Influencing Attributions of Responsibility to Rape Victims: A Meta-Analysis." *Aggression and Violent Behavior* 1: 81–96.

Wolff, Craig. April 21, 1989. "Youths Rape and Beat Central Park Jogger." *The New York Times*, B1.

The Social Construction of
Serial Murder Victims:
A Multivariate Level Analysis

JANELLE M. ELIASSON-NANNINI
AND DEIRDRE SOMMERLAD-ROGERS

Serial homicide cases and their perpetrators have been common topics in pop culture in America for some time now. They are the inspiration for books, movies, television series, and reality or news-entertainment shows. Starting in the mid–1980s, there was a change from fact-based reports of homicide to more sensationalistic "tabloidization" forms of reporting (Gibson 2006; Krajicek 1998; Schmid 2005). This was especially true for serial murder stories (Donovan 1998; Fox and Levin 2005; Jenkins 1994; Schmid 2005). Indeed, stories concerning serial murder are considered especially choice by most forms of news media (Fisher 1997; Gibson 2006; Jenkins 1994). The sensational nature of the coverage of such crimes is particularly salient as media reports, regardless of accuracy, have been shown to have a measurable effect on public perceptions (Wenger, James, and Faupel 1985) especially in times of concern or fear.

The body of academic research on the media's reporting of serial murder victims has increased. Most of the work to date has focused on why offenders choose certain targets, such as female college students (Cameron and Frazer 1987; Leyton 1996).[1] One of the main differences in media coverage of serial murder victims and single homicide victims is the likelihood of coverage. When homicides are covered in the media, it is usually because of the victim's characteristics or a sensationalistic nature to the crime, including multiple victims (Soothill et al. 2004). Media coverage tends to be more likely when the victims are children, women, elderly, or are white and are killed by a minority (Johnstone, Hawkins, and Michener 1994; Soothill et al. 2004; Sorenson, Manz, and Burk 1998). If readers are accustomed to the single homicide coverage style, when a rare serial homicide string of deaths occurs, the changes in media coverage signal that this case and its victims are different. The change also accentuates the vile nature of the killer. All of these elements heighten the sensationalism that surrounds a given case, which sets it apart from the reporting of other types of homicide cases (Soothill et al. 2004).

Until Eliasson-Nannini et al. (2010), little was known about the type of media coverage given to the victims of serial murderers. There were a number of interesting findings that came about from their research. Qualitatively, Eliasson-Nannini et al. (2010) found a systematic pattern in victim representations in print media coverage that changed over the course of the case, from the first murder to the resolution of the trial. Coverage progresses from fairly unsympathetic and factual when the victim was a solo victim to more sensational and in depth when the media realizes that there was a serial killer active. Finally, Eliasson-Nannini et al. found little to no coverage at all of victims once the serial killer is caught. In other words, when the murder was a single homicide, coverage of victims was more unsympathetic and few details were offered about the victims, unless there is some sensational quality about the victim, like they were a child. Once the case was classified as a serial homicide, the coverage was more sympathetic and details of the victims' lives were published. In several instances when victims were qualified as newsworthy or were especially sensational, secondary information stories (Soothill et al. 2004) were also published. These included interviews with family and friends, information about victims' employment or hobbies, and interesting facts about or accomplishments of the victim. The final phase of the pattern occurred once the serial murderer's identity became known. In this phase, victims were relegated to the background of the story, often becoming a laundry list of names at the end of a newspaper article (Eliasson-Nannini et al. 2010). These findings are also supported to some degree by the work of Curtis (2001) in his study of the famous serial killer, Jack the Ripper.

The research on the media coverage of serial murder victims dovetails with the idea of the "newsworthy victim" as articulated by Sorenson et al. (1998). Sorenson et al. (1998) found that coverage of crime victims sometimes varies as a function of the "worthiness of the victim," with women, whites, the wealthy, children and the elderly receiving a greater volume of coverage as compared to men, the poor and minorities. Eliasson-Nannini et al (2010) found that women and younger individuals were more likely to receive sympathetic coverage, whereas men, older individuals, and homosexuals were more likely to receive unsympathetic coverage. This also fits into the theoretical framework as outlined by Jenkins (1988; 1994) concerning the social construction of serial murder as a moral panic. He argued that the social construction of serial murder is related in part to a conservative philosophy of criminal justice that emerged in the 1980s and 1990s. This philosophy has a bifurcated view of the world: on one side is evil, and on the other side good. According to this view, women, children and younger victims are innocent and pure, and their fate as victims are undeserved and worthy of sympathy. In contrast, males and homosexuals are more closely aligned with evil; therefore, their deaths are not as tragic.

A logical next step in understanding the portrayal of serial homicide victims in print media is to explore the type of coverage victims receive in a multivariate manner, which will allow for a comparison between multiple victim character-istics. Certain lifestyles or traits are considered inherently deviant within soci-ety. Racism still exists in many domains of life and discrimination happens on a daily basis for a myriad of reasons. But the question remains as to which of these characteristics matter the most when it comes to the newspaper coverage of victims. As such, the current study focuses on the relationship between each victim characteristic type and its influence on the type of portrayal the victim receives in the newspaper coverage of the case.

The majority of past victimology research examines similar questions using other crime data, looking at the level and type of representation of victims based on various gender, socio-economic, and age categories. Past research shows that there is indeed a disparity in the level of coverage, whether or not that coverage is positive or negative with regard to the victim (Abrams et al. 2007; Dixon, Azocar, and Casas 2003; Howard 1984; Johansson, Anderson, and Persson 2007; Mastro et al. 2009; Salfati, James, and Ferguson 2008; Smith and Kuchta 1995; Taylor 2009; Wardle 2007). These findings will guide us as we use two different theoretical orientations to frame the current investigation: blam-ing the victim and moral panic.

When considering blame of the victim, we anticipate that stigmatizing char-acteristics will receive unsympathetic coverage compared to the balance of the sample. Work by Meyers (1994; 1997) found that when the victim of a crime was female, newspaper reporting would sometimes portray the female victim as hav-ing provoked the attack. Additionally, crime victims whose activities fall outside of societal norms, such as sex workers and drug users, are also covered differently by the news media than those whose lifestyles are within the norms of societal propriety (Lundman 2003; Roberts 1978; Van Brunschot, Sydie, and Krull 1999).

The response of the public, the media, political leaders and law enforce-ment to serial murder demonstrates how it is a classic example of what Cohen (1972) has defined as a socially constructed "moral panic." Simply put, a moral panic is a disproportionate reaction to a perceived social threat, one that is often presented in a "stylized and stereotypical fashion" (Cohen 1972, 9) to the public by the media, elected officials, law enforcement and opinion makers. As Best (1999) notes, moral panics often feature "exaggerated claims and intense concerns" (163) about threats to society, with public awareness of these threats usually being promulgated in large part by sensationalistic media reporting. Without a doubt, the media is often the key player in defining and promoting a moral panic (Ben-Yehuda 1990; Goode and Ben-Yehuda 1994), as the social construction of the panic often hinges on whether or not a few isolated events receive media coverage (Schmid 2005). The amount and type of coverage by the mass media of these isolated events often serves to widen the scope and speed of a moral panic, as well as reinforce the permanence of the panic, pro-vided that as part of its coverage the media distorts and exaggerates the extent of the isolated acts (Barron and Lacombe 2005; Cauthen and Jasper 1994; Jenkins 1994). Following this, we hypothesize that stigmatizing characteristics will not affect the type of coverage victims received. This fits within the framework of a moral panic as any victim pads a killer's resume, increases fear, and is easily distorted to give momentum to the panic, no matter the victim's worthiness or legitimacy in life.

Research Methodology

Sample

As denoted in Eliasson-Nannini et al. (2010), several methodological decisions were made prior to the original data collection of the Victims of Serial Homicide Newspaper Coverage dataset. First, a content analysis method was used to gather the information that ultimately comprised the dataset, as this technique is optimal when seeking to study and analyze messages contained in media (Berg 2001; Kaid and Wadsworth 1989; Valls-Fernández and Martínez-Vicente 2007). The second methodological decision is related to the sources from which the Victims of Serial Homicide Newspaper Coverage dataset was culled; specifically, the information which was eventually included in the dataset focused solely on newspaper coverage of serial murder for reasons related to the findings of Lee and DeHart (2007). Their work indicates that radio and television is more likely to distort the true threat of a situation through their choice of sources, such as anecdotal accounts and/or "person on the street" interviews. Prior work has found (Beasley 2004; Castle and Hensley 2002; Fisher 1997; Herkov and Biernat 1997; Hickey 2006; Lee and DeHart 2007; Schmid 2005) that this is especially true for stories that concern serial murder, as broadcast news has chased ratings by hyping the sensationalism that surrounds serial killers and/or serial murder cases. In contrast, most forms of print media (Burgoon, Burgoon, and Wilkinson 1981; O'Keefe and Reid-Nash 1987; Picard and Adams 1987) tend to be less sensationalistic and more likely to provide better approximations of actual crime statistics and information than broadcast media.

Several steps were followed by Eliasson-Nannini et al. (2010) in the creation of the data set. Data collection started by compiling a list of serial killers who committed murder during the time period under investigation, with the time period falling between January 1989 and August 2007. Although the print news media has covered serial killers since the first stories on Jack the Ripper in the late 1800s (Odell 2006), the last twenty years alone contains a volume of printed news devoted to serial murder which is vast in scope. From the works of Hickey (*Serial Murderers and their Victims*, 2006), Newton (*The Encyclopedia of Serial Killers*, 2000) and Schmid (*Natural Born Celebrities: Serial Killers in American Culture*, 2005) a list of serial murderers was compiled that was further refined as a function of several criteria. This stage of collection yielded 39 different serial killers who committed murder between 1989 and 2007.

Excluded from the list of serial killers were both spree killers and 'angel of death' killers, as neither fit the traditional definition of serial murder (for an explanation, see Fox and Levin 2005; Hickey 2006). Additionally, the Victims of Serial Homicide Newspaper Coverage dataset focuses only on male serial murderers, as female serial murderers are somewhat rare and tend to only target their own children, partners and the elderly as opposed to the more usual victims of serial murder (Egger 1998; Fox and Levin 2005). Additionally, any serial killer who had not committed, or been identified with, at least three different murders over the course of their homicide career are not part of this dataset.

Once the list of serial murderers was compiled, a LexisNexis search was conducted using each murderer's name and/or pseudonyms in order to generate information on each serial murderer's victims. Included in this stage of the data collection were all non-editorial newspaper articles covering each homicide. At times an article was reprinted in several neighborhood sections of a large metropolitan newspaper or reprinted to make a correction. When this occurred only one version of the story was included in the analysis.

With respect to the data collection specifications mentioned above, the dataset includes 1,585 unique articles on the 39 serial killers from forty-five different newspapers, as well as 183 different serial murder victims that were given some form of newspaper coverage in the aforementioned number of articles.

Variables and Coding

The dependent variable used in the quantitative analysis portion of this project was the type of coverage given to the victims of serial murder in newspaper articles. In order to best operationalize this concept, we elected to distinguish between two broad types of coverage; namely, coverage which was sympathetic to the victim of a serial murderer versus coverage that was unsympathetic towards the victim.

Admittedly, our chosen method of content analysis has the potential to be somewhat subjective on the part of a researcher, thus increasing the possibility that the bias of whoever is coding the data may influence the results. In order to overcome this potential obstacle, both manifest content analysis and latent content analysis techniques were employed. As noted by Berg (2001), manifest content analysis involves identifying certain elements that can be enumerated, whereas latent content analysis centers on articulating the deeper structural meaning and tone conveyed by the data.

We first employed latent content analysis. That is to say, we started by first reading each article to see if certain patterns in the tone of the coverage could be recognized. We rapidly discovered that the use of certain words and phrases in each article were critical in determining whether or not a given article conveyed a tenor of sympathy towards the victim. For example, we typically found that if the person killed by a serial murderer was more often than not referred to in a particular newspaper article as "the victim," or if he or she was more often referred to as having been "slain," the overall tone of the coverage he or she received in the article tended to be sympathetic in nature. In contrast, if a person was more bluntly referred to in an article as having been "killed," having "died" or "was found dead," the coverage tended to have a more unsympathetic tone.

Using the information gleaned via our latent content analysis, we then proceeded to use a manifest content analysis technique by enumerating the aforementioned terms and phrases in each article. If an article contained more sympathetic terms (such as "victim" or "slain") than unsympathetic terms, that article was flagged as being sympathetic in terms of the coverage given to victims of serial murder. In contrast, if the article contained less sympathetic and more unsympathetic terms, it was adjudicated as being unsympathetic in its coverage. One finding associated with our manifest content analysis that should be noted here is that thirty-two percent of all of the articles in the sample were dedicated to covering a given victim of a particular serial killer.

In an effort to increase intercoder reliability (and thereby reduce the potential subjective rater bias mentioned above), each article was analyzed according to the previously discussed criteria by two independent raters (the primary and secondary authors) before coverage was deemed to be either sympathetic or unsympathetic in nature. Calculation of Scott's Pi (Scott 1955), a statistic that is a measure of the agreement between raters, shows the intercoder reliability of the dependent variable to be .96, which is close to its maximum value of 1.0. Finally, the dependent variable was coded as 0 for sympathetic coverage and 1 for unsympathetic coverage.

With respect to the independent variables used in the investigation, the following procedures were utilized. The age of the victim was left continuous and ranged from 4 years of age to 87 years of age. The sex of the victim was coded 1 for female, and 0 for male. A series of dummy variables were created to report if a victim was identified as white, black or Hispanic in a given newspaper article. Along these same lines, three variables were also created as flags to indicate whether or not a victim was identified as employed, unemployed or a student in a given article. All of the remaining independent variables used in the statistical analyses were dichotomized, with the categories of interest being flagged as 1.

Statistical Analysis

Analysis of the data was conducted using binary logistic regression[2]. Three models were estimated: the first included the demographic and statistical controls (age, race, etc.); the second included respondent characteristics (drug usage, affluent status, etc.); the third model included all variables under investigation[3].

Results

Table 1 presents the means and standard deviations for all variables used in the quantitative portion of our investigation. As Table 1 reveals, fifty-seven percent of the victims of serial murders received sympathetic coverage in the newspapers we sampled, while forty-three percent received unsympathetic coverage. The average age of the victims was about 32-years-old; we also found that the majority of victims were female (85 percent). Very few of the victims were referred to as either having been poor (6 percent), affluent (7 percent) or homosexual (3 percent); along these same lines, only ten percent of victims were reported to have had an arrest history. In all, only 39 percent of the articles in the dataset indicated the victim's racial or ethnic background, with 20 percent of the victims being White, 16 percent being Black, and 6 percent being Hispanic. Six percent of victims were a student at the time of their death; interestingly, 6 percent of victims were also unemployed when killed. Twenty-one percent of victims were employed in an occupation other than sex worker, with 27 percent of victims engaging in some form of sex work. Finally, about one in every four articles (23 percent) mentioned the victims as having had either a history of drug use or that drugs were a factor in the victim's murder.

Table 1. Means and Standard Deviations for All Variables

Variable	Mean	Std. Dev.
Newspaper Coverage (Dependent Variable)		
Sympathetic	0.57	0.50
Unsympathetic	0.43	0.50
Independent Variables		
Age of victim	31.79	16.22
Sex of victim (1 = female)	0.85	0.35
Victim's race denoted as White (1 = yes)	0.20	0.40
Victim's race denoted as Black (1 = yes)	0.16	0.36
Victim's race denoted as Hispanic (1 = yes)	0.03	0.16
Victim was a student (1 = yes)	0.06	0.24
Victim was employed (1 = yes)	0.21	0.41
Victim was unemployed (1 = yes)	0.06	0.23
Victim was a sex worker (1 = yes)	0.27	0.44
Drug use mentioned (1 = yes)	0.23	0.42
Arrest history mentioned (1 = yes)	0.10	0.30
Referred to as affluent (1 = yes)	0.07	0.26
Referred to as poor (1 = yes)	0.06	0.24
Referred to as homosexual (1 = yes)	0.03	0.16

Table 2 presents the binary logistic results for the regression of newspaper coverage on respondent characteristics and statistical controls. Three different statistical models were estimated, with models one and two being combined and compared together in model three. In other words, each previous model appears within each subsequent model.

Table 2. Binary Logistic Regression Results for Prediction of Sympathetic versus Unsympathetic Newspaper Coverage

Explanatory Variables	Model 1	Model 2	Model 3
Intercept	-0.218	0.126	-0.368
Statistical/Demographic Controls			
Age of Respondent (1 = Female)	0.036†		0.051‡
Sex of Respondent (1 = Female)	-1.253*		-0.483
Victim's race denoted as White (1 = yes)	-1.640*		-2.523‡
Victim's race denoted as Black (1 = yes)	-0.302		-0.718
Victim's race denoted as Hispanic (1 = yes)	-0.497		-0.996
Victim was a student (1 = yes)	-0.719		-1.256
Victim was employed (1 = yes)	0.913*		-0.049
Victim was unemployed (1 = yes)	0.495		-0.394
Respondent Characteristics			
Drug use mentioned (1 = yes)		-1.090	-1.021
Arrest history mentioned (1 = yes)		-19.268	-19.231
Referred to as affluent (1 = yes)		21.077	21.745
Referred to as poor (1 = yes)		-0.280	-0.366
Referred to as homosexual (1 = yes)		-19.435	-20.770
Victim was a sex worker (1 = yes)		-0.515	-0.723
Model Chi-Square	38.301‡	41.984‡	79.055‡
Model df	8	6	14
R2 nagelkereke	.254	.275	471

Note: N = 183,* = p<.05,† = p<.01,‡ = p<.001. Coefficients presented above are unexponentiated

Model one regressed the dependent variable on the various statistical and demographic controls. As seen in Table 2, among the variables in model one only the respondent's age, biological sex, classification as White and employment status predicted newspaper coverage. Specifically, we found that older victims and men were more likely to receive unsympathetic newspaper coverage, whereas victims who were White were more likely to receive sympathetic coverage. Interestingly, victims who were employed at a job at the time of their death were more likely to receive unsympathetic coverage.

Model two regressed the dependent variable on the various respondent characteristics, such as drug usage, arrest history, whether the victim was affluent, poor, homosexual and/or a sex worker. Remarkably, none of these factors affect newspaper coverage when considered in a multivariate model.

Model three included all independent variables under examination. In this model only two variables significantly predict the type of newspaper coverage a victim receives: age and being White. As before in model one, older respondents are found to enjoy less sympathetic coverage than younger respondents; along these same lines, Whites in the sample were again found to be more likely to receive more sympathetic coverage. Indeed, the exponentiation of the coefficient for Whites in model 3 shows that Whites have a 92 percent increase in the odds for the occurrence of sympathetic news coverage as opposed to nonwhites. A curious finding is that all other factors in the multivariate analysis are nonsignificant predictors of newspaper coverage.

Discussion

The primary purpose of this project was to further clarify the social construction of serial homicide victims through newspaper coverage. To achieve this goal, the current project extended the previous line of work undertaken by Eliasson-Nannini et al. (2010) by evaluating the impact that several sociodemographic factors have on the prediction of sympathetic versus unsympathetic newspaper coverage in a multivariate analysis.

Previous work in this area (Eliasson-Nannini et al. 2010) suggested that, at the bivariate level, a victim's biological sex, age, race, arrest history, sexual orientation and socioeconomic status (i.e., identified as either poor or affluent) influenced the type of coverage in newspapers. Multivariate results in the current investigation contradict previous findings. When considered together, the impact of a victim's sexual orientation, arrest history, drug use history and socioeconomic status have no impact on the type of newspaper coverage given them. Indeed, any impact that a person's sex and employment status may have on whether they receive sympathetic versus unsympathetic coverage is completely attenuated when all factors in Model 2 are estimated simultaneously. The only two consistent factors that seem to predict the type of newspaper coverage a victim receives is their age and whether or not the victim is white.

One of the more interesting findings within our research was the fact that none of the predictors in model two played any role in the prediction of coverage given to a serial murder victim. We anticipated that among victims, their drug usage, arrest history, sex worker status, and whether the victim was poor or homosexual would play a part in predicting what type of media coverage they received. At first glance, these results would seem to be incongruent with Sorenson et al.'s (1998) notion of the newsworthy victim and Jenkins' (1988; 1994) theoretical framework on serial murder as a socially constructed moral panic. However, it may be the case that both newspaper editors and news reporters recognize that people in society generally devalue drug users, the poor, homosexuals, sex workers and people who have an arrest record. In an effort to compensate, editors and reporters may therefore go out of their way to provide more neutral coverage for these types of victims who would otherwise be dismissed as deserving of their fate because of their devalued and stigmatizing traits, histories and behaviors. Although speculative, future researchers may wish to expound on this line of thought, especially in light of the fact that there has been little research to date that analyzes the reporting of sensational stories in general (Carpenter, Lacy, and Fico 2006) and the coverage devoted to the victims of serial murder in particular. Given the lack of research in this area, it is difficult to explicate whether or not the traits of the victim of serial murder definitively influence the type of coverage he or she receives beyond what we have discovered in our investigation.

These findings question whether "blaming the victim" for their deaths suggested in previous work (Filak and Pritchard 2007; Lundman 2003; Meyers 1994, 1997; Roberts 1978; Van Brunschot et al. 1999) is appropriate, given that a priori characteristics (age and racial classification) seem to operate as the sole indicators of sympathetic versus unsympathetic coverage. An alternative theory advanced in the literature, that of the social construction of serial murder as a moral panic, would seem to suggest that sex worker victims, those with a homosexual identity, drug users and an arrest record should receive just as much sympathetic coverage as their counterparts without these traits. Results support this line of thought, as no differential impact of these factors can be found on the prediction of newspaper coverage suggesting that the potential for victimization is being emphasized over the victim's worthiness.

Ultimately our research suggests that the type of newspaper coverage given to the victims of serial murderers hinges on the characteristics of the victims. Our data also lend credence to the argument that the role of the victim plays an important part in framing serial murder as a socially constructed moral panic. But unlike other forms of moral panics, serial murder is rather unique in that it waxes and wanes over time. Indeed, one of the key characteristics of a moral panic is its volatility:

> Moral panics are *volatile*; they erupt fairly suddenly (although they may lie dormant or latent for long periods of time, and may reappear from time to time) and, nearly as suddenly, subside. Some moral panics may become *routinized* or *institutionalized*, that is, the moral concern about the target behavior results in, or remains in place in the form of, social movement organizations, legislation, enforcement practices, informal interpersonal norms or practices for publishing transgressors, after it has run its course. Others merely vanish, almost without a trace; the legal, cultural, moral, and social fabric of the society after the panic is essentially no different from the way it was before; no new social control mechanism are instituted as a consequence of its eruption [Goode and Ben-Yehuda 1994, 38–9].

When put another way, serial murder can be said to slumber within the popular consciousness until a high-profile event reignites our awareness of serial homicide as a social problem. Right now, serial murder continues to receive attention from certain forms of popular media (such as television shows and movies) and scholars (Best 1999; Fox and Levin 2005; Hickey 2006; Schmid 2005).

Beyond this, the understanding that serial murder is a real and present danger is simply not part of the current zeitgeist. Thus serial murder as a socially constructed moral panic will most likely remain in a steady state until policy leaders and/or policing agencies have need of it again. This was the case during the last "epidemic" of serial homicide in the United States during the 1980s and 1990s (Fox and Levin 2005; Hickey 2002; 2006; Jenkins 1994; Kappeler and Potter 2005); since that time, policing agencies have withdrawn their support of a disproportionate response to serial murder. In fact, a recent publication by the FBI's Behavioral Analysis Unit (a unit that grew out of the public concern about serial murder) identifies several issues about serial murder that stem from moral panic and underscores the fact that these issues are myths (Morton 2008). Furthermore, the document cautions those who investigate potential serial murder about the dangers presented by the media:

> When individuals appear in the media and discuss ongoing cases, they have an enormous potential to negatively influence investigations and may even cause irreversible damage. They often speculate on the motive for the murders and the possible characteristics of the offender. Such statements can misinform the public and may heighten fears in a community. They may contribute to mistrust and a lack of confidence in law enforcement and, more importantly, may taint potential jury pools [Morton 2008, 43].

This position by the FBI on the dangers of media speculation and misinformation is in stark contrast to the relationship that existed between law enforcement and the media two decades ago, a relationship that undoubtedly increased fear of serial murder among the public. Instead, the contemporary reaction to serial murders by law enforcement seems more proportionate to the actual danger posed by serial homicide, and today the discussion by the FBI is much more rational. Future researchers may wish to consider this by looking at how the role of the victim in serial murder has changed as a function of the waxing and waning of serial murder as a moral panic, both in terms of the amount and type of coverage given to a serial murder victim.

Previous research suggests that there is a push to create victim narratives that allow the audience to experience a "virtual victimhood" through a stylized writing technique known as "mediated witness," in which the reader personally feels the loss of the victims' life but, unlike the victims, the reader can then walk away from the incident (Peelo 2006). Peelo's concept of virtual victimhood is drawn from Katz's work "What Makes Crime 'News'?" (1987) where the nature of the relationship between the reader and this stylized material is described as follows:

> The reading of crime is a collective, ritual experience. Read daily by a large portion of the population, crime news generates emotional experiences in individual readers, experiences which each reader can assume are shared by many others. Although each may read in isolation, phenomenologically the experience may be a collective, emotional "effervescence" of moral indignation [64].

It may be the case that the writers of the articles which comprised our dataset were merely using the technique described by Katz (1987) to provide the opportunity for their readers to experience the crime in a "safe environment" by giving focus to those characteristics that are defined as more newsworthy. This line of thought would support Jenkins (1988; 1994) idea of the "newsworthy victim" of serial homicide. Based on his research, the ideal victim is often defined as a middle-aged white person (most often a woman) who is free from social stigmas who should receive more media attention than other homicide victims (Jenkins 1988; 1994). With respect to the paucity of significant factors which predict sympathetic coverage versus unsympathetic coverage among victims, a future project questioning the existence of an ideal victim in serial homicide cases would be justified to consider the work of Jenkins.

One noteworthy limitation inherent in the current study is the inability to ascertain whether coverage of a murdered individual would have been more or less sympathetic depending on the perspective of the journalist who covered the story. That is to say, would the reporting have varied if a journalist had started their coverage of a victim with the presumption that the individual was the prey of a serial murderer, and not just the fatality of a single episode of murder? Along these same lines, does affiliation with certain wire services, like Associated Press, United Press International, Reuters or Knight Ridder influence the coverage given to the victims of serial murderers, especially in light of the fact that these wire services have the ability to share stories and resources? These are questions that we were unable to address in the current investigation. Future researchers may wish to examine whether these factors impact the amount and type of coverage a serial murder victim receives.

While this project cannot definitively state the motivations and reasoning of newspaper writers, it is clear that just more than one rationale is likely. Previous researchers have well established the sensationalistic nature of media coverage in serial homicide cases (Beasley 2004; Castle and Hensley 2002; Fisher 1997; Herkov and Biernat 1997; Hickey 2006; Lee and DeHart 2007; Schmid 2005) and how its exaggerations contribute to moral panic (Barron and Lacombe 2005; Cauthen and Jasper 1994; Jenkins 1994). With serial homicide media reports being sensationalized and distorted, the coverage and details of the victims given within the media accounts hold salience with consumers and provides an ideal platform for the perpetuation of subtle discrimination in the name of public dissemination of information.

NOTES

1. Leyton (1996) as well as Caputi (1990) have applied a feminist perspective to serial murder. They specifically explain that the women who have made social gains, especially female college students, may appear to the modern serial killer as a threat to his social position, leading some killers to target these upwardly mobile women as a way to reclaim their own status.
2. Binary logistic regression is an analysis technique whereby a dependent variable that is

dichotomized (i.e., coded as 0/1) is regressed on one or more independent variables. For more information on binary logistic regression, please see DeMaris (1995; 2003; 2004).

3. Multicollinearity problems were checked by examining the variance inflation factor (VIF) associated with each coefficient in both the main-effects and interaction models. A VIF of 10 or above typically indicates multicollinearity problems (Myers 1986). However, all of the VIFs in our models were under.4.

REFERENCES

Abrams, Robert, Andrew Leon, Kenneth Tardiff, Peter Marzuk, and Kari Sutherland. 2007. "'Gray Murder': Characteristics of Elderly Compared with Nonelderly Homicide Victims in New York City." *American Journal of Public Health* 97(9): 1666–1670.

Barron, Christie, and Dany Lacombe. 2005. "Moral Panic and the Nasty Girl." *Canadian Review of Sociology and Anthropology* 42(1): 51–69.

Beasley, James. 2004. "Serial Murder in America: Case Studies of Seven Offenders." *Behavioral Sciences and the Law* 22: 395–414.

Ben-Yehuda, Nachman. 1990. *The Politics and Morality of Deviance: Moral Panics, Drug Abuse, Deviant Science, and Reversed Stigmatization*. Albany: State University of New York Press.

Berg, Bruce. 2001. *Qualitative Research Methods for the Social Sciences, Fourth Edition*. Boston: Allyn & Bacon.

Best, Joel. 1999. *Random Violence: How We Talk about New Crimes and New Violence*. Berkeley: University of California Press.

Burgoon, Michael, Judee Burgoon, and Miriam Wilkinson. 1981. "Newspaper Image and Evaluation." *Journalism Quarterly* 58(3): 411–419.

Cameron, Deborah, and Elizabeth Frazer. 1987. *The Lust to Kill: A Feminist Investigation of Sexual Murder*. New York: New York University Press.

Caputi, Jane. 1990. "The New Founding Fathers: The Lore and Lure of the Serial Killer in Contemporary Culture." *Journal of American Culture* 13(3): 1–12.

Carpenter, Serena, Stephen Lacy, and Fredrick Fico. 2006. "Network News Coverage of High-Profile Crimes During 2004: A Study of Source Use and Reporter Context." *Journal of Mass Communication Quarterly* 83(4): 901–916.

Castle, Tammy, and Christopher Hensley. 2002. "Serial Killers with Military Experience: Applying Learning Theory to Serial Murder." *International Journal of Offender Therapy and Comparative Criminology* 46(4): 453–465.

Cauthen, Nancy, and James Jasper. 1994. "Culture, Politics, and Moral Panics." *Sociological Forum* 9(3): 495–503.

Cohen, Stanley. 1972. *Folk Devils and Moral Panics: The Creation of the Mods and Rockers*. London: MacGibbon and Kee.

Curtis, L. Perry. 2001. *Jack the Ripper and the London Press*. New Haven: Yale University Press.

DeMaris, Alfred. 1995. "A Tutorial in Logistic Regression." *Journal of Marriage and the Family* 57(4): 956–968.

_____. 2003. "Logistic Regression." In John Shinka and Wayne Velicer (eds.), *Handbook of Psychology, Volume 2: Research Methods in Psychology*: 509–531. New York: Wiley.

_____. 2004. *Regression with Social Data Modeling Continuous and Limited Response Variables*. Hoboken: John Wiley and Sons.

Dixon, Travis, Cristina Azocar, and Michael Casas. 2003. "The Portrayal of Race and Crime on Television Network News." *Journal of Broadcasting & Electronic Media* 47(4): 498–523.

Donovan, Pamela. 1998. "Armed with the Power of Television: Reality Crime Programming and the Reconstruction of Law and Order in the United States." In Mark Fishman and Gray Cavender (eds.), *Entertaining Crime: Television Reality Programs*: 117–140. New York: Aldine De Gruyter.

Egger, Steven. 1998. *The Killers Among Us: An Examination of Serial Murder and its Investigation*. Upper Saddle River, NJ: Prentice Hall.

Eliasson-Nannini, Janelle, Christopher Bradley, Deirdre Sommerlad-Rogers, and Benjamin Pearson-Nelson. 2010. "The Social Construction of Serial Murder Victims: A Content Analysis of Newspaper Coverage." *Sociological Imagination*, forthcoming.

Filak, Vincent, and Robert Pritchard. 2007. "News (un)scripted." *Journalism* 8(1): 66–82.

Fisher, Joseph. 1997. *Killer Among Us: Public Reactions to Serial Murder*. Westport, CT: Praeger.

Fox, James, and Jack Levin. 2005. *Extreme Killing: Understanding Serial and Mass Murder*. Thousand Oaks, CA: Sage.

Gibson, Dirk. 2006. *Serial Murder and Media Circuses*. Westport, CT: Praeger.

Goode, Erich, and Nachman Ben-Yehuda. 1994. *Moral Panics: The Social Construction of Deviance.* Cambridge, MA: Blackwell.

Herkov, Michael, and Monica Biernat. 1997. "Perceptions of the Media in a Community Exposed to Serial Murder." *Journal of Clinical Psychology* 53(8): 909–915.

Hickey, Eric. 2002. *Serial Murderers and Their Victims, Third Edition.* Belmont, CA: Wadsworth.

_____. 2006. *Serial Murderers and Their Victims, Fourth Edition.* Belmont, CA: Wadsworth.

Howard, Judith. 1984. "Societal Influences on Attribution: Blaming Some Victims More than Others." *Journal of Personality and Social Psychology* 47(3): 494–505.

Jenkins, Philip. 1988. "Myth and Murder: The Serial Murder Panic of 1983–1985." *Criminal Justice Research Bulletin* 3(11): 1–7.

_____. 1994. *Using Murder: The Social Construction of Serial Homicide.* New York: Aldine de Gruyter.

Johansson, Anders, Susanne Andersson, and Maj-Liz Persson. 2007. "A Psychiatric and Social Matched Case Series Comparison of Victims of Criminal Homicide and Homicide Perpetrators in Sweden." *Nordic Journal of Psychiatry* 61(6): 427–432.

Johnstone, John, Darnell Hawkins, and Arthur Michener. 1994. "Homicide Reporting in Chicago Dailies." *Journalism Quarterly* 71(4): 860–72.

Kaid, Larry, and A.J. Wadsworth. 1989. "Content Analysis." In Larry Barker and Phillip Emmert (eds.), *Measurement of Communication Behavior*: 197–217. New York: Longman.

Kappeler, Victor, and Gary Potter. 2005. *The Mythology of Crime and Criminal Justice, Fourth Edition.* Long Grove, IL: Waveland Press.

Katz, Jack. 1987. "What Makes Crime 'News'?" *Media, Culture and Society* 9(1): 47–75.

Krajicek, David. 1998. *Scooped! Median Miss Real Story on Crime While Chasing Sex, Sleaze and Celebrities.* New York: Columbia University Press.

Lee, Matthew, and Erica DeHart. 2007. "The Influence of a Serial Killer on Changes in Fear of Crime and the Use of Protective Measures: A Survey-Based Case Study of Baton Rouge." *Deviant Behavior* 28(1): 1–28.

Leyton, Elliott. 1996. "Second Thoughts on Theoretical Approaches to Multiple Murder." In Thomas O'Reilly-Fleming (ed.), *Serial and Mass Murder: Theory, Research and Policy*: 37–51. Toronto: Canadian Scholars' Press.

Lundman, Richard. 2003. "The Newsworthiness and Selection Bias in News about Murder: Comparative and Relative Effects of Novelty and Race and Bender Typifications on Newspaper Coverage of Homicide." *Sociological Forum* 18(3): 357–386.

Mastro, Dana, Maria Knight Lapinski, Maria Kopacz, and Elizabeth Behm-Morawitz. 2009. "The Influence of Exposure to Depictions of Race and Crime in TV News on Viewer's Social Judgments." *Journal of Broadcasting & Electronic Media* 53(4): 615–635.

Meyers, Marian. 1994. "News of Battering." *Journal of Communication*, 44: 47–63.

_____. 1997. *News Coverage of Violence Against Women: Engendering Blame.* Thousand Oaks, CA: Sage.

Morton, Robert J. 2008. *Serial Murder: Multi-Disciplinary Perspectives for Investigators.* Retrieved October 27, 2008, from http://www.fbi.gov/publications/serial_murder.pdf.

Newton, Michael. 2000. *The Encyclopedia of Serial Killers.* New York: Facts on File.

Odell, Robin. 2006. *Ripperology: A Study of the World's First Serial Killer and a Literary Phenomenon.* Kent, OH: Kent State University Press.

O'Keefe, Garrett, and Kathleen Reid-Nash. 1987. "Crime News and Real-World Blues." *Communication Research* 14(2): 147–163.

Peelo, Moira. 2006. "Framing Homicide Narratives in Newspapers: Mediated Witness and the Construction of Virtual Victimhood." *Crime, Media, Culture* 2: 159–175.

Picard, Robert, and Paul Adams. 1987. "Characterizations of Acts and Perpetrators of Political Violence in Three Elite U. S. Daily Newspapers." *Political Communication and Persuasion* 4(1): 1–9.

Roberts, Helen. 1978. "Trap the Ripper." *New Society* 44(809): 11–12.

Salfati, C. Gabrielle, Alison James, and Lynn Ferguson. 2008. "Prostitute Homicides: A Descriptive Study." *Journal of Interpersonal Violence* 23: 505–543.

Schmid, David. 2005. *Natural Born Celebrities: Serial Killers in American Culture.* Chicago: The University of Chicago Press.

Scott, William. 1955. "Reliability of Content Analysis: The Case of Nominal Scale Coding." *The Public Opinion Quarterly* 19(3): 321–325.

Smith, M. Dwayne, and Ellen Kuchta. 1995. "Female Homicide Victimization in the United States: Trends in Relative Risk, 1946–1990." *Social Science Quarterly* 76(3): 665–672.

Soothill, Keith, Moira Peelo, Jayn Pearson, and Brian Francis. 2004. "The Reporting Trajectories of Top Homicide Cases in the Media: A Case Study of The Times." *The Howard Journal of Criminal Justice* 43(1): 1–14.

Sorenson, Susan, Julie Manz, and Richard Berk. 1998. "News Media Coverage and the Epidemiology of Homicide." *American Journal of Public Health* 88: 1510–1514.

Taylor, Rae. 2009. "Slain and Slandered: A Content Analysis of the Portrayal of Femicide in Crime News." *Homicide Studies* 13(1): 21–49.

Valls-Fernandez, Federico, and Jose Manuel Martinez-Vicente. 2007. "Gender Stereotypes in Spanish Television Commercials." *Sex Roles* 56: 691–699.

Van Brunschot, Erin, Rosalind Sydie, and Catherine Krull. 1999. "Images of Prostitution: The Prostitute and Print Media." *Women and Criminal Justice* 10(4): 47–72.

Wardle, Claire. 2007. "Monsters and Angels: Visual Press Coverage of Child Murders in the USA and UK, 1930–2000." *Journalism* 8(3): 263–284.

Wenger, Dennis, Thomas James, and Charles Faupel. 1985. *Disaster Beliefs and Emergency Planning.* New York: Irvington.

"These kids are killing each other": Gender-Neutral vs. Gender-Specific Framing in the School Shooting Media Discourse

BRIAN KNOP

Over the past ten years, numerous school shootings have occurred at colleges, high schools, and even middle schools all across the nation. Although there are various forms of violence and gun related incidences that have happened on school campuses, what the media define as "school shootings" is a rather specific case. The school shootings that often gain the most public attention are *rampages*, meaning that they are expressive, non-targeted attacks on a school (Muschert 2007). The young men who commit this type of shooting often see their act of violence as a symbolic retaliation against their community. They target their own school because it personifies what they see as a world that has wronged them. Evan Ramsey, who killed two classmates and wounded several others at Bethel Regional High School in 1997, described why he thought his actions were justifiable:

> I want people, the world, or maybe just Bethel, to know how mean and cruel the world is or can be.... The main reason why I did this is because I'm sick and tired of being treated this way everyday [Miller 2008].

Similarly, in a video sent to NBC News just before his attack, Virginia Tech shooter Seung-Hui Cho proclaimed:

> You forced me into a corner and gave me only one option.... You just loved to crucify me. You loved inducing cancer in my head, terror in my heart and ripping my soul all this time [Fantz and Meserve, 2007].

These planned attacks are violent public declarations intended to capture national attention. Not surprisingly, then, rampage shootings receive more attention from the mainstream news media than any other form of school violence (Muschert 2007). In the aftermath of school shootings, journalists often spend days outlining everything that happened during the incident. After this period of initial shock has ended, the media begin to incorporate discussions about the catalyst for the shooting. These discussions within the news have likely contributed to the moral panic over school shootings within the United States in the past two decades.

Moral Panics

Moral panics are widespread fears within a population about a person, a group, a movement, or a condition that is seen as threatening to a society's stable order (Thompson 1998). The moral panic over school shootings is based on a fear of youth being more violent than ever (Burns and Crawford 1999). This moral panic is continually being constructed and reworked through media discussions about the causes of school shootings. In the late 1990s, for example, the moral panic over school shootings centered around fears about violent video games and trench-coat-wearing students who were social outcasts (Samuels 2000; Ogle et al. 2003). Between 2000 and 2006, fear about school shootings in the media focused on gun control policies (Haider-Markel and Joslyn 2001). Since the Virginia Tech massacre in 2007, concerns about school shootings have focused on mental health issues (Kolenic 2009).

These various debates within the media about potential causes of school shootings all share a similar concern about young people in general. Muschert (2007) notes that there has been somewhat of a Rashomon effect in the sociological and public discussions about school shootings in which a multitude of different explanations about the causes and motives of this phenomenon have been given. Instead of unified and consistent dialogue, the scholarly and news media discussions about the causes of school shootings are characterized by inharmonious, simplified solutions. In September of 2008, the online news website Salon.com ran an article that outlined various characteristics among school shooters. The title of the article was "When Kids Become Mass Murderers" (Miller 2008). The mistake being made in these discussions within the media is that talking about *kids* negates the fact that nearly all school shootings in the last two decades have been committed by boys and young men (Langman 2009a). Scholars have shown that discussions about gender are often left out of the mainstream media's discourse about the causes and motives behind school shootings (Mai and Alpert 2000; Neroni 2000; Newman 2004). However, gender-oriented dialogue will never be integrated into the media's discourse about this issue if the media do not even recognize school shootings as a gender-specific problem — one that is perpetrated almost exclusively by boys and young men. This chapter analyzes whether the media frame discussions about the causes of school shootings in a gender-specific or a gender-neutral way. Are the media talking specifically about boys and young men or just kids and young adults?

Gender, Violence, and the Media

General research on media coverage of violent crimes by women demonstrates that violence is assumed to be "natural" for men and "unnatural" for women. Berrington and Honkatukia (2002) analyzed the media coverage around a woman who murdered several people and found that the media framed her as a "mad woman" because it was "unnatural" for a woman to be violent. Because she was a woman using lethal violence, the media presumed that she was mentally ill. Many sociologists have found that the discourse about violent men, on the other hand, does not involve explicit discussions about gender. This is especially apparent in the literature on school shootings.

Watson (2007) argues that because school shooters are usually middle class, white males, the media and the general public cannot seem to make the connection between gender and the crimes. Sociologists have used the term male privilege to describe the unearned benefits and exemptions that men receive (McIntosh 2004). In the case of school shootings, male privilege makes the young men's gender become invisible in discussions about causes. Watson notes that we blame easy access to guns, lack of parental supervision, and the media, even though girls experience these things just as much as boys, and yet, school shootings are overwhelmingly committed by boys and young men.

Some gender scholars have analyzed school shooting media discourse in order to uncover how homophobia plays a role in these shootings. Kimmel and Mahler (2003) suggest that masculinity and homophobia should be at the center of discussions about the causes of school shootings. They analyzed media coverage of school shootings and focused on discussions about bullying to show that the young men behind most school shootings were frequently bullied and picked on.

Other sociologists have tried to uncover why gender is not talked about in media discourse about school shootings. One reason why gender is overlooked by the media is because the young men who commit school shootings are often framed as individual deviants, which overshadows social problems that may be linked to these events. Consalvo (2003) argues that the media ignore discussions about school culture, race, and masculinity. She analyzed news coverage that immediately followed the Columbine High School shooting and found that the two young men involved in the shooting were framed as "monsters." As a result, the media failed to analyze how societal issues, such as violence and masculinity, played a role in the events.

Scholars have pointed out that the media fail to give any attention to gender when discussing school shootings. This article attempts to expand on this literature by focusing on whether the media talk about the causes of school shootings through a gender-neutral frame or through a gender-specific frame. That is, do they use neutral words such as kids, teenagers, young people, killer, or attacker, or do they use gender-specific words such as boys, young men, gunman, or even he? It is worth looking specifically at media reports that discuss causes and motives because they have major implications. They supposedly provide the answers or the solutions to the problem of school shootings. And, if these articles fail to recognize this as a gendered issue — one that is specifically about boys and young men — then these "answers" will be missing the point.

Data and Methods

In this study I used content analysis, a method for examining the symbolic content of media communication (Singleton and Straits 2010). I coded and analyzed media coverage of school shootings that specifically discussed causes or motives behind the shootings. My population was newspaper articles and television and radio reports discussing motives and causes. I collected my data using the LexisNexis academic search engine, using the keyword "school shooting." Because there were a large number of news reports on school shootings, I used a non-random convenience sample method to collect my data. I read the first 250 newspaper articles and the first 250 television and radio transcripts that I came across and selected all the news reports that discussed causes or motives for rampage school shootings. In those I found 20 newspaper articles and 17 television and radio transcripts that discussed causes and motives behind school shootings. Within those articles and transcripts, I coded 52 discussions about the causes and motives behind school shootings. Some of the most frequently discussed school shootings within the articles included: the 1999 Columbine High School shooting, in which 18-year-old Eric Harris and 17-year-old Dylan Klebold shot and killed 12 of their peers and one teacher before killing themselves; the 2001 Santana High School shooting, in which 15-year-old Charles Andrew Williams killed two fellow students and wounded 13 others; and the 2007 Virginia Tech shooting, in which 23-year-old Seung-Hui Cho killed 32 people before killing himself (Langman 2009b).

I searched within the timeframe of the past 10 years (1999–2009) because I wanted to analyze the current discourse on school shootings. Because the media discussions often focus on school shootings that occur within the United States—and, to a lesser extent, Canada — I limited my sample to North American media. The news sources were selected based on availability in the LexisNexis database. The newspaper articles that I collected came from *The St. Petersburg Times, The Washington Post, The Boston Globe, The New York Times, Daily News, Christian Science Monitor* and *USA Today*. I specifically used these newspapers because they are national in coverage and in circulation. The television and radio transcripts that I analyzed came from CNN, CBS News, MSNBC, ABC News, CTV Newsnet, and NPR News. Similar to the newspaper publications, the television and radio sources searched were selected because they are broadcasted nationwide and participate in national discussions.

If an article devoted at least one paragraph to a cause of school shootings, or a specific motive of one of the young men, then I identified the article as having a discussion about causes and motives. Some articles, then, had more than one discussion. Within those paragraphs that discussed causes and motives, I coded the nouns and pronouns as either gender-neutral or gender-specific.

Table 1. Gender-Specific versus Gender-Neutral Words

Type of Word	Gender-Specific Words	Gender-Neutral Words
Pronoun	He	They
		Everyone
Violence-Related	Gunman/Gunmen	Shooter(s)
		Killer(s)
Youth-Related	Boy(s)	Child/Children
	Young man/Young men	Young Person/ Young People
		Student(s)
		Teenager(s)

Nouns and pronouns that were coded as gender neutral included *they, everyone, shooter(s), killer(s), child/children, young person/young people, student(s),* and *teenager(s)*. Nouns and pronouns that were coded as gender-specific included *he, gunman/gunmen, boy*(s), and *young man/young men*. The word *gunman* was particularly interesting because in some ways it implies a gender-neutral frame. However, I coded it as gender-specific because it is the equivalent to the gender-neutral word *shooter*. If the discussions used only gender-neutral nouns and pronouns, this indicated that school shootings were projected as a non-gendered issue. On the other hand, if there were any gender-specific nouns or pronouns used in the discussions, this indicated that school shootings were projected as an issue specific to boys and young men.

I also coded for what types of issues were talked about within the discussions that might offer explanations for the shootings. I coded conversations about issues of adolescent bullying and teasing, or about the boys and young men involved in the shootings being picked on or harassed, as discussions about bullying. Some media reports suggested that school shootings were the result of young men emulating other school shootings that they have seen or heard about. I coded these conversations as discussions about "copy cat" attacks. Some of the most recurring topics in the reporting on school shootings revolved around gun policies and the boys' and young men's access to firearms. I coded these conversations as discussions about access to guns. Some of the articles on school shootings discussed depression, social anxiety and other mental disorders, as well as the need to improve counseling of adolescent mental issues. I coded examinations of these issues within the articles as discussions about behavioral and mental disorders. Other articles focused on exposure to violent media and mainstream news media coverage of school shootings as a possible cause. These were coded as discussions about media. Any cause or motive that was discussed in two or fewer articles was put into the "other" category. Some of the discussions in this category included video games, seeking attention, and lack of parental guidance.

Results and Discussion

In all, only 19 percent of the discussions that I coded used a gendered frame. The remaining 81 percent of the discussions were completely gender-neutral in their language. This shows that the media do not seem to recognize school shootings as an issue that is specifically about boys and young men. Gender-neutral words such as *student* and *shooter* were the most commonly used words to talk about the young men. When speaking broadly about the causes of school shootings, the media used the words *young people*, *children*, and *kids* the most often.

I broke the discussions down by specific causes and motives (see Table 2). I found that bullying was discussed through a gender-specific frame more than any other issue. For reporters, there is perhaps a connection between bullying and boys and young men. This relates to Kimmel and Mahler's (2003) study, which analyzed media coverage to show that the young men and boys behind the school shootings were often bullied. Not only do the media seem to give a fair amount of attention to bullying, but they also do it through a more gender-specific frame compared to other issues. Copy cat attacks (28 percent) and access to guns (28 percent) were close behind in terms of the use of gender-specific language.

Table 2. Gender-Specific vs Gender-Neutral Framing by Discussion

Cause/Motive	Gender Specific	Gender Neutral	Total
Bullying	3 (30%)	7 (70%)	10
"Copy Cat" Attacks	2 (28%)	5 (72%)	7
Access to Guns	4 (28%)	10 (72%)	14
Behavioral and Mental Disorders	1 (10%)	9 (90%)	10
Media		6 (100%)	6
Other		5 (100%)	5
Total	10 (19%)	42 (81%)	52

Behavioral and mental disorders was one of the most frequently discussed issues (10 discussions), and yet, there was only one discussion of this issue that incorporated gender-specific language. This is particularly interesting, as it relates to Berrington and Honkatukia's (2002) analysis of media framings of violent women. When reporting on violent women, the media often seem to connect gender and mental disorders. Conscious or not, the media construct the idea that women are naturally non-violent, and any woman who deviates from this assumption is presumed to be mentally ill. When it comes to boys and young men, however, these data show that the media do not make the same connection between gender and mental illness. In the midst of two school shootings in March of 2001 (the Santana High shooting and a school shooting in El Cajon, California, in which five students were injured) one CNN news anchor asked, "How to keep something like this from happening again? The government's put together a guide to help adults identify warning signs in troubled children" (Chen 2001). The media considers mental and behavioral disorders to be an issue associated with school shootings, but not because of the boys' and young mens' gender. This reinforces the idea that violence is "natural" or expected for boys, and that concerns over psychological problems only arise if the violent act is extreme, such as a school shooting.

I coded for the type of media in order to analyze possible differences between print media (newspapers) and non-print media (television and radio) in the use of gendered language.

Table 3. Gender-Specific vs Gender-Neutral Framing by Media Type

	Gender-Specific	Gender-Neutral	Total
Newspaper	3 (9%)	30 (91%)	33
Television and Radio	7 (37%)	12 (63%)	19
Total	10 (19%)	42 (81%)	52

Although there were more discussions about causes and motives in the newspapers compared to television and radio, there was a much higher chance of gender-specific discussions in the TV and radio reports. There was a positive correlation between type of media and use of gender-specific frame (chi square = 5.98 level of significance). One explanation for the differences in the use of gendered language by the print and non-print media is that newspapers may be more likely to discuss school shootings from a more broad perspective, whereas television and radio discussions may focus more on specific incidences. In the wake of the 2001 school shooting at Santana High, NBC News ran a segment entitled "Shooting at Santana High; Terror and Tears at Schools Across the Country; Questions About Cause, Copycats, and Whether Anything Can be Done to Prevent This Kind of Tragedy in the Future" (O'Donnell 2001). The piece recounted the attack and described the community's reaction to the incident before exploring possible causes for the shooting. Several weeks after that, the newspaper publication Christian Science Monitor ran an article entitled "Are Media Acting as a Publicity Machine for Shooters?" (Wood 2001). Instead of reporting on one specific incident, the newspaper article examined school shootings more broadly in its conversation about the catalyst behind such attacks. By talking broadly about school shootings, the newspaper articles may be more likely to use abstract references such as "kids" and "young people." The television and radio reports may discuss specific incidents more often and therefore may be more likely to use gender-specific language in their assessment of possible causes.

I also examined who exactly was using gender-specific frames. Reporters often quoted other people within their discussions about the causes and motives of school shootings. In 2001, for example, U.S. Attorney General John Ashcroft was quoted in a *Washington Times* article, urging the public to adopt a more comprehensive approach to addressing the "ethic of violence that young people seem to embrace" (Seper 2001). Just days after a shooting in El Cajon, California, California Governor Gray Davis appeared on CNN, suggesting that in order to prevent such violent occurrences from happening again, we must "be alert to the possibility of a child feeling alienated, distraught and left out" (Cornish 2001). I coded the discussions to see if there was any variation among experts (sociologists, psychologists, criminologists), non-experts (politicians, police officers, witnesses, prosecutors), and the reporters themselves in the use of gender-specific versus gender-neutral frames. I did not find a significant difference among experts, non-experts, and reporters with respect to gender framing. However, I did find that when using a gender-specific frame, experts often made it a point to mention gender. The following two quotes came from Dr. William Pollack, a psychologist who was interviewed by two different media outlets:

> Well, I think there's definitely a code of silence, particularly for boys, as part of what I have called the Boy Code [Edwards and Corley 2001].
> These young men — and they were all men in this case, had come to the attention of those in authority for having emotional problems or causing problems for others before the events occurred [McFadden 2008].

When they were interviewed, experts brought up gendered issues such as the "Boy Code." Experts, however, were very rarely interviewed for discussions about the causes and motives behind school shootings.

Conclusion and Analysis

This chapter has attempted to re-conceptualize the way we analyze the media's lack of attention given to gender in school shooting discourse. The argument being made is that we should analyze whether or not the media use gender-specific language in discussions about the causes of school shootings. If the media do not recognize school shootings as a gender-specific issue — one that is about boys and young men — then they are very unlikely to talk explicitly about gender and masculinity as potential causes. These results show that most of the mainstream media do not talk about school shootings through a gender-specific frame.

Why does the media discourse about school shootings overwhelmingly use gender-neutral language? One possible reason is that it may be assumed that the reporter, witness, or expert is talking specifically about boys and young men when they say kids and teenagers. In her groundbreaking book, *The Second Sex* (1989), Simone de Beauvoir argues that women have been defined as the "other" sex throughout history. This has no doubt been the case in the realm of language where male is the unmarked sex and female is the marked. If femaleness is the "other" in our culture, then maleness is defined by its place as the norm. This may help to explain why nearly four out of five discussions about causes and motives within this study used completely gender-neutral language. The implicit message within media discussion about school shootings is that the boys' and young men's gender does not need to be examined — they are just kids and teenages. Besides being male, most of the boys and young men behind school shootings were also white, heterosexual, middle-class, and from suburban areas (Kimmel and Mahler 2003). These characteristics may be what come to mind when someone uses abstract words such as *kids* and *young people*. Such may have been the case for the newspaper articles in this study, which were more likely than other types of media to talk about the causes of school shootings from a gender-neutral frame. It may be assumed, then, that the conversation is about young men whenever gender-neutral language is used in the media to talk about school shootings. This is problematic, however, because this type of assumption causes gender to become invisible in discussions about school shootings. Gender-neutral discussions about the causes of school shootings imply gender-neutral solutions.

The normalization of violence for boys and young men in our culture may also contribute to the lack of gender-specific language in discussions about school shootings. The media may be using neutral language because masculinity and violence are so intertwined that gender may become hidden in such cases. Aggressive behavior by boys and young men in our culture is often explained by arguments that suggest that men are "genetically programmed" to be violent (Katz 1999). Violence is assumed to be a normal part of the boyhood experience in America. If violence is expected for boys and young men, then the media have no reason to make a point of using gender-specific language when talking about school shootings. If girls and young women were committing similar violent acts at school, gender would most likely be at the center of media attention (Katz 1999). In the early 2000s, for example, the media exploded with speculations about alarming rates of violence brought about by a hostile new generation of "bad girls" after an incident at a suburban Illinois high school left several girls hospitalized (Chesney-Lind and Irwin 2004).

While these findings should be of concern to sociologists, they are equally relevant for the journalistic community. When the mainstream media discuss issues such as bulimia and anorexia — which are much more likely to affect girls and young women — they generally use a gender-specific frame. And yet, although nearly all school shootings are carried out by boys and young men (Langman 2009a), this study found that less than 20 percent of discussions in the media used a gender-specific frame. There is evidence to suggest that journalists would benefit from training in this area. For example, to address the issue of gender and reporting on domestic violence, the Washington State Coalition Against Domestic Violence issued a "Guide for Journalists and other Media Professionals" (Starr 2002). This report helped to improve journalists' understanding of gender when they report on domestic violence. It also gave tips for accurately reporting on domestic violence, as well as things to avoid. This type of report would be extremely beneficial for media coverage of school shootings.

Although males have committed nearly all school shootings, there have been a few violence and gun related incidences involving a female perpetrator. Future research could analyze incidences committed by females to see if gender-specific language is used in discussions of those cases. Future research on gender and media discourse could also compare coverage of school shootings with other gendered issues, such as anorexia and women, and acts of terrorism and men. When it comes to discussions about mental disorders and violence, this study, along with Berrington and Honkatukia's (2002) has shown that there are major differences in the ways that the media talk about violent women and violent men. However, there may be other ways in which the media report differently on gendered issues as they relate to women and men.

REFERENCES

Beauvoir, Simone de. 1989. *The Second Sex.* Translated by H. M. Parshley. New York: Vintage Books.

Berrington, Eileen, and Paivi Honkatukia. 2002. "An Evil Monster and a Poor Thing: Female Violence in the Media." *Journal of Scandinavian Studies in Criminology and Crime Prevention* 3 (1): 50–72.

Burns, Ronald, and Charles Crawford. 1999. "School Shootings, the Media, and Public Fear: Ingredients for a Moral Panic." *Crime, Law & Social Change* 32 (2): 147–168.

Chen, Joie. 2001. "The Nation Reacts to Santana High School Shooting." *CNN*, March 6.

Chesney-Lind, Meda, and Katherine Irwin. 2004. "From Badness to Meanness: Popular Constructions of Contemporary Girlhood." In Anita Harris (ed.), *All About the Girl: Culture, Power, and Identity:* 45–56. New York: Routledge.

Consalvo, Mia. 2003. "The Monsters Next Door: Media Construction of Boys and Masculinity." *Feminist Media Studies* 3 (1): 27–41.

Cornish, Eileen. 2001. "Only Shooter Seriously Injured in Assault on California School." *CNN*, March 23.

Edwards, Bob, and Cheryl Corley. 2001. "School Officials Across The Country Trying to Prevent School Shootings By Encouraging Students to Speak Out Against Fellow Classmates Who Make Threats." *NPR, Morning Edition.*

Fantz, Ashley, and Jeanne Meserve. 2007. "Witness Survives by Pretending to be Dead." *CNN.com,* April 17.

Haider-Markel, Donald P., and Mark R. Joslyn. 2001. "Gun Policy, Opinion, Tragedy, and Blame Attribution: The Conditional Influence of Issue Frames." *Journal of Politics* 63 (2): 520–543.

Katz, Jackson 1999. *Tough Guise* Video. Media Education Foundation.
Kimmel, Michael, and Matthew Mahler. 2003. "Adolescent Masculinity, Homophobia, and Violence." *The American Behavioral Scientist* 45(10): 1439–1456.
Kolenic, Anthony J. 2009. "Madness in the Making: Creating and Denying Narratives from Virginia Tech to Gotham City." *Journal of Popular Culture* 42 (6): 1023–1039.
Langman, Peter. 2009a. *Why Kids Kill: Inside the Mind of School Shooters.* New York: Palgrave Macmillan.
_____. 2009b. "Rampage School Shooter: A Typology." *Aggression and Violent Behavior* 14(1): 79–86.
Mai, Rebecca, and Judith Alpert. 2000. "Separation and Socialization: A Feminist Analysis of the School Shootings at Columbine." *Journal for the Psychoanalysis of Culture and Society* 5 (2): 264–275.
McFadden, Cynthia. 2008. "Mind of a Shooter; Preventing Tragedy." *ABC News.*
McIntosh, Peggy. 2004. "White Privilege: Unpacking The Invisible Knapsack." In Paula S. Rothenberg (ed.), *Race, Class, and Gender in the United States:* 188–192. New York: Worth.
Miller, Laura. 2008. "When Kids Become Mass Murderers." *Salon.com.*
Muschert, W. Glenn. 2007. "Research in School Shootings." *Sociological Compass* 1(1): 60–80.
Neroni, Hilary. 2000. "The Men of Columbine: Violence and Masculinity in American Culture and Film." *Journal for the Psychoanalysis of Culture and Society* 5(2): 256–263.
Newman, Katherine. 2004. *Rampage: The Social Roots of School Shootings.* New York: Basic Books.
O'Donnell, Norah. 2001. "Shooting at Santana High; Terror and Tears at Schools Across the Country; Questions About Cause, Copycats, and Whether Anything Can be Done to Prevent this Kind of Tragedy in the Future." *NBC News,* March 11.
Ogle, Jennifer Paff, Molly Eckman, and Catherine Amoroso Leslie. 2003. "Appearance Cues and the Shootings at Columbine High: Construction of a Social Problem in the Print Media." *Sociological Inquiry* 73(1): 1–27.
Samuels, Robert. 2000. "From Columbine to Professional Wrestling: Psychoanalysis of Postmodern Media Violence." *Journal for the Psychoanalysis of Culture and Society* 5 (2): 312–318.
Seper, Jerry. 2001. "Ashcroft Urges Era of Responsibility." *The Washington Times,* March 24.
Singleton, Jr., Royce A., and Bruce C. Straits. 2005. *Approaches to Social Research.* 4th Ed. New York: Oxford University Press.
Starr, Kelly. 2002. "Covering Domestic Violence: A Guide for Journalists and Other Media Professionals." *Washington State Coalition Against Domestic Violence.*
Thompson, Kenneth. 1998. *Moral Panics.* New York: Routledge.
Watson, Sandy White. 2007. "Boys, Masculinity and School Violence: Reaping What We Sow." *Gender and Education* 19(6): 729–737.
Wood, Daniel. 2001. "Are Media Acting as a Publicity Machine for Shooters?" *The Christian Science Monitor,* March 26.

The Social Construction of
Methamphetamine in the Print Media

TERESA ROACH

A Sunday, July 27, 2002, *Los Angeles Times* article runs the headline "Complaint Paints Desperate Picture of Blaze Suspect" with the subheading "Sequoia: Woman allegedly used drugs, stalked husband before setting campfire that grew out of control" (Arax and Boxall). The article goes on to report that this woman "allegedly smoked methamphetamine before setting the fire." What do we (the readers) learn from this headline and subsequent article? We learn that not only is this methamphetamine user destructive, uncontrollable, and dangerous, but perhaps most importantly — we learn that she is violent and we do not want to be like her.

Throughout American history, different drugs have been demonized. For instance in the past 100 years, heroin, marijuana, and crack are all drugs that at one point were a focus for law enforcement efforts and that endured an overall "demonization" in the public arena (King 2006; Musto 1999; Reinarman and Levine 1997). It now appears methamphetamine may be the next drug of "attack" by the federal government and policy makers. Additionally, it has become a major focus for law enforcement officials in rural America (Armstrong 2007) and has also received considerable coverage in the media. For example, in 2005 the Meth Project was created to target methamphetamine use with an implicit focus on prevention. The Meth Project was launched in Montana and uses graphic television descriptions of the "consequences" of methamphetamine as well as billboard prevention ads to focus on prevention of using methamphetamine. Since 2005 the Meth Project has expanded from Montana to other states including Georgia, Illinois, and Arizona (The Meth Project 2010).

It is important to better understand the presentation of drug-related events in the news media. Research suggests that people use information that they receive from the media to construct a vision of the world. These media effects, although subtle, may influence readers' perceptions to the extent that they can affect the audiences' political consciousness (Herda-Rapp 2003). Additionally, social construction can be best understood as the way in which social phenomena are created, institutionalized and made into tradition by humans (Berger and Luckman 1966). Therefore, when methamphetamine is mentioned continually in the news media, individuals cannot help but internalize what they encounter from news reports (Kappeler, Blumberg and Potter 1996). As Reinarman and Levine (1995) suggest, the media perform an agenda-setting function, by influencing what we think about, and consumers of the news media are actively involved in investing the news with meaning (Williams and Dickinson 1993).

This study broadly examines how methamphetamine and methamphetamine users are portrayed in the print media. The print media sources the *Los Angeles Times* and the *Boston Globe* were examined for the three-year period ranging from 2000 to 2002. Fundamentally, wider social and cultural factors are explored that may influence the presentation and representation of methamphetamine and methamphetamine users within the *Los Angeles Times* and the *Boston Globe* and how these representations work to shape constructions of methamphetamine use and users.

Methamphetamine in the United States

Methamphetamine is a synthetic drug that is a stimulant of the central nervous system; as a street drug it is often known as "speed" or "crank" (Jenkins 1994). Methamphetamine was first used in the 1930s for a variety of medical purposes (Miller 1997). However, by the 1960s demand for methamphetamine had far outstripped recognized medical treatment options and the federal government took notice. The Controlled Substance Act of 1970 classified methamphetamine as a Schedule II illegal substance and as a result of these increased restrictions the production and use of methamphetamine in the late 1960s and 1970s declined (Hunt, Kuck, and Truitt 2006).

However, this limitation of legal avenues for methamphetamine fostered an environment for the illegal production of methamphetamine, which proved cheap and extremely easy to make. Recently, methamphetamine has come under even tighter federal controls intended to further curb the illegal use and distribution of the drug. The 1996 Methamphetamine Control Act strengthened penalties for possession, distribution, and manufacturing (Hunt, Kuck and Truitt 2006). Additionally, methamphetamine has been a focus for both federal and state governments. In 2004, a number of states banned over-the-counter selling of cold tablets because the active ingredient (pseudoephedrine) can be used in the production of illegal methamphetamine (Drug Enforcement Administration 2006) and in 2006 Congress passed the Combat Methamphetamine Epidemic Act of 2005 (U.S. Drug Enforcement Administration 2006) to tighten regulations on the chemicals used to manufacture methamphetamine as well as to increase the penalties for the distribution and possession of methamphetamine (Hunt, Kuck and Truitt 2006). A direct consequence of these new regulations can be seen in the recent fining of CVS Pharmacy Inc. According to news reports (Girion and Glover 2010), CVS has agreed to pay $75 million in fines and to forfeit $2.6 million in profits for allowing repeated purchases of pseudoephedrine. Prosecutors allege that the violation of the law has led to a "spike" in Southern California drug trafficking.

Despite this increased attention and direct law making efforts that would suggest that, perhaps, there has been an increase in the use of methamphetamine. This appears to not be the case as methamphetamine still remains one of the least commonly used and abused drugs. Only .2 percent of Americans are regular users of methamphetamine, while 30 times as many Americans use marijuana and four times as many Americans use cocaine on a regular basis (King 2006). Statistics from the 2007 National Survey on Drug Use and Health report that the number of current methamphetamine users aged 18–25 decreased from .6 percent in 2006 to .4 percent in 2007. Further, lifetime use of methamphetamine for individuals aged 26 or older witnessed the same decline in usage: .6 percent in 2006 to .4 percent in 2007 (National Survey on Drug Use and Health 2007). However, not all drug use is on the decline. Findings from the 2007 National Survey on Drug Use and Health report increases in current use of prescription pain relievers among individuals aged 18–25, and adults aged 26 or older reported increases in lifetime use of marijuana. Further, when examining the use of illegal drugs among racial and ethnic minorities, a 2003 report from the National Institute on Drug Abuse estimates that 6.4 percent of whites have recently engaged in illegal drug use and the rates for non–Hispanic blacks and Hispanic whites are virtually the same.

Additionally, findings from the 2003 National Institute on Drug Abuse report cite statistics from the 2000 Drug Abuse Warning Network (DAWN) with respect to minority drug use. The Drug Abuse Warning Network is a public health surveillance system that monitors drug-related visits to hospital emergency departments and drug-related deaths that are investigated by medical examiners and coroners. DAWN reports that when methamphetamine was mentioned in emergency department visits it was mentioned 63.7 percent by whites compared to 6.2 percent by blacks and 16.1 percent by Hispanics. Thus, national statistics report variation within drug use with respect to minority and white users.

Social Construction, the Media, and Drug Use

As Berger and Luckman (1966) suggest, all human activity is subject to habitualization. Actions, such as reading the newspaper, become meaningful (habitualized) when they become embedded as routine. Thus, the mass media represents an institution in daily life and as a consequence of continual mentions of methamphetamine in the print media, individuals cannot help but internalize what they encounter. People use information that they receive from the media to construct a view of their world (Surette 1992).

Historically, studies of drug policy detail how certain drugs associated with particular races or classes were prohibited while others condoned (Musto 1999; Reinarman and Levine 1997). White middle class women largely used morphine and other narcotics in the early 1900s, but it was not until narcotic use shifted to the lower classes that its use became highly criminalized (Musto 1999). Other examples include crack use in the 1980s by black Americans. Crack use by blacks was largely criminalized and targeted by law enforcement and drug policy, yet use of powder cocaine by upper-middle class white Americans was not criminalized with such extreme measures (Reinarman and Levine 1997). Drug policy that only targets one group of individuals leads to an overwhelming perception of "us" and "them" (Elliott and Chapman 2000). Essentially, drug users become constructed as socially deviant and this marginalization likely contributes to the stigmatization of the user. Researchers Granfield and Cloud (1996) suggest classifying addicts as "other" has contributed to a "ghettoization" of drug users and the media plays an important role in shaping these public attitudes, opinions and constructions (Welch, Fenwick, and Roberts 1998).

Word choice in media presentation can also contribute to the construction of a problem. When the media associate methamphetamine with words such as "epidemic" or "plague" (Jenkins 1994; Orcutt and Turner 1993), a theme of problematic and dangerous drug use develops as represented by the media, which is then internalized by the reader. Jenkins (1994) convincingly demonstrates in his 1994 research study on the presentation of crystal methamphetamine in the media that the employment of rhetoric such as "Police chilled by New In-Drug Ice" and "The hidden methamphetamine plague" (see Jenkins 1994, 15–16) contributed to a social construction of "ice." Jenkins (1994) argues that these statements increased the national fear that ice would infiltrate all areas of the United States. Therefore, the use of rhetoric such as this is problematic because it may cause the reader to believe that methamphetamine use is more frequent and challenging than it actually is.

Thus, when we consider these concepts in the context of methamphetamine it is not hard to draw the conclusion that an association between methamphetamine and consistent negative images may contribute to a social construction of use and users. This study attempts to decipher the role that the print media has in shaping constructions about methamphetamine use and users.

Data and Method

To address how the media presented methamphetamine and methamphetamine use, a content analysis of newspaper articles from the *Los Angeles Times* and the *Boston Globe* was used. The *Los Angeles Times* and the *Boston Globe* were selected as data sources as they are two newspapers that are read in large cities in the United States. However, the *Los Angeles Times* has a more national circulation network than the *Boston Globe;* therefore, the *Los Angeles Times* localized Metro/Los Angeles area (Home Edition) version was used in this study with the expectation that the types of articles presented in both newspapers would be similar.

The sampling frame of the two primary data sources covered the three-year period from 2000 to 2002. This time frame is prior to the ban on selling of over the counter cold tablets in 2004 and the passing of the 2006 anti-methamphetamine legislation. A time frame prior to these actions was selected to examine how methamphetamine and users were portrayed in the print media prior to the passing of such legislation. The third full week of each month of each newspaper was reviewed for a representative sampling of newspaper articles. This yielded a total of 504 newspapers. Only sections A (Nation) and B (Metro/News) were examined in each of the newspapers because these were the two sections that matched the most closely across the newspapers in terms of content. All years of the newspapers were viewed on microfilm.

The newspapers were reviewed for mentions of the word methamphetamine, meth, any street slang derivative of the word methamphetamine (i.e., ice, crank, speed, etc.) as well as any chemical makeup terms that contained the word methamphetamine (i.e,. dioxymethaphetamine), as well as the words stimulant, amphetamine, pseudoephedrine, and for mentions of Ritalin (a synthetic amphetamine that mimics the effects of methamphetamine). This yielded a total of 96 newspaper articles, 77 from the *Los Angeles Times* and 19 from the *Boston Globe.* A content analysis was then performed on this subset of newspaper articles.

Table 1.
Frequency of Articles Included in Study Sample
by Newspaper and Year

	The Los Angeles Times	*The Boston Globe*
2000	78.1% (25)	21.7% (7)
2001	89.7% (26)	10.3% (3)
2002	74.3% (26)	25.7% (9)
n	77	19
N	96	

Overall, methamphetamine was mentioned more frequently in the *Los Angeles Times* than the *Boston Globe.* Eighty percent (n=77) of the sample is comprised of *Los Angeles Times* articles, while the remaining twenty percent (n=19) come from the *Boston Globe.* Further, methamphetamine mentions did not vary considerably over the three-year period. In 2000, 25 articles in the *Los Angeles Times* and 7 articles in the *Boston Globe* were included in the sample, in 2001 26 articles and 3 articles were included from the *Los Angeles Times* and *the Boston Globe* respectively, and finally, in 2002, 25 articles from the *Los Angeles Times* and 9 from the *Boston Globe*, were included in the data set for a total of 96 articles.

Initial thoughts about the data were structured around methamphetamine and drug use and users following a grounded theory approach (Charmaz 2006). The articles were read and then coded and memos were taken that identified the most salient themes that were present in each article. As the articles were being coded, themes started to evolve from the data. Broadly, mentions of methamphetamine occurred in the context of crime and law enforcement and methamphetamine mentions occurred more frequently in the *Los Angeles Times* than the *Boston Globe*. Once, the initial context of crime and law enforcement was broken down the broad category construction of sensationalism of methamphetamine in the print media became apparent and the subcategories of methamphetamine as harmful, methamphetamine as a social problem and methamphetamine as a perceived threat were developed.

Findings and Analysis

Table 2.
Frequency of Newspaper Themes

	N	%
Methamphetamine as Harmful	30	31.3
Methamphetamine as Social Problem	16	16.7
Methamphetamine as Perceived Threat	18	18.8
N	64	66.7

Methamphetamine as Harmful

Methamphetamine was frequently mentioned in the context of harm. Thirty-one percent (N=30) of the sample reflected a main theme of harm as the result of methamphetamine. For example, harm as a consequence of methamphetamine could be directed at the environment, as a May 25, 2000, *Boston Globe* article reported: "Drug lab suspected at site of blast" (Associated Press).

However, overwhelmingly, this harm was directed towards children. Roughly, two-thirds of the harm sample (n=19) explicitly referenced methamphetamine as having harmful consequences for children. Further, the majority of harm towards children was reported in the *Los Angeles Times* (n=16) and in the year 2000 sample (n=12). Evidence of harm towards children can be found in news reports such as the following September 20, 2000, *Los Angeles Times* article:

> "Three arrested in a raid at an alleged methamphetamine lab ... police said they found a handgun and a small amount of methamphetamine. Three children were taken into protective custody"

an April 16, 2000, *Boston Globe* article that reported:

> "Police say the two men who lived in the apartment had sodomized the boy repeatedly for hours before he died ... police who searched the apartment later found small quantities of a prescription drug they say the boy was forced to take and a small amount of what they believe is methamphetamine" [Haddigan].

Further, a November 23, 2000 *Los Angeles Times* article reported, "A man was convicted Wednesday of sexually molesting a girl for 10 years and operating a methamphetamine lab in his home."

Finally, an April 27, 2002, *Los Angeles Times* article ran the following: "Convictions of child workers to be revealed.... The preschool teacher was convicted of methamphetamine possession seven years ago and served several days in jail" (Murillo). Because the article mentions both methamphetamine use and harmful acts towards children the reader associates the two together — methamphetamine users and harm to children, thus methamphetamine users harm children. This problem is further complicated by the fact that individuals who read newspapers do not read objectively.

As Williams and Dickinson (1993) suggest, readers bring their own predispositions that influence their reading of news accounts. Further, children represent a population in society that ideologically is viewed as vulnerable and innocent. Therefore, the May 25, 2000, *Los Angeles Times* headline that reports, "School worker held on charges of selling speed" (B4) is problematic. The reader does not know if the drugs were actively being sold to children but the association of speed and school together allows the reader to construct a picture of who methamphetamine users are.

Further, sensational media constructions around harm include associations with mothers and parents harming their children. As a May 23, 2002, *Los Angeles Times* article reported, "Couple sentenced in death of infant son authorities say had been exposed to methamphetamine" and the September 23, 2000, *Los Angeles Times* article reported, "Mother sentenced in car wreck that killed son ... Julien had been charged with second-degree murder, gross vehicular manslaughter, child abuse, and possession of methamphetamine." Thus, the presentation of methamphetamine, harm, and children, may as Potter and Kappeler (2006) state, incite an emotional reaction from the reader because mothers and parents are supposed to protect and shield their children from danger and as a result the construction of methamphetamine users as harming children is formed.

Methamphetamine as a Social Problem

News reports that referenced methamphetamine frequently did so in the context of other "social problems," thus creating a duality of issues. Seventeen percent of the articles included in the sample referenced methamphetamine in the context of other social problems. For example, the *Boston Globe* or the *Los Angeles Times* would have a report on education, public health, or an opinion or editorial piece and there would be a mention of methamphetamine thus placing methamphetamine in the context of other issues that have already been deemed worthy of media attention. As a consequence, the sensational mention of methamphetamine diverts attention away from the actual issue that is being reported. An April 19, 2001, article in the *Los Angeles Times* illustrates this issue. The article is primarily a report about stolen credit cards and identity theft. The article, however, also reports, "Yamashiro was charged with methamphetamine possession.... They [suspects] are believed to be a part of a Southern California group known as 'the circulation'" (Blankstein and Fausset, B5). Thus, methamphetamine use is framed in the context of other recognized social problems—crime and gang affiliation.

Additionally, a February 23, 2001, *Los Angeles Times* article entitled "Report on Syphilis Reinforces concern about Sex Practices" (Rhone B3), fundamentally a news report focused on the public health ramifications of unsafe sex by gay and bisexual men, provides further evidence of the framing of methamphetamine with other social problems. The article mentions methamphetamine in the following way: "According to the report illicit drugs were used by 40 percent with crystal methamphetamine used the most frequently." Furthermore, a July 17, 2001, *Los Angeles Times* article that is a report on the homicide of a woman as a result of a dispute about a smuggling fee for undocumented immigrants also reports the following: "At the time of his arrest, Rodriguez was wanted by police for driving with a suspended license and possession of methamphetamine" (Piccalo). Thus, the reader is left with a lasting mention of methamphetamine and the implied connection with homicide and illegal immigration. This implicit association with methamphetamine and other social problems is continued in the July 17, 2001, *Los Angeles Times* report about the rape of two teenage girls and assault on two boys: "Suspect was preparing himself for a night out by taking crystal methamphetamine" [Tran and Leonard B10].

Similarly, a July 26, 2002, *Los Angeles Times* article on a Sequoia forest fire and the woman who allegedly set the forest fire reports the following: "VanBrunt has no criminal history related to fires. In 1998, a judge sentenced her to 16 months in state prison after she pleaded guilty to a methamphetamine charge" [Boxall and Arax]. Here, the *Los Angeles Times* reports on a forest fire and highlights the fact that the woman who is suspected of setting the fire has no criminal record related to fires *yet* she did plead guilty to a methamphetamine charge. Thus, methamphetamine once again is framed in the context of another social problem — environmental destruction.

Fundamentally, methamphetamine is framed, constructed and associated with easily identifiable social problems—homicide, HIV/AIDS, the environment, rape, unsafe sex, illegal immigration — and all of these issues have negative connotations in the public sphere.

The newspaper accounts also presented minority groups as using and abusing methamphetamine. The rape and assault of the girls and boys was committed by Latino men, the homicide of the woman was at the hands of a Latino man and the public health report on unsafe sex practices deals with sexual minorities. Thus, crime reports in the media inflame racial tensions and fears through bias and selective coverage (Potter and Kappeler 2006). Media accounts such as this allow for the reader to think that Latinos engage in a disproportionate amount of crime *and* methamphetamine use. Statistics show that this is just not the case. Statistics from the 2003 National Institute of Drug Abuse report "Drug Use Among Racial/Ethnic Minorities" report that 13–15 percent of white arrestees are likely to test positive for methamphetamine use whereas 6 percent of Hispanic arrestees are likely to test positive for methamphetamine and just .8 percent of Black arrestees are likely to test positive for methamphetamine. Thus, media constructions of methamphetamine in the context of other social problems are influential and harmful.

Methamphetamine as a Perceived Threat

Finally, methamphetamine was portrayed in the news media as a perceived threat. This was evidenced by the continual use of sensational rhetoric in relation to methamphetamine use and users. In a December 21, 2002, *Boston Globe* article methamphetamine is called "Nazi Dope" and methamphetamine users are equated to Nazis.

> "In the lexicon of meth, those who make the drug are 'cookers,' though they prefer to think of themselves as modern-day moonshiners. The drug they make is often called 'Nazi dope,' because it is widely believed that the Nazis were given methamphetamine. It's a good drug if you're a Nazi soldier, It makes you paranoid, aggressive, and keeps you from being hungry" [Aitchison, A3].

In seeking to portray a new problem as serious or dangerous, one well-known rhetorical device is to stigmatize that problem by associating it with another already familiar issue, thus placing it into an existing context (Jenkins 1994). The association of Nazis and methamphetamine conjures up negative, highly demonized images in society. A January 20, 2002, *Los Angeles Times* article whose headline states, "We are the Colombia of methamphetamine manufacturing" (Tempest) associates methamphetamine with Colombia and this association may conjure up images and reactions to the "crack scare" in the 1980s and early 1990s, which sociological research has argued was overblown and exacerbated by unfounded claims and media reports (Kappeler and Potter 2005; Reinarman and Levine 1997).

Thus, the word choices that media presentations utilize contribute to the social construction of a problem as evidenced by the following rhetoric employed by newspaper accounts.

"Methamphetamine is slowly coming this way. The labs are popping up in Maine, New Hampshire. It is only a matter of time" [Jiang, October 26, 2002].

"Methamphetamine was a far greater problem than marijuana" [Bailey, Los Angeles Times November 21, 2002].

"As the popularity and production of meth soar" [Seewer, February 19, 2002].

"Clearly Southern California is the Methamphetamine Capital of the world" [Los Angeles Times, April 21, 2000].

From these news portrayals the reader sees that methamphetamine is associated with rhetoric that suggests that methamphetamine is an impending problem and that it is "only a matter of time" before methamphetamine wreaks havoc on society. However, the use of sensational rhetoric in conjunction with methamphetamine is used to incite fear in the reader. Newspaper accounts such as the following contribute to the perceived threat.

"Last year saw a fourfold jump in meth operations and dumps found on public lands" [Murphy, May 21, 2001].

"Methamphetamine is a new and terrible challenge to the United States" [Chu, June 20, 2000].

Consequently, this linkage of methamphetamine with words such as "skyrocketed," "problem" or "spread" contribute to a theme of problematic and dangerous drug use, which is illustrated by the newspaper accounts below:

"Drug Enforcement officials consider methamphetamine the fastest growing illegal drug in the country — and its' use has skyrocketed" [Murphy May 20, 2001 A16].

"Methamphetamine is a growing problem in the South Bay ... fight the spread of methamphetamine use" [Los Angeles Times, April 21, 2000 B4].

The newsreader may actively engage and derive his or her own meaning from accounts such as these (Jenkins 1994; Orcutt and Turner 1993).

Rhetoric such as this contributes to negative constructions of methamphetamine and methamphetamine users. The question remains not whether illegal drugs such as methamphetamine are dangerous but whether or not they are dangerous enough to justify legal prohibition and the social outrage associated with their use (Kappeler, Blumberg, and Potter 1996). Further, methamphetamine is not a "new" drug. As Armstrong (2007) reports, the constant focus on meth and the use of the term "meth" itself, as if a new drug has appeared on the scene, ignores the essential equivalence of methamphetamine and other amphetamines. Therefore, news reports that reference methamphetamine as a "new" drug and couch the reference with inflammatory language contribute to the perception of methamphetamine as a new and threatening problem.

Overall, thirty-five percent (n=34) of the articles in the sample either referenced methamphetamine in the context of other identifiable social problems or utilized provocative rhetoric when reporting a methamphetamine news story. Consequently, as Altheide (1997) reports, this contributes to the linkage of the mass media and individuals perceptions of social problems. Further, given that the average citizen knows little about social problems, the information from the news media is taken at face value, though reports may be biased or reporting on special interests (Altheide 2002; Kupchik and Bracy 2009).

Discussion and Conclusion

What are the ramifications of these news reports? As shown by usage statistics, methamphetamine is a drug that does not have a large population of users. However, these consistent associations with methamphetamine and this sensationalism of media constructions of methamphetamine may contribute to a social construction of use and users that overstates the problem and the need for resources to fix the problem. The continual mentions of methamphetamine in the print media facilitate the internalization of these print media images by the news consumer.

Further, as Berger and Luckman (1966) suggest this habitualization of contact with the news media allows for the news media to become a social institution, which results in the media becoming an effective agent of social control. This effect is possible because the media is similar to other dominant social institutions in that it will reflect the ideology and messages of the dominant culture. Similarly, as Reinarman (2003) argues, the United States has a pattern of historically re-occurring anti-drug crusades and repressive anti-drug policies. For example, the legislation passed to ban over-the-counter selling of cold medication along with the Combat Methamphetamine Epidemic Act of 2005 explicitly exemplifies the conception that methamphetamine is a "problem" that needs to be controlled. Framing legislation around methamphetamine specifically contributes to increasing social control of drug use (Reinarman 2003).

Additionally, the role of the media in contributing to increases in social control related to methamphetamine cannot be ignored. In this study over half of the articles included in this analysis (n=53[1]) sensationalized the presentation of methamphetamine use and users. Whether methamphetamine was framed in the context of harm, as a perceived threat, or reported along with other social problems, the focus was not on the illegal use of methamphetamine but rather centered on evoking an emotional reaction from the reader (Potter and Kappeler 2006) which contributes to a social construction of methamphetamine use and users. This allows for the use of methamphetamine as a general scapegoat for the other social problems (Kappeler, Blumberg, and Potter 1996; Reinarman 2003).

If we recognize that the media represents an important social institution it is important to be wary of the agenda setting purpose that news media accounts may perform (Reinarman and Levine 1995). As research has shown, consumers of the news media are not static readers of news accounts and they interactively engage with what they read. Williams and Dickinson (1993) suggest that readers "actively" interact and create meaning from what they read. Thus, news accounts that portray minority groups in a negative light or associate methamphetamine with words such as "spread" and "problem" set the reader up to believe that methamphetamine use is higher than it is and that users are of minority status. Further, Potter and Kappeler (2006) assert that constructed reality does far more damage than good to understanding the reality of crime. This is evident with the coverage of methamphetamine use in conjunction with other social problems. The obscuring of reality does not allow for an objective opinion of what the *real* problem is. It is not that the use of illegal drugs such as methamphetamine should be condoned; rather, social structural issues such as poverty or the lack of educational opportunities and job resources are largely neglected in favor of blaming illegal drugs as the source of social problems.[2]

NOTES

1. This total includes only the articles that were coded for methamphetamine as harmful towards children. If all methamphetamine as harmful articles are included, n=64.
2. Limitations of this study include the small sample size and that only two newspapers for a select number of years were analyzed. As a result, the findings of this study cannot be generalized to other print media sources in respect to the social construction of methamphetamine in the print media. Thus, this study does not allow for a generalizability of findings regarding the social construction of methamphetamine in the print media. Further, in order for more compelling findings this study should be repeated with a more contemporary sample of current print media sources. Although, there are limitations of this study the findings regarding the sensationalism of media social constructions of methamphetamine are thought provoking nonetheless.

REFERENCES

Aitchison, Diana. Dec. 21, 2002. "Rural Drug Makers Vex Authorities 'Meth Cookers' Exert Potent Impact in Ozarks." *Boston Globe*, A3.
Altheide, David L.1997. "The News Media, the Problem Frame, and the Production of Fear." *The Sociological Quarterly* 38: 647–68.
_____. 2002. *Creating Fear: News and the Construction of Crisis.* New York: Aldine de Gruyter.
Arax, Mark, and Bettina Boxall. July 27, 2002. "Complaint Paints Desperate Picture of Blaze Suspect." *Los Angeles Times*, B10.
Armstrong, Edward G. 2007. "Moral Panic Over Meth." *Contemporary Justice Review* 10: 427–42.
Associated Press. May 25, 2000. "Drug Lab Suspected at Site of Blast." *Boston Globe*, A15.
Bailey, Eric. Nov. 21, 2002. "Pot Raids Spur Calls to Quit Working With DEA." *Los Angeles Times*, B10.
Berger, Peter L., and Thomas Luckman. 1966. *The Social Construction of Reality: A Treatise in the Sociology of Knowledge.* New York: Anchor Books.
Blankstein, Andrew, and Richard Fausset. April 19, 2001. "2 Arrested in Credit Card, Identity Theft." *Los Angeles Times*, B5.
Boxall, Bettina, and Mark Arax. July 26, 2002. "Sequoia Blaze Keeps on Burning." *Los Angeles Times*, B8.
Charmaz, Kathy. 2006. *Constructing Grounded Theory. A Practical Guide Through Qualitative Analysis.* Thousand Oaks, CA: Sage.
Chu, Henry. June 20, 2000. "U.S., China Will Pool Resources in Drug Fight." *Los Angeles Times*, A4.

Drug Administration Agency. 2006. "Fact Sheet: The Department of Justice's Efforts to Combat Methamphetamine." Accessed April 25, 2010. http://www.dea.gov/pubs/pressrel/pr061606. html.

Elliott, Amanda J., and Simon Chapman. 2000. "'Heroin Hell Their Own Making' Construction of Heroin Users in the Australian Press 1992–1997." Drug and Alcohol Review 19: 191–201.

Girion, Lisa, and Scott Glover. Oct. 15 2010. "CVS will play record fine for drug's sale." Los Angeles Times, A1.

Granfield, Robert, and William Cloud. 1996. "The Elephant that No One Sees: Natural Recovery Among Middle-Class Addicts." Journal of Drug Issues 26: 45–61

Haddigan, Michael. April 16, 2000. "AntiGay Groups Seize on Slaying To Make Point On Media Coverage." Boston Globe, A29.

Herda-Rapp, Ann. 2003. "The Social Construction of Local School Violence Threats by the News Media and Professional Organizations." Sociological Inquiry 73: 545–74.

Hunt, Dana, Sarah Kuck, and Linda Truitt. 2006. Methamphetamine Use: Lessons Learned. National Criminal Justice Reference Service, Publication No, 209730. http://www.ncjrs.gov/pdffiles1/ nij/grants/209730.pdf.

Jenkins, Philip. 1994. "The Ice Age: The Social Construction of a Drug Panic." Justice Quarterly 11: 7–31.

Jiang, Jenny. Oct. 26, 2002. "Police Seize 200,000 Worth of Designer Drugs." Boston Globe, B7.

Kappeler, Victor E., and Gary W. Potter. 2005. The Mythology of Crime and Criminal Justice: Fourth Edition. Long Grove, IL: Waveland Press.

Kappeler, Victor E., Mark Blumberg, and Gary W. Potter. 1996. The Mythology of Criminal Justice. Long Grove, IL: Waveland Press.

King, Ryan S. 2006. The Next Big Thing? Methamphetamine in the United States. The Sentencing Project, Washington, D.C. http://www.sentencingproject.org/Admin/Documents/publica tions/dp_netbigthing_meth.pdf.

Kupchik, Aaron, and Nicole Bracy. 2009. "The News Media on School Crime and Violence: Constructing Dangerousness and Fueling Fear." Youth Violence and Juvenile Justice 7: 136–55.

Los Angeles Times Staff and Wire Reports. April 21, 2000. "Methamphetamine is Focus of Hearing." Los Angeles Times, Section B.

_____. May 25, 2000. "School Worker Held on Charges of Selling Speed." Los Angeles Times, Section B.

_____. Sept. 20, 2000. "3 Arrested in Raid at Alleged Methamphetamine Lab." Los Angeles Times, Section B.

_____. Sept. 23, 2000. "Mother Sentenced in Car Wreck That Killed Son." Los Angeles Times, Section B.

_____. Nov. 23, 2000. "Man Convicted of Sexually Abusing Girl for 10 Years." Los Angeles Times, Section B.

The Meth Project. 2010. "Methamphetamine" Accessed July 19. http://www.methproject.org/index. php

Miller, Marissa A. 1997. "History and Epidemiology of Amphetamine Abuse in the United States." In The American Drug Scene: An Anthology, 4th Edition, edited by James A. Inciardi and Karen McElrath, 252–66. Los Angeles: Roxbury.

Murillo, Sandra. April 27, 2002. "Convictions of Child Workers to Be Revealed." Los Angeles Times, B8.

Murphy, Kim. May 20, 2001. "Urban Biohazard Invading Forests." Los Angeles Times, A16.

Musto, David F. 1999. The American Disease: Origins of Narcotic Control, Third Edition. New York: Oxford University Press.

National Institute of Drug Abuse. 2003. Drug Use Among Racial/Ethnic Minorities, Revised. U.S. Department of Health and Human Services, National Institutes of Health. http://archives.dru gabuse.gov/pubs/minorities/.

National Survey on Drug Abuse and Health. 2007. National Findings. Department of Health and Human Services, Substance Abuse and Mental Health Services Administration, Office of Applied Studies. http://www.oas.samhsa.gov/NSDUH/2k7NSDUH/2k7results.cfm#Ch2

Orcutt, James D., and Blake Turner. 1993. "Shocking Numbers and Graphic Accounts: Quantified Images of Drug Problems in the Print Media." Social Problems 40: 190–206.

Piccalo, Gina. July 17, 2000. "Police Say Man Admits Killing Woman Over Smuggling Fee." Los Angeles Times, B4.

Potter, Gary W., and Victor E. Kappeler. 2006. Constructing Crime: Perspectives on Making News and Social Problems, Second Edition. Long Grove IL: Waveland Press.

Reinarman, Craig. 2003. "The Social Construction of Drug Scares." In Patricia A. Adler and Peter

Adler (eds.), *Constructions of Deviance: Social Power, Context, and Interaction: Fourth Edition*: 137–46. Belmont CA: Wadsworth.

Reinarman, Craig, and Harry G. Levine. 1995. "The Crack Attack: America's Latest Drug Scare, 1986–1992." In Joel Best (ed.), *Images of Issues: Typifying Contemporary Social Problems*: 147–86. New York: Aldine de Gruyter.

_____. 1997. *Crack in America: Demon Drugs and Social Justice*. Berkley: University of California Press.

Rhone, Nedra. Feb. 23, 2001. "Report on Syphilis Reinforces Concern About Sex Practices." *Los Angeles Times*, B3.

Seewer, John. Feb. 19, 2002. "Drug's Popularity Produces Spike in Theft of Dangerous Fertilizer." *Boston Globe*, A3.

Surette, Ray. 1992. *Media, Crime, and Criminal Justice: Images and Realities*. Belmont, CA: Wadsworth.

Tempest, Rone. Jan. 20, 2002. "Meth Lab Crackdown Dealt a Setback." *Los Angeles Times*, B1.

_____. May 23, 2002. "Couple Sentenced in Death of Infant Son." *Los Angeles Times*, Section B.

Tran, Mai, and Jack Leonard. July 17, 2001. "Two Men Detail Night of Rapes, Beatings." *Los Angeles Times*, B10.

U.S. Drug Enforcement Administration. 2006. "President Bush Signs USA Patriot Act: A n t i - Meth Provisions Take Aim at Methamphetamine Production, Trafficking, Use." Accessed May 12, 2010. http://www.justice.gov/dea/pubs/pressrel/pr030906a.html

Welch, Michael, Melissa Fenwick, and Meredith Roberts. 1998. "State Managers, Intellectuals, and the Media: A Content Analysis of Ideology in Experts' Quotes in Feature Newspaper Articles on Crime." *Justice Quarterly* 15: 219–41. Williams, Paul, and Julie Dickinson. 1993. "Fear of Crime: Read All About It: The Relationship between Newspaper Reporting and Fear of Crime." *British Journal of Sociology* 33: 33–56.

Media vs. Reality: Who Is the Real Female Sex Offender?

Bridget A. Hepner-Williamson

Breaking news: "A Polk County jury found former 6th grade science teacher Danielle Jones guilty Thursday afternoon on eight felony counts of having sex with four teenage boys" (Baynews9 2009). This type of headline regarding female sex offenders seems to flood television news, the Internet, and newspapers around the country. This is not a random headline, but rather a commonplace media description of a female sexual offender. While most people consider sex offenders to be male (O'Connor 1987), there is a growing recognition that some sexual offenders are female (Davin 1993; Faller 1987; Vandiver and Kercher 2004). According to Pearson (1997), female sex offenders account for one in four of all child sexual abuse occurrences. Between 1994 and 1997, the U.S. Department of Justice reported a 7 percent increase in official accounts of female sex offenders, from 1 percent to 8 percent (Management, Myths and Facts about Sex Offenders 2000) and as a result there has been an increase in academic research on female sex offenders (Davin 1993; K. C. Faller 1987; Vandiver and Kercher 2004. Since the late 1990s the numbers of female sex offenders has remained somewhat stable. The Uniform Crime Report (Federal Bureau of Investigation 2004) concluded in 2004 females account for 283 (~1.5 percent) of forcible rape arrests and 5,414 (~8.4 percent)[1] of all other sex offenses.[2] While in 2009, the overall number of women arrested for forcible rape was slightly down to 208 (~1.3 percent)[3] (Federal Bureau of Investigation 2009) the number of women arrested for all other sex offenses[4] rose slightly to 6,186 (~8.8 percent)[5] (Federal Bureau of Investigation 2009). Likewise, the National Crime Victimization Survey (Bureau of Justice Statistics 2005) concluded that in 2005 females accounted for 6 percent of independent offender sex offenses and 40 percent of multi-offender acts. Finally, the National Incident Based Reporting System (National Archive of Criminal Justice Data 2008) reported that in 2007 females were responsible for approximately 5.1 percent of sexual assaults. NIBRS also reported in 2007 that if the victim of a sexual assault was a juvenile, a female was the offender approximately 6 percent of the time but only approximately

1 percent if the victim was an adult. The numbers of reported female sex offenders may seem small overall, but we must ask ourselves if the official reported rates of female sex offending are a true account of the phenomenon. We should also ask what this female sex offender looks like in reality versus media portrayals.

Muraskin and Domash (2007) tell us that the media have the greatest influence on our perception of crime, while Jerin and Fields (1994) report that the media distort the true picture of crime. These distorted beliefs can ultimately influence policy-making decisions (Muraskin and Domash 2007). While most media accounts tend to overstate the threat of crime (Muraskin and Domash 2007) this does not seem to be the case with female sex offenders. For example, a recent news article reports, "Law enforcement officers say they found Tamara Ryman, 37, in a parked van with her former 16-year-old student, in a compromising situation" (Viren 2007). Reading the article we see that this offender was caught having sex with her former student in her car. It is this depiction of a female sex offender that is explored in this research and is compared to the academic research on female sex offenders to see if the media indeed, as Muraskin (2007) asserts, distorts the true picture of crime. The expectation is that while the media do indeed distort the true picture of a female sex offender, the distortion is more likely to be positive rather than negative. I argue that the media are not making us more afraid of a female sex offender; rather, they are making us question if the offender is a real offender and if victim is truly victimized.

While the increase in academic research has provided us with a view of what the female sex offender looks like we still are bombarded with media representations of a female sex offender that do not seem to match the demographics of actual female sex offenders, or do they? The purpose of this paper is to conduct a mixed methods review of media accounts of female sex offenders and compare the results to actual statistics of incarcerated women in treatment for sex offenses. The possibility that a media-driven perspective of an offender that is misleading may allow for decreased awareness, an increase in potential for harm and a decreased detection of a sexual victimizer is scary to say the least. To date, we are lacking a comprehensive understanding of female sex offenders, their victims and the offense.

Literature Review

What we know about female sex offenders is limited. Most of the current research focusing of female sex offenders is focused on typology creation, descriptive analysis of the offender and victim, and clinical research (Faller 1987; Mathews, Matthews and Speltz 1989; McCarty 1986). The corpus of literature tells us that female sex offenders are a heterogeneous population, that ages can and do range from adolescent to geriatric, that differences exist with regard to relationship status and whether or not the offender is a parent (Ferguson and Meehan 2005; Center for Sex Offender Management, 2000; Mathews, Matthews, and Speltz 1989). Clinical research examining female sex offenders suggests that many of these offenders present with some type of mental health history (Grier, Clark and Stoner 1994; Green and Kaplan 1994; Cooper et al. 1990; Chow and Choy 2002).

The clinical research tends to focus on personality disorders and psychological problems of female sex offenders; results suggest that there is a high occurrence of psychiatric history, substance abuse, past victimization, and lowered mental functioning present (Cooper et al. 1990; Chow and Choy 2002; Davin 1993; Faller 1987; Mathews, Matthews, and Speltz 1989). For instance, two different studies compared types of female sex offenders (McCarty 1986; Davin 1993) and found similar results of higher levels of emotional instability and more traumatic child sexual abuse histories in independent offenders. Conversely, some studies were contradictory concerning their results of mental, personality, or clinical factors (Grier, Clark and Stoner 1994; Green and Kaplan 1994; Cooper, et al. 1990; Chow and Choy 2002). Other studies (Faller 1987, 1995; Rowan, Rowan, and Langelier 1988; Travin, Cullen, and Protter 1990; Lewis and Stanley 2000) support assertions by some researchers that female sex offenders have poor social skills (McCarty 1986; Mathews, Matthews, and Speltz 1989), and high incidences of mental/emotional problems (O'Connor 1987; Mayer 1992; Nathan and Ward 2001; Nathan and Ward 2002). However, caution must be taken when assessing the generalizability of these results to the general female sexual offender population as most of the research was (a) clinically-based,[6] (b) was conducted with small sample sizes, or were (c) were results from judicial cases in which the offenders are being evaluated for competency to stand trial.

The other area female perpetrated sex offending research is focused on is typology formation. The literature provides about nine different typologies with several overlapping categories, yet many of these typologies are based on small samples sizes.[7] The existence of so many "types" of female sex offenders supports assertions by researchers that female sex offending patterns are heterogeneous in nature (Mayer 1992; Saradjian and Hanks 1996; Nathan and Ward 2002; Vandiver and Kercher 2004; Ferguson and Meehan 2005). While many typologies exist, generalizability is a problem as is reliability and validity. Another area of concern is that very few, if any typologies consider motivation when developing types.

Methodology

The purpose of this paper is to utilize a mixed methods approach to compare media accounts of female sex offenders with a known sample of convicted female sex offenders to assess if the image portrayed by the media is representative of a sample of incarcerated female sex offenders. Thus, there are two comparison groups in the sample: women accused or convicted of sex offending from newspaper reports and an incarcerated sample of female sex offenders. The mixed methods approach taken in this study will utilize qualitative and quantitative methods. The qualitative method is a content analysis of newspapers to determine the image of a female sex offender as portrayed by the media. These data were then turned into quantitative data to compare with the incarcerated sample. The quantitative portion of the paper is a descriptive analysis from official Texas Department of Criminal Justice (TDCJ) mental health and sex offender treatment records of a sample of incarcerated female sex offenders. These two samples where then assessed quantitatively to determine if the images of female sex offenders as represented by the media are valid when compared with an incarcerated sample of female sex offenders. A mixed methods approach was utilized to increase the descriptive and analytical power of the results. By combining two methods, descriptive statistical analysis and content analysis, these data have increased reliability and validity. For purposes of this paper, female perpetrated sex offending is any illegal sexual boundary violation between a female and her victim (Hepner 2007).

Sample

As a part of a larger sex-offender research project, access to a purposive sample of incarcerated female sex offenders was possible. This population sample included 129 current and past participants in the TDCJ Female Sex Offender Treatment Program (SOTP) located at the Hilltop Prison in Gatesville, Texas. This is the only female SOTP in the state of Texas; therefore, the data garnered from this unit contains the population of female sex offenders treated by this program. The SOTP program is an involuntary 18-month rehabilitation program for female sexual offenders who are within 24 months of release. The curriculum utilizes a cognitive-behavioral modification model with an emphasis on relapse-prevention skill development. The program includes a combination of group and individual treatments with the goal of lowering the recidivism risk upon the offenders' release. The offenders in the program have offenses ranging from failure to register as a sex offender to aggravated sexual assault.

The procedure for this research included a chart review of the treatment records of the offenders where all relevant data were coded for the 129 current and past participants in TDCJ female SOTP. The charts were reviewed for demographic data regarding the offense, the victim, past criminal activity, victimization history of the offender, and mental health histories. The data collection process occurred at the Hilltop women's prison in Gatesville, Texas, for the current participants as well as at facilities in Huntsville, Texas, for data on the past participants. Officials from the TDCJ SOTP archive maintained and located the charts of the past participants and the data were recorded on site. The charts of the current participants located at the Hilltop unit were accessed via prison officials and these data were recorded on site. The data collection process included the creation of an SPSS database and occurred over a two-year span from 2006 to 2008.

For the qualitative comparative sample, a LexisNexis newspaper search was performed using the key phrases "female/woman sex offender" and "female/woman pedophile." Initially, careful attention was paid to terminology regarding the relationship between the female and her victim. For example, it was hypothesized that the use of the key phrase "female teacher sex" would likely return more biased results than that of the key phrase "female sex offender." However, a search was run on the term "female teacher sex" and the results were analogous to those of "female/woman sex offender" and "female/woman pedophile" so these results were included as well. Only newspaper accounts were included in the analysis. With regard to the sample period, articles were to be accessed from 1980, since the academic research on female sex offenders began about that time and extend to 2008. However, the articles returned by LexisNexis only dated back to 1996 at the earliest, so the sample included news reports from 1996 to 2008. Only accounts specifically describing a female sex offender were reviewed. A "case" contained information on one female offender. If there were multiple articles related to one case the multiple articles were only counted as one case, for example, there were 12 articles related to Mary Kay LeTourneau, all 12 articles counted as one offender case. Data were coded from all 12 articles for analysis as one case. Thirty-eight cases were accepted for final review. Specific article exclusions were:

1. articles about female sex offenders in general due to lack of data;
2. articles that mentioned but did not detail an offender in depth; and
3. editorials regarding female sex offenders due to a potential for bias.

A codebook of terms and phrases was created to facilitate the data collection process. A test-retest method was utilized to help enhance reliability. The test-retest method is a process by which the articles were first coded, then at a later time recoded to assess that measurement of the codes were stable and that the data remained reliable. For example, a positive description of an offender should be positive the first and second time the article was coded to be reliable. An SPSS statistics file was then created and used for the comparison analysis of the details of the media accounts and the incarcerated female sex offenders, their victims, and their crimes along with descriptors of the offender and the co-offender if one was mentioned.

Analysis

Demographics of the female sex offender sample from the TDCJ SOTP (n= 129) shows a typical female sex offender in a Texas sex offender treatment program is an employed (58 percent), 31-year-old (SD 8.8), white (65 percent) woman with approximately10 years of education (SD 2.2). She was usually single (69 percent) and a victim of abuse (80 percent sexual abuse, 70 percent physical abuse). She often has some type of prior mental health issues (53 percent.). In most cases, she does not have multiple victims (78 percent), and she usually offends alone (57 percent). This offender usually does not have a history of sexual arrests (84 percent) but does have a history of general arrests (74 percent). The average sentence for this offender was 9.8 years. The most common offense was sexual assault of a child or aggravated sexual assault[8] of a child (67 percent). There were 162 victims from this sample and the typical victim was 11 years old (SD 4.8) and a majority of the victims were under the age of 16 (60 percent). More of the victims were female (54 percent) and about half were either the biological child (31 percent) or an acquaintance (23 percent) of the offender. On only 7 percent of the incarcerated sample were teachers the offender with half of their victims being male and half being female.

In the media reports (n=38), the average age of female sex offenders[9] is 31 years old (See Table 1 for a summary comparison of the two samples of offenders). Race could not be determined from the articles. While accurate data regarding the offender's education level could not be ascertained from the articles, it is safe to assume that since 24 of the 38 offenders were teachers, more than half have at least a college education. Only two articles mentioned mental health issues, but none mentioned prior arrests unless they were connected to the current case. Only one article discussed the past sexual abuse of an offender, and half of the offenders were married. The average victim age was 13, most victims were male (73 percent) and most offenders only had one victim (81 percent). Most of the media accounts describe the victim as having a consensual sexual relationship with their alleged offender (60 percent). However, 80 percent of the crimes/charges dealt with some type of sexual assault including rape, child rape, and molestation. Finally, only two offenders had a co-offender mentioned; both of the male co-offenders were described in negative terms and were portrayed as having worse compulsions to offend than their female counterparts have. For example, one male co-offender was described as a "slave master" (Hunter and Greene 2001, 23) and the other demonstrated "high levels of arousal by minors" (Jensen 1999, b5) while their female partners were described as having a "consensual relationship with the victim" (Jensen 1999, b5) and the other was "in love and forced to offend" (Hunter and Greene 2001, 23). In both of these instances, the men received lengthier sentences than the females.

Table 1.
Comparison of Average Incarcerated Female Sex Offenders and Media
Accounts of Female Sex Offenders

	Incarcerated	*Media*
Age	31	31
Education	~10	~14*
Co-Offender	No	No
Married	No	Yes
Employed	Yes	Yes
Mental Health Problems	Yes	No†
Prior Victimization	Yes	No‡
Relationship with Victim	Biological Parent (31%)	Teacher (63%)
Victim Age	11	13
Victim Gender	Female	Male

*Assumed based on employment as teachers.
†Only two articles of 38 mentioned mental health issues.
‡Only one article mentioned offender victimization.

In comparing the two samples, the findings show agreement with several descriptors and disagreement on other descriptors. In both groups the average age of the offender was 31, they often acted alone, and were employed. However, the groups differed in ways that are more substantial. While the incarcerated sample was a single woman, in the media she was married. The incarcerated sample had a lower education level than the media sample. Most importantly to the assertions of the paper, the victimology is different. For the incarcerated offender the victim was usually her biological daughter of about 11 years of age yet the media portrayal of the victim was a 13-year-old male student of the offender.

An interesting phenomenon is that most of the media accounts (81.5 percent) of the female sex offenders describe the female sex offenders in a positive light or neutral light. Even the judges in some cases thought they were "easier to rehabilitate" (Hunter and Greene 2001, 23) and non-violent (Taylor 1996). Some of the women were described as "young attractive, professionals" (Krause 2008, 1) or "the prom queen, salutatorian, class president, a great dancer and basketball player" (Krause 2008, 1) or a petite suburban mother of six (Gutowski 2003) or "[simply] in love with the boy" (Lyons 1999, B1). There were seven negative depictions of the women. Of the seven, three of the women were called pedophiles (for example, Hancock 2005) yet only two were reportedly diagnosed as a pedophile (for example, Bell 2003). The harshest accounts of the women came from the description of the two women who were pretending to be males to abuse their female victims and of the two women who were classified by their states as high-risk offenders; "sexually dangerous" was the term used to describe all four women (for example, Snowden 2005; Hopkins 1997).

While most of the media women (63 percent) were accused of sexual offenses[10] against children or convicted (36 percent) of criminal sexual acts against children; most of the women offenders were portrayed in a positive/neutral manner (81.5 percent). Most victims in the media portrayals were male (86 percent) and most of the offenses were described in a positive way. Examples include phrases such as they "ran away together" (Wagner 2002) or they were "having a sexual relationship" (Associated Press and Local Wire 2008) or there was "no criminal activity" (Van Bronkhorst 2002) or they "were in love" (Lyons 1999, B1). Interestingly, most of the descriptions of female victims were neutral or they were not described at all; for example, one article described the criminal activity as an "incident with the girl" (*Buffalo News* 1998, 5C).

Discussion

If it is true that the media have the greatest influence on our perception (Muraskin and Domash 2007) and that our perception is distorted by the media (Jerin and Fields 1994), this research proves that we indeed need to be worried. We should be worried, not in the traditional sense that crime is on the rise but rather in the opposite direction, worried that we have a false sense of security when it comes to the sexual victimization of children. At a time when statistics are showing a stabilization and in some instances a general increase in reported female sex offenses, increases in prison populations of female sex offenders, and national victimization studies showing increases in sexual assaults committed by females, we should be concerned that we are not getting a true picture of the female sex offender from the media.

We see two different women presented in this study, mostly with regard to victimization. The incarcerated female sex offender (on average), is a mother who is in prison for sexual abuse of her biological daughter. She is contrasted with a media portrayal (on average) of a teacher having sex with her teenaged male student. While both types of offenders present with significant criminal accusations and convictions for serious sexual offenses, the media tend to dismiss the significance of the victimization perpetrated by the female sex offender especially when she has a male victim. The overall impact of media accounts of female sex offenders with male victims tend to be positive, describing women who are in "consensual sexual relationships" (Times 1998) or are simply "having sex" (Times Publishing Company 2008) with boys.

These media accounts reinforce the notion that "it's not a child being victimized by an adult; it's a boy getting all his desires and dreams" (Hallissy 2002). Much of the same thinking is demonstrated by a judge who found that a 13-year-old boy suffered little harm after being sexually assaulted by his teacher (Lima 2002). The notion of little or no harm to male victims is yet again reinforced by quotes such as "I wish she'd been **MY** [emphasis in article] sixth grade teacher" (Van Bronkhorst 2002). This is a dangerous assumption especially if the sentencing policies of judges are based on this notion of teens contributing to their victimization or judges presuming a lack of victimization.

David Finkelhor, director of the University of new Hampshire Crimes Against Children Research Center, was quoted in one news story that "judges and jurors and prosecutors tend to see teens (male) as having contributed to their victimization" (Gutowski 2003, 1). This thinking is especially dangerous for the victim. For example, this news story was about a 16-year-old boy that was reportedly having a "sexual relationship" (Gutowski 2003) with a 41-year-old library aide, who claims that he was raped and no one believes him. As a result of the sexual assault, he sees a therapist for depression. He claims that he is not seen as a victim by his peers; rather they describe him as a sexual predator who went after the library aide and is claiming rape. By reducing the importance of the victimization by female sex offenders we allow harm to come to a portion of society that needs our protection the most—children. We appear to justify the consequences of female sex offending by blaming the male victim.

While the media downplay the impact of male victimization by a female offender, the media are much more critical of the short sentences given by judges when there is a female victim. One of the most striking cases in the newspapers was entitled "Outrage over four-year plea deal in Long Island sex-torture case" (Hunter and Greene 2001, 23). In this report the judge released a female sex offender for the Thanksgiving holiday after she pleaded guilty to the kidnapping, sexually assualt and sexual trafficking of a 15-year-old girl. The media suggested that the only reason this offender was released for the holiday was because she was a woman. In this article the judge justified the sentence and release because he felt that a female sexual offender is "easier to rehabilitate" (Hunter and Greene 2001, 23). When an offender is seen as easier to rehabilitate, they are more likely to get a lesser sentence for an equivalent crime and are seen as less culpable due to her co-offender forcing her to sexually abuse a child (Center for Sex Offender Management 2007). The sentencing for her male co-offender was not mentioned in the article.

Though this research does not address length of sentencing in detail, the findings from the media suggest that there is leniencey with regard to female sex offender sentencing. It is problematic when courts are lenient on female sex offenders. When judges justify relaxed sentencing practices on the notion that there is "not enough research into the risk that female sex offenders will commit new sex crimes" (Bell 2003, B2) a door is opened for discriminatory sentencing practices between male and female offenders. There is little literature regarding female sex offender recidivism, and currently there are no valid risk assesments for prediciting female sex offender recidivism. One potential problem with this justification is that we may have fewer female sex offenders to include in female sex offender recidivism studies. Additionally, we may never find out what types of treatment are useful for these offenders.

What is lacking in the reporting of female sex offenders in the media is the truth of who is sexually abusing children, and who the victims are. The purpose of comparing a media sample with an incarcerated sample of female sex offenders was to not only highlight the differences between the reality of incarcerated female sex offenders and the stereotype promoted by the media, but also to give a voice to the victims of female sex offending. It seems that the victims of female sex offenders seem to have less of a voice than victims of male sex offending. Since newspaper accounts generally report on the story of the teacher and her male student (only 7 percent of the incarcerated population) the true victim, on average an 11-year-old girl has no voice. Ironically, the rare accounts of the offender as "dangerous" (Snowden 2005) and "predatory" (Hopkins 1997, B1) were used in the media accounts for offenders with female victims, which are the most common type of victim of the incarcerated sample.

Theoretically, we tend to think of women as less responsible for crimes than male offenders, and as a result we give them less severe sentences and consequently discount the victimization experience. Muraskin and Domash (2007) conclude, "It is clear that the general public is getting incorrect information about women and the criminal justice system" (116). With the media reporting on the "little harm" (Lima 2002) victims of female sex offenders experience, we are blind to the most a dangerous offender that might exist, the one we don't acknowledge. Sensationalizing the female sex offender is a way to justify the actions that many see as just a rite of passage for a typical teen boy (Van Bronkhorst 2002). As Muraskin (2007) suggests our perceptions of crime, justice and offenders are shaped by the media. If media accounts continue to provide the image a of a "young attractive, professional" that "was [simply] in love with the boy" as a sex offender, our policies will continue to disregard the victimization this type of offender is allowed to perpetrate.

Perhaps the media sensationalize the accounts of female sex offenders and young boys because it is not seen as a taboo in the way that a male sex offender and a female victim are (Muraskin and Domash 2007). Perhaps the rareness of the crime is enough to garner the headlines, but unlike the female victim of a male offender, we are not worried about our children being victimized by the teacher, the neighbor, or the babysitter. The nurturing stereotype of a woman keeps us from seeing her as an offender, as someone to be afraid of. We willingly send our children off with no worries of possible victimization because the media have socially constructed a female sex offender to be aberrantly fulfilling their gender roles in a way that is somewhat, acceptable to a large portion of society, including obviously the media and our criminal justice system. This research suggests that perhaps the media ought to be more accountable for the image they portray of offenders. If we construct our images of offenders from media reports that are more positive than negative, we become accepting of a crime because we perceive the harm to be so minimal, that we can dismiss it without regard. As a result, we allow harm to truly vulnerable victims to continue.

This research introduced potential research topics that should be explored in the future. For example, the idea of perceived/actual harm experienced by victims of female sexual offenders as well as research into the extent of males contributing to their victimization would contribute to the literature. Additional research regarding sentence disparity among male/female sex offenders would also be useful.

Like all research on female sex offenders, this work has its limitations. Though some of the offenders in the media sample contained women who were convicted and incarcerated, it is likely that using an incarcerated sample creates a bias. Ideally, a matched sample including female sex offenders who were also given probation or a deferred sentence would provide for a better comparison, as would the utilization of more types of media sources. Likewise, an increase in sample size would help with generalizability, as this research should not be generalized to the broader population of female sex offenders.

NOTES

1. A 10 percent increase from 1995 to 2004
2. Not including forcible rape or prostitution.
3. Down 12.4 percent from 2000–2009
4. Not including rape or prostitution.
5. An increase of 4.9 percent between 2000 and 2009; see note 7.
6. As a part of a mental health evaluation or a mental health treatment program.
7. Sample sizes range from 11to 51 with one exception of 471.
8. Sexual assault was defined as the intentional or knowing engagement in any sexual contact with a child less than 17-years old as defined by 1999 Texas Penal Code §22.011. Aggravated sexual assault was defined as the intentional or knowing engagement in any sexual contact with a child less than 17-years old and includes the aggravating factors of physical injury, death, the use of a weapon, threats that create fear of loss of life, or sexual assault of a child less than 14 years of age. Defined by the 1999 Texas Penal Code §22.021.
9. Note not all women in the media accounts had been convicted of a sexual crime.
10. Sexual offenses include acts such as rape, indecency, sexual assault, child rape.

REFERENCES

Associated Press and Local Wire. 2008. "Police Say Female Teacher Had Sex with High School Boy." May 13.
Baynews9. 2009. "Polk Teacher Found Guilty of Having Sex with Students." Aug. 20. Accessed Jan. 11, 2011. http://www.baynews9.com/article/news/2009/august/55786/Polk-teacher-found-guilty-of-having-sex-with-students.
Bell, Kim. 2003. "Coffel Shouldn't Have Been Held at All, Expert Says." St. Louis Post-Dispatch, Nov. 7, B2.
Buffalo News. 1998. "Female Sex Offender Rearrested." Feb. 7, 5C.
Bureau of Justice Statistics. 2005. National Crime Victim Survey. Accessed Jan. 15, 2007. http://bjs.ojp.usdoj.gov/index.cfm?ty=pbdetail&iid=1743.
Catalanello, Rebecca. 2008. "Teacher-student Sex Alleged." St. Petersburg Times, March 21, 1B.
Center for Sex Offender Management. 2000. Myths and Facts about Sex Offenders. August. Accessed Nov. 15, 2007. http:www.csom.org/pubs/mythsfacts.html.
_____. 2007. Female Sex Offenders. March. Accessed Nov. 1, 2010. http://www.csom.org/pubs/female_sex_offenders_brief.pdf.
Chow, Eva W.C., and Alberto L. Choy. 2002. "Clinical Characteristics and Treatment Responses to SSRI in a Female Pedophile." Archives of Sexual Behavior 31, no. 2: 211–215.
Contra Costa Times. 1998. "Woman Arrested on Charge of Molesting Boy." Feb. 25.
Cooper, A.J., S. Swaminath, D. Baxter, and C. Poulin. 1990. "A Female Sex Offender With Multiple Paraphilias: A Psychological, Physiologic (Laboratory Sexual Arousal) and Endocrine Case Study." Canadian Journal of Psychiatry: 334–337.

Davin, Patricia A, 1993, "The Best Kept Secret: A Study of Female Sex Offenders." PhD diss., The Fielding Institute.

Faller, Kathleen C. 1987. "Women Who Sexually Abuse Children." *Violence & Victims* 2, no. 4: 263–276.

_____. 1995. "A Clinical Sample of Women Who Have Sexually Abused Children." *Journal of Child Sexual Abuse* 4: 13–30.

Federal Bureau of Investigation. 2004. Crime in the United States. *http://www2.fbi.gov/ucr/cius_04/index.html.*

_____. 2009. Uniform Crime Report 2009. Accessed Nov. 1, 2010. http://www.fbi.gov/aboutus/cjis/ucr/ucr.

Ferguson, Chritopher H., and D. Cricket Meehan. 2005. "An Analysis of Females Convicted of Sex Crimes in the State of Florida." *Journal of Child Sexual Abuse* 14, no. 1: 75–89.

Green, Arthur, and Meg S. Kaplan. 1994. "Psychiatric Impairment and Childhood Victimization Experiences in Female Child Molesters." *Journal of the American Academy of Child and Adolescent Psychiatry* 33, no. 7: 954–961.

Grier, Priscilla E., Marie Clark, and Sue B. Stoner. 1994. "Comparative Study of Personality Traits of Female Offenders." *Psychological Reports* 73: 1378.

Gutowski, Christy. 2003. "Is He Less of a Victim? Teen Who Says He Was Raped by Library Aide Says He's Been Ostracized Because He's Male." *Chicago Daily Herald*, Sept. 21, 1.

Hallissy, Erin. 2002. "Teacher Accused of Sex with Teen." *San Francisco Chronicle*, Oct. 12, A19.

Hepner, Bridget A. 2007. "An Exploratory Study of Types and Characteristics of Incarcerted Female Sex Offenders." Master's thesis, Sam Houston State University.

Hopkins, Jack. 1997. "State's First Female Sex Predator Is Locked Away: Woman Has Violent Fantasies About Tots." *Seattle Post-Intelligencer*, Jan. 23, B1.

Hunter, Brad, and Leonard Greene. 2001. "Outrage Over Four Year Plea Deal in Long Island Sex Torture Case." *New York Post*, Nov. 25, 23.

Jensen, Derek. 1999. "Sex Abuse of Minor Results in One Year Jail Term." *Deseret News*, May 22, b5.

Jerin, Robert, and Charles Fields. 1994. "Murder and Mayhem in the USA Today: A Quantitative Analysis of The Reporting of State's News." In G. Barak (ed.), *Media, Process, and the Social Construction of Crime: Studies in Newsmaking Criminology*: New York: Garland.

Krause, Thomas W. 2008. "What's Behind the Teacher's Grin?" *Tampa Tribune*, April 30, 1.

Lima, Paulo. 2002. "Teacher in Tryst Is Spared Prison." *The Record*. May 23.

Lyons, Brendan, 1999. "Woman Teacher Has Sex with Boy, 15, Cops Say." *The Times Union*, Feb. 26, B1.

Mathews, Ruth, Jane K. Matthews, and Kathleen Speltz. 1989. *Female Sex Offenders: An Exploratory Study.* Orwell, VT: Safer Society Press.

Mayer, Adele. 1992. *Women Sex Offenders.* Holmes Beach, FL: Learning Publications.

McCarty, Loretta. 1986. "Mother Child Incest: Characteristics of the Offender." *Child Welfare* 65: 447–458.

Muraskin, Roslyn, and Shelly F Domash. 2007. *Crime & The Media: Headllines vs. Reality.* Upper Saddle River: Pearson.

Nathan, Pamela, and Tony Ward. 2002. "Female Sex Offenders: Clinical and Demographic Features." *Journal of Sexual Aggression* 8: 5–21.

Nathan, Pamela, and Tony Ward. 2001. "Females Who Sexually Abuse Children: Assesment and Treatment Issues." *Psychiatry, Psychology and Law; An Interdisciplinary Journal of the Australian and New Zeland Association of Psychiatry, Psychology and Law* 8, no. 1: 44–55.

National Archive of Criminal Justice Data. 2008. National Incident-Based Reporting System. Accessed Nov. 15, 2010. http://www.icpsr.umich.edu/cocoon/NACJD/STUDY/27741.xml.

O'Connor, Art A. 1987. "Female Sex Offenders." *British Journal of Psychiatry* 150: 615–620.

Pearson, Patricia. 1997. *When She Was Bad: Violent Women and the Myth of Innocence.* New York: Viking Press.

Rowan, Edward L., Judith B. Rowan, and Pamela Langelier. 1988. "Women Who Molest Children." *Bulletin of the American Academy of Psychiatry and Law* 18, no. 1: 79–83.

Saradjian, Jacqui, and Helga Hanks. 1996. *Women Who Sexually Abuse Chidren.* New York: Wiley and Sons.

Snowden, Richard. 2005. "Girl, 17, Marked as First Female Sex Offender in Illinois." University Wire, Nov. 2.

Taylor, Kate. 1996. "Girl, 13, Charged with Raping Boy, 9, in Jackson County." *The Oregonian*, August 17, B1.

Travin, Sheldon, Ken Cullen, and Barry Protter. 1990. "Female Sex Offenders: Severe Victims and Victimizers." *Journal of Forensic Sciences* 35: 140–150.

Van Bronkhorst, Erin. 2002. "Detective Says Mother Was Unconcerned After Son Found with Teacher." Associated Press State and Local Wire. April 3.

Vandiver, Donna M. and Glen Kercher. 2004. "Offender and Victim Charcteristics of Registered Female Sexual Offenders: A Proposed Typology of Female Sex Offenders." *Sexual Abuse: A Journal of Research and Treatment* 16, no. 2: 121–137.

Viren, Sarah. 2007. "Teacher Under Investigation After Being Found with Teen." *Houston Chronicle*, March 21. Accessed April 10, 2008. http://www.chron.com/disp/story.mpl/headline/metro/4648220.html.

Wagner, Angie. 2002. "Female Teacher Who Took Student to Vegas Highlights Problem." Associated Press State and Local Wire. May 11.

Monstrous, Demonic and Evil: Media Constructs of Women Who Kill

Kate Whiteley

A woman who kills is a rare breed. Her primary victims are abusive male partners followed closely by her children. Rarely does a woman commit serial murder (Cluff, Hunter, and Hinch 1997; Scott 2005; Hickey 2006). Western societies struggle to comprehend this act of aberrance from this, the gentler sex. However, feminist criminology looks to discourses of victimization (Chan 2001) and more recently agency (Morrissey 2003; Pearson 1997) or willingness (Laub 2006) for explanation. The societal construct of the woman who kills unlawfully is one wherein the woman breaks the fundamental natural laws of femininity. However, societal perceptions range from labeling her monstrous, evil, and wicked, to gestures of compassion as she is a victim or suffers from illness. Therefore, in these cases she is to be treated, not punished.

The bias towards pathologizing female homicide offenders is reflected in research conducted by Tilley (1989). Her research with males and females who committed filicide disclosed that males more often suffered consequences classified within a legal or *punishment model*, whereas females received sentences that fell within the welfare or medical *treatment model*. This practice aligns with Worrall's (1981) assertion that a killing of a child by a male is presented as an egregious criminal act, but the same action by a female is contexualized as pathological. An additional study is Wilczynski's (1997) work with homicide offenders and their psychiatric pleas. Wilczynski (1997) recognized that 87.5 percent of women submitting a psychiatric plea received sentence of hospitalization or non-custodial judgments. Their male counterparts submitting psychiatric pleas witnessed 84.2 percent being sentenced directly to prison.[1]

Another voice that seeks to describe the phenomenon of the woman who kills is that of the news media, whose discourse often conflicts with the narratives of the female homicide offender and can distort the realities of female perpetrated violence (Chesney-Lind and Irwin 2004). This essay addresses which discourses of female homicide offending are identified or rejected by the media as revealed in their coverage of this act.

An Exceptional Act

It is reported by Jensen (2001), that males commit approximately 90 percent of the total homicides within western cultures. In agreement, Mann (1996) reports that across Australia, Canada, England and the United States, women commit 10 to 14 percent of the overall homicides. In an analysis of homicide rates occurring within England and Wales between the years of 1995 to 2001, Chan (2001) found that 11 percent of the total homicides were committed by women. The New South Wales Bureau of Crime, Statistics, and Research, Australia, reported that 9 percent of the total homicides committed across 2008–09 were female perpetrated. Lastly, the United States' Bureau of Justice Statistics (2008) conveyed that 8.9 percent of the total U.S. homicides were committed by females. Therefore, homicide is largely a male activity (Brookman 2005), and the rates of female homicide offending have remained relatively constant at approximately 10 percent of the total homicide during the last three decades, across western societies (Chan 2001; Jensen 2001; Yourstone, Lindholm and Kristiansson 2008).

When women kill it tends to be within the domestic setting (Brookman 2005; Jensen 2001; Peterson 1999; Silverman and Kennedy 1988). The vast majority of female homicide victims are intimate partners (Davies 2008; Fox and Levin 2001; Jensen 2001; Leonard 2001; Messing and Heeren, 2004; Websdale 1999), followed by their children (Abel 1986; Warren 1989). More specifically, women kill those closest to them. In consideration of homicide statistics from England during the years 1995 to 2001, Brookman (2005) found intimate partners accounted for 32 percent of the total female perpetrated homicides and their sons and daughters comprised another 30 percent.

A further breakdown of categories and rates of female perpetrated homicide (see Stanko et al. 1998), report a marked descending rate moving from intimate partners, family members, friends, and lastly to strangers. Statistics such as these buttress the statement of Blum and Fisher (1978) that female homicide offending is indeed an intimate act. In contrast Jensen (2001) asserts, when men kill, they are least likely to kill intimates, but women who kill are most likely to kill intimates.

Universal Explanations for
Female Homicide Offending

There exists a paucity of research regarding women who kill. Feminist criminologists (Chan 2001; Jensen 2001; Leonard 2001; Morrissey 2003), concur that this dearth of research is related to two primary rationales. First, the numbers of female offenders are too small to allow generalizations to be drawn. Secondly, homicide has been designated as a male domain; therefore we have sought to understand all homicide offending through the male lens (Jurik and Winn 1990). From the 1980s forward, three constructs have dominated as explanations for female homicide offending. Identified within criminological and feminist realms has been the influence of the victim, mad, and bad constructs (Ferraro 2006; Jensen 2001; Morrissey 2003). However, earliest rationales for a woman who killed were delivered in biological theory and hinted of the mad and bad constructs as evidenced in the quote from Lombroso and Ferraro (1895, 148), "To kill her enemy does not satisfy her, she needs to see him suffer and know the full taste of death." The early 20th century found criminology looking to the psychoanalytic in efforts to understand the woman who kills (Alexander and Healy 1935) heavily influenced by Freudian theory.

The psychoanalytic dominance yielded to the discourse of victimization which found its way into criminological and feminist research in the late 1970s with Walker's (1979) seminal work, *The Battered Woman*. Her subsequent theory, the Cycle of Violence, established firmly the construct of the woman who kills as a victim. Walker's thoughts and efforts were instrumental in bringing from the shadows the plight of the battered woman and played a pivotal role in the subsequent public and legislative response to this criminal act. Feminist criminological researchers (Browne 1987; Goetting 1988, Leonard 2001) concur that men perpetrate far more intimate partner violence than women. In addition, a lengthy history of physical, sexual, and emotional violence is associated with female perpetrated intimate partner homicide. Furthermore, others contend that females are also perpetrators of domestic violence (Archer 2002; Nicholls and Dutton 2001). The evidence however strongly supports females are more often the victims of intimate partner violence. Demonstrated by statistics from Australia, Ferrante et al. (1996), found that women are eight times more likely to be victims of domestic violence than their male counterparts.

The second most prevalent explanation for a woman who kills is that of *mad* or *pathological*. Prior to the introduction of the Battered Woman Syndrome (BWS) in the late 1970s, Chesler (1972) and Ehrenreich and English (1973) depicted how common practice was to ascribe a deep-seated disease of the mind and body to the woman who murdered. No other act of female homicide draws such absolute reliance upon pathology as the act of female perpetrated infanticide or filicide (Peter 2006). Serious dialogue regarding these acts will inevitably include the influence of the mental illnesses of post-partum depression and post-partum psychosis (Reece 1991). Additionally, Wilczynski (1997) draws the distinction between men who kill their children and women. Men are considered "bad and normal" and women are deemed "mad and abnormal."

Prominent homicide offending researcher Chan (2001) concludes from her research that when a woman murders, she is far more likely to be categorized as mad than her male counterpart who kills. Many are the detractors to the universalizing of women who kill as mad. Concerns are raised by Rosencrans

(1997) and Jensen (2001), both of whom point out that not all women who kill are mentally ill and such labeling may excuse their behaviors and strip them of agency. Feminist psychological scholar Worrall (1990) made the observation that the more serious the crime, the more likely the woman will be labeled mentally ill. Similarly, Morrissey (2003) contends that by the gravitating to the mad discourse, we fail to further explore the phenomenon of the woman who kills and our understanding is thereby incomplete. Lastly, in an analysis of Canadian incarcerated violent female offenders, to include female homicide, Laishes (2002) reports that significantly more of these offenders were in possession of mental illness diagnoses. In fact, Laishes (2002) found female offenders were overrepresented in every diagnostic category, with just one exception, antisocial personality disorder (Allen 1987; Jensen 2001; Peter 2006; Rosencrans 1997; Walker 1989).

The third universal explanation which is not grounded in empirical science and one which defies theory and statistical analysis is the discourse of *evil* and *bad*. This construct however, has found its way into the dialogue regarding female perpetrated homicide. This discourse has its underpinnings in the gendered role expectations for female behaviors. A woman who transgresses these qualities is stereotyped as "bad" or in the case of a woman committing infanticide; she is labeled evil or monstrous. An example provided below is by Meyer et al. (2001) of this practice as it relates to a mother who kills:

> Women characterized as bad are depicted as cold, callous, evil mothers who have often been neglectful of their children of their domestic responsibilities.... These mothers are often portrayed as sexually promiscuous, non-remorseful and even nonfeminine [70].

Furthermore, gender roles are based upon the biologic sex (Brennan 2002), but are learned socially. They are then granted legitimacy and are enabled by values and assumptions that take hold within societal institutions and social stratifications.

The long held conception in western thought is that women are docile, passive, and nurturing mothers (Pearson 1997). In the socialization of females is the notion that the nurturing mothering instinct somehow mysteriously arrives when a woman reaches out to hold her newborn. Males kill, and as Carlen (1985) claims, violence is ascribed as innate to them, just as care giving and nurturing is to women. Based upon this prevailing stereotype of the passive and gentle woman who is instinctually a caregiver, a significant blow to our construct of appropriate femininity is leveled when a woman violently offends. A woman who engages in unlawful killing is, as Kruttschnitt and Carbon-Lopez (2006) argue, guilty of an act of aberrance far more objectionable than for a male who kills. When a woman commits homicide, she has transgressed two fundamental laws (Lloyd 1995).

The first is the general law wherein violence is forbidden. The second is the natural law wherein women are ascribed roles of passivity and care giving.

Scholars such as Chan (2001), Morrissey (2003), and Pollock and Davis (2005) contend the prevailing perceptions of a woman who kills unlawfully, situate the act as shear deviance, more vicious, and more unscrupulous, than her male murderous counterpart. The women who kills her children defies description and adjectives such as evil and demonic are applied to this act (Morrissey 2003). In summation, a woman who kills offends our societal myths of maternal grace and the love of a mother (Oberman 1996).

The universal explanations for female homicide offending are three: the women who kills is a victim, she is mad or sick, and she is bad or evil or a combination of these. With what discourse does the media identify in their narratives regarding the woman who kills? Does the news media reflect biases in its depiction of violent women and in particular, women who kill? Is a woman who kills of significant newsworthiness and if so, what is it about this behavior that sells stories?

In a more recent study by Whiteley (2011), lengthy interviews were conducted with Australian women incarcerated for murder. Overall, it was revealed that each woman to varying degrees accused the media of over indulgence and gross misrepresentations (Whiteley 2011, unpublished manuscript). The following quotes are provided from two of the women:

> Yeah, the media got it all wrong you know. They said I killed him because he wouldn't stop smoking in my dying mother's room. This was in all of the papers. This is so far from the truth, you know, and it had absolutely nothing to do with what I did. It was ridiculous what they said about me! I was called the "evil woman who killed her stepfather" and another paper called me a "vicious drunk" [Lil].

> Wicked, just wicked was the way the newspaper here, wrote about me! I felt so betrayed! They put headlines like I was this wicked, elderly and evil grandmother ... that was one headline. Another paper called me the "killer grandmother" [Wendy].

Newsworthiness of Female Homicide Offending: The *Curse* of Femininity

Well established is the news media's infatuation with the theme of murder (Chermak 1995; Gilliam and Iyengar 2000; Meyers 1997). Murder stories are not just granted status by the printed page, but as suggested by Gilliam et al. (1996), they find their way to lead stories on the evening news. Female homicide is a favorite front page feature in major urban newspapers (Blau 1991; Pritchard 1985). According to Naylor (2001), British newspapers devote approximately 65 percent of the overall crime news to acts of personal violence in which homicide is most eminent. It stands to reason, that for working journalists, the usual and commonplace are not newsworthy. Rather, it is the unusual that leaps out and shatters the mundane (Oliver and Meyers 1999).

Far from mundane was the act of homicide committed by a young Australian woman identified as Sarah, who killed a teenage girl.

I was on the front page of nearly all the Australian newspapers and who knows, I could have been in other papers and magazines around the world ... you know.They wrote that I killed this young girl to steal her personality, can you believe that? Lots of the women in here killed ... but none of them grabbed the headlines like I did ... typical bloody media. Men kill all the time ... and might not even make it into the papers like I did! [Whiteley 2011, unpublished].

In speaking of homicide offending, Blau (1991) contends that there are those murders that are the "normal" murders. An example would be the story of an urban murder in which there is a Black victim. The more common murders were found by Simon (1991) to be overlooked by the media. However, Pritchard and Bagley (2001) reported that in contrast, an urban murder in which the perpetrator is a female will more likely be deemed worthy of frequent and prominent coverage.

Women who kill are in general more newsworthy (Nyawanza 2007). The question therefore is are men and women who kill reported in similar fashion or is one more embellished than the other? Feminist criminologist Morrissey (2003) argues that the news media's response to women who kill is indeed inflated. In comprehensive examination of the media coverage of men who kill, men are depicted as perpetrators across a wide range of violent behaviors including simple assault, bizarre sexual acts, and homicide. Interestingly, minimal references to these acts as being unnatural and or un-masculine are cited. Further, Morrissey (2003) contends that the acts are presented in such a fashion as to be imaginable. A woman who kills an intimate partner is a victim who kills in self defense (Walker 1979). A woman who kills a child must be mad and a victim of mental illness (Chan 2001; Jensen 2001). Lastly, sensational horror stories make front page news largely in relation to the draw of *bad* and *evil*. Clearly, the explanations for male homicide are more varied and the act deemed more natural as violence is thought innate to males, while women who kill are cast into the three universally held stereotypes.

A resolute display of this tack is found in Morrissey's (2003) accounting of the media's coverage in 1989, of the Australian female homicide offender Tracey Wigginton. This case was well publicized in mainstream media with repeated references to the "lesbian vampire killing." Wigginton was particularly demonized as the alleged ringleader of the four women involved in the crime. The coverage exploited the lives of Wigginton, her three female associates, their alleged sexual behaviors and engagement in vampirism. Examples of media headlines surrounding this particular homicide case, as noted by Gillespie and Hansen (1989), included that it was a bizarre act and they were a satanic group, and devil worshippers. It is argued by Creed (1993) and Morrissey (2003) that such headlines sought to calm the terror and dissipate the uncertainties by portraying these women as mythical or outside of the human realm.

The primary issue does not lie in the alleged tantalizing rituals of vampire killing (the taste for blood), but is more situated in the seeming inability to embrace the act of murder at the hand of a female. A woman who commits a homicide is operating outside of the normative framework of appropriate femininity. Homicide is depicted as a masculine phenomenon (Kirkwood 2000). Men kill because they possess the propensity to kill (Worrall 1981), whereas societal constructs deny women an inherent propensity to kill (Morrissey 2003). The biologic and evolutionary theorists posit that violence is natural and instinctive to men (Daly and Wilson 1988).

The double standard is well articulated in Cavaglion's (2008) analysis of media coverage of filicide committed by mothers and fathers across Israel between 1991 and 2002. She identified in the media coverage that fathers as murderers, were deemed rationale in their premeditative act. Cavaglion (2008) notes language that depicted the male perpetrators acting in a machine-like and emotionless fashion. In concluding her analysis of a double standard of reporting, male to female filicide, Cavaglion (2008) cited coverage that attempted to persuade the reader that the murder was an extreme act of evil and strongly resisted any references to pathology as a cause.

Subsequently, the reaction to women who murder reveals more extreme societal objection than that of their male counterparts, particularly when the act is as sensational as serial killing or deemed as sexually motivated (Chan 2001; Ferraro 2006; Pollack and Davis 2005). According to Godwin (1978, 113), "When women commit violence, they are worse than their male counterparts, more bloodthirsty, more vicious more unscrupulous and more deadly than the male." Although dated, this description parallels the media depictions as found in Morrissey's (2003) summation of the 1989 Australian media coverage of the Wigginton killing. While Wigginton herself decried her life riddled with victimization (Morrissey 2003), the media ignored her cumulative victimizations and chose to emphasize her evilness and wicked nature. Interestingly, as Cavaglion's (2008) study suggests, women who kill their children are less demonized than their male counterparts.

Media Coverage of Female Homicide Offenders: Race and Ethnic Bias

There exist well documented studies from the Juristat Canadian Centre for Justice Statistics (2005), the Australian National Homicide Monitoring Program Annual Report (2007) and the United States' Bureau of Justice Statistics (2006), that find Aboriginal women in Canada and Australia and African American women within the United States, are overrepresented in homicide offending. If female ethnic minorities commit more homicide, it would be expected that statistically, there be more media coverage of this group. The question is, despite this higher incidence of homicide amongst these groups, are they covered by the media accordingly or does a bias in coverage prevail?

In a comprehensive content analysis of two major newspapers, the *Los Angeles Times* and the *New York Times*, Brennan and Vandenberg (2009) surveyed front page articles to assess an entire year's coverage to determine how many of the stories featured white women versus minority women offenders. This study, while considering *any* criminal offense has relevance, found that 39 percent of the stories covered were of murder or attempted murder and 13 percent addressed other acts of violence. This research aids the understanding of the media's representation of female offending based on its sampling of two major urban newspapers. This study of the media and the depiction of female offenders calls to our attention the bias towards white women and further details how this bias is situated within the media narratives.

Newsworthiness is determined largely by the targeting of people who purchase the news and the appeal to advertisers that underwrite the news media (see Meyers 1997; Chermack 1995). In consideration of the magnitude of news occurrences, journalists must choose news and write in a fashion that will attract the largest number of consumers in a demographic area that appeals to local advertisers (Lundman 2003). Marketing considerations clearly reflect a selection bias in relation to race and gender (Lundman 2003). An example of this is reflected in that the largest share of the media market targets Caucasians that possess higher disposable incomes (Entman and Rojecki 2000). In terms of race and violence, Shah and Thorton (1994) suggest that Caucasians' fear of Black crime is more newsworthy than violent crime committed by Caucasians. The prevailing constructs of homicide as a male phenomenon finds stories of female homicide running counter to gendered beliefs and therefore less newsworthy (Meyers 1997).

The biological sex and the race of an individual are both highly visible. It can be argued the size or shape of one's nose or the texture of one's hair is not any more prominent than one's skin color (Healey 1997). However, at first glance such features are important pieces of information in regards to recognition of one another. There exists more sensitivity to skin color which is based in our socialization as dictated by our residence in a race conscious society. Classifications assumed on one's race or ethnicity afford a basic means to differentiate among people (Rattner 1996). Stereotypes are attached to specific races and ethnicities and these become highly problematic when discrepant behavioral expectations are ascribed (Brennan 2002).

Racial disparities are situated within the media representations of female homicide offenders. Researchers including Barak (1994), Dates and Pease (1997), and Hurwitz and Peffley (1997) argue such discrepancies within U. S. media are rooted in notions of white ethnocentrism. There exists a specific set of negative stereotypes ascribed to Black women that stand in stark contrast to the stereotypes of white women. Landrine (1985) cited attributes of competent, emotional, intelligent and warm as associated with white women, while such traits as hostile and dirty often define black women. Adding to the list of negative stereotypes for Black female offenders, Farr (2000), Brennan (2002), and Young (1986) cite such descriptors as hyper-sexed, welfare queens, and aggressive. In another study of the newsworthiness of female homicide, Lundman (2003) found that homicides were more often covered when particular race and gender combinations were present. For example, a white perpetrator and Black victim or a white woman who kills received more front page coverage than a Black on Black homicide or a Black woman who kills. Researchers Anderson (1999), Cobb (1992), and Feagin (1991) concur such stories are newsworthy in that they convey the constructs rooted in white racism and notions of Black criminality.

There may be less coverage of female minority offenders, but the coverage is also different and more negative for minority offenders. Brennan and Vandenberg's (2009) study found much more favorable accountings of white female offenders than of female minorities; across the measures studied, the bias held true. They found the favorable tone rating for white female offenders was 49 percent compared to the minority offenders who were largely of African American and Latina backgrounds at 17 percent. In terms of the measure ascribing personal responsibility for the crime, white women were "excused" 56 percent of the time, compared to 21 percent for their female minority counterparts. Brennan and Vandenberg (2009) cite the measure of minimizing of the harm done by the female offender, referred to as the neutralizer. In consideration of white female offenders, 30 percent of the time the harm done to the victim and family was neutralized as compared to just 8 percent for female minorities.

Cavaglion's (2008) findings in Israel were similar to Brennan and Vandenberg's (2009) research, to the extent that marginalized ethnic female minorities were depicted in more negative narratives. As Cavaglion (2008) explains these groups, particularly women of Arab descent were defined by Israeli media as deviant and criminal. She further described that ethnic minority women who killed were not referenced as good mothers which many of their white female counterparts who killed were. Also, she found it noteworthy that white female homicide offenders were significantly more often deemed pathologic or mentally ill. Subsequently, their homicide was then understood and more readily accepted, wherein the Arab women were rarely deemed as mentally ill. Cavaglion (2008) as previously noted, recognized the societal stereotypes as negative towards Arab women. Additionally, Rattner and Fishman (1998) found that Arab women are in general were treated more severely within the criminal justice system than Jewish women.

Women Deemed Bad!

The International Federation of Journalists (1986) in its code of ethics calls upon journalists to respect the truth and further to always report stories that are accurate, fair, and balanced. It has been speculated that journalists may fall prey to myths or familiar social constructs and that their narratives may then become entangled in truth and myth (Bird and Dardenne 1997; Hanson 2001; Kitch 2002; Lule 2001). A deep-running cultural construct associated with a woman who commits infanticide or filicide is that of the flawed mother or the bad mother (Lule 2001). Do media embrace the constructs of femininity, the nurturing mother, or the evil and unnatural being who commits the unthinkable, and is this then reflected in their narratives?

In their analysis of front page stories of female offenders, Brennan and Vandenberg (2009) identified frequent references to these offenders as bad. Such women are those who have crossed the boundary of appropriate gender role expectations and did so of their own accord. Women who do so are demonized (Ballinger 1996) and according to Naylor (2001) they are at times depicted by the media in masculine terms, as it is the male who owns the rights to violence. When their homicide is of a heinous and grotesque nature, highly unfavorable narratives are sure to follow. It could be argued that such stinging narratives serve the purpose of banishing the woman from the community of proper motherhood.

Research undertaken in 2006 with seven women incarcerated in an Australian prison for convictions of murder revealed that the majority of the women were deemed bad or evil within media depictions (Whiteley 2011). One of the women was repeatedly referred to by the media as the drug abusing prostitute who deserted her children. The eldest offender in this study was framed by the media as the evil murdering grandmother. The media in relying upon the discourses of appropriate femininity situated both female offenders far outside of the constructs of domesticity. A good mother does not abandon her children and a loving *elderly* grandmother does not engage in violence (Whiteley 2011).

Two dichotomous terms that reside within media narratives surrounding women who kill their children are the "perfect mother" and the "flawed mother" (Barnett 2005). In an article that critiques the newspaper coverage of two infamous United States cases of mothers who killed, the media's depiction of good mothering and bad mothering stands in stark contrast. In her review of the media coverage of the Andrea Yates trial, a mother who drowned her five children, and Khoua Her, a mother who strangled her six children and then attempted suicide, Huckerby (2003) reveals some telling findings. Her extensive analyses lead Huckerby (2003) to recognize and then utilize the terms good mothers and out-group mothers. The media depictions surrounding Andrea Yates reflected the good mother construct which is directed at white-middle class women. Huckerby (2003) defines the out-group as single mothers, women of color, and lesbian women.

Huckerby (2003) found that Khoua Her's "otherness" as a Cambodian woman was frequently referenced. Her singleness and teen motherhood were frequently cited. There was a persistent effort to suggest that her eight years of experience in a refugee camp where she was raped would situate her life as something foreign and primeval to "us" as westerners. In giving birth to a child at age 13, Her subsequently conceived four more children, which was communicated by the media as a lack of control over her sexuality and again situated Her within the realm of "otherness." Huckerby (2003) concludes that Her was portrayed as failing as a mother within her Asian cultural constructs of good mothering.

In direct contrast was the depiction of Andrea Yates, who Huckerby (2003) found was frequently referred to as a nurse who had devoted her life to caring. The media frequently cited how she cared for her father in his terminal illness. Her beliefs rooted in fundamental Christianity were repeatedly mentioned and her home schooling of her children reinforced her Christianity and her nurturing nature. Interestingly, Huckerby (2003) disclosed that Her professed similar fundamentalist Christian beliefs, but her beliefs were absent from the media narratives. Yates had invested her life in her domesticity as a loving wife who chose to be a homemaker. Yates' marriage to a NASA engineer and the fact that the couple had just moved into a new home further served to reinforce her near ideal identification with the prevailing notions of femininity and motherhood. In consideration of Her's life and the lives of many women who kill violent intimate partners, rarely are the social inequalities highlighted.

Feminists Macdonald (1995), Sanger (1999), and Showalter (1982) have argued how ancient myths of women as creators, destroyers and the Victorian ideals of female virtues have served to propagate the modern perceptions of motherhood. This myth of the perfect mother has saturated the media as it presents narratives of woman who kill. However, if one considers the harsh actualities of their lives, the majority of women who kill (Douglas and Michaels 2004) are far removed from the nirvana-like portrayals of societal constructs of appropriate femininity and motherhood.

Is She Mad or Ill?

Women who kill have been understood through the three universal explanations previously cited, one of which is "she kills because she is mad or mentally ill." Has the media embraced or rejected the construct of mad as an explanation in its narratives of women who kill? In her study of women in Israel that killed their children, Cavaligon (2008), found that mother's who kill their children are more often depicted as mentally ill than fathers, guilty of the same crime. She also described the media's tendency to ignore madness or psychopathology even when suspected in ethnic female minorities and those women who are marginalized economically, single, and undereducated.

In a comparison of the case of an 18-year-old Israeli girl who killed her infant and two Arab women who killed their children, the media again demonstrated an obvious bias. Cavaligon (2008) describes in detail how insanity was found within the narratives of the media coupled with descriptions of harsh environmental conditions that evolved over the course of the case. The depictions clearly reflected a softening in the media's perception of the young Israeli mother. However, in the two cases of Arab mothers who killed their children, Cavaligon (2008) found no references to insanity rationales and little reference to their aspects of marginalization. One woman's behavior was described as inexcusable and heinous while the others had no explanation and was deemed monstrous.

If we return to Huckerby's (2003) analyses of the two sensationalized cases of Her and Yates, both were interestingly portrayed by the press as failing to cope with motherhood. As noted, Her had been a resident of a Cambodian refugee camp for eight years where she had been raped. She was pregnant at 13 with the first of her six children. Her struggled with depression and expressed feeling overwhelmed with her singleness and overwhelming responsibilities. Yates was also depicted by the media as feeling inadequate as a mother of five. Some media highlighted her struggles with low self-esteem and how she was too immobilized to reach out for help. Despite similarities in the two women's struggles to cope with motherhood, the parallels end here. Throughout the course of their criminal trials, Huckerby (2003) found the media narratives largely supporting the biological discourse of insanity to account for Yates' homicide. Her was not afforded the discourse of mad. In an analysis of the media portrayal of Her, Huckerby (2003) finds she was in addition to being a flawed mother also labeled as a disagreeable human.

Parallel to Huckerby's contention of media bias situated within the Yates and Her murder cases is an assertion by Whiteley (2011). One woman in this study shared several characteristics of Andrea Yates, to include a strong work ethic and caring for her grandmother and later her own mother. The media chose to focus upon her struggles with chronic depression and her use of alcohol to self medicate and to relieve the psychosocial stressors associated with the burdens of care giving. In the same study, Whiteley (2011) identified an offender who had a history of drug addiction and more extensive depression to include hospitalization following a suicide attempt found the media ignoring her depression and emphasizing her drug addiction. This woman received no acknowledgement by the media of her struggles as a single mother and harsh and abusive childhood. It can be argued the media was biased towards the care giving and nurturing of one woman who further minimized her use of alcohol while the other woman's drug abuse could not be equated with appropriate femininity and domesticity (Whiteley 2011).

Victimized by the Media

Violent female offending, more specifically homicide, has long been associated with a woman's status as a "victim" (Brookman 2005; Davies 2005; Whiteley 2011). The majority of women who kill, kill intimates who are often abusive partners (Jensen 2001). An overarching explanation for women who violently offend in the killing of intimates is that they have been subject to cumulative victimizations to include child abuse, economic marginalization, and educational deficits to mention a few (Wesely 2006).

It can be argued the media have also served to victimize women who kill in the impact their characterizations have upon their sentencing and their person. The full extent of media coverage upon outcomes of trials and sentencing is difficult to surmise (Morrissey 2003). Furthermore, the impact to the woman's self esteem, her family, and her future when the media has sensationalized her act of murder, and saturated the printed page with what the women term as gross misrepresentations of their lives and crime is another victimization (Whiteley 2011). The youngest homicide offender in Whiteley's (2011) study was 27 at the time she was interviewed. In reflecting upon her future when released from prison, she said:

> You know in a few years I could be released. I would have done my time ... and paid my debt. But you know I will never have any kind of normal life. After what the press said about me ... and the book and a movie, do you think I will ever be able to live out there and not be harassed? We know men murder all the time ... and a few weeks later you don't read a thing about it. No one gives a shit! But, a woman who kills ... makes news headlines.
> If a bloke killed a younger guy, trust me, he wouldn't receive the coverage I got, no ... nothing close to it. What's fair about this? What this bloke did you can say was just as bad as any of us. Sometimes I think I will be safer to stay here in this hell hole. It scares me to think that I am safer here. You know, I have the media to thank for this. I am sorry for what I did but the news has taken my life. I bet they had fun with my story and made money and yeah, it's not right [Sarah].

In her study, Whiteley (2011) asserts the voice of the media and the voice of the woman who murders habitually conflict. In her extensive interviews with seven women incarcerated for convictions of murder, repeatedly heard was the notion that the media grossly misrepresented the women and their lives. One of the women identified as Bella shared:

> The media got it all wrong you know. All the papers kept referring to me as this drug abusing prostitute, or something like that. They never mentioned the rest of my life. What about the repeated rapes and beatings I endured as a child? Never did I read anything about my former husband and how he beat me so badly I kept ending up in the emergency room and once was admitted for my injuries.
> My life was so bad I tried to kill myself and spent three months on a psych unit you know. What about the rest of my life? I lived a good life and was never in trouble with the law until I got caught up in drugs two years ago. What about the first 30 years of my life, I was a good mother, daughter and friend. Why didn't they talk about that? I guess it wouldn't sell papers, would it?

Another woman in Whiteley's (2011) study was 19 years of age when she killed a young girl who was a family acquaintance. As with Bella, Sarah calls to our attention the tendency to sensationalize violent female offending that transgresses perceptions of appropriate femininity.

The newspapers said I killed this young girl to steal her personality. I mean how stupid is that! They said I was obsessed with her and lured her into my flat so I could kill her and take over her identity. Yeah, it was in all of the papers and magazines all over Australia. I got all this hate mail and people harassed my family. No one wrote about me and my life. I wanted to scream; would someone please tell the whole story. I wanted them to know that yes, what I did was terrible, but I am more than a person who did a really bad thing. I was never in trouble with the law, never! I never had a beer or took drugs. I was made out to be this monster ... this evil person and that's all the public knew about me. The media was not interested in the rest of my life ... I guess that wouldn't sell papers you know. [Sarah]

These statements from women who murder reinforce Morrissey's (2003) assertion, that if the women did not kill in self defense, if her offending is not related to mental illness, she is vilified by the media. The media continue to rely upon the construct of appropriate femininity and women as passive and nurturing beings. Therefore, the ultimate act of violence, such as murder, committed by a woman challenges the construct. Approximately four decades ago, Chesler (1972) decried the construct of motherhood in which women are intended to embrace frustrations, humiliations, and dire circumstances, and dare not transgress notions of good mother and loving wife.

What both the victim and pathology explanations fail to reconcile is that when a women kills, the act is a complex behavior. Labels such as mad, bad, victim and evil, cannot adequately account for this behavior. The women in Whiteley's (2011) study who committed homicide, within their narratives, referred to their social contexts, their multifaceted roles and complex lives, suggesting their commission of murder cannot be essentialized. She is victimized by the printed page and further victimized when the media relies solely upon explanations of pathology or killing. A reliance on these two constructs further victimizes the woman as it denies her agency.

Conclusion

It can be concluded that women who kill have indeed proven newsworthy subjects. Women who kill challenge prevailing societal expectations regarding appropriate femininity and violent female offending. Armstrong (1999) argues they are substance for good cover stories. For example, the construct of motherhood is woven tightly into the psyche of western societies, to the extent that a woman who kills her child or children is the greatest affront to domesticity and such an aberrant act sells papers (Gans 1980). Chesney-Lind (1989) contends the media intentionally or unintentionally convey a staunch warning to women who engage in extreme violence will be vilified accordingly.

Well established in the media's coverage are the race and ethnic biases toward women who kill. Cited was the Brennan and Vandenberg (2009) study which suggests that white women are more favorably portrayed in homicide coverage than their ethnic minority counterparts. This bias extends beyond the United States as demonstrated by Morrissey (2003) in Australia, and the Cavaglion (2008) findings within Israel. This chapter explains that when men kill, they are not depicted by the media as engaging in the unnatural or unmasculine (Morrissey 2003; Whiteley 2011). For men, societal constructs and criminology have regarded violence as more natural or innate.

Women largely kill intimate male partners (Jensen 2001). Typically, the male victim was assumed to have been abusive (Walker 1979). However, if the victim was her child the woman was deemed as mentally ill (Chan 2001). The media, it appears, follows these two rationales in their reporting. Having two widely embraced explanations for the majority of the victims of women who kill serves to allay societal anxieties and is consistently reported.

Where society and the media are most challenged is in their representation of women who kill outside the realm of intimates. This is the case wherein women kill like men with intent and for such motives as jealousy or for financial gain. If rationales such as postpartum depression and Battered Woman Syndrome are not applicable, what other discourses are there to draw from?

In Whiteley's (2011) study all seven women were convicted of murder, which presupposes premeditation and intent. Without a universal explanation such as mental illness or Battered Woman Syndrome, the women in her study were demonized and vilified by media. Interestingly, even though the majority of the women had lengthy histories of victimizations and mental illness, these were not included in the media portrayals. Was the gravitation to the demonization an exercise at selling stories or a reflection of an inability to grapple with a woman who kills, because she chose to (Morrissey 2003)?

Female homicide offending is a complex act. In the media portrayals of the women in the Whiteley (2011) study, it appears no genuine effort to express the complexities and entirety of the female offenders' lives was made. One of the women provides an example of this practice:

> I followed our traditional ways you know and served my mother in law and brother in law and husband first. I could not speak English for a few years. I worked as a cleaner across town and had no friends. He was abusive and he would force me to have sex every day. I can't tell you why I did what I did, it was complex ... it was complex. The papers said I killed him to get him out of the way. No one ... no one asked me why, it was just complex [Jennifer].

Reflected in Jennifer's narrative is her perception that when a woman kills, it is not as simple as a psychiatric diagnosis or an abusive relationship or in Jennifer's case a desire to remove someone from the landscape of their life. Such an act is more multifaceted and it seems the media largely fails to acknowledge this (Whiteley 2011).

A woman who kills is newsworthy. Demonstrated is that some acts of female perpetrated homicide are better understood and then less sensationalized. Biases in portrayals are evident. Far reaching are the constructs of normative femininity and as such, a woman who kills is measured by these. In Whiteley's (2011) study, when asked about her portrayal by the media, Bella responded:

> I wanted to cry out to the media ... won't you try to understand me! No one asked me what my life was like, you know. They were in the courtroom, they heard about what I went through ... but no one reported that you know. They only wanted to talk about the man I killed ... and how I did it. But, if they told the whole story, they wouldn't sell many papers would they? [Bella].

A journalist who supports the complexities hypothesis is Barnett (2006). Barnett is a journalism professor who spent many years writing prior to engaging in academia. Her research interest has been the portrayals of violent female offending in the media, particularly in relation to constructs of normative femininity. The following quote is taken from her study of women who kill their children as portrayed by the media:

> As a former journalist, I recognize that deadlines, source availability, economic resources and community norms shape news coverage. However, I invite journalists to move beyond simplistic explanations of infanticide as the outburst of one demented individual and to consider this crime as a larger problem affected by romanticized notions of motherhood, gender norms that delegate child care responsibilities primarily to women, lack of recognition of the hard work involved in daily child care, lack of understanding about postpartum depression, and lack of family, community, and institutional support for mothers [Barnett 2006, 427].

Here, Barnett (2006) has captured the complex nature of a woman's life and in doing so discourages any depictions that stop short of such considerations. She couches her remarks with recognition that a journalist faces obstacles in gathering information, but she decries simplistic explanations.

In closing, the review of the scant literature pertaining to the media's coverage of women who kill reinforces the societal discomfort with this aberrant act, rendering it highly newsworthy. Obvious is the media's adherence to the universal explanations for women who kill but just as transparent are its biases in reporting. Lastly, a standing challenge for the media is to broadly consider the depth of complexities of the female homicide offender's life and avoid what Barnett (2006) refers to as simplistic explanations.

Notes

1. An interesting finding of Wilczynski (1997) lies in the fact that many of these females had psychiatric evaluations prior to entering their psychiatric pleas as compared to their male counterparts. [0]

References

Abel, Ernest L. 1986. "Childhood Homicide in Erie County, New York." *Pediatrics* 77(5): 709–713.

Alexander, Franz, and William Healy. 1935. *Roots of Crime*. New York: Alfred A. Knopf.

Allen, Hillary. 1987. "Rendering Them Harmless: The Professional Portrayal of Women Charged with Serious Offences." In Patricia Carlen and Anne Worrall (eds.), *Gender, Crime and Justice*. Milton Keynes: Open University Press.

Anderson, Elijah. 1999. *Code of the Street: Decency, Violence, and the Moral Life of the Innercity.* New York: W. W. Norton.

Archer, John. 2002. "Sex Differences in Physically Aggressive Acts Between Heterosexual Patterns: A Meta-analytic Review." *Aggression and Violent Behavior* 7: 313–351.

Armstrong, Irene. 1999. "Women and Their Uncontrollable Impulses: The Medicalisation of Women's Crime Differential Gender Sentencing." *Psychiatry, Psychology, and Law* 6(1): 67–77.

Australian National Homicide Monitoring Program Annual Report. 2007.

Australian Government; Australian Institute of Criminology. *National Homicide Monitoring Program, 2005–2006.* http://www.aic.gov.au/about_aic/research_programs/nmp/0001.aspx

Ballinger, Anette. 1996. "The Guilt of the Innocent, and the Innocence of the Guilty: The Cases of Marie Fahmy and Ruth Ellis." In Alice Meyers and Sarah Wight (eds.), *No Angels: Women who Commit Violence*: 1028. San Francisco: Harper Collins.

Barak, Gregg. 1994. "Between the Waves: Mass-mediated Themes of Crime and Justice." *Berkeley Journal of Sociology* 21(3): 133–147.

Barnett, Barbara. 2005. "Accountable Mothers, Blameless Fathers: Narratives of Gender and Responsibility in News Articles About Maternal Violence." Paper presented at meeting for the Association for Education in Journalism and Mass Communication. Texas, August.

Barnett, Barbara. 2006. "*Medea* in the Media: Narrative and Myth in Newspaper Coverage of Women Who Kill Their Children." *Journalism* 7(4): 411–432.

Bird, Elizabeth S., and Robert W. Dardenne. 1997. "Myth, Chronicle and Story: Exploring the Narrative Qualitative of News." In Daniel Berkowitz (ed.), *Social Meanings of News: A Text Reader*: 333–350. Thousand Oaks, CA: LexisNexis.

Blau, Robert. 1991. *The Cop Shop: True Crime on the Streets of Chicago.* Reading, MA: Addison-Wesley.

Blum, Alan and Gary Fisher. 1978. "Women Who Kill." In Irwin L. Kutash (ed.), *Violence: Perspectives on Murder and Aggression.* San Francisco: Jossey-Bass.

Bond-Maupin, Lisa. 1998. "That Wasn't Even Me They Showed: Women as Criminals on *America's Most Wanted. Violence Against Women* 41(1): 30–44.

Brennan, Pauline K. 2002. *Women Sentenced to Jail in New York City.* New York: LFB Scholarly Publishing.

Brennan, Pauline K., and Abby L. Vandenberg. 2009. "Depictions of Female Offenders in Front-page Newspaper Stories: The Importance of Race/ethnicity." *International Journal of Social Inquiry* 2(2): 141–175.

Brookman, Fiona. 2005. *Understanding Homicide.* London: Sage.

Browne, Angela. 1987. *When battered Women Kill.* New York: The Free Press.

_____. 1997. "Violence in Marriage: Until Death Do Us Part? In Albert P. Cardarelli (ed.), *Violence between Intimate Partners: Patterns, Causes, and Effects*: 16–28. Boston: Allyn & Bacon.

Carlen, Patricia. 1985. "Law, Psychiatry and Women's Imprisonment: A Sociological View." *British Journal of Psychiatry* 146: 618–621.

Cavaglion, Gabriel. 2008. "Bad, Mad, or Sad? Mothers Who Kill and Press Coverage in Israel." *Crime, Media, Culture* 4(2): 271–278.

Chan, Wendy. 2001. *Women, Murder and Justice.* New York: Palgrave.

Chermak, Steven M. 1995. *Victims in the News: Crime and the American News Media.* Boulder, CO: Westview Press.

Chesler, Phyllis. 1972. *Women and Madness.* New York: Four Walls Eight Windows.

Chesney-Lind, Meda. 1989. "Girls' Crime and Woman's Place: Toward a Feminist Model of Female Delinquency." *Crime and Delinquency* 35: 5–30.

Chesney-Lind, Meda, and Katherine Irwin. 2004. "From Badness to Meanness: Popular Constructions of Contemporary Girlhood." In Anita Harris (ed.), *All About the Girl: Culture, Power and Identity.* New York, Routledge.

Cluff, Julie., Allison Hunter, and Ronald Hinch. 1997. Feminist Perspectives on Serial Murder: A Critical Analysis. *Homicide Studies* 1(3): 291–308.

Cobb, James. C. 1992. *The Most Southern Place on Earth: The Mississippi Delta and the Roots of Regional Identity.* New York: Oxford University Press.

Coughlin, Anne M. 1994. "Excusing Women." *California Law Review* 82(1): 57.

Creed, Barbara. 1993. *The Monstrous-feminine: Film, Feminism and Psychoanalysis.* London: Routledge.

Daly, Martin, and Margo Wilson. 1988. *Homicide.* New York: Aldine.

Dates, Jannette L., and Edward C. Pease. 1997. "Warping the World: Media's Mangled Images of Race. In Everette E. Dennis and Edward C. Pease (eds.), *The Media in Black and White*: 77–82. New Brunswick: Transaction.

Davies, Kim. 2008. *The Murder Book: Examining Homicide*. Upper Saddle River, NJ: Pearson Education.

Douglas, Susan J., and Meredith W, Michaels. 2004. *The Mommy Myth: The Idealization of Motherhood and How it Has Undermined Women*. New York: Routledge.

Ehrenreich, Barbara, and Deirdre English. 1973. *Witches, Midwives and Nurses: A history of Women Healers*. New York: Feminist Press.

Entman, Robert, and Andrew A. Rojecki. 2000. *The Black Image in the White Mind: Race and Media in America*. Chicago: University of Chicago Press.

Farr, Kathryn A. 1997. "Aggravating and Differentiating Factors in the Cases of White and Minority Women on Death Row." *Crime & Delinquency* 43(3): 260–278.

_____. 2000. "Defeminizing and Dehumanizing Female Murderers: Depictions of Lesbians on Death Row." *Women & Criminal Justice* 11(1): 49–66.

Feagin, Joe R. 1991. "The Continuing Significance of Race: Anti-black Discrimination in Public Places." *American Sociological Review* 56: 101–116.

Ferrante, Anna, Frank Morgan, David Indermanur, and Richard Harding. 1996. *Measuring the Extent of Domestic Violence*. Sydney: Hawkins Press.

Ferraro, Kathleen. 2006. *Neither Angels nor Demons*. Lebanon, NH: Northeastern University Press.

Fox, James, and Jack Levin. 2001. *The Will to Kill: Making Sense of Senseless Murder*. Boston: Allyn & Bacon.

Gans, Herbert J. 1980. *Deciding What's News. A Study of* CBS Evening News, NBC Nightly News, Newsweek *and* Time. New York: Vintage.

Gilliam, Franklin D., and Shanto Iyengar. 2000. "Prime Suspects: The Influence of Local Television News on Viewing Public." *American Journal of Political Science* 44: 560–573.

Gilliam, Franklin., Shanto Iyengar, Adam Simon and Oliver Wright. 1996. "Crime in Black and White: The Violent, Scary World of Local News." *Harvard International Journal of Press/Politics* 1(3): 6–23.

Godwin, John. 1978. *Murder U.S.A.: The Ways We Kill Each Other*. New York: Ballantine.

Goetting, Ann. 1988. "Patterns of Homicide Among Women." *Journal of Interpersonal Violence* 3(1): 3–19.

Hanson, Christopher. 2001. "All the News That Fits the Myth." *Columbia Journalism Review* Jan.–Feb.: 50–53.

Healey, Joseph F. 1997. *Race, Ethnicity, and Gender in the United States: Inequality, Group Conflict, and Power*. Thousand Oaks, CA: Pine Forge Press.

Hickey, Eric. 2006. *Serial Murderers and Their Victims*. Belmont, CA: Thompson Higher Education.

Huckerby, Jane. 2003. "Women Who Kill Their Children: Case Study and Conclusions Concerning the Differences in the Fall from Maternal Grace by Khoua Her and Andrea Yates." *Duke Journal of Gender Law & Policy* 10(147): 149–172.

Hurwitz, Jonathon, and Mark Peffley. 1997. "Public Perceptions of Race and Crime: The Role of Racial Stereotypes." *American Journal of Political Science*. 41(2): 375–401.

The International Federation of Journalists. 1986. *http://www.ifj.org/ed*.

_____. 1986 [1954]. *Journalism Ethics*.

Jensen, Vickie. 2001. *Why Women Kill: Homicide and Gender Equality*. London: Lynne Rienner.

Johnson-Cartee, Karen S. 2005. *News Narratives and News Framing: Constituting Political Reality*. Lanham, MD: Rowman and Littlefield.

Jurik, Nancy C., and Russ Winn. 1990. "Gender and Homicide: A Comparison of Men and Women Who Kill." *Violence and Victims* 5(4): 227–242.

Juristat Canadian Centre for Justice Statistics. 2005. *http://www.thefreeradical.ca/Violent_crime_statistics_Canada.htm*

Kirkwood, Debbie. 2000. "Women Who Kill: A Study of Female Homicide Perpetrators in Victoria Between 1985 and 1995." Unpublished dissertation, Monash University, Victoria, Australia.

Kitch, Carolyn. 2002. "A Death in the American Family: Myth, Memory, and National Values in the Media Mourning of John F. Kennedy Jr." *Journalism and Mass Communication Quarterly* 79(2): 294–309.

Kruttschnitt, Candace, and Kristin Carbone-Lopez. 2006. "Moving Beyond the Stereotypes: Women's Subjective Accounts of Their Violent Crime." *Criminology* 44(2): 321–352.

Laishes, Jane. 2002. *Women Offender Programs and Issues: The 2002 Mental Health Strategy for Women Offenders*. Correctional Service of Canada.

Landrine, Hope. 1985. "Race and Class Stereotypes of Women." *Sex Roles* 13(1/2): 65–75.

Laub, Karin. 2006. "Group Says Palestinian Women Victims of Societal Violence: Activists Say State Doesn't Protect." *Boston Globe*. *http://www.boston.com/news/world/middleeast/articles/2006/11/07*

Leonard, Elizabeth D. 2001. "Convicted Survivors: Comparing and Describing California's Battered Women Inmates." *The Prison Journal* 8(1): 73–86.

Lloyd, Ann. 1995. *Doubly Deviant Doubly Damned: Society's Treatment of Violent Women.* London: Penguin.

Lombroso, Cesare, and William Ferraro. 1895. *The Female Offender.* London: T. Fisher Unwin.

Lule, Jack. 2001. *Daily News, Eternal Stories: The Mythological Role of Journalism.* New York: Guilford.

Lundman, Richard J. 2003. "The Newsworthiness and Selection Dias in News About Murder: Comparative and Relative Effects of Novelty and Race and Gender Typifications on Newspaper Coverage of Homicide." *Sociological Forum* 18(3): 357–386.

Macdonald, Myra. 1995. *Representing Women: Myths of Femininity in the Popular Media.* London: Edward Arnold.

Mann, Coramae R. 1996. *When Women Kill.* New York: State University of New York Press.

Meyer, Cheryl L., Michelle Oberman, Kelly White, Michelle Rone, Priya Batra, and Tara C. Proana. 2001. *Mothers Who Kill Their Children: Understanding the Acts of Moms from Susan Smith to the "Prom Mom."* New York: New York University.

Messing Jill T., and John W. Heeren. 2004. "Another Side of Multiple Murder: Women Killers in the Domestic Context." *Homicide Studies* 8: 123–158.

Meyers, Marian. 1997. *News Coverage of Violence Against Women: Engendering Blame.* Thousand Oaks, CA: Sage.

Morrissey, Belinda. 2003. *When Women Kill: Questions of Agency and Subjectivity.* London: Routledge.

Naylor, Bronwyn. 1990. "Media Images of Women Who Kill." *Legal Service Bulletin* 15(1): 4–8.

Naylor, Bronwyn. 2001. "Reporting Violence in the British Print Media: Gendered Stories." *The Howard Journal of Criminal Justice* 40(2): 180–194.

Nicholls, Tonia L., and Don G. Dutton. 2001. "Abuse Committed by Women Against Male Intimates." *Journal of Couples Therapy,* 10: 41–57.

Nyawanza, Mercy. 2007. "Women and Criminality: The Reporting of Crime News in the British Press." *ERCES Journal* 3(4).

Oberman, Michelle. 1996. "Mothers Who Kill: Coming to Terms with Modern American Infanticide." *American Criminal Law Review* 34: 1–110.

Oliver, Pamela E., and Daniel J. Meyers. 1999. "How Events Enter the Sphere: Conflict, Location, and Sponsorship in Local Newspaper Coverage of Public Events." *American Journal of Sociology* 105: 38–87.

Pearson, Patricia. 1997. *When She was Bad: Violent Women and the Myth of Innocence.* Toronto: Random House of Canada.

Peter, Tracey. 2006. "Mad, Bad, or Victim? Making Sense of Mother-Daughter Sexual Abuse." *Feminist Criminology* 1(4): 283–302.

Peterson, Elicka S. L. 1999. "Murder as Self-help: Women and Intimate Partner Homicide. *Homicide Studies* 3(1): 30–46.

Pollock, Joycelyn, and Sareta Davis. 2005. "The Continuing Myth of the Violent Female Offender." *Criminal Justice Review.* 30(1): 5–29.

Pritchard, Colin, and Christopher Bagley. 2001. "Suicide and Murder in Child Murderers and Child Sexual Abusers." *Journal of Forensic Psychiatry & Psychology* 12(2): 269–286.

Pritchard, David. 1985. "Race, Homicide, and Newspapers." *Journalism Quarterly* 62: 500–507.

Rattner Arye. 1996. "Is There a Prima Facie Obligation to Obey the Law? An Empirical Examination of the Question in Israeli Society." *European Journal of Crime, Criminal Law and Justice* 4(4): 348–360.

Rattner, Arye, and Gideon Fishman. 1998. *Justice for Everybody? Jews and Arabs in the Israel Justice System.* Jerusalem: Abraham Fund Organization.

Reece, Laura E. 1991. "Mothers Who Kill: Postpartum Disorders and Criminal Infanticide." *UCLA Law Review* 699(38): 754–757.

Rosencrans, Bobbie. 1997. *The Last Secret: Daughters Sexually Abused by Mothers.* Brandon, VT: Safer Society Press.

Sanger, Carol. 1999. "Leaving Children for Work." In Julia D. Hanigsberg and Sara Ruddick (eds.), *Mother Troubles: Rethinking contemporary maternal dilemmas:* 97–116. Boston: Beacon.

Scott, Hannah. 2005. *The Female Serial Murderer: A Sociological Study of Homicide and the "Gentler Sex."* Queenstown, ON: Edwin Mellen Press.

Shah, Hemant, and Michel C. Thorton. 1994. "Racial ideology in the U.S. Mainstream News Magazine Coverage of Black Latino Interaction, 1980–1992." *Critical Studies in Mass Communication* 31: 141–161.

Showalter, Elaine. 1982. "Women Writers and the Double Standard: Victorian Notions of Motherhood." In Susan Cahill (ed.), *Motherhood: A reader for men and women:* 67–71. New York: Avon.

Silverman, Robert A., and Leslie W. Kennedy. 1988. "Women Who Kill Their Children." *Violence and Victim,* 3(2): 113–127.

Simon, David. 1991. *Homicide: A Year on the Killing Streets.* Boston: Houghton Mifflin.

Stanko, Betsy, Louise Marian, Rachel Manning, Jonathan Smith, and Sharon Cowan. 1998. *http://www.ncjrs.gov/App/Publications/abstract.asp?ID=195714.*

Tilley, Nick. 1989. "The Abuser — Punishment or Treatment." In Wendy, Stainton-Rogers., Denise Hevey and Elizabeth Ash (eds.), *Child Abuse and Neglect.* London: Batsford.

United States Department of Justice's Bureau of Justice Statistics. 2006. *http://www.ojp.usdoj.gov/nij/welcome.html*

_____. 2008. *http://www.ojp.usdoj.gov/nij/welcome.html*

Walker, Lenore. 1979. *The Battered Woman.* New York: Harper & Row.

_____. 1989. *Terrifying Love: Why Battered Women Kill and How Society Responds.* New York: Harper Collins.

Warren, Janet. 1989. "Women Who Murder: Violence in America." Paper presented at FBI Academy, 158th Session, Quantico: VA.

Websdale, Neil. 1999. *Understanding Domestic Homicide.* Boston: Northern University Press.

Wesely, Jennifer K. 2006. "Considering the Context of Women's Violence: Gender, Lived Experiences, and Cumulative Victimization." *Feminist Criminology* 1(4): 303–328.

Whiteley, Kate M. 2011. "Women Incarcerated for Homicide: In the Australian Criminal Justice System." Unpublished doctoral dissertation, Queensland University of Technology, Brisbane, Australia.

Wilczynski, Ania. 1997. "Mad or Bad: Child-killers, Gender and the Courts." *British Journal of Criminology* 37(3): 419–436.

Worrall, Anne. 1981. "Out of Place: Female Offenders in Court." *Probation Journal* 28(3): 90–93.

_____. 1990. *Offending Women.* London: Routledge.

Young, Vernetta D. 1986. "Gender Expectations and Their Impact on Black Female Offenders and Victims. *Justice Quarterly* 3(3): 305–327.

Yourstone, Jenny, Torun Lindholm, and Marianne Kristiansson. 2008. "Women Who Kill: A Comparison of the Psychosocial Background of Female and Male Perpetrators. *International Journal of Law and Psychiatry,* Aug.–Sept. 31(4): 374–383.

Gangs, Politics and Media: Lessons from the New York Chapter of the Almighty Latin King and Queen Nation

Louis Kontos

In the 1990s, New York City ended its streak of rapidly increasingly crime rates. It began to lead the nation in a significant drop in crime. However, while the city looked cleaner and felt safer, there was a growing gang problem. Gangs that originated on the West Coast and in the midwest now appeared in the streets of New York City. The New York City Police Department identified the Almighty Latin King and Queen Nation (ALKQN) as the biggest, most organized, most secretive and most violent of these groups. In 1996 the ALKQN began to generate sensational headlines. Its leader was found guilty of racketeering and of ordering a string of murders from jail. Shocking details about the group were revealed during the trial by co-defendants who cut deals with the prosecution, including that the punishment for violating its code of secrecy was death. But just after the ALKQN shocked the public, it captured its imagination. The new leader proclaimed that the group had lost its way, that it had been led astray into the underworld and it was now time for the ALKQN to reclaim direction and purpose. Its members were already caught up in the growing unrest of the inner-city communities in response to police harassment and brutality. The ALKQN itself eventually became a significant part of the unrest.

The ALKQN did not jump into the fray without reservations. There was an ongoing concern about public exposure. It wanted to make itself known but not transparent. Its position with regard to media coverage and publicity became less ambiguous toward the end of its political phase. In those days, journalists were around all the time and not only could ask questions and debate the answers with group members, but could see practically anything they needed to see. Yet, there was always an issue of trust. Media coverage raised doubt about the credibility of the ALKQN, time and again. This became the angle. The ALKQN thought it possible to strike a bargain. It offered less secrecy with the expectation of greater coverage of its grievances, its role in political events, its alliances with community organizations, its struggle to keep the peace with rival groups, and its attempts to dissuade thousands of members from engaging in criminal activity (even though many of them struggled to make a living and many had a criminal background). The ALKQN thought it could get its story out despite the antipathy of the media. The results were mixed.

This essay examines the attempt of the ALKQN to rework its public image. The research is ethnographic, drawn from a larger study involving the group in NYC and Long Island (cf. Kontos 2007, 2003; Kontos, Brotherton, and Barrios 2003). The members that are quoted were interviewed between 1998 and 2000. Several, including the retired leader of the ALKQN, were recently re-interviewed for this essay. Members were initially paid a nominal fee for lengthy semi-structured interviews, but not for being re-interviewed. The other people quoted below were either interviewed by me or observed directly by me in ALKQN meetings or public venues. The media coverage was selected on the basis of its importance as a topic of discussion and object of strategy within the group. Extensive and comprehensive coverage was always the most important. ALKQN members tried increasingly to facilitate this type of coverage. They got it in the pages of the *New York Times* and *New York Magazine*, and on the national stage with *Dateline*, *ABC Primetime*, and *HBO*.

Secrecy and Publicity

The ALKQN had an ambivalent relationship to media through most of its political phase. The group was not initially forthcoming with details about itself, especially with regard to its codes, rituals or beliefs. Most members avoided the media. Part of the problem for them was that the code of secrecy had been replaced with something contradictory — the idea of a more open secret-society. The literature of the group — the Latin King Bible — was revised several times, which included eliminating references to beatings and killings as punishments for transgressions, and formalizing the exit process. But references to secrecy remained in place. The Latin King Bible begins with the sentence: "You are entering into the depths and secrets of the ALKQN. This secret elite society is made up of great men of honor, courage, boldness, self-respect, pride and most importantly 'silence.'" In addition, the ALKQN in Chicago was not enthusiastic about what the New York chapter was doing. Nobody knew how this conflict would play out. In this kind of world, it was better to be safe than sorry. Yet, the New York chapter gained a fair amount of publicity, and became an active participant in the construction of its public image.

In response, the NYPD maintained that the political activism of the ALKQN amounted to a sophisticated public relations campaign — that the public was being duped through the media into supporting and protecting a sophisticated criminal organization. The problem with this ominous warning was that the ALKQN did not seem particularly sophisticated to anybody that observed it directly for any length of time. It seemed to be inventing itself as it went along; it seemed rather disorganized in most respects. Debates about strategy were usually settled not in days or weeks, but in a few hours during weekly (local) and monthly (general or "universal") meetings. And it was never clear what it meant for the ALKQN to settle anything. There was significant ongoing disagreement within the group about the new direction because the trade-offs were many. As a secret society the ALKQN could take care of its problems any way it saw fit—violence was a constant option. No matter the true intentions of the ALKQN during its political phase, it still had to deal with various rival gangs in its neighborhoods and the prison system. Whatever it proclaimed about itself was irrelevant in this context.

Yet, the group got caught up in events and publicity. What seemingly began as a commitment to rediscovering its purpose and adding its voice to popular grievances, turned into a radical reevaluation of every aspect of its identity, including its literature, ideology and history. The transformation of the ALKQN was neither smooth nor consistent. It eventually failed. It is possible to say, in retrospect, that the movement collapsed under the weight of its own contradictions. But outside forces played a role, the media most of all. The fascination that the mainstream media developed with the ALKQN ultimately worked against the group. ALKQN tried to tell a compelling story about gangs, crime, politics, and the police. But the journalists with which it engaged for the most part had other things in mind. They already had the angle that suited them: trust. And increasingly it became possible to develop a good human interest story in which the new leader, Antonio Fernandez, "King Tone," could assume the role of flawed protagonist, in which a secular morality play could unfold.

The ALKQN

The ALKQN is the oldest Latino/a gang in the country. It was founded in Chicago in the 1940s. The New York chapter was founded in 1986 in Collins Correctional Facility by King Blood (Luis Felipe), who was part of the Muriel Boat Lift and joined the ALKQN in Chicago. In Collins, racial and ethnic conflict had reached crisis proportions. The majority of inmates were Black, and the Black gangs were larger and better organized than the various Latino gangs. King Blood offered not only a solution but a vision. The solution was organization. The vision was embodied in the doctrine of Kingism. Kingism asserts the need for Latino/as to reclaim their history and culture; to recognize that their lands have been stolen and that their peoples have been oppressed by colonial forces that have rewritten and whitewashed history. Kingism includes religious eschatology, where the oppressed finally receive justice after hundreds of years' worth of trials and tribulations.

The ALKQN began to appear on the streets of NYC as inmates returned from prison with crown-positions given to them by King Blood and other prison leaders. Throughout the late 1980s, Latino youth were entering prison in sizable numbers, largely due to the War on Drugs, and they were coming out in substantial numbers as members of the ALKQN. Outside of these impacted areas in the city, however, the ALKQN was relatively unknown. The situation changed in 1996, when the group was introduced to the larger public by the local media as being responsible for some of the most gruesome murders ever seen in NYC (Smith 1996a, 1996b; Kocieniewski 1996). King Blood had ordered the execution of rival members and provided the hit men with instructions that included mutilation and decapitation. The courtroom drama included the attendance of dozens of Latin Kings and Queens that supported their Godfather. It was made complete when King Blood transferred leadership of the ALKQN during courtroom proceedings, naming his successor, King Tone. It was during the trial of King Blood that King Tone announced that the ALKQN was ready to change its ways. Within the group King Tone was known as a moralist and a true believer. The doctrine of belief was Kingism.

Kingism

The Latin King Bible originates from a set of principles—including honesty, loyalty and discipline. Narrative was added over time. A manifesto took form, together with various lessons, rules and prayers. Although the contents of the Latin King Bible have long ago been discovered and disseminated by law enforcement, including in excerpted form in various websites, the text is shrouded in mystery and maintains an aura of sacredness and authenticity for the group. The Latin King Bible invents a subculture in its pages. Members are expected not only to commit themselves to the ALKQN in a total way—to pledge their lives—but to become believers and to keep its ideals and past alive through specific rituals and rites. The ritualistic aspect of the ALKQN could be seen by outsiders when members greeted each other in public. Their greeting involves a series of steps that includes the gesture of forming a crown with the right hand and placing it over the chest (the heart) to signify total commitment and willingness to sacrifice. The gesture communicates "I will die for you." It alone provided journalists with sufficient reason to doubt the claim that the ALKQN was no longer a "gang." Media coverage that included reference to the way in which Latin Kings and Queens greet each other, invariably failed to explain it. In this coverage, gang signs, symbols and codes were all the same, even if some were more elaborate than others (e.g., Palmer 1999; Richardson 1996).

The meetings became increasingly politicized events in the late 1990s and began to include outsiders as presenters, including Puerto Rican Nationalists, former Black Panthers and Young Lords, and members of the clergy. Father Luis

Barrios' brand of liberation theology was especially appealing to the group (see Brotherton and Barrios 2004). He welcomed them into St Mary's Church in Harlem. Other churches also did that, but what was unique about St. Mary's was that ALKQN members were able to attend in large numbers and to represent their group with colors and insignia. And they were able to perform their identity by praying in their own way and throwing-the-crown when they felt the need as well. St. Mary's became especially important in 1998 when King Tone was placed under house arrest. He needed permission to travel but was allowed to go to church on Sundays. The churchyard of St. Mary's thus became the permanent site of the universals. That is usually also where the ALKQN received visitors.

By 1998, it seemed that every radical group in NYC sought a potential alliance with the ALKQN. But the ALKQN could not accommodate the demands of most them; especially any demand to change its name or put away its colors and insignia. A great deal of pride was associated with being a member of a group in which everybody commits his/her life to everybody else; a group that outsiders had to take seriously, if only because there was reason to fear it. At the same time, ALKQN members were becoming image conscious. They did not like being called a "gang" anymore because they associated that term with a sordid history from which they were trying to make a break; and because they did not like the comparison it evoked with other groups that were labeled gangs. It made no difference except in media coverage of the group that dealt explicitly with the question of whether its claims about reforms were real. At the same time, the ALKQN could not easily extricate itself from gangland. It had an image to maintain among its rivals and enemies, where it could not afford to be seen as weak, even as it tried to change its image in its dealings with the community and the larger public.

Politics: Grievances and Elevation

During his trial, King Blood asked the judge not to blame the ALKQN for his misdeeds. He stated that the ALKQN should be allowed to "elevate." Elevation to the next level, King Blood said, was now happening with the appointment of King Tone. Outsiders could hardly make sense of these remarks but there was no misunderstanding their significance within the group. Members knew the phraseology — levels are eschatological in the Latin King Bible. They knew that King Tone had received official blessing for change; and they knew he was a zealot. He created public drama instantly by announcing that Kings that were into crime and violence should just leave, they were no longer welcome. Seemingly everything had changed in that moment. But in private conversations with King Tone and other members, reality was acknowledged to be more complex. It was acknowledged, for instance, that some unspecified portion of the membership was consistently involved in crime and that unless jobs were more widely available there was no real way to change that fact. Journalists who asked the group about itself got the same private conversation. The idea of "elevation" was made plain to a whole bunch of people that got involved with the group. But it did not translate well into media coverage or public discourse.

New York City was becoming an unforgiving place. It was now a test site for the theory of Broken Windows, which presumes that people react to signs of disorder by withdrawing from public space and abandoning neighborhoods, resulting in a decrease of informal social control. Petty offenses became suddenly hugely important. Policing policy became indistinguishable from political policy in that respect. It was the dawn of a new age, a veritable renaissance, where there was no room for any kind of sympathy for the unemployed and the poor, especially not for the ne'er do wells that joined gangs; they were simply not welcome. The dark side of this policy quickly became apparent in the inner-city. The NYPD had adopted an aggressive stance toward people who lived there, especially young people. Civilian complaints against the police doubled in a few years (Kontos 2001). Community forums were absorbed by the issue of police harassment and brutality. Meeting after meeting in churches, schools, and community centers had become occasions for members of the community to state grievances against the police and to look for solutions. Very little of what was happening found its way into the local mainstream media. Former NYPD Commissioner William Bratton recounts it dismissively in his autobiography, where names of community organizations and leaders appear like a punch line to a joke. They are portrayed as foolhardy and, alternatively, as opportunistic in their criticisms of the NYPD. The problem in Bratton's estimation was that for twenty-five years African Americans "and other groups in the city had been treated gingerly" (Bratton 1998, xiv).

The feeling in the communities of the inner-city that the ALKQN tapped into was that the NYPD and the mayor were holding them for ransom; that they were being expected to give the police carte blanche authority and allow it endless indiscretions in exchange for greater public safety. Unprecedented numbers of residents were being stopped-and-frisked without special reason. People were now being arrested for minor offenses that previously would have resulted in nothing more than a desk-ticket. Summonses went up from 100,000 in 1993 to 600,000 in 1994 (Cole 2001). Hanging out in street corners became a public order offense. Disorderly conduct became a crime anyone could commit without knowing it. It was routinely applied to young people whose social life was tied up with the streets. Members of the ALKQN were always vulnerable, even with reporters in the background (Bearak, 1997). Such offenses, in turn, provided a pretext for investigations in which the offender's record and associates became an issue, leading to further entanglement in the criminal justice system. In addition, NYPD officers made the unprecedented move of establishing permanent surveillance and guard posts throughout inner-city schools.

Police were arresting kids in school for crimes that would have been dealt with internally by school security and principles in previous times. Getting a police record was becoming easier in NYC. The President of the Police Benevolent Society described this set of policies as a "map for a police state" (Cole 2001).

Broken Windows and Police Politics

The Giuliani administration redefined the public discourse in NYC about gangs. We were told that it was no longer necessary to be concerned with them as anything other than public enemy. People who thought otherwise were labeled "advocates" and "romantics" (Cole, 2001). Giuliani mocked his opponent Ruth Messinger in a similar way in a televised debate for suggesting that social programs were needed alongside policing strategies to deal with a growing gang problem. "These are violent repeat career criminals and I don't think that giving them sewing lessons is going to help. ... [I]t is almost an inappropriate thing to start taking about youth programs for them" (*New York Times* 1997). It was clearly not okay to "start talking" about youth programs or anything else that brought to mind the bad old days. What Messinger and other liberals did not get apparently was that the public discourse had already shifted. Their kind of talk had become passé. Receptivity in the media to Giuliani's relentless tough talk and abrasive demeanor signaled the change. The *New York Post* and *Daily News* referred to him simply by his first name, Rudy — like a rock star. The *New York Times* mostly treated Giuliani like medicine that had to be taken no matter how it tasted.

The perception that crime rates skyrocketed in the 1980s because "activists" and "romantics" had kept the NYPD from being as aggressive as it needed to be, and that it no longer had that problem, was facilitated by media coverage that adopted the administration's narrative regarding crime and disorder. In this narrative, small offenses lead directly to big offenses and therefore aggressive policing becomes simply a requirement of a safe and decent society.

Counter Narrative: Police Brutality

The counter-narrative that embodied a concern with the conditions that cause crime had lost traction in the local mainstream media and political discourse. But another counter-narrative began to materialize around brutality and the administration's response to it. The problem that the new administration faced within barely its first year was the perception that the NYPD was no longer playing by any rules that as a consequence rogue cops were able to do as they pleased.

Officer Francis Livoti became the face of the problem in 1994. Livoti murdered Anthony Baez, 29, by applying a choke hold which is explicitly forbidden by the NYPD. Baez was playing football with his three brothers in front of his parents' home in the Bronx. After the ball hit the cruiser of Livoti a second time, Livoti choked Baez to death. The incident caught the attention of New Yorkers because of the brutality involved and the cover-up that followed. Six of ten officers who appeared on the scene testified that Baez was resisting Livoti's attempt to put him in handcuffs, and that it took several of them to restrain the 270-pound Baez. The officers described a struggle that could have ended at any point with Baez' cooperation; each of them said that they did not see Baez being choked. Livoti was acquitted. Yet, the presiding judge who found Livoti not guilty referred to the testimony of the six officers as "a nest of perjury." The "nest of perjury" conclusion was later affirmed in a trial by the NYPD, where it was determined that Livoti met with the officers to concoct a scenario that would protect him from criminal prosecution. It was reaffirmed in a second criminal trial. Livoti was found guilty of violating the civil rights of Anthony Baez.

Questions remained. It turns out that Livoti had nine previous complaints against him for police brutality, and that he had been previously disciplined for assaulting a police lieutenant. Yet he was still on the force. Why? Why were none of the six officers (the nest of perjury) disciplined? Perhaps the biggest problem for the public image of the NYPD around the Baez murder was that an officer who broke ranks and testified against Livoti had now made public statements to the effect that she feared for her life. She was receiving death threats from fellow officers. She had to be assigned 24-hour police protection. Her locker had to be checked every day with bomb sniffing dogs. Eventually she resigned from the force. The headlines provided an interesting contrast with pictures of hundreds of NYPD officers showing up repeatedly at the court-house in support of Livoti: "Her Bravery Shatters Blue Wall" (Gonzales 1996), "Witness Cop Fears for Life" (McQuillan and Garcilazo 1996).

Another unlikely source of heroism was Anthony Baez' mother, Iris Baez. Iris Baez was the quintessential version of a conservative, church-going mother who worked hard and sacrificed to provide a better life for her children. She had no particular prior concern with political activism until the stonewalling she experienced from the NYPD and municipal authorities following the murder of her son. She decided to take matters into her own hands. She turned to the National Congress for Puerto Rican Rights. The founder of this organization, Richie Perez, was a founding member of the New York Young Lords Party. He sought out the Kings after hearing King Tone speak on the radio. Perez set up a meeting between the Kings, Baez and the group of mothers that then founded Mothers Against Police Brutality. When the Latin Kings told Baez that they were willing to fight alongside her group to make the police accountable to the community, she was open to them.

They showed up by the hundreds in rallies against police brutality, quickly becoming associated with that issue and the Baez case in particular. Latin Kings and Queens were uniquely able to support the Mothers' movement, which lacked organizational resources and experience, and which did things spontaneously in response to new cases of police brutality or responses to them by NYPD officials or Mayor Giuliani. King Tone recounts these early events as follows:

> One time three mothers called a rally at the same day that I had a universal. I sent Queens to the Queens rally, 300 people. I sent Brooklyn to the Brooklyn rally. Two hundred people. I sent a church full of a thousand kids who waited and then went to Manhattan with Richie [Perez]. They all got in around the city, and finished the rally. Took the train to 126th St. And at my meeting I still had 1,200. There ain't an organization right now in New York that could do that. You go find it for me. The mayor can't call it. Ain't a thousand people showing up for him. [...] I get on the phone, I say we got a rally. I need you there. We got 500. If it's a bad day, we'll get 200. And they'll be there. Regardless of what you say, when you can say to these youth, "come on and let's march with this lady," and 900 of them show up, there's something goin' on. They wasn't cold. Something in their heart said we need it, and somebody's giving us the opportunity to save our own.

The association between the ALKQN and the Mothers was controversial from the start. One of the mothers whose son was a Latin King, who was killed execution style in the back of the head by an NYPD officer, was the first to object to their involvement because she feared that the murder would be taken less seriously if it was discovered that her son belonged to the group. To this day, the ALKQN prides itself over the fact that it did not disclose any information to the public regarding this matter; even though members felt it would have helped their cause. Stigma by association also complicated matters for other groups who wanted to help the Baez family, including the Latino Officers Association (LOA). This group was the only faction within the NYPD to publicly support Officer Boria. It was then publicly vilified by police officials when it took the stage with the ALKQN at the invitation of the Baez family at a rally against police brutality (Fitz-Gibbon 1996).

October 19, 1996, eleven days after Livoti's acquittal, Captain Steven Plavnick was shot outside the 46th Precinct stationhouse in the Bronx. NYPD officials blamed the ALKQN. They were apparently expecting a violent response from the ALKQN based on threats that NYPD officers claim to have overheard after the trial. None of the reporters who covered the event mentioned anything about threats. The initial round of coverage of the NYPD's claims was skeptical. October 22, three days after the shooting, The *Daily News* quoted Mayor Giuliani as saying that there was "no evidence" to link it with "the Baez demonstrations" (McQuillan and Garcilazo 1996, 8). December 22, the *New York Times* quoted anonymous sources in the NYPD as saying that three drug dealers had been arrested for the shooting and that "no affiliation" between this group and the ALKQN was found. But the official NYPD version, which remained the same except for added detail and intrigue, gained the support of the district attorney's office. The *New York Times* states this version in full on January 8, without any reference to its earlier coverage: "After Officer Livoti was found not guilty in the 1994 death of Anthony Baez, a criminal whom prosecutors would not name offered $5,000 to the Latin Kings in exchange for killing a police captain, said Dawn Florio, an assistant district attorney in the Bronx. The Latin Kings subcontracted the work out to a smaller gang called the Netas, she said, and four men carried out the plan on October 19, 1996 by shooting Capt. Steven Plavnick in the back as he arrived at the station house of the 46th Precinct in an unmarked patrol car" (Cooper 1997, B1). A few days later, ALKQN and Neta leaders held a joint press conference to deny that their groups had anything to do with the shooting. King Tone accused the prosecutor and NYPD of "slandering" the ALKQN and Neta. His lawyer, Ron Kuby, accused the NYPD of trying to divide them (Fitz-Gibbon 1997, 1).

Media Coverage

In the midst of this drama, King Tone decided to grant unprecedented access to a reporter from *New York Magazine* (Richardson 1997). He believed that *New York* would provide the ALKQN with a new and different audience — the educated; he was aiming at the educated and influential classes of New York City. But the story that resulted could have been written by the NYPD or the district attorney's office, sources that are quoted throughout as authoritative and objective. King Tone's answers to provocative questions were dismissed as propaganda, not even worth engaging. For instance, he was asked how he could now claim to stand for anything positive when he got his position by rising through the ranks of the group during its most violent and criminal phase. Did he participate in physicals (beatings)? Yes. Did he order them? Yes. The Kings were not Boy Scouts. King Tone added that he never had anyone murdered. He was not like previous leaders. He believed in Kingism and thought he could lead the group in a positive direction, etc. The reporter was not buying a word of it. After listening to Tone say that history was being made and that had he not become leader of the ALKQN history would be different, the reporter "burst out laughing" (Richardson 1997). That's his account. Latin Kings did not like to see their brothers and leader ridiculed when they could have simply avoided dealing with unsympathetic reporters, or avoided reporters altogether. But, with regard to this story, what caused the biggest controversy within the group was King Tone's statement that he encouraged a few members to go to the district attorney with facts about a murder case in which a Latin King was the victim and the boyfriend of a Latin Queen the assailant. King Tone's statement was treated by the reporter as yet more propaganda (Richardson 1997). Whereas the Kings themselves believed it and they were not happy. The prison leadership of the group made the strongest condemnation of the First Supreme Crown saying that it's okay to talk with the district attorney. King Tone developed a reputation as a "snitch" among a segment of the ALKQN as a result of this coverage.

A few months later the ALKQN made another attempt to reach a broader audience, this time nationally. They appeared on *Nightline* (April 8, 1997). Ted Koppel begins the program with the question: "The Latin Kings: can they be trusted?" He proceeds to list the crimes of King Blood and to point out that the ALKQN has never dissociated itself from him. U.S. Attorney Mary Jo White appears several times in the program to make the point that the ALKQN cannot be trusted because it maintains "rigid rules and codes" and "cult-like devotion to King Blood." Bernard Kerik, First Deputy Commissioner of the Department of Corrections, appears on the program to say much the same; adding that he and his staff should be credited with the reduction in gang violence at Rikers Island. The ALKQN should not be credited with anything besides criminal violence and now a clever public relations campaign, Kerik said. Later in the program, David Marsh interviews King Tone and a few other members of the ALKQN. Each of them talks about their struggles and admits to a learning curve. King Tone is then shown confronting Latin Kings selling drugs in a street corner. "This isn't what we do anymore." "Either you stop flying the colors or you come in righteous." Marsh asks: "is any of this real?" Toward the end, Father Barrios makes the dramatic statement: "In my theology, King Tone is a prophet. What is a prophet? A prophet is someone who first denounces injustice and second goes against injustice." ALKQN members generally liked the program because it seemed balanced and because it showed something of their spirit and zeal.

But publicity remained controversial within the ALKQN. Many of the members did not like the idea that media coverage had invited greater scrutiny and possible public backlash from sectors of society that would never accept them no matter what they did or what they became. Hundreds of members preferred the underground, though it was rare to hear statements to that effect unless they involved a direct challenge to King Tone — there were several of them, including three assassination attempts from within the group. The argument they heard repeatedly from King Tone was that increased public scrutiny was coming their way anyway and that it was coming with increased repression. In this scenario the ALKQN had few choices and only one of them was morally and strategically right; namely to take a public stand.

Positive media coverage appeared to empower the progressive forces within the group — the members that thought it necessary and possible to transform the ALKQN into a political organization. Coverage did not have to be totally positive to serve this purpose, as long as it captured something real about the Kings and Queens and their struggle as part of a larger movement. The coverage that was produced by *ABC Primetime* (*ABC Primetime Live* 1998) was their favorite because it displayed them as united, powerful, capable of great violence, and peaceful by choice. That was the right mixture of elements for them. The director had given members of the ALKQN seven cameras to film themselves over a period of six months. But very little of what was filmed appeared in the final cut. Gone were the rallies and demonstrations. Gone also was an interview segment with John Quinones, who asked an assembled group of 30 Latin Kings questions about a range of topics for over an hour. Coverage took form around King Tone. The highlight of the program is a scene where he is accompanied by a few dozen members as he confronts a rival from the old guard whom the ALKQN tried and convicted of rape. In earlier times, a conviction by the ALKQN meant either beating or death. If the accused was also a rival of the leader, it would have almost certainly meant the latter. Here King Tone is shown making peace. He says: "I ain't fighting you because I'm the Inca of New York State, Supreme Crown of this Nation. I ain't fighting you because when my hands lift up, it's for war. It's for people to die and nobody to live." "I won't do that because I love you" (*ABC Primetime Live* 1998). The Kings were never happy over the fact that what they thought was important, the rallies and demonstrations especially, became secondary or non-existent topics in media coverage of their group. In the next year, great expectations were built up after the ALKQN was approached by HBO (Home Box Office). Director Jon Alpert spent five months with the ALKQN. He had virtually unrestricted access. Yet the HBO documentary special on the ALKQN is comprised mostly of interviews with King Tone, his mother, girlfriend, and lawyer Ron Kuby. Audiences get to see the mother break down repeatedly. She says to Alpert that she never understood why her son joined the ALKQN, though she believed he tried to do some good as its leader. At one point she seems outraged that King Tone professed Kingism. There was 'only one King' in her eyes—Jesus. On the way to visit her father, King Tone's toddler daughter is asked by Alpert if she knows where she's going. She replies, "Daddy's in a cage." Every time the documentary seems to move away from the personal life of King Tone, toward ALKQN itself, the audience is brought right back again into the same voyeuristic, wrenching drama.

In 2003, when the HBO Documentary *The Latin Kings: A Gang Story* was released, it was too late to make any difference to the internal struggles of the group—they had already been settled. Nonetheless it did receive attention and reaction. The first question that members asked was what happened to all the footage? What happened to the rallies? Nowadays these types of questions are not asked. Rather, there are plenty of members (the majority) who know the political phase of their group only through media coverage and documentaries. Even among the members who weren't there, there is a sense of nostalgia.

Politics and Crime

The transition of the ALKQN from gang to political organization did not strike people in affected communities as being as odd as the mainstream media had made it out to be. The questions were different. Among outsiders living in the Upper East Side of Manhattan or Park Slope, Brooklyn, there was a question about whether the Kings could be trusted to transform themselves into anything other than a violent gang — it was the same question posed repeatedly by journalists in the mainstream media. It seems that the concern followed the coverage, though it would be wrong to attribute any significant concern about the ALKQN within these communities aside from their general concern about crime. Within the inner-city the question about the Kings was more poignantly simple: could they succeed? Could this group of ne'er do wells get its act together and stop victimizing the communities of which they were a part? Would the NYPD simply harass them or, instead, attack them in an extraordinary way?

According to Richie Perez, extraordinary measures were to be expected. The ALKQN, in his estimation, had become the biggest public relations problem that the NYPD had yet endured; since, it had thrown into question the NYPD's claim to speak for the community and to frame opposition to its policies in terms of nothing more than inchoate grievances from bad-guys. He had a point. Latin Kings and Queens gained a voice through which they amplified and dramatized the grievances of the community, which were neither inchoate nor ill-informed. But Perez had few illusions. There were many historical examples of activist groups with confrontational politics that were targeted by the FBI and NYPD, including the Black Panthers and Young Lords. None of them had the sordid background of the ALKQN. Yet they were treated as gangs and persecuted for real and imaginary offenses. The Latin Kings and Queens, by contrast, were like babes in the woods. So it seemed.

Still, support materialized in ways that mattered. It mattered, for instance, when supporters could offer the ALKQN places to meet, since the NYPD had become determined to offset this possibility by invading every available place. St. Mary's Church in Harlem served this purpose for the entire group. Father Eddie Lopez and Father Gordon Duggins also provided church space in Brooklyn and the Bronx. Richie Perez provided use of his office. But the most important resource came when Willie Morales offered use of Charas/El Bohio, a community center in the Lower East Side. Charas allowed the Latin Kings and Queens to mingle with others— outsiders— on a regular basis. They enjoyed being there. Morales, a former member of the X-Men, a Boston gang, said he believed that the Latin Kings and Queens were the real deal. "I saw them at a public speakout in New York City a year and a half ago. It was a pretty positive event. I saw it as legit from the get-go," Morales said. "I admire them. They're not saying we're former Latin Kings. They are saying, 'We are Latin Kings.' They're not trying to hide their past. I think their past makes them more credible with young people'" (Rodriguez 1999). Charas, which began in 1979, closed its doors in 1999 when a real-estate developer bought the building in which it was housed. ALKQN members usually describe the loss of Charas as the beginning of the end. They fought publicly against its closing every step of the way (Allon 1997).

Like every social movement, the success of the ALKQN in mobilizing sup-port and participation was predicated on its ability to produce results. When momentum is lost or setbacks become too many, internal conflicts usually more clearly manifest. The ALKQN was not exceptional in this respect. Members of the old guard had credibility within the group because they had made all the sacrifices that were required of them; the fact that they were still around meant that they had paid their dues. Reaction to the new direction came mostly from their ranks. After the last of a series of police sting operations, internal reaction became intense. Over a thousand NYPD and FBI agents invaded the homes of high-ranking members of the ALKQN in 1998. Operation Crown was the largest coordinated police effort in the history of NYC. Many members now asked openly about why only their group was targeted and, more importantly, about the timing — why now? Community activists were asking the same question. Mainstream journalists, by contrast, had now found an answer to the question of whether the ALKQN could be trusted (McFadden 1998; Peterson, Rashbaum, and Smith 1998). Reactionary forces within the group were empowered. They held up the past against the present; King Blood against King Tone. Challenges to King Tone, including of the kind that appeared in the HBO documentary, were now routine. The new direction of the ALKQN made the group weak and vulnerable — that was the main line of dissent. These members would not have been allowed to voice dissent against King Blood. The irony was not lost on anybody present.

Discussion

King Tone was sentenced to 12–15 years for conspiracy to traffic heroin. His role in the conspiracy did not support the image that the NYPD had con-structed of him as an organized crime boss. It basically involved weighing and packaging (bagging) the heroin. It netted him approximately $700. It was hard to believe that King Tone would jeopardize a movement and the goodwill of collaborators and supporters over an opportunistic crime of this nature. But it made sense that something had to give. Bills were not getting paid with the money that King Tone was receiving from the ALKQN. He tried to differentiate himself from earlier leaders by taking a stipend from members' dues — which were collected in a box. ("The box" became a constant reference, a type of coded reference, in criminal trials involving ALKQN members, notwithstanding the fact that it was literally a box that was mostly always empty.) He sought employment everywhere he could, so it seemed; including at one point by trying to distribute Amway products, which the court did not allow because it accepted the argument of the FBI that Amway could be used as a cover to further criminal activity. The Amway incident became newsworthy (e.g., Peterson 1998), but there was no coverage related to the problem itself. The problem was always finding jobs that got the bills paid — not only King Tone's problem but the ALKQN's problem. What made King Tone's situation different from that of other members was that the job prospects were even fewer; not too many employers wanted anything to do with someone who was under constant surveillance and whose presence invited the police, gang rivals and every imaginable kind of trouble. At the end day, however, none of this makes a difference. With the incarceration of King Tone, everything stopped as quickly as it began. HBO was barred, as were researchers and journalists.

The ALKQN has now gone back, more or less, to what it was before 1996. Only its annual attempt to participate in the Puerto Rican Day Parade causes any stir. There is nothing particularly controversial otherwise about media coverage of the ALKQN nowadays. It makes headlines routinely for stereotypical gang activity, and occasionally when another sting operation (nothing ever again on the scale of Operation Crown) takes down a whole new set of its leaders. The human interest story that developed within the mainstream media during the political phase of the ALKQN did not do justice to the people involved. Rather, it reinforced a reactionary political narrative about crime and disorder along with the stereotype that gang members can never be trusted. It also did something worse; it obscured the nature and causes of the social unrest of which the ALKQN was a part.

REFERENCES

ABC Nightline. 1997. "The Latin Kings—Can They be Trusted?" Narrated by Dave Marash and Ted Koppel. April 8.
ABC Primetime Live. 1998. "All the Kings Men." Jan. 14.
Allon, Janet. 1997. "Neighborhood Report: East Village / Lower East Side; At Hearing, Gang Shows New Colors." *The New York Times*, Section 13, page 7 March 23.
Bearak, Barry. 1997. "Man of Vision or of Violence? Where Gang Leader Talks Peace, Police See Just Talk." *The New York Times*, Section B, page 1 Nov. 20.
Bratton, William. 1998. *Turnaround: How America's Top Cop Reversed the Crime Epidemic.* New York: Random House.
Brotherton, David, and Luis Barrios. 2004. *The Almighty Latin King and Queen Nation.* New York: Columbia University Press.
Cole, Williams. 2001. "Against the Giuliani Legacy." *The Brooklyn Rail.* www.brooklynrail.org/ 2001/05/local/against-the-giuliani-legacy-part-one.
Cooper, Michael. 1997. "Revenge Cited in Shooting Of a Captain," *The New York Times.* Section B, Page 1 Jan. 8.
Fitz-Gibbon, Jorge. 1996. "Gang-Link Talk Riles Cop Unit," *Daily News,* Suburban, page 1 Nov.13.
_____. 1997. "Gangs Deny Role in Cop Shoot." *Daily News* Suburban, page 1 Jan. 14..
Gonzales, Juan. 1996. "Her Bravery Shatters Blue Wall." *Daily News.* Sept. 27. Dailynews.com.
Hagedorn, John. 2001. "Institutionalized Gangs and Violence in Chicago." *New Guerra New Paz.* www.coav.org.br/ publique/media/chicagoing.pdf.
Kocieniewski, David. 1996. "Gang Rivalry Cited in Police Captain's Shooting." *New York Times,* Section 1, Page 40. Dec. 22.
Kontos, Louis. 2001. "Review of William Bratton's *Turnaround.*" *Humanity and Society.* 24, no. 4, pp. 241–245.
_____. 2003. "Between Criminal and Political Deviance: A Sociological Analysis of the New York Chapter of the Almighty Latin King and Queen Nation." *The Post-Subcultures Reader.* Edited by David Muggleton and Rupert Weinzierl. Oxford: Berg.
_____. 2007. "The Latin King Bible," *Encyclopedia of Gangs.* Edited by Louis Kontos and David Brotherton. Westport CT: Greenwood Press.

_____. 2011. "Latino Activism." *Encyclopedia of Latinos and Criminal Justice*. Edited by Jose Luis Morin. Santa Barbara, CA: ABC-CLIO.

_____. David Brotherton, and Luis Barrios. 2003. *Gangs and Society*. New York: Columbia University Press.

McFadden, Robert D. 1998. "94 in Latin Kings Are Arrested Citywide." *The New York Times*, Section B, Page 4. May 15.

McQuillan, Alice, and Miguel Garcilazo. 1996. "Witness Cop Fears for Life; She Testified Against Livoti." *Daily News*, Page 8. Oct. 10.

Miller, Walter B. 1982. *Crime by Youth Gangs and Groups in the United States*. Washington, D.C.: Office of Juvenile Delinquency Prevention, U.S. Department of Justice.

New York Times. 1992. "A Police Protest Gets Out of Hand." Section 4, page 2 Sept. 20.

_____. 1997. "Race For City Hall; Candidates in Mayoral Race Touch on Education, Gangs, and Unemployment." Section B, Page 4. Oct. 10.

Palmer, Brian. 1999. "The Way We Live Now: 8–15–99: Campaign Stops: Gang Uniforms; True Colors." *New York Times Magazine*. Aug. 15.

Peterson, Helen. 1998. "I Sell Sope, Not Dope, Latin Kings Chief Sez." *Daily News*, page 8. July 3.

Peterson, Helen, William K. Rashbaum, and Greg B. Smith. 1998. "Cop Coup Takes Latin Kings Down." *Daily News*, page 6. May 15.

Richardson, H. John. 1997. "The Latin Kings Sing Songs of Love." *New York Magazine*, pages 30–37. Feb. 17.

Richardson, Lynda. 1996. "An Inside Look at a Gang's Grisly Drama; Trial of Deposed Leader Offers Contrasting Views of the Latin Kings." *New York Times*, Section B, page 1 Nov. 18.

Rodriguez, Cindy. 1999. "Have the Latin Kings Reformed?" *Boston Globe*, April 23. Bostonglobe.com.

Smith, Greg B. 1996a. "Killer Describes Grisly Litany of Latin Kings." *Daily News*, page 8. Nov. 1.

_____. 1996b. "Indicted Latin King is Greeted Royally." *Daily News*, page 22. Nov. 19.

Williams, Cole. 2001. "Against the Giuliani Legacy." *The Brooklyn Rail*. www.brooklynrail.org/2001/05/local/against-the-giuliani-legacy-part-one.

Inequalities in CSI: Crime Scene Investigation: *Stereotypes in the CSI Investigators*

Denise L. Bissler and Joan L. Conners

CSI: Crime Scene Investigation (*CSI*) has proven itself a popular program since its launch in 2000, as evidenced by its number one Nielsen ratings, as well as successful spin-off programs. While the series' popularity suggests that it contributes to our fascination with crime, little critical analysis of the series has taken place. Crime media (including dramas) are problematic in that that they tend to sensationalize rare violent crimes, increase fear and overstate the crime problem (Potter and Kappeler 1998). *CSI*, in particular, has been purported to influence viewers' expectations of real crime cases and trials, what some call the "CSI Effect," in that it may affect potential jurors' expectations about evidence (Roane and Morrison 2000).

It is our argument that *CSI* perpetuates gender, race, and class stereotypes through its depictions of the main characters. *CSI* consistently represents its primary characters in traditional gender roles in the workplace, in the field, and in their rarely shown private lives. Racial and class stereotypes are similarly reinforced, although gender distinctions appear to be most prominent of these categories.

Literature Review

Images of gender, race, and class in the media can have lasting effects on the audience. Butsch notes recurring patterns or "stock images" (p. 17) influence how we perceive people on television, but also how we perceive others in real life as well (Butsch 2003, 17). What we see in the news and on TV helps us shape our view of reality (Rome 2004; Butsch 2003; Surette 2003). The human socialization process is heavily influenced by media (Rome 2004). Portrayals involving race, class, and gender often serve to reinforce rather than challenge existing stereotypes concerning those on the margins of these groups (Dines and Humez 2003). Constant viewing of stereotypical, monolithic images concerning various groups helps to perpetuate a culture or ideology in which one is more likely to view all members of that group in that light, ignoring any evidence to the contrary and accepting any evidence in support (Zatz and Richey Mann 2006).

In terms of gender, typical media images of women show females being objectified (Kilbourne 1999; Katz 1999) in traditional gender roles (Abt and Seesholtz 1994; Gamson et al. 1992), and being subordinate to men (Kilbourne 1999). Above all else, females must look good (Kilbourne 1999) and the standard for looking good is narrow: thin, young, small features, tall, long hair, flawless skin, etc. Although women are now depicted in the workforce, the stereotypical image is still one of conventional attractiveness (Dow 1996). Thus, women might be viewed in seemingly less traditional roles (in the workforce vs. home) but upon closer examination, female characters often still have traditional roles/traits: emotional, nurturer, conventionally attractive, flirty, and subordinate (Croteau and Hoynes 2003; Gamson et al. 1992).

Images of men also tend to hold to traditional stereotypes although this continuum often has more variation than for women. Male characters fall into the hegemonic masculine ideal — powerful, paid, strong, tough, hypersexual (Katz 1999; Messerschmidt 1997). The "good guys" typically meet the masculine ideal in some form but the "bad guys" are often portrayed as hypermasculine (Scharrer 2001). But, men are typically allowed more variation in the way they look and the way they act especially if they playing an antagonistic role.

The same holds true for images of minority characters. Representations of minority characters tend to fall into stereotypical, monolithic images or typologies (Rome 2004). One of the main stereotypical images for African Americans in the media (especially the news) is that of "the black demon" or male criminal (Rome 2004, 78) or, more generally, "bad boy." It is noted that television avoided the black male criminal stereotype in the 1970s and 1980s as black viewers became an important audience; however, images were still not positive (Rome 2004). When African Americans are shown as criminal they are more likely to be cuffed and in custody of police (Entman 1990). Again, the image of African Americans in the media is often negative. The black character is more often depicted using profanity and being violent (Entman 1990).

Class is a bit more difficult to study in media images as it is not always made clear, but lower classes are commonly absent altogether. However, some have argued that when shown, the lower class is depicted as uneducated (Ehrenreich 2000), irresponsible (Butsch 1995), uncouth (Benhoff and Griffin 2004), and dangerous/criminal (Reinarman 2006). In addition, crime shows often focus on street crime which tends to be associated more with lower class offenders (Potter and Kappeler 1998).

What does this gender, race, and class inequality have to do with crime shows specifically? It has been argued that

> the media have the greatest influence on public attitudes about crime; control of information to the public represents control of the public, because people structure many of their views of the world around media information and crime dramatization [Rome 2004, 65].

If media have the greatest effect on views about crime, then it is logical to think that crime shows specifically have a huge influence. Certainly the news is not the only important socializing force in the media. Given the popularity of crime shows such as *CSI*, it is logical to assume that these shows have socializing effects as well. Thus, our research question focused on the representations of main characters in crime shows. Specifically, we investigated whether gender, race, and class stereotypes (female as subordinate, emotional, irrational, attractive; male as authoritative, tough, unemotional, hypersexual; black as criminal/bad boy, street-wise, lower-class; lower class status as criminal, focus on street crime) were being challenged or reinforced. It seems that crime shows could be a place to challenge stereotypes given their popularity regardless of gender, race, and class status of the viewer. If each show did a better job of representing the reality and complexity involved in gender, race, and class inequality, this socializing agent might be able to challenge rather than reinforce stereotypes. Thus, we set out to test whether one very popular show, *CSI* in its first season, developed complex main characters and challenged stereotypes or vice versa.

Method

We were interested in character development and how the characters were represented to audiences when this popular series began. Thus, we conducted a qualitative content analysis of the main characters or character investigation (Holtzman 2000) by scrutinizing representations of gender, race, and class, noting instances that both support and contradict traditional gender, racial, and class labels (Lofland and Lofland 1995).

A critical content analysis of the portrayals of the main characters in the 23 episodes from the first season (2000) of the original series was conducted by the two researchers. The following aspects of the show were examined: workplace relations; perpetuation of gender, race, and class stereotypes; and possible effects of these representations. All the episodes in season one were viewed separately by each researcher. The researchers watched the episodes taking notes on conventional categorizations of gender, race, and class. In addition, evidence that worked against these typical characterizations was noted. Notes were then compared to discern analytical codes and themes in the material at several times throughout the research process.

Findings

The findings illustrated that stereotypical representations manifested in both what the characters said or did, and what others said about or to them. By stereotype, we mean "oversimplified generalized images of members of a particular group. Stereotyping essentially categorizes all members of a particular group as having a specific set of characteristics" (McIntyre 2002, 223). In general, stereotypes do not tend to be grounded in empirical evidence. Rather they are created and perpetuated based on anecdotal evidence and ignore any difference among individuals that belong to certain groups.

The analysis revealed that traditional gender, race, and class cultural representations were abundant in the first season of *CSI*. Although the show aims to counteract some of the more common stereotypical images of women and minorities (for example, having females with strong demeanors in lead investigator roles), it fails to do so in a meaningful manner. In trying to work against stereotypes (e.g., by having a 40 percent female cast in the typically male dominated field of crime scene investigation; the second-in-command is a female), *CSI* manages to perpetuate several traditional gender roles and racial categorizations.

On the surface, *CSI* should be praised for offering such diversity within its lead characters, particularly two strong women (Catherine Willows and Sara Sidle), and an African American investigator (Warrick Brown). However, on closer examination of the portrayal of the main characters in the introduction of *CSI* in 2000, we found a number of traditional and disconcerting stereotypes being reinforced. As Butsch notes, recurring patterns within characters or "stock images" (Butsch 2003, 17) may not only influence how we perceive people on television, but also how we perceive others in real life as well. Offering examples from the first season as evidence, we analyze the patterns in the portrayal based primarily on gender, but we also discuss the race and class of main characters when made relevant in episodes and storylines. Below, we illustrate stereotypes that were present in the first and integral season of this widely popular crime show. As stated above, we argue that televisual portrayals of gendered, raced, and classed characters can serve to perpetuate negative stereotypes. Following a brief description of each character[1] below, we describe various patterns and concerns found in each character's representations.

Gil Grissom

Gil Grissom joined the Las Vegas crime lab when he was 30 years old, and takes over running the lab in season one at the age of 44. He became L.A. County's youngest coroner when he was just 22, and as a child would conduct autopsies on dead seagulls and other dead animals he discovered. Grissom's CSI specialty is entomology. Grissom has never been married.

Several traditional stereotypes in Gil's character emerge in season one. These stereotypical images serve partially to develop his character and help audiences relate. However, these static, traditional representations also serve to reinforce stereotypes of a hegemonic masculine leader who has to be male, unemotional, overtly intellectual, and protective to be effective. By omission, this gives the view the sense that leadership roles in crime venues are inherently masculine roles.

The Science Nerd: Affectionately nicknamed "Gruesome Grissom" by his co-workers ("Friends and Lovers"), Gil is a freaky, eccentric entomologist, or "bug guy" as he's called in "To Halve and To Hold," and he even owns a tarantula ("Pledging Mr. Johnson"). Gil's character enacts a televisual version of the science-nerd stereotype. He has the intelligence of the stereotypical nerd, even making his own fingerprint powder ("Anonymous") and referring to himself as a "science geek" ("Fahrenheit 932"). However, he is also considered good-looking, as evidenced by flirtations with female characters, such as lab tech Charlotte in "Pilot," and Teri Miller in "To Halve and to Hold." He does not personify the "geeky look or air," but rather he often comes across as either cocky or socially awkward. For instance, he constantly alienates others with his fascination with bugs, specifically maggots ("Friends and Lovers"). In the episode "Boom" he licks a piece of rock found in the desert to see if it is bone. While he can be socially awkward, he is "appropriately" masculine as outlined below and part of that masculinity is his superior intelligence and fascination with insects.

The Omniscient Wise Man: Grissom's character fits the all-knowing masculine ideal. Gil knows everything from bugs to Shakespeare. He is the archetypal, masculine, leading character of television dramas in that he is constantly correcting the other investigators, or giving them sage advice. We rarely see him second guessing himself, or apologizing for making errors. For instance, he is usually so confident that when he admits he is wrong, other characters are shocked ("Justice is Served"). In that episode, he explains that being wrong eventually leads him to the truth. In other words, even if he is wrong at first, he is confident in his ability to discern the truth from the evidence, and solve the case.

In this vein, the leader is portrayed as having the traits of the ideal male: confidence and knowledge (Kimmel 2009). In "Cool Change" Nick questions how Grissom knows so much and he responds, "It's our job to know stuff." Again, Grissom has expertise in a rather wide range of areas. He is represented as an audio specialist, a psychoanalyst, and an amateur arson expert. In "Anonymous," he hears just a few seconds of an audiotape and recognizes it as English being spoken backwards. In "Unfriendly Skies," he cites a fact from the *Psychoanalysis and Forensic* magazine, and offers to get Sara Sidle a subscription when she doubts him. In "Fahrenheit 932," he solves an arson case, even though other experts were stumped.

The Quiet Leader: Males are stereotypically portrayed as having stronger leadership skills than women. Steenland concludes in her analysis of 1990s television, "It's the norm for men to talk more, give orders, solve problems, and run things" (Steenland 1995, 187). Even when television fiction presents strong female characters, there is often a male who guides them. *CSI* is no exception. Gil is the quiet leader who leads by example ("Crate 'n Burial"). He almost always maintains his composure, even when his underlings directly challenge him. He is strong and stoic in his leadership, doling out wisdom like a paternal sage. The "Pilot" establishes Grissom's objective role, when he responds to Warrick, "Yes, you had him and the minute you started thinking about yourself instead of the case, you lost him. There is no room in this department for subjectivity. You know that, Warrick, we handle every case objectively and without presupposition regardless of race, color, creed or bubble-gum flavor. Okay?" His leadership is fair-handed but strong and powerful.

The Protector: It is common for Gil to play the "protector" role in relation to the series' female characters but not in relation to the males. Grissom is a character quick to react to the damsel in distress and he has plenty of opportunities to do so, even though the female investigators appear outwardly strong. In one scene, he touches Sara's face and asks if she "is all right" ("Crate 'n Burial"). In "Friends and Lovers," he is described by a coroner as "Gruesome Grissom. Tin man with a heart. Who knew." At another point, he protects Catherine by intervening during a fight between her and her ex-husband ("Who Are You?").

Conversely, he serves as a mentor to Warrick, who faces professional and personal challenges, such as being blackmailed by a judge in "Cool Change." His leadership of males seems to be more in the role of a mentor compared to his "protection" of females both emotionally and physically. Of course, this depiction serves to perpetuate the notion that females need protection by males even if they can succeed in male-dominated workplaces.

The Emotionless Workaholic: Gil perpetuates conventional masculine representations in his unemotional approach to any situation. Although he is supportive of his staff, he himself is never shaken or emotionally overwrought even in the midst of shocking crime scenes. While he is protective of his coworkers as cited above, he does not empathize with them, but rather he supports them. Even in the face of adversity, he is strong, articulate and unmoved. For example, in "Pilot" a new CSI is killed. The other CSIs deal with it by supporting each other emotionally, but Gil does not interact with the others as they are mourning. Similarly, in "Pledging Mr. Johnson," he criticizes Catherine for her personal involvement in her cases and she responds by berating him for having no personal life. He maintains his austere posture seemingly unfazed by the personal and inappropriate mention of his private life. In "Face Lift," he admits to Catherine that he does not have rapport with people. When his professional subordinates confront him about his ability to shut off his emotions ("Sex,

Lies, and Larvae" and "I-15 Murders"), he shows no anger or frustration at their insubordination. Rather than contest their allegations, he agrees with them, but also identifies that his detachment helps him do his job. Again, supporting the need for a masculine leadership style.

Issues of Gil Grissom's Portrayal: Given the above examples, Gil Grissom's character perpetuates traditional or hegemonic masculine norms: he is stoic, unemotional, and omniscient (Messerschmidt 1997). The way he is represented gives the impression that leaders in this field must be bookish (but also good looking), married to the job, calm in all situations, but also strong and all-knowing. These stereotypes insinuate that the characteristics of a leader in this field coincide with those of a traditional male who has no ties (e.g., to family) that would interfere with his professional work and no emotions to interfere with the alleged objectivity of science. Grissom also perpetuates the label of the tough, emotionally-void male. This depiction is problematic in its own right but is even more so when taken in conjunction to how the other characters are depicted.

Catherine Willows

In the pilot episode, we learn that Catherine Willows was recruited to be an assistant technician by Gil Grissom more than 10 years ago. Her specialty is blood spatter analysis. While going to college at University of Nevada, Las Vegas to study medical technology, she worked as an exotic dancer. Catherine is 37 years old in season one, the divorced mother of Lindsey, who is 5 years old. Her character is depicted as strong-willed but emotional. Moreover, her conventional attractiveness, rather than her skill as an investigator, is a focus of most of her interactions. Thus, while breaking a stereotype by succeeding in a male-dominated field, she perpetuates the notion that females should be attractive, sensual, emotional, motherly, and non-confrontational to authority.

The Superwoman: Catherine contradicts the stereotype of the weak, fragile woman who acquiesces to male needs. At the same time, she sets a nearly unachievable standard as a female role model. For instance, she is a divorced, single mother who says she works "24/7" ("Crate 'n Burial") in a male-dominated field. In contrast to many female portrayals, she is able to compete with her male colleagues both verbally and mentally. However, her appearance comes to the forefront in many of her interactions. She is very thin, her hair is always perfectly done, and her lipstick is flawless. Throughout season one, she wears high-heeled boots to crime scenes even when called out in the middle of the night. For example, while other investigators are wearing T-shirts and jeans, Catherine is often wearing a professional suit and turtleneck sweater or blouse ("Crate 'n Burial," "Pledging Mr. Johnson"). Female viewers get the sense that if one is to succeed in this male-dominated field they must be smart, strong, and above all else, look attractive. More importantly, instead of confronting men for inappropriate comments about her looks, she flirts with them.

The Seductress: Despite her tough demeanor, Catherine relishes her attractiveness and enjoys attention from men. In developing her character, the audience learns that she used to be an exotic dancer. The audience is reminded of this in more than one episode. Perhaps in an empowering way, she seems to be proud of this past. However, instead of telling co-workers that her past as a dancer is not an appropriate conversation in the workplace, she seems to appreciate the fascination her male co-workers have with her past. In "Table Stakes," Greg (a lab technician) asks with reference to lingerie from an investigation, "Did you wear things like this when you danced?" Catherine replies, "I wore nothing but skin" and smiles coyly. In "Who Are You?" she visits the bar where she used to dance to investigate a case. She flirtatiously admits to a cop that she used to dance there. Later, Greg says, "I used to go to that bar, maybe I saw you dance." She replies, "No, you would have remembered me." This might be a way to reframe the stripping profession in a "feminist" way, with Catherine implying "I was a stripper and I'm proud of it." However, she might also be interpreted as saying "It is okay to comment on my sexuality instead of how well I do my work." Not only does she avoid confronting this sexual harassment, her character seems to encourage it.

Catherine is not above using seduction to trap suspects or get the job done. In one episode, she convinces a suspect to meet her by flirting with him over the phone ("Cool Change"). In "To Halve and to Hold," Warrick complains that she has contradicted her own advice. Catherine replies, "I was probably saying that to get you to service my needs at the time." Not only is Catherine's language laden with sexual innuendo, but also with manipulation, insinuating that attractive women will use their looks to get men to do their bidding (even at work). Rather than reinforcing her status as a CSI given her knowledge and experience, examples like these confirm perceptions of getting by on one's looks. While other characters might have flirtatious interactions, Catherine does so more often and with more people. Every male from a studio sound mixer ("Anonymous") to a cop dressed in riot gear ("Anonymous") feels the need to flirt with Catherine. In addition, the ramifications are different for men and women who flirt. Women who flirt in their workplaces might perpetuate the notion that women should act sexual even while working and use their sexuality to manipulate men. Thus, their work-life becomes connected to their ability to enact femininity in a conventional way. The conventional female role is not only about good looks but also about being emotional and motherly. Importantly, a message is sent in this representation that in order to succeed in the male-dominated world of law enforcement, a woman must look conventionally attractive and not only ignore, but encourage sexual harassment. In other words, she cannot be "one of the guys" because that is not an appropriate feminine role and she also cannot protest when the guys are acting inappropriately because then she becomes the "emotional woman."

The Emotional Woman: Another feminine stereotype that is perpetuated in this character is Catherine's emotional side, which is a repeated element in the show's storylines. Unlike Gil, Warrick, and Nick, she cannot approach some cases devoid of emotion. Male characters show some emotion but it is less pronounced and less often. The audience is often reminded that Catherine is a single mother and that this affects her job. As a mother, she is deeply affected by cases involving children; for example, in one scene of "Pilot," she hears a baby crying while Warrick is completely unaware of it. In another case involving the death of young child, Warrick offers to take the lead because she is visibly upset ("Crate 'n Burial"). In "Justice Is Served," Sara suggests that Catherine is taking a case more seriously than normal because she is a mother. In the process of conducting interviews in a molestation investigation, she is so disturbed that she leaves work in the middle of a workday to go home to hug her daughter ("Pilot").

Catherine also appears to be the only CSI whose past intimate relationships are explored in any depth in season one. While the others have had past romantic relationships only Catherine was previously married and it is her former marriage that is the personal relationship of primary attention in the first season. During "Pledging Mr. Johnson," she reveals to a victim's husband that his dead wife was cheating on him, against Grissom's advice. She does so because her husband cheated on her and she empathizes. Not only does Catherine have empathy for people involved in the cases she investigates, but she willingly reveals it while male characters are more reluctant to reveal empathy or emotional involvement

While Catherine seems to be the "superwoman" juggling a career and raising a child alone, she is not adept at separating her emotional and professional lives. She is torn between striving for success and the emotional impact of dealing with death and crime. The male characters do not seem to have this battle. They see the crime scene as a puzzle to be solved almost void of any emotional element. In "Crate 'n Burial," Catherine wants to pursue her emotional hunch about a case, but Warrick reminds her that they have to "follow the evidence" regardless of where it leads. When she has to show a woman her dead son's body in "I-15 Murders," she cries. Emotional sensitivity as a female attribute is not necessarily a negative representation, but it can be problematic if it is portrayed as a solely feminine trait and as interfering with professionalism. While the male CSIs also have emotional moments in some cases, Catherine's emotional reactions are portrayed more frequently during investigations than are her coworkers.

Issues of Catherine Willows' Portrayal: Catherine's character was perhaps constructed to rebuff feminine stereotypes; unfortunately, these findings suggest that she does the opposite. On one hand, she is presented as the career-oriented, hard-working rebel who fought her way to the top under conditions of adversity. On the other hand, she is portrayed as passively accepting sexual harassment, being overly emotional, and not able to separate work and family issues. These elements of her character give the impression that a woman has to try to excel by being as strong as a man without failing to look feminine/attractive and that success will come only at the cost of a family life.

Characters can reify traditional notions of femininity by depicting white middle-class femininity in a post feminist era in which they are allowed to work, but cannot ignore conventional standards for how women should look (Dow 1996). At first glance Catherine appears to be a tough modern woman: rebellious, strong, and not afraid to confront authority. Thus, she might seem to be an ideal role model. However, she sets the unrealistic standard of having to look perfect on the job, while also being the seductress who is flattered by sexual harassment. This is common in televisual representations of female characters who are competent, performing professionals but as in *CSI*, they "are almost always conventionally attractive and often beautiful" (Dow 1996, 98). In addition, she is also portrayed as being overwhelmingly emotional to the degree that it can interfere with doing her job. Catherine's character contributes to the commonly depicted post feminist theme that a successful career woman struggles with her personal life which is a version of women's issues that supports status quo and does not adequately reflect the complexity of women's issues (Dow 1996).

Interestingly, Sara Sidle's characterization depicts another type of femininity. Again, while her characterization might seem to contradict feminine stereotypes on the surface, further analysis illustrates how her representation serves to reinforce stereotypes of the angry woman, feminist, and hypocrite.

Sara Sidle

Sara Sidle is a 29-year-old investigator originally from California. She went to college at Harvard University and then returned to California to work in the San Francisco coroner's office and then the crime lab before arriving to Las Vegas in the second episode of season one. She is single. She specializes in material and element analysis.

The Angry Feminist: Sara comes across as a no-nonsense investigator who is very serious about her job. Unfortunately, she perpetuates the idea that strong, career-oriented women are angry and bitter (Dow 1996). She does not seem to hate *all* men but she bashes those that she deems (often without evidence) to have contributed to the mistreatment of women. She seems to male-bash in the sense that she pigeonholes some men as being "players." For instance, she accuses a group of fraternity men of murder without evidence and is critical of their hazing rituals ("Pledging Mr. Johnson"). She is repeatedly shown to assume the worst about male suspects (more so than female suspects) before there is evidence to support her opinion. In "Sex, Lies and Larvae," she is highly confrontational with a suspect whom she believes abused his wife, but does not have strong evidence of abuse. Superficially, one might award such condemnation of the objectification and devaluation of women. However, a sound critique of misogyny would include a more systematic analysis of evidence and an exploration of the system of oppression rather than the targeting of individual behavior.

In addition, she is often rude to her male colleagues and superiors. While she may also be rude or impatient with women, Sara is portrayed clashing with men more often. In "Crate 'n Burial," she tells the male cops, "If anyone touches anything, I'll break their fingers." In "I-15 Murders," she is abrupt and rude to a male robbery victim whose brother was murdered. She is also presented as bossy and commanding. However, this does not come across as a leadership style (like it might for Grissom) instead it conveys as an emotional "loose-cannon."

The Emotional Woman, Part 2: Like Catherine, Sara also embodies the emotional feminine cultural representation, but in her characterization the emotionality is presented in a self-righteous way instead of as a sign of weakness. She uses her emotions to comment on the shamefulness of other people's behavior. Sara gets emotionally involved when a woman is abducted, raped, and left for dead ("Too Tough to Die,") promising the victim she will catch the killer. In "Crate 'n Burial," she illustrates her sadness and disbelief at the things people are capable of and states, "It never ceases to amaze me what people do to each other" as she and Grissom rescue a woman who was buried alive. In "Sex, Lies and Larvae," she is highly emotional when dealing with a case in which an abusive husband kills his wife. Grissom implies that her emotions interfere because she relates too much with the victims. She confronts him and argues that her emotions help her do her job. While for Sara her emotions are a source of confidence, to her colleagues, her emotions are presented as clouding her judgment. Her emotions interfere with her ability to objectively judge evidence, and cause her to appear confrontational, irrational, and judgmental. The negative label of the dangerous, emotional female is perpetuated in these examples because her emotions affect her ability to do her job. Not only do her emotions cloud her judgment but she is also depicted as being difficult to get along with.

The Handful: Sara is opinionated, but she voices her opinions with a tone of superiority and accusation. She is fiery and strong, but this makes her seem bitchy instead of inspiring. In "Sex, Lies and Larvae," an abusive husband looks at Grissom and says, "You've got your hands full with her" to which Grissom replies, "So do you," suggesting Sara's tenaciousness in cases. To some extent, she is a loose cannon. In "Pledging Mr. Johnson," Nick has to calm Sara down because she is going, in his words, "80 miles per hour in second gear." In "Table Stakes," Sara makes a grumpy remark and Greg suggests that Nick should give her Valium. Nick replies, "Yeah, I'm with sunshine all night." This illustrates not only Sara's inability to handle cases rationally and professionally but also, that she should be kept in check by her male colleagues. Because she is presented as a loose cannon she comes across as hypocritical and a bit frightening.

The Hypocrite: Sara is the kind of woman that frightens men — the hypocritical "feminazi." She is the hypocrite because she flirts with men when it suits her, but might be judgmental if she witnessed the same behavior from a man. She corrects others' use of sexist language, but uses it herself. In "Friends and Lovers," a lab technician hits on her and she says, "I'm going to give you some advice ... if you want to 'pull chicks,' you have to get aggressive, drop the glasses, lose the coat, and grow some scruff. You get a 'c' for cute though."

Sara's language is often sexually suggestive and if she were a man would probably be considered sexual harassment in the real work world. In "Pledging Mr. Johnson," she compliments Warrick's looks by saying, "That's a fine suit and you look fine in it." More strikingly, the relationship between Sara and Grissom involves ongoing sexual tension, and she overtly uses sexual double entendres in their interactions. In "Crate 'n Burial," she asks Grissom to "come tape me up" in the process of reconstructing a crime scene. In "Unfriendly Skies," she tells Grissom about her experience in the "mile high club" recounting everything from her sexual partner's name to the flight number. She remarks that her partner was "overrated in every aspect." This conventional portrayal of the angry, hypocrite is dangerous because it confuses the viewer as to what behavior is harassment and who is allowed to engage in flirtation and who is not. Her depiction might also allow people to generalize this hypocritical behavior to all women who enter more traditionally male professions such as law enforcement and perpetuate the idea that even if women say they do not enjoy being sexualized, they really want to be. This can contribute to the existing fear of working with women especially in male-dominated fields because co-workers do not know how to handle interactions with someone who is inconsistent in their behavior.

Issues of Sara Sidle's Portrayal: Sara's character seems to contradict the fragile feminine conventional stereotype. Unfortunately, she perpetuates the "feminazi" categorization instead, being tough, demanding, and in some cases openly hostile. This furthers the televisual representation that powerful women are evil, backstabbing, and untrustworthy (Dow 1996). Perhaps in an effort to soften her character, she is flirtatious, which weakens an otherwise strong female role because this sexualizes her and seems to contradict her own belief system. Thus, she comes across as inconsistent, unstable and hypocritical. Co-workers cannot relate and do not know how to interact. Sara embodies a negative characterization by being opinionated, touchy, uptight, and irrationally emotional whereas she could have been presented as strong, articulate, competent, and rational.

Nick Stokes

Nick Stokes is a 29-year-old investigator from Texas, where his parents were both involved in law enforcement, his father first as a state district attorney before being appointed to the Texas State Supreme Court, and his mother as a public defender. He joined the Dallas police force after college, and then worked one year with the Dallas crime lab before moving to Las Vegas. His specialty is hair and fiber analysis. The youngest of seven children, Nick has never been married.

The Player: Nick is the quintessential lady-killer. He is portrayed as the good looking, flirtatious, successful, career-conscious, all–American boy next door — a heart-breaker. The viewer discovers his player status when the other cast members tease him about being a "womanizer." Grissom calls him a "ladies' man" ("Who Are You"). In one episode, the viewer witnesses a flirtatious Nick when he tells a "hooker" to show him her skin "discolorations" (he suspects her of drugging a client and robbing him) which happen to be on her breasts ("Pilot"). Nick's background of one-night stands is subtly referred to throughout the season. He seems to have a pattern of leading women on and women continue to fall for his game. For instance, at one crime scene Nick talks to a visibly tense female detective ("Sex, Lies and Larvae"). She quickly expresses her disappointment with Nick because "we had dinner and I thought it went well, but you never called back." Nick is able to deflect her disappointment by ambiguously promising another date.

The Frat-boy: Nick also has the typical fraternity boy persona. He is clean-cut, good-looking, charming, and adept at womanizing. As it turns out, Nick's past includes belonging to a fraternity, partying, and hazing. It is implied that he has outgrown the partying (in "Boom," he turns down a college friend for a round of drinks in order to complete paperwork), but he still identifies with this privileged and elite part of his past. In "Pledging Mr. Johnson," he uses his brotherhood ties to get a confession from two fraternity members who murdered one of their pledges.

A common representation of fraternity men is that they objectify women. Nick is no exception. In "Boom," Nick gets involved with a sex-worker who is later attacked by a security guard. Nick comes to her defense and helps her prove that the guard attacked her. When a lab technician asks why he wants to help her he holds up her shirt that he is having analyzed and replies, "If you saw the girl who went into this shirt, you'd help too." He further objectifies the woman in order to trick the security guard into confessing. In an attempt at male bonding, Nick tells the guard, "She's a pain, but she's a babe. I helped her because I thought I'd get lucky, but all I got was trouble." In this instance, he is only pretending to fulfill the stereotype, whereas in other instances, he embodies stereotypical images. Nick's attitude contributes to the stereotype of the shallow man who only cares about the way women look. This is part of the hegemonic male stereotype or traditional masculinity being enacted. It is theorized that traditional (or hegemonic) male behavior is rewarded, thus men must be tough, in the paid labor force, womanizers, and heterosexual to be considered real men (Messerschmidt 1997). To achieve an ideal masculine image, one must perpetuate the stereotype of males being emotionless in general and especially to women. Women are only there as a means of sexual release and to be pursued in sexual conquest.

The Competitor: Now that Nick is past his fraternity days, he has turned his energy to his career. Of all of the cast's characters, Nick most enacts the masculine cultural expectation that men turn everything into a competition. He frequently bets with Warrick about who can solve a case first, and in "Fahrenheit 932" he even instigates a bet with a potential suspect (over whether the other suspects are innocent). He and Warrick also compete in order to see who will be promoted first ("Crate 'n Burial"). Nick wins and when he celebrates his 100th case being solved, and is promoted to "Investigator Level Three" ("Crate 'n Burial). In "Evaluation Day," he reminds Grissom that he was promoted before Warrick. He does not limit his competition to men, in "To Halve and To Hold," Nick is happy to show Catherine that he has a better memory than she does because he has better retained his Latin lessons from the academy.

The Supportive Man: Whereas Grissom's character is a protector of the female characters, Nick provides more of a support system for them. Nick comforts Catherine as she struggles with guilt when a new CSI is killed on her shift ("Cool Change"). In another episode, Nick is supportive of a sex worker and defends her to other characters who denigrate her occupation ("I-15 Murders"). Later, he intervenes in a fight between this woman and her pimp, and is her champion in an incident that she seemed to have instigated ("Boom"). Notably, as much as Nick supports this woman, he does not sleep with her until she says that she is giving up prostitution. Apparently, he sees the prostitute as a more suitable partner once she has found a new career. Nick is obsessed with the way she looks but cannot get past her chosen profession. Thus, while he is supportive in many instances, his character's perpetuation of the representation of the womanizing, frat-boy devalues women and belittles men.

Issues of Nick Stokes' Portrayal: Nick's character is the charming boy next door, who is polite, smart, subordinate (but not weak), and good at his job. He is sensitive, but does not let his emotions interfere in his work, he maintains his rationality during investigations, and uses humor to lighten the mood. His most notable characteristic is that he is the stereotypical ladies' man who seems to attract women but does not date them for very long. In addition, his character contributes to the idea that men are shallow and can be manipulated by good-looking women and that women should not trust good-looking men. The viewer is privy to his private life in terms of his short-lived relationships with women and his philosophy that some women might just want a guy to take care of them. His portrayal, while admittedly has some complexity between shallow and supportive, oversimplifies the masculine ideal. Again, given the impression that in order to be accepted in the field (if not the stoic leader like Grissom), a man must be hypersexual, competitive, and demeaning to women (while also offering support/protection to attractive women in distress). The other male leading character is not as sexual but represents other stereotypes.

Warrick Brown

Warrick Brown is single, African American, and 30 years old in season one, and was born and raised in Las Vegas. He was a casino "runner" (runs chips between dealers/cashiers) as a teenager, and held a variety of jobs including a taxi driver, a hotel bell captain at the Sahara, and even a grave digger to put himself through school at University of Nevada, Las Vegas. After his mother's death when Warrick was 7 years old, he was raised by his grandmother. His specialty is audio/visual analysis.

The Urban Cool Minority: Warrick is the character the other CSIs want to emulate. He is smooth, confident, hip, urban, and cool. He is ultra-masculine, but dresses in flashy colors and current styles. He sports a large silver chain proudly on the outside of his shirt (supporting a stereotype that African American urban youth wear large jewelry to look "cool"). Warrick is privy to the knowledge of a young "party" crowd and rave sub-culture in Vegas. In "Friends & Lovers," when the other CSIs are confused, Warrick explains the protocol of "raves." He knows all the details, such as the lingo and the hand stamp that indicates which DJ is playing at which venue.

Warrick's cool, urban persona is also enacted through his use of slang in a professional setting. For instance, he uses terms like "dome" to refer to a suspect's head ("To Have and To Hold") and "the bomb" to praise Catherine's motherhood skills ("Sex, Lies, and Larvae"). He tells Sara that she has said too much to a suspect by stating, "You showed him all your cards ... sucker play" ("I-15 Murders"). In "Fahrenheit 932," he tells a suspect, "Roll with your attorney," meaning that the suspect should leave with the attorney.

The Disadvantaged Youth: Warrick seems like the kid from a disadvantaged background that succeeded in the middle or working-class career[2] of crime scene investigation. His disadvantaged background is a recurrent theme through which the audience is reminded of his struggle to become "straight" after a misspent youth.[3] The writers never clearly state his background but insinuations to disadvantage are prevalent. For instance, he worked as a runner as a teen which he had to hide from his grandmother.[4] Later, the audience learns that he paid his way through college by placing bets at Las Vegas casinos ("Fahrenheit 932). Warrick is called upon to interpret the Vegas underworld for the other investigators, none of whom are originally from the city. In "Fahrenheit 932," he helps explain the details of betting to Nick and Catherine (who apparently are not aware of them even though they too live in Las Vegas). Although he is constantly reminded of his difficult past, it makes him the "cool, quiet hero" who has difficult moral decisions to make. For instance, he struggles with a gambling addiction and in one instance he is bullied by a judge (Warrick lost a large amount of the judge's money on a bad bet) who wants him to sacrifice the evidence in a case ("Pledging Mr. Johnson"). He usually makes the more moral choice. However, it often takes an entire episode for him to find the moral high road. In "Sex, Lies and Larvae," Sara shows Grissom a videotape of Warrick entering a casino (after he promised Grissom he would not gamble). We do not learn until the next episode that his actions were legitimate because he was not gambling but collecting on a past debt so he could help a friend. The audience is led to assume that Warrick will regress to his old ways. The viewer is led to believe that he will fail because of his past.

His street persona is marked by the use of slang and harsh language (he does the most swearing in the first few episodes). His toughness is reflective of a street upbringing which includes having to constantly vie for respect from peers and having to prove that he cannot be taken advantage of (Anderson 1999). In "Pledging Mr. Johnson," he tells a judge who is blackmailing him, "Nobody owns me." Later, he gets the judge arrested and says, "See, I told you, nobody owns me." Our interpretation of this statement was that Warrick took the blackmail as a personal attack. Not only was he stating that he would not be bullied, he was also illustrating that he would retaliate if threatened. In a street environment, this ability and willingness to retaliate is of utmost importance. One earns respect by proving that they will not be taken advantage of. If respect is not earned and a threat goes unanswered, then the person sets themselves up for further attack (Anderson 1999).

The street stereotype is reinforced in another scene in which Warrick is listening to rap music loudly ("Crate 'n Burial"). Again, this perpetuates negative racial stereotypes by implying that urban African Americans are inconsiderate of other people. Further, no one seems annoyed when Grissom plays classical music loudly but Warrick's rap is clearly annoying to Catherine in this scene. This affirms the notion that Warrick's character feels the need to assert his independence by listening to the music loudly and perhaps identification with his racial community. However, the viewer is left with the common stereotype that all African Americans enjoy rap and play it at high decibels. There is no acknowledgement of individual difference presented in this scenario. Lastly, Warrick is aware of his minority status, but is not afraid to play on it. In "Pilot," he states, "I took this job because I always could tell when whitey is talking out his ass."

The African American as Criminal: Not surprisingly, the only main character on *CSI* who is a racial minority has a troubled past that apparently affects his current job. Whereas Catherine's use of cocaine is mentioned in season one, it does not seem to reflect on her current ability to do her job. Conversely, Warrick's job is in jeopardy due to his addiction. Early in season one, Warrick loses a promotion and almost loses his job over his gambling problem. In "Pilot," a judge blackmails Warrick in order to make him do unscrupulous favors. These representations reflect negatively by perpetuating the idea that African Americans have questionable principles and weak work ethics. Warrick cannot escape the constant reminders of his struggle with his working-class upbringing and his gambling addiction. Others categorize Warrick as criminal; for example, when he visits the black-mailing judge late at night, the neighbors call the police because they saw "a black man outside your house" ("Pilot"). The cops arrive and harass Warrick, assuming he is committing a crime. This blatant racism is not really addressed on the show except the Judge sarcastically congratulates the officers.

The Empathizer: Warrick has a sensitive side, and tries to help troubled, disadvantaged teens. He is shown trying to save adolescents from repeating his mistakes, and in doing so, he unselfishly supports these kids and acts as a role model. In "I-15 Murders," when Sara berates him for being in a casino, we later find out that he is there to collect on a debt owed to him so he can help a young boy who is in trouble. In "Crate 'n Burial," a teenager is sent to a detention center for vehicular homicide. Warrick writes his cell phone number on the boy's hand and tells him, "The first few days are going to be the roughest." This insinuates that he may have had experience with detention or corrections (apart from his current job). Regardless, it also shows Warrick's integrity and good-hearted nature in that he is trying to help the young boy cope.

Issues of Warrick Brown's Portrayal: Warrick Brown is the only main character on *CSI* who is a person of color. Race does not seem to be an issue for anyone but Warrick. The others do not appear to recognize their white privilege. As earlier shows have done, *CSI* privileges white-middle class audiences in both character representations and content (Gray 1995). Bell hooks notes that blacks who fulfill racist stereotypes receive more support in the culture (bell hooks 1992). Further, when a black minority is depicted, the character often gives the impression that the identity is monolithic. Diversity and complexity of African American identity is often ignored (bell hooks 1992). In *CSI*, this complexity is masked both by the lack of diversity in the main characters and by Warrick's adherence to stereotypes. It seems that the writers tried to contradict stereotypes such as lazy, unemployed and criminal by making him the "favorite CSI" (as Sara referred to him in "Sex, Lies and Larvae"), hard-working, career-oriented, and ambitious. Unfortunately, the writers of *CSI* reinforce several common cultural categorizations concerning African American males. For instance, the writers make a point to emphasize his lower-class background when they do not emphasize the class background of the other characters. In addition, while Warrick is not a criminal he does struggle with an addiction to gambling and connections to the underground world of sports betting while the other characters' struggles seem to be more of a conventional, legitimate nature (e.g., Catherine's ex-husband, Gil's social ineptness, Nick's womanizing). Warrick's character reflects what Majors (1995) identifies as Black men acting out a "cool pose," presenting a defensive posture to the rest of society through one's attitudes and behaviors.

Concluding Concerns

We have tried to illustrate that *CSI* perpetuates some basic representations of traditional gender, race, and class stereotypes. The way that *CSI* represents gender, race, and class stereotypes via its characters is indicative of a larger pattern that underlies the series' content. Through their interaction with each other, and with victims or suspects, the characters manage to reinforce cultural representations that misrepresent reality and may adversely affect efforts to improve equality. Through its representations of gender, race, and class, *CSI* undermines the advances that have been made by increasing diversity in the workforce. By relying on stereotypes as the basis for the main characters' identities, viewers are led to believe that the crux of their personalities reflect common sense ideologies about gender, race, and class that can be derogatory and damaging if they are read as reflecting social realities outside of *CSI*'s televisual world.

Gender Representations

Traditional gender representations are clearly observable in the characters' interactions with one another. The men are cold, unemotional, strong, and protective while the women are emotional, prissy, and motherly. For instance, the female characters are disgusted by normal aspects of their jobs such as bugs and dead skin, more so than male CSIs. For example, in "Sex, Lies, and Larvae" Sara comments to Grissom, "I never get used to this part, you know, when the bugs get going." In addition, they are victims of sexual harassment but they do not seem to recognize the harassment and, in some cases, even engage in the inappropriate conversation. These representations are especially damaging because, on the surface, it appears that these women are strong, career-oriented and overcoming odds to excel in a male-dominated field. However, upon closer examination, they perpetuate many myths about female workers.

Some may interpret the fact that female characters embrace their sexuality as a form of empowerment, but in this context it seems more of an objectification of women (Fiske 1987). *CSI* characters Catherine and Sara perpetuate the stereotype that career-oriented females must excel but also look good or they are considered to be more masculine and angry/irrational. *CSI* focuses predominantly on the workplace which contradicts the patterns of gender representation in other television in which women are typically portrayed in the context of their personal relationships and men are often portrayed in the context of their careers (Holtzman 2000). However, the focus on Catherine's struggle to be a good investigator as well as a single mother weakens what otherwise would be a portrayal of equity between men and women in the workplace because the men are not shown as having a similar personal struggle. Dyer would acknowledge the intersection of race and gender of these characters, stating, "White women do not have the same relation to power as white men" (Dyer 1997, 30). While *CSI* attempts to offer female characters in a more equal way, gender differences in the context of power and relationships continue to be reflected in Catherine's and Sara's portrayals. These representations depict powerful women, but their power is relative to men and does nothing to challenge the existing power structure (Dow 1996). *CSI*, like other television shows, may seem to proclaim women's success in the workplace even while serving to make problems faced by female characters seem to be of an individual nature rather than as a social problem. In addition, they trivialize problems encountered by working women (Dow 1996), reducing them to emotional reactions versus the more logistic struggle. For instance, they do not show the logistical challenge of finding a baby sitter when Catherine is called to crime scenes at 3:00 A.M.

The male characters also perpetuate traditional masculine categorizations by objectifying women, belittling the work of women, and by viewing their female co-workers' strong wills as burdensome. Male victims and suspects often ignore the female investigators. When Sara interrogates some fraternity brothers, they do not answer her until Nick tells them to do so ("Pledging Mr. Johnson"). This perpetuates the idea that a male needs to stand up for female coworkers in order for the female to be taken seriously. Nick plays the protector-role here and the men listen to him rather than her, suggesting that information and orders are more official coming from men. In "Unfriendly Skies," Nick commits the same error the fraternity brothers did. Sara suggests that more than one perpetrator committed the crime; Nick ignores her comment and asks for Grissom's opinion.

Male stereotypes also abound. The men on *CSI* are competitive, which perpetuates the idea that men are obsessed with winning, competing, and watching and betting on sports. Nick and Warrick constantly compete over cases and chastise each other. This perpetuates the idea that men will bet and compete over petty things for amusement.

A double standard regarding gender is apparent in an episode when Nick becomes involved with a prostitute ("I-15 Murders"). He is encouraged not to do so because it would reflect negatively on the CSI unit. Many of the other male characters show disdain for his relationship. However, they joke with Catherine about her past as a stripper. Nick's indiscretion is seen as tarnishing the integrity of the uniform, while Catherine's indiscreet past is seen as a way for the male characters to objectify her. Both serve to degrade females.

Conversely, despite the evidence presented here, not all of the gender representations in *CSI* are based on traditional stereotypes. For instance, the female CSIs often solve crimes more quickly than their male colleagues. They take on a large portion of the interrogation process. Thus, they *are* presented as strong women who are good at their jobs and trusted to do their jobs well. However, as illustrated by gender stereotypes discussed above, these characters perpetuate many of the biases that still surround women in the workplace (e.g., emotionality, instability, edginess). The nature of character representations is complex and multifaceted. Thus, while some aspects of a character may seem to work against traditional representations, other aspects reinforce these stereotypes.

Racial Representations

Not only are conventional gender roles depicted in *CSI*, traditional racial characterizations are also present. Televisual media often seemingly represent diversity but at the same time manage to reinforce racial characterizations or ignore diversity within a racial population.[5] Perhaps most notable is the glaring lack of diversity among the main characters. There is only one character that is identifiable as a member of a racial minority. When a minority is included in a television show, an assimilationist approach is often portrayed. Like many other shows, *CSI* does little to deal with complex issues of race and assumes assimilation of minorities. Gray notes that

> assimilationist programs construct a United States where the historic and contemporary consequences of structured social inequality and a culture deeply inflected and defined by racism are invisible and inconsequential to the lives of its citizens. Seldom on these shows is there ever any sustained engagement with the messiness, confusion, and tension caused by racism and inequality that punctuate the daily experience of so many members of our society [Gray 1995, 86].

CSI trivializes the lived-experience of minority characters. When *CSI* does deal with race, the situation is presented at the individual-level and as an isolated incident. Gray noted these issues in his analysis:

> When they exist, race class, and gender inequalities seem quite extraordinary, and they always seem to operate at the level of individual experience. Put differently, to the extent that the these tensions and conflicts are addressed at all, they figure primarily through individual characters (white and black) with prejudiced attitudes, who then become the focus of the symbolic transformation required to restore narrative balance [Gray 1995, 86].

Similarly, Hall (2002) may conclude the racism on *CSI* is not overt with Warrick's character, but is instead inferential racism. Warrick Brown is the token African American who reaffirms many of the common cultural representations about African American men.[6] In the first season, he nearly ruins his career over a gambling problem. His background includes being raised by his grandmother due to the death of his mother and abandonment by his father. This reflects racial patterns of an increasing number of children being raised by their grandparents, and in particular African Americans being more likely to raise their grandchildren than other racial groups (Casper and Bryson 1998). He has connections to both the legitimate and illegitimate sides of the city, allowing him to use his street smarts to advance his career.[7] As has been identified in other prime time television analyses (Means Coleman 2000), race is often linked to the underclass, as the challenges in Warrick's background suggest.

Class Representations

Class inequality is much less obvious in the series, perhaps because limited attention is paid to the characters' personal lives. Many of the victims and/or suspects in the *CSI* cases seem to be "high rollers" in contrast to the middle-class representations of the investigators. They have taken middle-class jobs and seem to be a little awe-struck at the wealth of some of their clients. However, these middle-class representations contradict many of the investigators' seemingly culturally privileged backgrounds. We are instructed that Grissom's family was involved in art dealing and importing, while Catherine's family owned horses. Nick's father is a State Supreme Court judge. Sara's parents were hippies, yet she managed to get her degree from Harvard, while Warrick had to support himself as a teenager by being a "runner." Warrick's character represents an intersection between race and class, in that he is the only main character of color, but also the only character who struggled financially while growing up.

Regardless of their middle-class salaries, the investigators know how the other half lives. In one episode the sheriff is attending a black tie benefit in a mansion. In "Fahrenheit 932," the investigators know that it costs $50,000 to be a member of a certain club. The show's main characters seem a little captivated by the high roller lifestyle. Warrick and Catherine get a case in "Somerlin" (which is apparently a wealthy community) and Catherine says, "Oooh Somerlin" to which Warrick responds, "Somerlin ... rich folks" ("Sex, Lies and Larvae"). Catherine's comment illustrates that she is impressed by the community. Warrick's comment intimates that this is "how the other half lives." The context of his statement is that he is delineating between "rich folk" and folk like themselves (more middle-class). His tone is not necessarily critical but more of an understanding of the class difference in that they move in two different worlds within the same city.

Regardless of the type of cultural categorization, there are consequences to these representations in that they may affect our views of gender, race, and class diversity. Stereotypical representations such as those discussed in this essay may have adverse effects in the way viewers understand women's role in the workplace and gender relations in the world of crime scene investigation. In other words, women are, once again, given the impression that in the workplace, the way they look matters as much, if not more, than their ability. They might expect to be hit on and to interact in a flirtatious manner with co-workers. Women might be discouraged by these stereotypical representations especially if they choose not to perpetuate them in their own interactions. Race and class representations can be damaging because they present these characterizations as monolithic. In other words, the stereotypical presentation ignores within-group diversity and the complexity involved in the intersection of gender, race, and class. Viewers may generalize these representations to the real world and use them as support for existing prejudices or for creating new ones. These prejudices may then translate to discriminatory behavior.

In addition, the depictions of these characters perpetuate general gender, race and class stereotypes that have been shown to be mythical and damaging to social mobility in the workplace (Reskin and Padavic 1994). While the program is original, creative, and popular, *CSI* could depict gender, race, and class relations in a manner that emphasizes equality. In addition, by relying on traditional cultural representations of gender, race, and class, individual differences are ignored or minimized. A more accurate depiction of gender, race, and class would include character development that is not limited to conventional stereotypical images. Additionally, while *CSI* offers diversity in its leading characters, it does not take advantage of the opportunity to explore issues of diversity within these characters and their relationships. In doing so, the program could work further to dispel myths regarding gender, race, and class and break down stereotypes and viewers' expectations of reality that may evolve from them. Others have noted the need for more complex analysis of television representations of race including more theorizing and more critical analysis (Gray 1995).

NOTES

1. Information in character descriptions was from *www.cbs.com/primetime/csi/bios* and can be accessed at *http://csithenightshift.tripod.com/characters.html.*

2. According to *http://forensics.rice.edu/html/characters.html* all of the characters have a B.S. except Grissom who has a Ph.D. Various web sites estimate the salary range of a Las Vegas CSI to be between $30,000 and $60,000. Thus, we categorize the job as middle-class although some might include it as working-class in that it is similar to law enforcement. This job requires more education but the pay is similar (police make $43,000 to $69,000, according to *http://www.theblueline. com/salary1.html*).

3. According to *http://csithenightshift.tripod.com/characters.html* and *http://www.imdb.com/char acter/ch0011023/bio* Warrick never met his father, his mother died when he was young and he was raised by his strict grandmother.

4. See *http://csithenightshift.tripod.com/characters.html.*

5. Gray asserts that the Cosby show was guilty of ignoring within-group differences. Gray, Herman. 1995. *Watching Race: Television and the Struggle for "Blackness."* Minneapolis: University of Minnesota Press.

6. Also, Gray notes that representations of African American men often reinforce stereotypes and the existing racial order. See Gray, Herman. 1995. *Watching Race: Television and the Struggle for "Blackness."* Minneapolis: University of Minnesota Press.

7. See *http://csithenightshift.tripod.com/characters.html*

REFERENCES

Abt, Vicki, and Mel Seesholtz. 1994. "The Shameless World of Phil, Sally, and Oprah: Television Talk Shows and the Deconstructing of Society." *Journal of Popular Culture* 28 (1): 195–215.

Anderson, Elijah. 1999. *Code of the Street: Decency, Violence, and the Moral Life of the Inner City.* New York: W. W. Norton.

Benhoff, Harry M., and Sean Griffin. 2004. *America on Film: Representing Race, Class, Gender, and Sexuality at the Movies.* Malden, MA: Blackwell.

Butsch, Richard. 1995. "Ralph, Fred, Archie, and Homer: Why Television Keeps Recreating the

White Male Working-class Buffoon." In G. Dines and J. M. Humez (eds.), *Gender, Race, and Class in Media*: 575–585. Thousand Oaks, CA: Sage.

Butsch, Richard, 2003. "A Half Century of Class and Gender in American TV Domestic Sitcoms." *Cercles* 8: 16–34.

Casper, Lynne M., and Kenneth R. Bryson. 1998. "Co-Resident Grandparents and Their Grandchildren: Grandparent Maintained Families." *U.S. Census Bureau*. Accessed December 2010. *http://www.census.gov/population/www/documentation/twps0026/twps0026.html.*

CBS. 2010. *http://www.cbs.com/primetime/csi/cast/*

Character Bios. 2010. Accessed December 2010. *http://csithenightshift.tripod.com/characters.html.*

CSI Web Adventures. 2010. *http://forensics.rice.edu/html/characters.html.* Accessed December 2010.

Croteau, David, and William Hoynes. 2003. *Media/Society: Industries, Images and Audiences*, 3d ed. Thousand Oaks, CA: Pine Forge Press.

Dow, Bonnie J. 1996. *Prime-Time Feminism: Television, Media Culture, and the Women's Movement since 1970*. Philadelphia: University of Pennsylvania Press.

Dyer, Richard. 1997. *White: Essays on Race and Culture*. New York: Routledge.

Ehrenreich, Barbara. 1989. "The Silenced Majority." In Margaret L. Andersen and Patricia Hill Collins (eds.), *Race, Class & Gender: An Anthology*, 3d ed.: 40–42. Belmont, CA: Wadsworth.

Entman, Robert. 1990. "Modern Racism and the Images of Blacks in Local Television News." *Critical Studies in Mass Communication* 7 (4): 332–345.

_____. 2000. *Black Image in the White Mind: Media and Race in America*. Chicago: The University of Chicago Press.

Fiske, John. 1987. *Television Culture*. London: Methuen.

Gamson, William A., David Croteau, William Hoynes, and Theodore Sasson. 1992. "Media Images and the Social Construction of Reality." *Annual Review of Sociology* 18: 373–393.

Gray, Herman. 1995. *Watching Race: Television and the Struggle for "Blackness."* Minneapolis: University of Minnesota Press.

Hall, Stuart. 2002. "The Whites of Their Eyes: Racist Ideologies and the Media." In Gail Dines and Jean M Humez, (eds.), *Gender, Race, and Class in Media: A Text-reader, 2d ed.*: 89–93. Thousand Oaks, CA: Sage.

Holtzman, Linda. 2000. *Media Messages: What Film, Television and Popular Music Teach Us About Race, Class, Gender, and Sexual Orientation*. New York: M. E. Sharpe.

hooks, bell. 1992. *Black Looks: Race and Representation*. Boston: South End Press.

IMBD. "Biography for Warrick Brown." Accessed December 2010. *http://www.imdb.com/character/ch0011023/bio.*

Katz, Jackson. 1999. *Tough Guise: Violence, Media & the Crisis of Masculinity*. Executive prod. and dir. Sut Jhally. Northampton, Ma: Media Education Project. DVD.

Kilbourne, Jean. 1999. *Deadly Persuasion: Why Women and Girls Must Fight the Addictive Power of Advertising*. New York: The Free Press.

Kimmel, Michael. *The Gendered Society*, 4th ed. New York: Oxford University Press.

Lofland, John, and Lyn H. Lofland. 1995. *Analyzing Social Settings: A Guide to Qualitative Observation and Analysis*. Belmont, CA: Wadsworth.

Majors, Richard, 1989. "The Cool Pose: The Proud Signature of Black Survival." In Michael S. Kimmel and Michael A. Messner (eds.), *Men's Lives*: 83–87. Boston: Allyn & Bacon.

McIntyre, Lisa J. 2002. *The Practical Skeptic: Core Concepts in Sociology, 2d ed.* Boston: McGraw Hill.

Means Coleman, Robin R. 2000. *African American Viewers and the Black Situation Comedy 2d ed.* New York: Garland.

Messerschmidt, W. James. 1997. *Crime As Structured Action: Gender, Race, Class and Crime in the Making*. Thousand Oaks, CA: Sage.

Police Pay Compensation Survey. 2004. *http://www.theblueline.com/salary1.html.* Accessed December 2010.

Potter, Gary, and Victor Kappeler. 1998. *Constructing Crime: Perspectives on Making News and Social Problems*. Prospect Heights, IL: Waveland Press.

Reinarman, Craig. 2006. "The Social Construction of Drug Scares." In Patricia A. Adler and Peter Adler (eds.), *Constructions of Deviance: Social Power, Context, and Interaction*: 139–150. Belmont, CA: Wadsworth.

Reskin, Barbara, and Irene Padavic. 1994. *Women and Men at Work*. Thousand Oaks, CA: Pine Forge Press.

Roane, Kit R., and Dan Morrison. 2000. "The CSI Effect: On TV, It's All Slam-dunk Evidence and Quick Convictions." *U.S. News and World Report*, April 25.

Rome, Dennis. 2004. *Black Demons: The Media's Depiction of the African American Male Criminal Stereotype*. Westport, CT: Praeger Press.

Scharrer, Erica. 2001. "Tough Guys: The Portrayal of Hypermasculinity and Aggression in Televised Police Drama." *Journal of Broadcasting & Electronic Media* 45 (4): 615–634.

Steenland, Sally. 1995. "Content analysis of the image of women on television." In Cynthia M. Lont (ed.), *Women and Media: Content/Careers/Criticism*: 179–189. Belmont, CA: Wadsworth.

Surette, Ray. 2007. *Media, Crime, and Criminal Justice: Images, Realities, and Polices*. Belmont, CA: Wadsworth.

Zatz, Marjorie S., and Coramae Richey Mann. 2006. "The Power of Images." In Coramae Richey Mann, Marjorie S. Zatz, and Nancy Rodriguez (eds.), *Images of Color, Images of Crime*: 1–17. Los Angeles: Roxbury.

"Who are you?"
Shared Responsibility and the Victims of CSI: Crime Scene Investigation

KATHERINE FOSS

From a young age, we are taught how to avoid becoming victims. School programs like McGruff and "Stranger Danger" warn children of predatory strangers luring kids with candy and puppies. Adults are advised to take precautions against crime, such as locking doors, guarding personal identification information, and zipping one's purse or wallet to prevent petty theft. Most crime prevention literature includes special sections for senior citizens, people with disabilities, and women, warning them to be extra careful in order to avoid attacks. For example, the police department in a Massachusetts town instructs senior citizens on how to safely ride public transportation (Beverly Police Department 2009). A brochure by the National Crime Prevention Council (2010b) cautions people with disabilities not to let con artists deceive them. Conventional crime prevention wisdom holds that women should travel in groups, avoid risky situations, such as dark alleys and parking garages, and dress appropriately so no one may get the "wrong idea." Targets of hate crime, including people of color and people who are gay, lesbian, bisexual, or transgendered, are also considered at-risk groups, although hate crime prevention focuses more on creating tolerant environments and less on individual safety tips (National Crime Prevention Council 2010a).

Obviously, offering practical advice on avoiding victimization helps reassure people that they likely will not become the next target. At the same time, prevention advice, particularly about "stranger danger" for children and adults is, at the very least, futile, given that in over half of all violent crimes and in most homicides, people knew their attackers (Bureau of Justice Statistics 2010b). In addition, this approach implicates victims in the crimes, suggesting that had they not behaved in a certain way, they would not have become victims. Furthermore, the construction of certain types of people as potential victims is problematic — it may reinforce unequal power structures in society and encourage differences in support and restitution, based on victims' characteristics. For example, the abundance of literature portraying women as vulnerable conveys that it is a woman's responsibility to amend her behavior for her own protection (Gordon and Riger 1991, 1–7). Thus, one might assume that a female victim must have ignored proper precautions and is therefore somewhat responsible for her attack (Karmen 1990, 105).

It is not just police departments and neighborhood task forces that tell us how to avoid becoming the next victim. News stories about crime often describe ways in which victims failed to protect themselves (Foss 2006). As a visual medium, television can also be especially powerful in disseminating messages about victimization. Reality crime programs, for example, use camera angles to create sympathy for a victim (Cavender and Bond-Maupin 1993, 20–30). Fictional programs can play out complex storylines, offering background information on assailants and victims that would not or could not be addressed in news media. Because most people do not work closely with crime victims, nor will they likely (and fortunately) ever personally experience crime, especially violent crime, these media messages can strongly shape how people perceive victimization. This chapter explores the inequality of messages about victimization in fictional television, using seasons one through four of the CBS program *CSI: Crime Scene Investigation* to discuss how television depicts victimization. This chapter will focus not on the investigators or assailants, but on who the victims are and why each character was chosen for victimization.

Victimology and the Rise of the Victim's Movement

To better understand the role of media in constructing victimization, it is helpful to examine theories of victimology, the study of the victim's role in a crime (Elias 1986, 17). In early criminology, crimes were considered as committed against society, not an individual, therefore the victim's behavior, along with the criminal's motive for the crime were thought of as irrelevant (Elias 1986, 13). The role of the victim was not empirically studied until the 1940s, when von Hentig (1948) argued that a victim "shapes and moulds the criminal," thereby playing a role in his/her victimization — a term referred to as "shared responsibility" (348). Von Hentig proposed that certain types of people, such as children, senior citizens, women, the mentally ill, and immigrants were more likely to suffer a criminal attack than others (1948, 348–404). Thus, by being of a certain age or sex, or possessing certain characteristics, such as having a disability, a victim was considered somewhat responsible for his/her victimization. As described by Schafer (1963), Mendelsohn created legal typologies to classify victims, ranging from completely innocent to those who fabricate their victimization (34–36). In the 1950s, adding to these typologies, Wolfgang (1958) concluded that certain traits and behaviors made a person more susceptible to becoming a victim (203–245). Building on von Hentig's typologies and Wolf-gang's research, Hindelang, Gottfredson, and Garofalo (1978) argued that additional factors influenced one's chances of victimization such as public exposure and one's association with known criminals (245).

In the 1970s, victim-centered thinking surfaced in political and legal discourse. Actions of the Second Wave Feminist movement, along with the Civil Rights movement, largely contributed to this focus on victim's rights. Its proponents pushed for victims' rights, especially for female victims, aiming to combat the perception of victim blaming through anti-rape campaigns (Elias 1986, 48). This "victim's movement" aimed to address the needs of crime victims and aid them in their recovery (Abell 1990, 216–225). During the 1970s and 1980s numerous legislative acts were proposed (and some enacted) to help victims participate in the legal process and compensate victims for their losses (Abell 1990, 216–225). On April 23, 1982, President Ronald Reagan created the Victims of Crime Task Force, designed to lead "the nation into a new era in the treatment of victims of crime" (President's Task Force 1982). Since that time, support for victims has come in other forms as well, with services like battered women's shelters, and financial restitution (Karmen 1990). Discussion of the impacts of victimization has also entered the public sphere, emphasizing traumatic social, physical, and psychological effects that can last long after the crime has occurred (Elias 1986, 107–131; Ochberg 1988, 3–20; Hartman and Burgess 1988, 152–174).

However, even with the efforts of the victim rights movement, victim blaming still occurs. As demonstrated with crime prevention tips, victims are often treated differently based on who they are, their lifestyles, and other behaviors. For example, in 1989, a jury trying a rape case in Lauderdale, Florida, found the defendant "not guilty" because the victim had "asked for it" by her choice of clothing (Baer 1991, 246). Unlike other types of crime, within rape cases, a woman's sexual history is scrutinized to determine whether or not the victim attracted her assailant through her behavior (Crenshaw 1992, 402–440). Hence, the perception of victim culpability continues to play a crucial role in real-life victimization (Karmen 1990, 105–106). The degree of shared responsibility, which is often framed by media coverage of the victimization, can have significant consequences, affecting public support for the victim and influencing the legal process—from the initial police arrest through the trial (Karmen 1990, 105–106).

Contemporary theories have been used to explain crime. For example, in 1979, Lawrence Cohen and Marcus Felson developed the theory of routine activity, which focuses on everyday activities and contexts. This theory posits that the occurrence of crime can be predicted by the convergence of three factors: *"motivated offenders, suitable targets, and the absence of capable guardians"* (Cohen and Felson 1979, 589). Thus, by preventing the meeting of potential criminals and victims, in an environment without authority figures (or even other citizens), crime rates can be reduced (Cohen and Felson 1979, 588–608). Certain people are more likely to become victims as predicted by demographics and lifestyles. For example, those who were unemployed, unmarried, or had physical disabilities were more likely to be victimized than their counterparts, because of their daily routines and interactions with other people (Cohen and Felson 1979, 588–608). And yet, while this theory has been used to explain patterns of criminal activity, it can be problematic in that it paints certain types of people as victims as vulnerable (Mustaine and Tewksbury 1999, 43–62; Schwartz and Pitts 1995, 9–31).

Andrew Karmen (1990) developed categories to describe different victims and the extent to which they may be considered responsible for their victimization (100–115).

1. *Repeated victims* become victims because they routinely place themselves in dangerous situations.
2. *Victim facilitation* describes those who can be considered somewhat responsible for their attacks because they "unknowingly, carelessly, negligently, foolishly, and unwillingly make it easier for the criminal to commit the crime" (Karmen 1990, 110).
3. *Victim precipitation*, in which the victim's behavior incites the action leading to the crime.
4. *The completely innocent victim*, referring to "crime-conscious people who tried not to be victimized" [Karmen 1990, 115].

While these perspectives have been considered useful in understanding victimology, like older victimology theories, they have been criticized for placing too much responsibility onto the victim (Schwartz and Pitts 1995, 9–31; Karmen 1990, 105). Some have argued that a better approach may be to use the macrolevel focus of Routine Activity Theory to enact programs that prevent crime from occurring (Cohen and Felson 1979, 588–608). At the same time, when crime does take place, the emphasis in the investigation and media coverage should be on the criminal, thus shifting responsibility away from traits or behaviors that assign responsibility to the victims (Schwartz and Pitts 1995, 9–31).

Media and Victimization

Crime and victimization has been a staple in popular culture products for the last century. Since crime reporting emerged with the Penny Press era in the 1800s, this genre has often been used to bolster ratings and circulation (Kobre 1964; Krajicek 1998, 7; Lipschultz, and Hilt 2002, 30–56). Fictional stories about crime have appeared in all media, from crime fiction at the turn of the 20th century, films, serial radio dramas of the 1930s and 1940s, film and, of course, television (Castleman and Padrazik 2003).

News and fictional stories about crime can impact victimization in many ways. First, crime stories can influence public perception. Cultivation theory posits that heavy viewers of television (which typically over represents crime) believe that the world is more violent than it actually is, and therefore, television can make people fearful of crime (Gerbner and Gross 1976, 173–99). For example, Romer and colleagues determined heavier viewers of television news reported greater fears and concerns about crime (Romer, Jamieson, and Aday 2003, 88–104). The cultivation effect also explains how different messages about victimization can shape public perception. For example, because television often perpetuates stories about women falsely accusing others of rape, Kahlor and Morrison (2007) found that college women who were heavy television viewers were less likely to believe that a sexual assault had actually occurred (729–39). Similarly, Franiuk and colleagues (2008) found that people who read news stories that questioned the sexual assault accusations in the 2003 Kobe Bryant case were less likely to believe that his actions were criminal (287– 309). With this cultivation effect, people may be less supportive of friends or family who were victims of sexual assault. At the macro-level, if the majority of people do not believe that rape is a crime, there may be fewer support networks for victims and criminals may face lesser or no charges or lighter sentences.

The repeated victimization of a particular group can also create stereotypes (i.e., "people with disabilities are easy targets"), reducing members of a certain group down to their classification. In this way, stereotyping creates a dichotomy between "normal" and its deviant subordinate counterpart — the stereotyped group, also known as "The Other" (Hall 1997, 258). The "otherness" of a group becomes important within the hegemonic structure. As long as a group is viewed as deviant, they will remain separate from the ruling class (Hall 1997, 258– 259). With crime, this distinction may mean that a victim of a particular group receives less public support, the criminal may not be legally punished, or the consequences may be less severe (i.e., a shorter sentence or probation instead of prison time) especially if it is believed that the victim contributed to the crime itself. For example, with the Kobe Bryant case, if people do not view sexual assault as a crime, there is no criminal, and therefore, no consequences for the victimization (Franiuk et al. 2008, 287–309). Media representations of crime perpetuate and reinforce stereotypes by defining who the typical victim is and why the person became a victim. Repeated messages linking one type of victim to a particular crime establish these stereotypes. These generalizations distort public perception of a group, and without sufficient education or countering messages, can lead to prejudice and discrimination (Lester and Ross 2003, 1– 6). As described by Hart (2000), Clark's (1969) stages of representation can help explain why limited depictions of a certain type of group in media can limit public acceptance of that group (59–79). Clark argued that to gain entry into the dominant group in society, a marginalized group must pass through four stages of representation in the media: First, nonrecognition, in which the group is absent from media. The second stage is ridicule, in which members of the marginalized group are targeted by the dominant group. Next comes regulation, in which the marginalized group is represented by authority figure characters (who serve as token depictions of that group). Finally, if members of the group begin playing an array of characters in many different situations, the group may reach the respect stage, in which there is no stereotypical role (Hart 2000, 59–79). Applying these stages to *CSI* may be useful in analyzing the "typical" victim of this program.

Victimization in *CSI:*
Crime Scene Investigation

With the popularity of crime dramas, representations of victimizations have become increasingly prevalent on television. In the traditional crime drama, police detectives attempt to solve a crime by interviewing suspects and gathering evidence in a linear progression, primarily through an oral narrative of what happened, as illustrated by the programs *Law and Order* and its spin-offs, *NYPD Blue*, and *Homicide: Life on the Streets* (Sumser 1996). In September 2000, *CSI: Crime Scene Investigation* premiered on CBS. A twist on the conventional crime drama, this program does not center on the detectives, but on those that collect and process evidence from a crime scene. Throughout the program, CSIs and others attempt to decipher what happened, as conveyed through vignettes—flashbacks of what was believed to have happened in the crime. Typically, the episode begins with the victim alive (i.e., sleeping or running through a park) or someone discovering a body. The shot cuts to the Crime Scene Investigators surrounding the body. For the rest of the episode, the CSIs attempt to deduce why and how the victim was attacked, guided by the forensic evidence and to a lesser extent, eyewitness testimony. With this format, viewers learn about the fictional crime through the authorities' verbal speculation and visual depictions of what the CSIs speculate may have happened.

Since *CSI* began, this program has been widely popular, often ranking first in television ratings. Even after ten seasons, *CSI* is the most internationally watched drama (Gorman 2010). After *CSI*'s success, similar programs have been developed, including *NCIS, Bones, Criminal Minds,* and *Dexter*, to name a few, as well as the two spin-offs for *CSI*. Its popularity and unique focus has increased interest in forensics at the high school and university levels (Bimbaum 2009; Abram 2005). And, in courtrooms, a "CSI effect" has been noted, in which juries expect more forensic evidence, although such an effect is difficult to measure[1] (Dakks 2005; Cole and Dioso-Villa 2007). Specific storylines have also clearly influenced viewers. For example, after a 2003 storyline featured a convention where humans dress as animals (who call themselves "furries"), participation in one annual "furries" convention grew dramatically, from 400 to 1700 participants (Shepherd 2005, E8).

Method

This research examined episodes of *CSI: Crime Scene Investigation* to explore how this program depicts victimization in regards to shared responsibility. The following questions guided the study:

1. What are the identifiable discourses in the representation of victims on *CSI: Crime Scene Investigation*?
2. How is the information about the victim's life and subsequent murder communicated to the audience?

To explore these questions, a textual analysis was conducted on the victims in episodes of the television show, *CSI: Crime Scene Investigation*. This method allows exploration into the "how" and "why" of textual messages, beyond frequency. In this case, using a textual analysis provided a look into how this program depicted victimization and why certain victims were chosen, while other types of people remain unharmed (or invisible in the program). In textual analysis, meaning is not fixed or inherent, but is shaped by the dominant values and ideologies present in society (Larsen 1991, 122). In other words, messages about victimizations in this fictional program reflect, reinforce, and perpetuate perceptions about victimization discourse in American society.

To conduct the analysis, seasons one through four of *CSI* were analyzed in detail, although all episodes in the remaining seasons were also examined (2000–spring 2010). For each episode, information about each victimization was noted, including any details provided about the victim (sex, approximate age, lifestyle, hobbies, etc.). In addition, all messages conveyed about the victimization itself were analyzed. Analysis was conducted using the following questions: What is the justification for the victimization (e.g., jealousy over an unfaithful spouse)? Why was this person chosen instead of another person (i.e., because this person cheated)? How was this information conveyed (e.g., Through a flashback? By the CSIs? By the assailant?)? What happened in the victimization? How is this information conveyed? After the preliminary analysis, the material was organized into recurring themes in the program.

Findings: The Victims of *CSI*

The focus of *CSI* is on the evidence produced during victimization, which occurs at least once per episode. Many times, episodes have several storylines with multiple unrelated (or sometimes related) victimizations. For example, in the episode "One Hit Wonder," the primary storyline addresses a series of sexual assaults (3.14). At the same time, in a secondary storyline, CSI Sara Sidle investigates an unsolved case involving a home invasion. Some episodes also had multiple victims from the same incident. For example, in "Crash and Burn," an elderly woman drives into a restaurant, killing several people (3.17). Storylines also carried over multiple episodes. Three serial killers are featured in multiple episodes: Paul Millander in seasons one and two, the blue paint killer in seasons three and five, and the "Miniature Killer" in season seven (1.1, 1.8, 2.13, 3.6, 5.6, season 7). The CSIs themselves also became victims. The female CSIs were victimized in four episodes (1.1, 1.2, 7.1, 7.24) and the male CSIs were attacked while on the job in five storylines over six episodes (5.24–5.25, 6.23, 7.4, 9.1, 10.23).

Even with numerous victimizations, certain types of people were repeatedly victimized. Karmen's (1990) classifications were used to organize the material into three categories: victim facilitation — lifestyle, victim facilitation — inherent traits and the completely innocent victim chance. Repeated victims and victim precipitation was rarely noted because of *CSI*'s episodic nature and the overall absence of victim resistance. These themes are analyzed in the following section.

Victim Facilitation — Lifestyle

Storylines of *CSI* convey that people risk becoming victims if they choose dangerous, risky, or morally questionable lifestyles. People were murdered because of drug use, mafia involvement, and illegal activities, in which greed became a motive. For example, in "And then there were none," after four people rob casinos, one of them kills the others so that he does not have to divide the money (2.9). Like other crime dramas, many of the victims of *CSI* have preexisting relationships with their assailants (Soulliere 2003, 12–38). For these victims, had they not participated in crime, they would not have become victims. These episodes repeatedly illustrated the Routine Activity Theory, demonstrating in which contexts and between which type of victims, crime often occurs.

Hobbies or ways of living typically considered "deviant" also heightened a person's chance of victimization. For example, in "Cats in the Cradle," a reclusive elderly woman is murdered because she would not give away one of her 21 cats (2.20). Imagery of the multiple cats gnawing at their owner, combined with the actual motive for the homicide, suggests that this woman died because she chose to live in a house full of cats— deviant, as least according to *CSI*. Other aberrant lifestyles that made one vulnerable to victimization included vampirism, killer robot competitions, and dressing up like an animal (4.13, 3.18, 4.5).

On *CSI*, a number of victims held sex-related jobs prior to their victimization. These jobs appear to bring together potential killers, more vulnerable people (usually women), and does so in a place unguarded by authority. Often, because no alternative explanation is offered, it is suggested that the victim's choice of career directly caused her death. In the episode "Boom," for example, a man strangles a prostitute, coming up from behind her and wrapping a curtain tie around her neck (1.13). The murderer explains, "I was her pimp. She was leaving me to start her own racket." Since no other information is known about the victim, save her occupation, this statement suggests that the woman died simply because she was a prostitute. Dancers, dominatrixes, and porn stars were also suggested to be more susceptible to victimization (3.23. 1.13, 2.8, 3.15, 3.8). In fact, a recurring place of victimization is Lady Heather's—a dominatrix and pleasure house. For example, in the episode "Slaves of Las Vegas," a client of Lady Heather's paints one of her employees in latex and then forces her to breathe through straws emerging from the black suit (2.8). He beats the woman and then accidentally suffocates her.

These ties between "deviant" lifestyles may be problematic. First, not all of the lifestyles that lead to victimization in *CSI* endanger society. Therefore, a slightly eccentric person in real-life may have difficulty receiving restitution because his or her harmless hobby had been featured in this program. Secondly, with sex crimes, instead of blaming the victim for becoming involved in dangerous occupations, a more productive approach would be to highlight reasons why people become involved in these submissive positions and seek to remedy those situations with funding for education or job training programs. The link between sex and death also reinforces the belief that women facilitate crime, especially sexual assault through their behavior, conveying the message that rape is not a crime. As demonstrated with the Kobe Bryant case, viewers may be less supportive of real-life victims of sexual assault (Franiuk et al. 2008, 287–309).

Victim Facilitation — Inherent Traits

Certain types of people are repeatedly presented as more susceptible to victimization than others. In these episodes, had the person not possessed the "risky" trait, s/he would not have been victimized, as indicated by a comparison with victims without the trait. Furthermore, the episode plots, aided by the CSI flashbacks, indicate that these victims should have been aware of their increased vulnerability and therefore, should have taken more precautions to prevent the crime. Victim facilitation due to the traits of physical disability, race, class, and sex will be discussed in detail.

Physical Difference: Although two main characters out of the 14 regular cast members in the ten seasons of the program appeared with physical disabilities,[2] it is rare for single-episode characters to exhibit difference. In fact, the issue of difference only comes up in two episodes: "Sound of Silence" (1.20) and "A Little Murder" (3.4). As these titles convey, these episodes address deafness and dwarfism, suggesting that that these conditions not only make a person more likely to be victimized but also serve as a justification for death. Early in "Sounds of Silence," the victim, Brian, is identified as a deaf college student (1.20). The victim's abnormality is visually displayed through a juxtaposition of a CSI shot of a healthy eardrum, followed by a shot of the victim's, whose eardrums are twisted and knotted. When the CSIs learn of the victim's deafness, they initially assume that he stepped into the street and was run over by a car he did not hear. Later, the CSIs deduce that two men deliberately assaulted and drove over the victim. Since only Brian's body is visible in the flashback, he seems more like a log than a man, as the truck drives over him. Throughout this scene, the lighting, combined with the camera angles, emphasize the fearful experience of the men in the truck, dehumanizing Brian. Since the men ultimately kill Brian because he does not respond to their initial calls, it is assumed that his deafness is the justification for his death. This link is reinforced in the final scene of the episode, when another character tells Grissom, "That's why they killed Brian, because he was different."

Likewise, in "A Little Murder," the vulnerability of the little person enables the assailant to subdue and then kill the man (3.4). In a CSI flashback, another little person hits the victim on the back of the neck, illustrated by a CSI shot of the man's spine severing, rendering him incapacitated. The coroner states that only a man with this particular form of dwarfism would be susceptible to this action. Since a "normal" person would have survived the attack, this flashback stresses the victim's vulnerability, especially considering the weakness of the assailant, another little person. Besides highlighting the victim's susceptibility, this close-up CSI shot of the bloodied severed brain stem, zoomed in to where nothing is visible except a faint blurred light on the left of the gruesome mess, also dehumanizes the little person, reducing him to his physical impairment. Following this attack, the man cannot defend himself, as the other little person slips a noose around the man's neck and hangs the man from the rafters. The assailant justifies the murder, stating, "I just couldn't let Jessica marry him. Any kid they have. Fifty percent chance it could be a dwarf," which both stresses the man's physical condition as motive for murder, as well as underscores dwarfism as an undesirable trait, making a person vulnerable to victimization.

This connection between disability and crime portrays people with disabilities as vulnerable. Furthermore, because people with disabilities only appear in episodes about the disability,[3] their representation is limited to a token appearance, which strengthens the stereotypes that disability means vulnerability and that people with disabilities cannot have regular occupations, such as being a police officer, or are regular people who sometimes witness crime. At the worst, one could consider these representations as exemplifying the ridicule stage of representation, in that people are ridiculed or punished because of their disabilities (Hart, 2000). At best, because the depictions are limited to these episodes, they could be considered illustrative of the token stage—far from respect and acceptance (Hart 2000, 59–79).

Race: Although *CSI* is set in Las Vegas, which has a somewhat diverse population, most victims and assailant characters are Caucasian. Multiple persons of color typically only appear in episodes focused on a subculture.[4] Thus, race among victims is largely ignored and members of most ethnic groups are invisible from the program. Only one episode directly addresses racially-motivated killing. In "Blood Lust," a group of Caucasian men beat a cabdriver of Indian descent to death after his cab runs over a Caucasian teenager (3.9). Unlike most episodes of *CSI*, this homicide is not presented as a CSI flashback or through a murderer's confession, but as "real" scenes of the show. During the assault, a close-up of the cabdriver emphasizes his vulnerability and agony as he begs them to stop, yet cannot physically protect himself from the endless blows and kicks. Finally, one slow-motion punch across the driver's face is made, causing dark red blood sprays from his face onto the street.

Later, a gang member justifies their attack: "We're heroes man. They have no respect for our loss." Another man adds, "He's not from here, this country." The CSIs also question the reason behind the assault. CSI Warrick Brown asks, "Do you think it was racially motivated?" His colleague, CSI Sara Sidle, responds, "I do. White mob. White kid. Dark-skinned cabbie," explicitly linking the victim's skin color to his murder. And because the attack is part of "real" scenes, the audience witnesses the situation, as it happened, not through CSI speculation. This allows the viewer to connect the man's ethnicity to his murder, aided, of course, by the juxtaposition of the mob and the accident, along with the emphasis on race.

This episode, along with the overrepresentation of Caucasian characters, reinforces a dominance of this group over the invisible others. In addition, the occupation of the victim supports the stereotype of the Indian cabdriver. Such a stereotype, paired with the absence of other representations of people from India (and other marginalized groups), implies that the "typical" person (i.e., lab specialist, CSI, coroner, eyewitness, assailant, etc.) is Caucasian — a problematic message in that this paints a large percentage of its viewing audience as "atypical."

Socioeconomic Class: Low socioeconomic class also increases one's risk of victimization in *CSI*. In "The Pilot," a man, described as an alcoholic drifter, is shot in the home of a middle-class family (1.1). Although the CSIs conclude that the family initially invited the man in and shot him in the back, the lighting during the CSI flashback demonizes the victim, not his assailant. The flashback shows a clean-cut, well-dressed man loading a gun as his wife opens the door. A disheveled, long-haired man enters from the dark shadows. The suburban couple is featured in white lights, which reflect off their light clothing. The lighting, along with the murder itself, implies that the murder of the alcoholic drifter was actually a blessing and that, for being a human leech, the victim brought the murder upon himself. Other episodes present lower-class or homeless people as more expendable than the general population. For example, in "Scuba Doobie Doo," a decomposed corpse is discovered in a duffle bag (2.5). The CSIs determine that because the homeless veteran bothered the customers of a posh restaurant, the manager killed the man and disposed of him like trash. Since these people often have no family or friends to mourn them or even report them missing, these storylines indicate that they are less valuable to society. They also emphasize the individual's plight, as opposed to creating empathy for the victim. A more prosocial approach would explore the conditions that led to the victimization.

Gender and Vulnerability: In *CSI*, unlike male victims, women were often careless about security, naïve and gullible in their decisions, and behave too provocatively, all of which significantly contributed to their victimizations. Many of these episodes with vulnerable women included more than one victim, such as "The Strip Strangler," "I-15 Murders," and "The Execution of Catherine Willows" (1.23, 1.11, 3.6). The gravity of these poor decisions is emphasized by the extreme brutality of the crimes themselves.

In several episodes, police officers, detectives, and CSIs link the female victim's behavior to her victimization. Assailants enter through open windows, attack women alone in public spaces, and those who open their doors to strangers. In one scene of "One Hit Wonder," for example, a detective describes how one woman blocked her door with a treadmill (3.14). Her next-door neighbor did not and was sexually assaulted. A male detective demonstrates how easily a person could break in, reaching through the window to unlock the victim's door. In "Too Tough to Die," a woman walks across a dark, empty parking garage (1.16). As she puts her key into the car door, a masked man appears behind her, sticks his gun into her side and slams her against the car. In the next shot, the woman is found unconscious on the side of the road, in the dirt, with her shirt off, exposing her bra. Authorities discover that the woman was sexually assaulted and shot multiple times. Similarly, women are presented as careless and vulnerable in "The Execution of Catherine Willows" and "What's Eating Gilbert Grissom?" in which the same serial killer attacks female college students (3.6, 5.6). In these episodes, the assailant attacks women who walk across campus alone at night. Had the women followed preventative measures, such as avoiding shortcuts at night, it is suggested that they would not have become victims. And yet, even the two episodes in which male victims exhibited "careless" behavior of hitchhiking and jogging alone, no authority figures comment on the dangerous choices of the victims.

Inherently "female" characteristics also make women more susceptible to victimization. For example, in "I-15 Murders," a couple abducts, rapes and murders gullible women (1.11). A CSI flashback shows the female suspect pleading to another woman, "My baby is in trouble." The naive woman willingly follows her to a refrigerated truck, where she is taken. Since no such ruse is used with male victims, this storyline conveys that only women would foolishly put themselves at risk. Ruses used on men are more light-hearted in tone. For example, in the "Pilot," a female prostitute drugs her male clients in order to rob them (1.1). Unlike the numerous episodes in which women are drugged and victimized (usually sexually assaulted and murdered), this episode has a lighter tone — the victim and the assailant both sheepishly admit how the drugs were administered (through her nipples). The victim gets his property returned.

Nick Stokes even flirts with the assailant and later dates her. This storyline paints the victimization as more of a prank than a punishment for the victim's foolish behavior, especially because the perpetrator is a prostitute who later has intimate relations with CSI Nick Stokes.

A woman's dress and behavior also are shown to increase her risk. Criminals argued that the female victims were so sexually provocative that they "couldn't help themselves." In "The Strip Strangler," for example, the serial killer explains how women "work out because they want us to look at them and then they parade around and you just want to say, 'Hello' (1.23). Because he thinks the women "ask" for his affection through their body language, the serial killer becomes enraged when women reject him so he invades their homes and brutally murders them. Likewise, the murderer in "Invisible Evidence" explains that the victim "answers the door in this sexy, little thing and stuff. Most of the time when a woman answers the door, it's in sweats.... This was not like that. I mean, what am I supposed to think?" (4.7). The killer argues that the victim's clothing was an indication of her desires to be intimate with him, thus justifying her rape. The CSI flashback stresses the victim's sexuality. As the victim answers the door, she has long blond hair and is wearing a small lacy dress. She smiles sweetly. It is at this point that he forces the door open and rapes her. The visual imagery of these events suggests that her displayed sexuality "invited" the killer's advances, resulting in her death.

A gender difference even exists in the victimizations of CSIs. In ten seasons, eight of the CSIs (male/female) become victims at some point. In fact, only Gil Grissom never becomes a victim. Three of the female CSIs become victims: new investigator Holly Gribbs is fatally shot, Catherine Willows is drugged, stripped naked, and taken to a motel, and Sarah Sidle is abducted and pinned under a car (1.1, 1.2, 7.1, 7.24). Unlike the male CSIs, though, storylines present these women as vulnerable and weak. For example, during the pilot episode, Gribbs winds up alone at a crime scene, due to another's negligence. Several people are blamed for Gribbs' death, with the assumption that she was too weak, unprepared, and new to the job to handle a scene alone. For Willows' attack, she is off-duty at a bar and accepts a drink from a stranger. She wakes up naked in a seedy motel. Willows appears to be so ashamed of putting herself at risk that she does not report her crime. CSI Sarah Sidle also becomes a victim of the "Miniature Killer," as she walks alone at night to her car. Despite their training, these plots suggest that the female CSIs violated basic crime prevention rules, leading to their victimization. They are not heroes willing to sacrifice themselves for the job. Instead, especially because they are off-duty, the female CSIs become vulnerable women.

CSI perpetuates a disparity between male and female victims, even with the Crime Scene Investigators. By showing CSI flashbacks of women walking alone, then becoming victims, for example, storylines imply that unaccompanied women put themselves at risk for victimization. Therefore, in real-life, when women become victims, especially of sexual assault, some may wonder if they ventured out alone or "violated" other tenets of crime safety. And because of this vulnerable behavior, one may question the extent to which they deserve support for their "decisions." These depictions reinforce the inequality of power in society and downplay a criminal's role in the attack. This program supports the myth that women are more fragile than men, thus reinforcing unequal positions of power between men and women, as the male killers torture and murder the "weaker" sex.

Nearly all cases of sexual assault occurred to women. In fact, when a male victim was sexually assaulted, the episode focused on the rarity of the attack. CSI Nick Stokes even personally contacts a professional on the victim's behalf, to ensure that he receives counseling. The absence of depictions of sexual assault to male victims reinforces a stigma toward male victims, which have been known to discourage male victims from reporting their crimes, for fear of being viewed as "gay" or weak (Sable et al. 2006, 157–162).

Other Vulnerable Groups: Besides lifestyle, disability, race, socio-economic class, and gender, other types of people were also victimized in *CSI*. Characters who were gay, lesbian, bisexual, or transgendered only appeared in episodes about victims with these traits. The absence of GLBT characters, except for these episodes, conveys that these characteristics make a person susceptible to victimization. For example, in the episode "Evaluation Day," a character who is gay murders his partner due to jealousy (1.22). Likewise, in "XX," a female prisoner kills another inmate, her lover, because she fears the woman loves another person (4.17). These representations may convey that people who are GLBT are more unfaithful than others, especially given that no positive depictions exist in this program. Like the "deviant" hobbies, the episode on transgenderism focused on this trait more than the crime itself. And in "Ch-Ch-Changes," a transgendered man murders a transgendered woman to protect his spouse (also transgendered) (5.8). The outcome of this episode (murder) implied that had the victim not been transgendered, she would have survived.

Senior citizens also seem to be more at risk, especially older women. For example, in the "Cats in the Cradle" episode previously discussed, a child murders the elderly woman with a pen — circumstances that emphasize her vulnerability (2.20). In "Homebodies," a man easily shuts an elderly woman in a closet (4.3). She attempts to escape, but cannot and dies in the closet. Senior citizens rarely appear in roles other than victim or grandmother, thus reinforcing stereotypes of elderly as weak, feeble or useless. This stereotype has also been perpetuated in other media, including advertising (Smythe 2003, 167–174).

Completely Innocent: The Crime-Conscious Victim

CSI only presents one type of victim as completely innocent in that the person did not contribute to the crime by engaging in risky lifestyles or by possessing traits that increased the risk of victimization. Storylines conveyed that typically only Caucasian, able-bodied, heterosexual men were sometimes chosen at random for victimization. Criminals kill these victims quickly, with no sexual assault or other torture prior to death, suggesting that the assailant murders these men for a purpose other than punishing the victims.

In "Fur and Loathing," the male victim is again shown to be chosen by chance (4.5). When a man interrupts another man robbing a vending machine, the thief turns and shoots the man. Had he entered a few moments later, it is implied that he would not have been killed. However, since the episode clearly shows that the man had no knowledge that a crime was occurring, he is not presented as careless about security. The victim's innocence is reinforced by the focus on finding the murderer in this episode. And in "Grissom Versus the Volcano," shortly after an African-American man rents a car, it explodes, killing him instantly (4.9). The CSIs determine that the car bomb was intended for the previous car renter and therefore, the victimization is random.

For these victims, CSIs or other authority figures never criticize the victim's behavior leading up to the crime. These episodes focus on why the killer attacked, not why the victim was chosen. For example, the episode, "Justice is Served" illustrates this "stroke of bad luck" (1.21). A male jogger is mauled and killed by a giant dog, and then has his organs removed and consumed by a woman who suffers from a vampire-like disorder. Once the CSIs establish that the assailant was, in fact, human, the man's involvement in his own death is not mentioned again. It is assumed that his actions were coincidental with his death; especially since no CSI flashback is shown, suggesting that the circumstances surrounding his death were irrelevant. The emphasis of this episode is not on the victimization, but on the abnormal behavior of the murderer. Throughout this show, the CSIs question what the killer does with the organs she harvested from the jogger. She eventually explains that she eats them to protect herself from a degenerative condition. A CSI flashback illustrates the progression of her disorder without consuming organs, showing the woman's skin peel off her face. This focus on the killer, not the victim, implies that his death was, in some ways, an accident and therefore he cannot be held responsible for jogging alone in the park at night. Even when male victims clearly make themselves susceptible to victimization, storylines do not frame them as responsible for their victimization. For example, in "Identity Crisis," a man becomes a victim after he picks up a hitchhiker, yet no comments are made about the dangers of hitchhiking (2.13). On the contrast, when female victims violate conventional wisdom about safety, storylines suggest that it is this behavior that made them susceptible to victimization.

The only serial killer to exclusively target men, Paul Millander, chooses his victims because of something they cannot control, in this case, their birthdays. This theme appears in three episodes: "The Pilot," "Anonymous," and "Identity Crisis" (1.1, 1.8, and 2.13). Throughout the course of their investigation, the CSIs determine that Millander kills men and then stages their suicides in order to reflect his father's death. Other than the role they play in Millander's presentation, the victims themselves are not important. In the three episodes with this serial killer, there is no indication of the victim's contribution to his own death. As mentioned, even in "Identity Crisis," where the victim picks up a hitchhiker (the killer) on a dark deserted road, there are no references to danger of this practice or that this action led to the man's death (although clearly it did). Instead, the emphasis is on the abnormality of the killer himself, who is discovered to be intersexed. The focus of the episode on the serial killer, combined with the assailant's victim selection process, implies that the men, even when they place themselves in dangerous situations, hold no responsibility for their attacks.

Similarly, the male CSIs are framed differently than the female CSIs when they become victims. Male CSI victims are framed as heroes, not victims, and their wounds appear to symbolize bravery, although all of the men were alone during the crime and seemingly could have protected themselves from the situation. While on the job, Jim Brass and Warrick Brown are shot, Greg Sanders is severely beaten, and Ray Langston is stabbed (6.23, 9.1, 7.4, 10.23). Nick Stokes actually becomes a victim twice. He is abducted and buried alive in "Grave Danger" and shot in "Meat Jekyll" (5.24–5.25, 10.23). None of these victims are chosen because of their vulnerability — they were all injured while responding to a call, interrogating a criminal, or going above and beyond the call of duty, seeking justice. For example, the randomness of Nick's victimization is a constant in the episode "Grave Danger," beginning with him losing a coin toss, and referred to by both Warrick and Grissom, who says that the criminal could not have known that Nick would arrive at the scene. Furthermore, no one mentions precautions Stokes could have taken to protect himself, such as attending to the scene with a partner or insisting that the responding officer stay nearby. Warrick Brown is depicted as a hero when he becomes a victim in "For Warrick," after he meets the primary suspect alone in a dark alley in the middle of the night, where a crooked police officer inflicts a fatal wound. The CSIs seek justice for Warrick, as they uncover the murder plot. The risk of his solo investigation and the choice and time of the meeting are never mentioned, even though it is this behavior that leads to Warrick's untimely death. Similar messages are conveyed about the other male victimizations. In fact, Jim Brass even receives a medal of recognition for his bravery after he is shot negotiating a hostage situation.

Implications of These Representations

The messages about victimization in *CSI* reinforce the early philosophies of victimology, which proposed that traits and lifestyles increased a person's risk of victimization and perpetuate varying degrees of shared responsibility (von Hentig 1948, 348–404; Hindelang 1973, 245; Karmen 1990). The connection between specific attributes, such as physical difference, and death is particularly interesting because contemporary victimologists repudiate this idea for real-life crime (Karmen 1990). We also see a demonstration of the Routine Activity Theory, in which criminal, target, and an absence of guardians lead to crime (Cohen and Felson 1979, 588–608).

Why does it matter that television presents some lifestyles as more risky or certain types of people as more likely to become victimized? By connecting victims' behavior to their attacks, storylines implicate the victims, suggesting they contributed to their crimes. While some may argue that associating certain lifestyles with risk could help deter people from these activities, this perpetuation of shared responsibility conveys that these victims should not receive public support or even sympathy for their plight.

In some ways, it is alarming that certain social groups were targeted above others, given the strides toward the equal treatment of people of color, those who are GLBT, women and people with disabilities. These representations counter efforts toward tolerance of difference and cultural awareness and imply that victims of these groups may not be as deserving of support and restitution as someone in the dominant group (i.e., able-bodied, Caucasian, heterosexual man who is not yet a senior citizen). In the later years of the show, one episode addresses the sexual assault of a man. Other than this storyline, little difference was noted over the years studied. For most of these types of people, characters with the traits only appear in episodes about the traits. Using Clark's stages of representation, by not depicting characters with these traits in an array of roles, these portrayals challenge acceptance of these marginalized groups (Hart 2000, 59–79). We don't see a little person play a police officer or a transgendered person play a coroner. And because the trait is the theme of the week, akin to the vampire-themed episode or the storyline with the man who dresses like a baby, it is presented almost as a spectacle. The dehumanizing visuals of the deaf victim in the shadows or the close-up of the fractured spinal column of the little person reinforce this notion of spectacle. Translated to real-life, these representations reinforce narrow definitions of what people of certain groups can achieve and the extent to which they should be supported if victimized.

From a cultivation perspective, these messages reinforce a "culture of fear," and may lead certain types of viewers to believe that they are at risk for crime (Romer, Jamieson, and Aday 2003, 88–104; Gordon and Riger 1989). Furthermore, the focus on individual action (that certain people must modify their behavior to avoid victimization), discourages awareness and support for macrochanges that could improve overall safety. In the episode "Too Tough to Die," for example, a woman becomes victimized after walking alone in a parking garage. Applying the Routine Activity Theory, more emphasis could be placed on improving the "guardian" factor by adding more security officers and better lighting in the garage (Cohen and Felson 1979, 588–608). Programs that target potential criminals could also help to reduce overall crime rates. This shift in emphasis would detract attention (and possible blame) on the victim and instead center on the location of crimes and potential victims. Storylines in *CSI* or other programs could address the positive effects of implementing Neighborhood Watch programs or other larger-scale efforts to reduce crime, thus reminding viewers that both criminals and their victims are influenced by the social, political and environmental contexts. Altering these factors may have a much greater impact than telling people to lock their doors or shy away from ruby-red lip gloss or other provocative make-up or clothing.

The Reality of *CSI*

Obviously, *CSI* is a fictional show, produced for television. And yet, themes identified in *CSI* do not exist in a bubble, but reinforce news coverage, reality cop shows, fictional programs, and other media products that present certain victims as more responsible for their crimes than others. This connection to real-life may explain why producers choose to reinforce many existing stereotypes, perhaps arguing that these stories, especially those that focus on deviance, spark strong ratings. Like *CSI*, other crime dramas also perpetuate these messages, often downplaying or ignoring victims with physical disabilities, people of color, and those who are elderly. For example, in "Silent Night" of *CSI: New York*, a teenager murders his girlfriend and abducts their baby so that she can grow up as a hearing child. In the 2008 episode of *Cold Case*, "Andy in C Minor," a Deaf student murders another student because he could not qualify for a Cochlear Implant and feared living with his deafness, while his friend could hear. Other programs also reinforce myths about rape, use transgenderism for spectacle, and focus on changing individual behavior instead of a system that leads to criminal activity. These messages, while channeled through fiction, draw from prevalent ideologies about power, what defines a crime, and what defines a victim. Without some connection to real-life, it is doubtful that people would tune in. That said, television representations have the potential to positively change perceptions toward victimization. With all the crime dramas airing these days, there is plenty of opportunity.

NOTES

1. The issue of the CSI effect has received widespread attention. Cole and Dioso-Villa (2007) found more than 400 media stories on the effect. Numerous law symposiums have been held to debate it.
2. Robert David Hall, who plays Doc Robbins, is a double-amputee. And, in the third season, CSI Gil Grissom experiences progressive hearing loss.
3. Again, Dr. Robbins is a double-amputee who walks with a crutch. However, other characters with disabilities only appear in the specific episodes with those storylines.
4. The episode "Snakes" (5.12) is about the Hispanic community or "Say Uncle" about violence in Korea town (9.6).

REFERENCES

Abell, Richard B. 1990. "A Federal Perspective on Victim Assistance in the United States of America." In Emilio C. Viano (ed.), *The Victimology Handbook: Research Findings, Treatment, and Public Policy*: 213–225. New York: Garland.

Abram, Susan. 2005. "Crime Scene Investigators: Who Are They? New Class Gives Students a Clue." *The Daily News of Los Angeles*. March 20, SC1.

Baer, Judith A. 1991. *Women in American Law: The Struggle Toward Equality From the New Deal to the Present*. New York: Holmes & Meier.

Beverly Police Department. 2009. "Crime Prevention Recommendations for Senior Citizens." Accessed 18 June 2010. *http://www.beverlypd.org/pdf/PERSONAL%20SAFETY/CRIME%20PRE VENTION%20FOR%20SENIORS.pdf.*

Bimbaum, Michael. 2009. "CSI: Landon School: Forensic Science Class Turns to 'Crime' to See Textbook Theories in Action." *The Washington Post*. October 24. Accessed June 18, 2010. *http:// www.washingtonpost.com/wp-dyn/content/article/2009/10/23/AR2009102302539.html.*

Bureau of Justice Statistics. 2010a. "Homicide Trends in the U.S." Accessed June 18, 2010. *http:// bjs.ojp.usdoj.gov/content/homicide/relationship.cfm.*

Bureau of Justice Statistics. 2010b. "Victims and Offenders." Accessed June 18, 2010. *http://bjs.ojp. usdoj.gov/index.cfm?ty=tp&tid=94.*

Castleman, Harry, and Walter J. Podrazik. 2003. *Watching TV: Six Decades of American Television*, 2d ed. Syracuse: Syracuse University Press.

Cavender, Gray, and Lisa Bond-Maupin. 1993. "Fear and Loathing on Reality Television: An Analysis of *America's Most Wanted* and *Unsolved Mysteries*." *Sociological Inquiry* 63: 20–30.

Clark, Cedric. 1969. Television and Social Controls: Some Observations of the Portrayal of Ethnic Minorities. *Television Quarterly* 9(2): 18–22.

Cohen, Lawrence E. and Marcus Felson. 1979. "Social Change and Crime Rate Trends: A Routine Activity Approach." *American Sociological Review* 44: 588–608.

Cole, Simon A., and Rachel Dioso-Villa. 2007. "Symposium: The CSI Effect: The True Effect of Crime Scene Television on the Justice System: CSI and Its Effects: Media, Juries, and the Burden of Proof." *New England School of Law Review* 41: 435.

Crenshaw, Kimberly. 1992. "'Whose Story is it Anyway?' Feminist and Antiracist Appropriations of Anita Hill." In Toni Morrison (ed.), *Race-ing Justice, En-gendering Power: Essays on Anita Hill, Clarence Thomas, and the Construction of Social Reality*: 402–440. New York: Pantheon.

Dakss, Brian. 2005. "The CSI Effect': Does the TV Crime Drama Influence How Jurors Think?" *CBSNews*. March 21. Accessed June 18, 2010. *http://www.cbsnews.com/stories/2005/03/21/early show/main681949.shtml.*

Elias, Robert. 1986. *The Politics of Victimization: Victims, Victimology and Human Rights*. Oxford: Oxford University Press.

Foss, Katherine. 2006. "Tracing the Blame Game: Constructions of Victimization in *The New York Times, 1920–2003*." Paper presented in an interactive session of the Critical and Cultural Studies Division of the Association for Education in Journalism and Mass Communication (AEJMC), San Francisco, CA, August 2–5.

Franiuk, Renae, Jennifer L. Seefelt, Sandy L. Cepress and Joseph A. Vandello. 2008. "Prevalence and Effects of Rape Myths in Print Journalism." *Violence Against Women* 14: 287–309.

Gerbner, George, and Larry Gross. 1976. "Living with Television: The Violence Profile." *Journal of Communications* 26: 173–99.

Gordon, Margaret T., and Stephanie Riger. 1991. *The Female Fear: The Social Cost of Rape*. New York: The Free Press.

Gorman, Bill. 2010. "*CSI: Crime Scene Investigation* is the Most Watched Show in the World!" *TV By the Numbers*. Accessed November 22, 2010. *http://tvbythenumbers.zap2it.com/2010/06/11/csi -crime-scene-investigation-is-the-most-watched-show-in-the-world/53833.*

Hall, Stuart (ed.). 1997. *Representation: Cultural Representations and Signifying Practices*. London: Sage.

Hart, Kylo-Patrick R. 2000. "Representing Gay Men on American Television." *Journal of Men's Studies* 9: 59–79.

Hartman, Carol R., and Ann Wolbert Burgess. 1988. "Rape Trauma and Treatment of the Victim." In Frank Ochberg (ed.), *Post-Traumatic Therapy and Victims of Violence*: 152–174. New York: Brunner/Mazel.

Hindelang, Michael J., Michael R. Gottfredson, and James Garofalo. 1978. *Victims of Personal Crime: An Empirical Foundation for a Theory of Personal Victimization*. Cambridge: Ballinger.

Kahlor, LeeAnn and Dan Morrison. 2007. "Television Viewing and Rape Myth Acceptance Among College Women." *Sex Roles* 56: 729–39.

Karmen, Andrew. 1990. *Crime Victims: An Introduction to Victimology* 2d ed. Pacific Grove, CA: Brooks/Cole.

Kobre, Sidney. 1964. *The Yellow Press and Gilded Age Journalism.* Tallahassee: Florida State University.

Krajicek, David J. 1998. *Scooped! Media Miss Real Story on Crime While Chasing Sex, Sleaze, and Celebrities.* New York: Columbia University Press.

Larsen, Peter. 1991. "Textual Analysis of Fictional Media Content." In K.B. Jensen and N.W. Jankowski (eds.), *A Handbook of Qualitative Methodologies for Mass Communication Research*: 121–134. London: Routledge.

Lester, Paul, and Susan Dente Ross. 2003. "Images That Injure: Introduction." In An Paul Lester and Susan Dente Ross, (eds.), *Images That Injure: Pictorial Stereotypes in the Media*: 1–6. Westport, CT: Praeger.

Lipschultz, Jeremy H., and Michael L. Hilt. 2002. *Crime and Local Television News: Dramatic, Breaking and Live From the Scene.* Mahwah, N.J.: Lawrence Erlbaum.

Mustaine, Elizabeth Ehrhardt, and Richard Tewksbury. 1999. "A Routine Activity Theory Explanation for Women's Stalking Victimizations." *Violence Against Women* 5: 43–62.

National Crime Prevention Council. 2010a. "Strategies." Accessed June 18, 2010. *http://www.ncpc.org/topics/hate-crime/strategies.*

National Crime Prevention Council. 2010b. "Crime Prevention for People with Disabilities." Accessed June 18, 2010. *http://www.ncpc.org/resources/files/pdf/violent-crime/crime%20prevention%20for%20people%20with%20disabilities.pdf.*

Ochberg, Frank (ed.). 1988. *Post-Traumatic Therapy and Victims of Violence.* New York: Brunner/Mazel.

President's Task Force on Victims of Crime. 1982. "President's Task Force on Victims of Crime: Final Report." Washington, D.C.

Romer, Daniel, Kathleen Hall Jamieson, and Sean Aday. 2003. "Television News and the Cultivation of Fear of Crime." *Journal of Communication* 53: 88–104.

Sable, Marjorie R., Fran Danis, Denise L. Mauzy, and Sarah K. Gallagher. 2006. "Barriers to Reporting Sexual Assault for Women and Men: Perspectives of College Students." *Journal of American College Health* 55: 157–162.

Schafer, Stephen. 1963. *Victimology.* Lexington, MA: D.C. Heath.

Schwartz, Martin D., and Victoria. L. Pitts. 1995. "Exploring a Feminist Routine Activities Approach to Explaining Sexual Assault." *Justice Quarterly* 12: 9–31.

Shepherd, Chuck. 2005. "Blasphemous 'Springer, the Opera' Bound for United States." *News of the Weird.* March 17.

Smythe, Ted Curtis. 2003. "Growing Old in Commercials: A Joke Not Shared." In Paul Lester and Susan Dente Ross (eds.), *Images That Injure: Pictorial Stereotypes in the Media*: 187–174. Westport, CT: Praeger.

Soulliere, Danielle M. 2003. "Prime-Time Murder: Presentations of Murder on Popular Television Justice programs." *Journal of Criminal Justice and Popular Culture* 10: 12–38.

Sumser, John. 1996. *Morality and Social Order in Television Crime Drama.* Jefferson, NC: McFarland.

von Hentig, Hans. 1948. *The Criminal and his Victim: Studies in the Sociobiology of Crime.* New Haven: Yale University Press.

Wolfgang, Marvin E. 1958. *Patterns in Criminal Homicide.* Philadelphia: University of Pennsylvania.

Macho Cops, Corner Boys and Soldiers: The Construction of Race and Masculinity on HBO's The Wire

Linda Waldron and Cheryl Chambers

In 2002, HBO aired its first season of *The Wire*, a police drama that ran for five seasons. During its run it was nominated for two Emmys and several TV Critic Awards, and won the ASCAP Top TV Series Award, a Peabody Award and a Writer's Guild Award. The storylines of the show included "police corruption, brutality and incompetence, a portrait of race and politics, the futile War on Drugs and an extraordinarily honest depiction of the gravitational pull of the streets and drug 'corners' for a generation of African American inner-city youth with few other prospects or opportunities" (Tyree 2008, 32). Unlike the typical cop drama that is based in Los Angeles or New York, this show was both based and filmed in Baltimore and relied heavily on local issues for its storylines (Zurawik 2006). The first season develops around the narcotics division's often-futile attempts to infiltrate one of the top drug gangs in West Baltimore. The Harbor serves as the backdrop for the second season, which explores crime, political corruption, unions and the plight of the working class. Season three refocuses on the Barksdale gang and addresses the legalization of drugs, while season four examines Baltimore city schools through the eyes of four young African American boys struggling to stay off the corners. The final season uses the newsroom to uncover crime, drugs, and politics in Baltimore. Unlike many TV crime dramas, *The Wire* does not offer any clear episode-based resolutions. Instead, as Marshall and Potter (2009) have argued, all five seasons form a "super-narrative" as "faces change, characters enter our awareness or drop from view, but the drug problem (which may be seen as the series' principal concern) persists" (Marshall and Potter 2009, 9).

The city of Baltimore itself becomes an integral part of this "super-narrative." As Tyree (2008) argues, the landscape of Baltimore actually serves as a "character" in the show; as the city of Baltimore changed so too did the setting and storyline of the show. This included incorporating storylines about actual condemned housing projects in season three or deciding to pick Monroe

Elementary School, an actual school that was closed down by the city due to budget cuts, as the site for filming school scenes in season four. These details and accuracy of life on the streets of Baltimore has led many critics to describe the show as having an "unparalleled degree of authenticity" (Kamalakar 2003, 69).

The "unparalleled degree of authenticity" and complex writing of the show combines to often blur the lines between reality and fiction. This provides a particularly interesting site for sociological analysis. Despite claims of authenticity, *The Wire* does not necessarily construct facts, but rather it constructs images that Gamson et al. (1992), would say frame the social world of Baltimore in a particular way. "With this conception, a frame is more like a storyline or unfolding narrative about an issue" (Gamson et al. 1992, 385). Although this storyline is most certainly about crime and drugs, police officers and gang members, city council and city students, it is also about ideologies of race and racism, sex and sexism, social class and discrimination. This paper explores what a show that has been touted as "authentic" teaches us about race and masculinity. Although this topic truly transcends any one season, for the purpose of this analysis, we will examine season three, which serves as the show's midpoint.

Background on *The Wire*

TV Cop Dramas and the Social Construction of Reality

The introduction of cable in the 1980s and the proliferation of target marketing introduced "quality" dramatic television programming aimed at an "upscale audience" that provided storylines that were "better, more sophisticated, and more artistic than the usual network fare" (Thompson 1996, 12). Thompson argues that in 1981, *Hill Street Blues* led the charge to a more serious, literary, writer-based drama. The conception of *Hill Street Blues* was not necessarily unique — NBC was looking for another gritty, police series when they picked up the show. Yet the show transcended a typical cop drama by innovatively borrowing from conventions of the documentary, the novel, the sitcom and even soap operas (Thompson 1996). *Hill Street Blues* started a trend of 'quality' dramatic television, which helped pave the way for new programs, such as the critically acclaimed *Cagney & Lacey, Moonlighting* and *L.A. Law* during the 1980s, *Homicide* and *NYPD Blue* in the 1990s. More recently, we argue that shows like *The Wire* fall under 'quality' dramatic programming. Thompson (1996) argues that these types of programs develop complicated characters that traverse complex storylines, storylines that can only be told in the serial format of television.

Croteau and Hoynes (2003) argue that much of the allure of television is that it seems real. "One reason why television is often considered to be so ideologically charged is that it relies, almost exclusively, on conventional 'realist' forms of image construction that mask the workings of the camera" (Crouteau and Hoynes 2003, 178). Much of the focus about the "authentic" nature of *The Wire* can be attributed to the intimate knowledge that the creators have of the city and the many years they spent living and working on the streets of Baltimore. The show's creator, David Simon, began writing for *The Baltimore Sun* after graduating from the University of Maryland and stayed on staff for 13 years. One of the head writers, Ed Burns, worked for twenty years on the Baltimore City Police Department and for several years as a Baltimore City teacher. Combined, they have written the majority of *The Wire* episodes.

In a final letter posted on HBO's website for the show, David Simon wrote that *The Wire* "demanded from viewers a delicate, patient consideration and a ridiculous degree of attention to detail" (Simon 2010). Unlike many current cop dramas like *Law & Order* or *CSI* that provide a formulaic routine to each episode, *The Wire* is often credited as constructing a more complex portrait of life on the streets of Baltimore, what Lanahan (2008) has called a "televised novel."

> Nothing ever resolved itself in an hour, and there were no good guys or bad guys. All were individuals constrained by their institutions, driven to compromise between conscience, greed, and ambition. Facets of their characters emerged slowly over time. They spoke in the sometimes-unintelligible vernaculars of their subcultures. All of this made unprecedented demands of viewers and provided an immense reward for those who stuck around [Lanahan 2008, 24].

The complexity of the show is perhaps based in its ability to uncover so many of the social problems that in fact exist in Baltimore. According to the U.S Census Bureau, in 2004, the year that season three aired, almost 24 percent of the Baltimore's residents lived in poverty and more than 78 percent of them were African American, although African Americans only made up two-thirds of the city's residents. Baltimore also had a substantially higher violent crime rate than the rest of the nation. In 2004, the national violent crime rate was 465.5 per 100,000 (Uniform Crime Report 2004), yet Baltimore was four times that rate (1839.4 per 100,000). In 2009, although the poverty rate and the violent crime rate for Baltimore have decreased slightly, the overall trends remain the same[1].

The plot lines throughout the five seasons of the show capture the complexity of these social problems for people living in Baltimore, yet the characters themselves also help to blur the lines between reality and fiction. In season three, for example, we are introduced to the Deacon, who was actually arrested by series co-creator Ed Burns when he worked as a Baltimore police officer (Marshall and Potter 2009). Felicia "Snoop" Pearson plays a character by her own name. She is a Baltimore native, born to two crack addicts, who became a drug dealer and eventually spent eight years in prison for killing someone in self-defense. Many of the characters also represent real life people. For example, co-creator Ed Burns was a police detective who became a city teacher, which is closely mirrored by the character of Roland Pryzbylewski in season four. In this regard, *The Wire* creates an "authenticity that bleeds through the screen" (Marshall and Potter 2009, 10) by incorporating elements of truth into fictional storylines.

Race and Masculinity on Television

The Wire provides not only a snapshot of social problems surrounding poverty, educational inequality and political corruption, but given its predominantly African American male cast, it also provides an important site for the analysis of race and gender. Television has come a long way since controversial programs like *Amos 'n Andy* in 1951. To some degree, the Civil Rights and Women's movements helped inspire change in Hollywood. For example, in the 1980s, *The Cosby Show* was often credited with transcending racial stereotypes of black families and presenting comedic middle class black characters with dignity (Jhally and Lewis 1992), allthough it has also been criticized for ignoring the significance of racism in the lives of African Americans (Watkins 1998). By the 1990s, television shows like *Homicide* also provided audiences with more positive and varied portrayals of African Americans (Mascaro 2004; Mascaro 2005).

In addition to studies of race and television, gender scholars have also begun to pay attention to the role of media in the construction of images. Although studies on gender and the media initially focused on the images of female characters, there has been an emerging field of scholarship related to the portrayal of men and masculinities in the media. As social movements helped improve the number and type of roles for females and historically marginalized characters, the result for male characters has been less progressive. In response to the progress of other social groups, there has been a backlash that has resulted in the proliferation of more hypermasculine images in film and advertisement, as the dominant group (read: white, male) tries to maintain some of its power and control (Katz 1999, 2003; Kimmel 1996; Watkins 2005). In the documentary *Tough Guise*, Jackson Katz (1999) argues that this "crisis of masculinity" is exemplified through popular film characters like Rambo and the Terminator whose depiction of large muscles, big weapons, aggression and violence works to "keep women in their place" (Katz 1999). Henry's (2004) analysis of John Singleton's 2000 remake of *Shaft* demonstrates how recent images of African American men are also becoming more aggressive and violent. For example, in the 2000 remake, Singleton actively removed the (already limited amount of) political acknowledgement of the Black Power Movement that was in the original 1971 release of the film (Henry 2004). Additionally, the original version of the film was built of Shaft's "legend of his sexual prowess" (Henry 2004, 121), yet the remake instead focused almost exclusively on vengeance and aggression (Henry 2004).

Despite burgeoning research on masculinity in film and advertising, there have been fewer studies examining masculinity in television. Scharrer (2001) takes up this topic directly with a study about hypermasculinity on police and detective dramas, utilizing Mosher and Sirkin's (1984) "hypermasculinity inventory" to examine TV images. She found a strong relationship between male characters who displayed the three components of hypermasculinity—callouse sex attitudes, danger as excitement, and violence as manly. "Bad guys" in particular, tended to display more hypermasculine traits than "good guys." Soulleire (2006) found similar results when examining episodes of the World Wresting Entertainment (WWE) programs, *Raw* and *Smackdown*. Similar to Scharrer (2001), she found that "proof of manhood" was displayed through aggression, violence and physicality. Soulleire also found that men displayed their manhood through emotional constraint (i.e., men accept defeat graciously) and through the emasculation of other men, in essence, the "low blow" of wrestling.

This research extends the growing body of research on the construction of race and masculinity in television. This chapter focuses on the male characters of the program that represent police officers, politicians and drug dealers. Our chapter asks how is masculinity constructed through the male characters on *The Wire?* How does the construction of white masculinity compare to black masculinity? How do images of masculinity for characters that comprise "the law" compare to that of "the streets"?[2]

Method

The Wire aired 60 total episodes on HBO, for five seasons, beginning on June 2, 2002, and running until the program finale on March 9, 2008. This research employed purposive sampling in order to focus on the 12 episodes that make up season three. The first episode of season three, "Time after Time," was the 26th episode of the show and aired on September 19, 2004 on *HBO*. The season finale, "Mission Accomplished," was Episode 37 of the program and aired on December 19, 2004. This season was chosen because it represents a "mid-point" of the show and the time period when the show was beginning to receive more national accolades. For example, season three's premiere began just shortly after it received an ASCAP and a Peabody for best television program, and the season went on to gain its first nomination for an Emmy for writing.

Season three focuses on the top drug gang from previous seasons, headed by Avon Barksdale and Stringer Bell, and their rivalry with a relative newcomer to the corner, Marlo Stanfield. As the tension and violence continue to escalate among the corner boys, so too does the pressure by the city police commissioner to lower crime rates. In response to this, Western District Major Bunny Colvin issues a plan that essentially forces all drug dealers into three, relatively unin-habited neighborhoods, an area that becomes known as "Hamsterdam." As long as the drug dealers operate without the use of guns or violence, they essentially get to continue the sale of drugs without repercussions from the police. Although Hamsterdam works to effectively lower crime statistics, when the commissioner and the mayor discover the plan, Hamsterdam is officially dis-mantled.

This paper uses qualitative content analysis to examine all 12 episodes of season three of *The Wire*. In order to provide intercoder reliability, both authors individually watched each episode, took notes, and then conferred on some possible research questions about race, gender and sexuality and its relationship to the street and the law. We individually watched and transcribed every episode, which increased the accuracy and detail of our final transcriptions, and then systematically coded each episode using an open coding method (Berg 1998), before conferring together on our codes. Open coding involves minute, line-by-line analysis of the data, consistent with Glaser and Strauss' (1967) grounded theory approach and the qualitative portion of ethnographic content analysis (Altheide 2004; Jernigan and Dorfman 1996). From open coding, dis-tinct patterns regarding the race and gender of the characters and the storylines began to emerge. Finally, we individually watched each episode a third time and then together modified our open coding with axial coding (Glaser and Strauss 1967), which involved intensive coding around the categories of race and masculinity. As patterns started to emerge from our codes, we searched for negative cases, or cases that might contradict our themes (Berg 1998), in an effort to make sure we were not misreading the data. From this coding process, we developed several analytical themes.

Findings

Male Characters: A Statistical Majority

A quick review of the list of cast members on *The Wire's* official website reveals the particular gendered and raced nature of the program. There are 25 characters listed under "The Law," most of whom are police officers. Twenty-two of the "law" characters are male. Of the three women in this category, one is a white police officer, one is an African American police detective, and one is a white lawyer. About two-thirds of the police officers are white males, although the police commissioner is an African American man. This serves in stark contrast to the list of characters under "The Street." Of the 21 characters featured in this area, all but two are African American and all are male, except one female character, Felicia "Snoop" Pearson. Two white male characters are also part of "The Street:" Walon, a Narcotics Anonymous sponsor, and Maury Levy, the white lawyer for the Barksdale drug gang. Although these do not represent all of the characters on the show, or all of the ones who are present in season three, they do represent an overwhelmingly male cast and a dominant African American presence, particularly for the men on the streets and those listed as the "main" characters.

Hegemonic Masculinity and the Baltimore Police

Power and Control of Bodies and Movement: Connell's book *Gender and Power* (1987) provided the first integrated and systematic theory of hegemonic masculinity. Although there are multiple forms of masculinity and a hierarchy of masculinity, masculinity is not based simply on domination and force, but also on a pattern of hegemony, which includes cultural consent, discursive centrality, institutionalization, and marginalization of alternatives (Connell and Messerschmidt 2005). Hegemonic masculinity embodies "the most honored way of being a man, it required all other men to position themselves in relation to it, and it ideologically legitimated the global subordination of women to men" (Connell and Messerschmidt 2005, 832). This form of masculinity is often associated with athleticism, competiveness, aggression, sexual desirability and virility, independence and self-reliance (Connell 1987; Gershick 1998/2004; Katz 2003; Soulliere 2006). Hegemonic masculinity becomes a symbol of authority and the standard by which all men are judged, albeit most men and boys actually do not obtain this hegemonic masculine ideal. Rather, it just requires men to position themselves in relationship to this normative construct, internalize these ideals, strive to demonstrate some of these hegemonic attributes, as well as judge other men using this construct (Gershick 1998/2004). Hegemonic masculinity is central to the construction of police characters on *The Wire*.

The institution of the police force is one that is inherently marked with power; the power to arrest and essentially control the movement and lives of people, especially that of corner boys, soldiers and gang leaders. The show is ripe with the traditional interrogation scenes, where police officers routinely remind African American men that the police are the ones in control of their lives. Interestingly, although it is a predominantly white police cast, many of the scenes that involve attempts at controlling corner boys involve African American police officers. This is exemplified in the introductory sequence in Episode 31, which includes several scenes that demonstrate the extent to which the police officers will go in their effort to relocate the low level drug dealers to Hamsterdam. The first scene is shot in daylight with an African American uniformed officer slamming a young African American boy against the wall of a building. The boy says "Man, I ain't even dirty. I got rights and shit." The officer replies "go with the one about staying silent" and then slams the boy into the wagon door, as seen below in our transcription of this sequence.

A uniformed African American officer repeatedly pushes a handcuffed African American boy up against a wall as he moves him towards the police wagon. The officer throws the boy in the wagon before another officer shuts the paddy wagon door. The officer then sprays the five or six African American boys with either mace or pepper spray through the steel cage "window." Meanwhile Sergeant Carver (who is African American) stands back and watches. The police wagon is then driven out of the city into a wooded area where the boys are let out and left to find their way back to the city on foot.

In the previous episode, a similar scene took place when Major Bunny Colvin (who is African American) also tries to relocate the drug dealers to a couple of uninhabited neighborhoods. Bodie (one of the drug dealers) asks what will happen if they don't relocate. Major Bunny Colvin replies:

I swear to God, I have over 200 sworn personnel and I will free them all up to brutalize every one of you they can. If you're on my corner in my district, it will not be just a humble or a loitering charge. It will be some Biblical shit that happens to you on the way into that jail wagon. You understand? We will not be playing by any rules that you recognize.

The power that the police have over the corner boys is represented through both dialogue and the positioning of officers in relationship to the men on the streets. This is symbolized in one of the scenes of the first episode of season three. Several police officers arrive on the corner, yielding their guns, before they begin to frisk all of the young African American men on the corner. One young man who carries a backpack, presumably filled with drugs, decides to run. Police attempt to chase him by foot, but the cops are unable to catch him. Sergeant Carver (who is African American) returns to the neighborhood and gets up on top of his car and, in what appears to be a performance for both the officers surrounding him and the men on the streets, he warns, "Hey, listen to me, you little fucking piece of shit! I'm gonna tell you one thing, and one thing only about the Western boys you are playing with! We do not lose! And we do not forget! And we do not give up! Ever! ... we will beat you longer and harder than you beat your own dick" (Episode 26). In this scene, power is positioned symbolically and literally, as the officer yells threats from the top of a car. Yet power is also gained through control of another person's body (i.e., frisking corner boys) and the ability to essentially emasculate another man through the use of sexualized language (i.e., "we will beat you longer and harder than you beat your own dick"). These "Western boys" gain power through the "Western way," a reference made throughout the season, which is as much about the location of this neighborhood in Western Baltimore, as it is symbolic of a way of doing police work.

This particular display of hegemonic masculinity is significant because the aggression and violence is constructed as "legitimate," particularly in contrast to the aggression and violence displayed by the corner boys. Their behavior could be read as a form of "institutionalized group violence" (Henslin 1996, 141) or "governmental deviance" (Ermann and Lundman 1996). This type of aggression and violence is carried out under the authority of legal officials, in this case, under the direction of Major Colvin. It is essentially what Simon (2006) refers to as official violence, which includes "overt acts by the government and subtle ways that the system operates to do harm" (265). "The Western way" is essentially this system in operation as constructed in *The Wire*. In this regard, police brutality is a normative part of the job. This is further demonstrated in a scene in Episode 28 when the police catch the shooter of a fellow police officer (Officer Dozerman). Detective Bunk (African American) brings a beaten and bloody suspect into the precinct interrogation room. McNulty (white) asks if the suspect is the cop shooter.

> Bunk replies, "Yeah, not much to him. But he did that job on the Dozerman kid last week. Gave it up in a full statement." McNulty asks, "Before or after you knocked the shit out of him?" Bunk then reads from the official police report, "Injuries were sustained while patrol officers were affecting pursuit and arrest of aforementioned suspects." McNulty asks, "He was caught in the East side right?" Bunk then says, "Yeah. But the wagon made a stop at the Western District for an unscheduled tune-up. It's dark on that back lot. Western boys mistook him for a piñata."

This scene exemplifies the common knowledge that the Western Way is the accepted way of enforcing the law.

The dynamics of power are not only exhibited between the police and the corner boys, but a hierarchy of power also exists within the police system. A dominant theme in Season three is decreasing the murder rate in Baltimore. The city police commissioner often sits in meetings with his top lieutenants, berating them for not effectively dealing with crime. In Episode 28, the deputy commissioner (who is white) tells the officers, "I don't care how many years you have on this job. If the felony rate doesn't fall, you most certainly will. The gods are fucking you, so you find a way to fuck them back. It's Baltimore, gentlemen, the gods will not save you." Again, sexualized language is used as a method of intimidation. In order to deal with the pressure to get the crime rates down, the Western District's Major Bunny Colvin orchestrates a plan to essentially move all of the drug dealers to largely uninhabited areas of the district, allowing drug deals to happen freely as long as they stay in those areas. The result was a substantial lowering of crime rates everywhere else in the district. By the end of the season, when the commissioner learns the real reason behind the falling crime rates, he demonstrates who really is boss. In Episode 37, he jeopardizes Bunny Colvin's retirement plans to work as a security guard at Johns Hopkins University by going to the Provost and disclosing Colvin's failed attempt at "Hamsterdam," the area that essentially came to represent the legalization of drugs.

Throughout the season, the hierarchy of the district is enforced in similar ways that control of the corner boys is garnered — through intimidations, threats and control over the freedom of movement. In Episode 31, Lieutenant Daniels (African American) reminds some of his officers in his squad of his power.

Daniels asks, "What is my rank, Detective Greggs?" No one responds. He then yells, "My rank!" Detective Kima Greggs responds, "Lieutenant." He then faces Detective McNulty and asks, "What is my rank McNulty?" When McNulty doesn't reply, he yes, "If you can't remember that much than you can go the hell back to narcotics and you can go back to whatever unit will have you. Now get the fuck out of my office."

It is not surprising that by the end of the season, Lieutenant Daniels is effectively promoted to Major Daniels. This is based, in part, on his ability to successfully control the movement of bodies (physically and symbolically) of the corner boys to "Hamsterdam," which lowers the crime rates, but also to control to actions of his lower ranked officers, through demotions out of his division and into other units.

Sexual Conquest and "The Law": Masculinity among police officers is tied to sexual conquest, another key attribute to hegemonic masculinity (Connell and Messerschmidt 2005). This is presented through both conversations about sex and sexuality, as well as the sexual behavior of the police officers. For example, in Episode 27, Detectives Carver and "Herc" engage in a rather lengthy conversation that transpired over several scenes about whether or not Herc would be willing to have sex with another man if it meant he could have sex with the Olsen twins (young celebrity actresses). Concerned about the implications of homosexuality, Herc questions Carver about the nature of the sexual act with another man, asking, "I'm pitching, not catching, right?" Carver replies, "No problem." With this assurance Herc spends the remainder of the episode deciding on which man. After much consideration he finally tells Carver his choice is Gus Triandos, the Baltimore Orioles' catcher. This disclosure of an actual person provides an avenue for his fellow officers to harass him, thus demonstrating how masculinity is strictly tied to heterosexuality. Even if the end result is to conquer two young attractive celebrities, crossing the boundary with homosexual acts is never an acceptable way to do it.

The sexual behavior of the officers often coincides with drinking at a local bar. In the same episode that Carver and Herc talk about "getting both twins," Officers McNulty and Bunk end the workday sitting at the local bar. As they glance over to a white woman at the jukebox McNulty says, "My turn, Bunk," referring to the woman. In what appears to be a scripted ritual of picking up women, Officer Bunk goes over and annoys the woman, and then McNulty sweeps in to "save" her, essentially "winning" the girl for the night. In Episode 29, a similar scene takes place, but this time, the characters refer to "number two," as they have several pre-scripted "pick up" lines. This time, Bunk gets to take the woman home. In this regard, part of the sexual conquest involves supporting others in their drive for a sexual conquest, "taking one for the team," so to speak, so your friend can pick up a woman at the bar. Interestingly, scenes of sexual behavior that involve police officers overwhelming involve them cheating on a spouse or partner. This is personified by Detective McNulty's adulterous character. In one scene, he's with his soon-to-be ex-wife at their children's school's open house when he begins a flirtatious interaction with Theresa D'A-gastino, a political campaign strategist for a Mayoral candidate. He ends up leaving his family at the open house to go to a hotel with Theresa. Other scenes that involve explicit sex acts among officers tend to involve unfaithful behavior as well. For example, Lieutenant Daniels is seen having sex with the assistant district attorney before he is officially divorced, as is Detective Kima Gregg who is seen cheating on her lesbian partner, Cheryl, shortly after Cheryl has a baby. (McNulty reinforces this behavior by covering for Kima when Cheryl calls looking for her.) In contrast, two other main characters, Detectives Carver and Herc, although they are shown in conversations that degrade women, do not cheat on their partners and are never shown in any explicit sex scenes.

Bars serve as a backdrop not just for sexual conquests, but also provide an avenue for a particular type of male bonding. The police officers often gather at Kavanagh Bar, a stereotypical Irish pub. In Episode 28, they are there for the wake of a fellow police officer, Ray Cole, who is laid out on the pool table with a bottle of Irish whiskey in one hand and a cigar in the other. As the officers drink in honor of their fallen friend, their drinking bonds them together while the bar and the wake provide a legitimate space for being emotional, something that is ultimately not part of hegemonic masculinity. While this scene represents a moment where perhaps hegemonic masculinity is being challenged, the scene that follows shortly after outside the bar minimizes this moment of resistance.

> Jimmy and Bunk have stepped outside the bar and in a drunken stupor are "waxing poetic" about the meaning of life. While Bunk sits on the curb, Jimmy is leaning on the fire hydrant in a position implying that he has just thrown up; however, they are both still drinking. Homicide detective Ed Norris comes out of the bar with a shot in both hands. He hands one shot to Jimmy and says "Wake up and die right, you cunts" and then hands the second shot to Bunk. Norris then proceeds to throw up while Bunk and Jimmy drink the shots.

The use of the word "cunt" implies that the men are being too emotional about Cole's death. In many ways throughout the season, alcohol is used as a way to help mask emotions and the problems that these officers face in their life — troubled marriages, low incomes, seeing death on the job, cases they can't solve. Although the police officers are constructed as being in a powerful position in the show, at moments when they feel like they might be losing control they disguise their fears and frustrations with alcohol, which often involves reasserting their masculinity whether by calling their fellow officers derogatory names or by picking up random women.

Hegemonic Masculinity, Sexual Conquest, and "The Streets"

There is also a dominant theme about sexual conquest among the men of "the streets," yet few of these men have any kind of committed relationships. Although women are decidedly absent from the streets, they are plentiful in scenes about the nightlife and are often used as objects of reward, particularly for getting out of prison. For example, in Episode 29, drug dealer Bodie takes ex-con Cutty to a party where countless topless and naked women casually strut through the hallways of the house. Bodie asks Cutty, "You still like females, don't you?" which seems to reference a stereotype about homosexual behavior that takes place in prisons. Cutty responds by following a girl down the hallway into a private room where a second woman is waiting for them.

Sexual conquest is part of hegemonic masculinity, yet is also tied to the "code of the streets" (Anderson 1999). Kubrin (2005), in a study of gangsta rap lyrics, argues that this code constructs a particular type of black masculinity that is centered on sexual conquest, materialism, nihilism, respect, violence and vengeance. A combination of materialism and sexual conquest can best be demonstrated through the scripting of gang leaders Stringer Bell and Avon Barksdale. In Episode 30, Avon Barksdale heads to the strip club he owns, "looking for some skirts," after being released from prison. Stringer Bell, who has been dabbling in real estate development as a way to bring legitimate money into the mix, has invited some investors there to meet Avon, which interrupts his ability to pick up any women. Afterwards, Stringer insists that Avon needs to come with him and Avon reluctantly agrees. They arrive at a luxury waterfront condominium, complete with a Lincoln Navigator in the basement garage. Stringer tells Avon, "This is all for you. In your name too. This piece of paper makes it legit." Avon soon switches the conversation back to sexual conquest, "Look man, I've been locked down...." So Stringer leaves, yet quickly returns with a knock on the door, saying, "I left something." As Avon opens the door, two provocatively dressed women enter. The overall scene epitomizes the value of material success and sexual rewards for the men of the "streets."

"Code of the Street" and Respect

Another perhaps more important "code of the street" that is intricately connected to black masculinity is respect.[3] Anderson (1999) argued that a lack of jobs, racism, inadequate school systems, lack of public services, and the growing drug trade have all contributed to real problems of crime and violence in urban communities. One of the consequences of all of this is a particular street culture, or "codes of the street" that govern public behavior (Anderson 1999, 33). Central to the code of the street is the issue of respect; being treated right and being given the deference that one deserves. "For many inner city youths, manhood and respect are two sides of the same coin; physical and psychological well-being are inseparable, and both require a sense of control, of being in charge" (Anderson 1999, 91). Gaining respect may sometimes involve the use of aggression and violence especially when competing for scarce resources.

Loyalty of Soldiers: Respect on the streets centers around the gang leaders, whether it be Avon Barksdale, Stringer Bell, Marlo Stanfield or Omar Little. Within the hierarchy of gangs, leaders demand unwavering respect from the corner boys and soldiers. "A soldier" is the term given to the men closest to and most loyal to the gang leaders. They enforce the gang leaders' demands to protect their corners, whether by punishing disloyal corner boys or taking out the competition. Corner boys are at the low end of the hierarchy, doing whatever they have to in order to move product on the streets, in hopes of one day rising in the ranks to become a soldier. Given the hierarchy of the gang, corner boys must demonstrate respect for not just the leaders, but also for the soldiers. In Episode 27, Cutty, a former soldier who has been in prison for the last 14 years, meets up with Slim Charles on a corner of his old neighborhood. Cutty is frustrated that a phone number he was given by Avon in prison is no longer working — he is unaware that drug dealers now use disposable cell phones to avoid the wiretap. Bodie, a young drug dealer who has never met Cutty before, responds somewhat arrogantly, "Don't you know that?" Slim Charles berates Bodie, "Respect, respect! Don't you know who you are talking to?" He then gives Cutty a new number and says, "Give Shamrock a call and tell him a soldier finally came to camp." The next episode is actually titled "Dead soldiers," which involves a gang shootout that leaves two Barksdale gang members and Tosha, one of Omar's crew, dead in the streets. Omar is the leader of a small group comprised of Tosha, Kimmy, and Dante, intent on disrupting the Barksdale monopoly on the drug trade. Part of being a good "soldier" involves not questioning the leader's authority. In Episode 28, when Tosha asks Omar, "Why do we have to keep up with the Barksdales?" His response is simply "Because."

The use of "soldier" is particularly telling. It provides a metaphor for someone who is in the military — loyal, patriotic, follows orders, adheres to a hierarchy, willing to serve and die for their leaders. The writers integrate war, in general, as a metaphor for life on the streets. In Episode 31, Bubbles (who is working as an informant for the police) tells McNulty and Gregory that Marlo killed two of Barksdales people up on the corner. "Marlo is flying his own colors. West side is about to become all Baghdad and shit." In Episode 35, gunshots go off as two boys rob a convenience store. Snoop pulls up to get some of her gang members and says, "What the fuck you're doing on the streets. Don't you know there's a war going on?" In Episode 33, gang leader Avon, who just got shot by one of Marlo's gang members, says, "We're going to see who has the bigger war chest," insinuating that he plans to get back at Marlo. It is clear that this "soldier" mentality is indoctrinated early on. There is not a single episode in the season that does not prominently feature a variety of images of young Black men, teenagers, and even children willing to work the corners selling drugs during a "war" as good, loyal "soldiers."

Interestingly, the theme of respect is also about adherence to a type of moral conduct that is understood on the streets. When Stringer Bell orders his soldiers to kill Omar while he's taking his grandmother to church on Sunday, the soldier questions this decision: "It's church day, String, Sunday morning you know" (Episode 34)—clearly Stringer is breaking the moral code of no violence on a church day. Nonetheless, Stringer orders the hit. The shooting is a failed attempt, and Omar is able to get his grandmother into a taxi with only her hat, or "crown," being hit. Barksdale's soldier, Slim Charles, again questions the decision to shoot Omar on Sunday.

> On a Sunday morning, y'all try to hit a nigga when he taking his wrinkle-ass grandmas to pray. And y'all don't hit the nigga, neither. All y'all kill is grandma's crown? (holding Omar's grandma's hat).... Ain't enough y'all done violated the Sunday morning truce. No! I'm standing here holding a torn-up church crown of a bona fide colored lady. Do you know what a colored lady is? Not your moms, for sure. 'Cause if they was that y'all would've known better than that bullshit. Y'all trifling with Avon Barksdale reputation here. You know that?

Omar reiterates this "Sunday morning truce" sentiment. "And, for as long as I been grown, once a month, I been with her on a church Sunday. Telling myself ain't no need to worry 'cause there ain't nobody in this city that low down to disrespect a Sunday morning." Obviously, Stringer Bell has broken this code of respect.

Guns as Symbolic Power: In Kubrin's (2005) study of codes in gangsta rap lyrics, respect was the most commonly referenced theme and this code was often connected to violence as an avenue to gain respect. In particular, rap songs would project a tough image, where exerting force was done in order to gain respect and guns were constructed as an "accessory" of the ghetto. Violence is seen as an acceptable way to enforce social control on the street. It can be used to respond to challenges, to resist victimization or to fight for "justice" to deter future assaults.

The willingness to use a gun to kill someone is often tied to issues of disrespect. For example, in Episode 34, one gang member kills someone who simply "laughed at his shoes." In Episode 26, Bubbles, who is a well-known heroin addict who sells t-shirts and other random items out of a shopping cart, is walking down the street with another homeless man, Johnny, when they accidently push his cart into drug dealer Marlo's SUV. Marlo's soldier, Fruit, gets out of the SUV and puts his gun to Johnny's head, but since Marlo has somewhere to go, rather than shoot them, Fruit takes their pants and makes them walk down the street half-naked. In this regard, men use guns to humiliate other men on the streets.

Being able to use a gun effectively to intimate and harm is intricately tied to manhood. In Episode 26 Avon arranges a meeting with Cutty, who is scheduled to be released from prison, to offer him a package of drugs to help him get a new start on the outside. Avon asks Cutty if he is "still a soldier." Cutty does not reply and just walks away, leading Avon to question if "the joint might have broken him." Avon's soldier replies "Boss, you talking about a homie who walked up and shot Elijah Davis. Broad daylight at Pennsie and Gould. Dude picked up a phone, called 911 and said 'I just shot a nigga. Come get him.' That dude ain't breaking." Again, anyone willing to use a gun to brazenly kill someone adheres to the codes of the street.

Cutty does eventually reach out to the Barksdale gang and becomes one of Avon's soldiers. In Episode 31, Cutty and Slim Charles seek revenge on one of Marlo's soldiers, Fruit. Cutty has Fruit in his sights and could have made the shot, but instead he hesitates and ultimately lowers his gun and allows Fruit to run away. Later Cutty and Slim Charles meet with Avon to discuss the shooting.

> SLIM CHARLES: We got one of the two of them motherfuckers, you know?
>
> AVON: You mean, you motherfuckers come strolling in here all walking tall and shit.
>
> SLIM CHARLES: Yo, B, man I'm saying, man we was blazing on them dudes. Man, you know what I'm saying? Just got in the heat, man. We was blazing, though. It was like...
>
> AVON INTERRUPTS: All right, all right. Relax, man. I already heard. Go sit down. I'm not tweaking behind none of this. That's one less motherfucker that's breathing than was yesterday. You know what I'm saying? So we all good. But I'm surprised at you (to Cutty), though, man. Shit didn't get by you, back when.
>
> SLIM CHARLES DEFENDS CUTTY: Wasn't my man's fault, man. I unloaded on the young 'un too soon, man. Gave him enough room to buck and run.

At this point, Cutty interjects, confessing to Avon that he had the shot but "couldn't squeeze the trigger." Avon still offers to put him back on the corner. Cutty replies, "I ain't making myself clear. The game ain't in me no more." In this scene, Cutty's inability to kill Fruit could be constructed as him being less of a soldier, less of a man, but because he stands up to Avon and tells him the truth, he is able to maintain Avon's respect. Avon accepts his desire to get out of the game, telling him that they are "straight." He shakes his hand, hugs him and allows him to leave. After he is gone, Slim Charles remarks that Cutty was "a man in his time," yet Avon corrects him, stating, "He a man today. He a man." This provides a somewhat interesting twist on masculinity that is not prevalent throughout most of the show. At this moment, being a man is still about respecting the leader (Avon), but he is respecting him by being honest that he can no longer be a soldier.

Revenge: Another strong theme of *The Wire* highlights the code of the street that ties black masculinity to revenge. Revenge is often depicted on the streets in a moralistic light because it is conceived as a legitimate form of justice. This is perhaps best exemplified when Stringer Bell is willing to kill his partner Avon's nephew, D'Angelo, who he fears is going to turn on them when he goes to trial. Stringer orchestrates his murder in prison, at first making it look like a suicide. He later confesses to Avon that he killed D'Angelo, defending his decision as something he did to protect Avon.

> Yo, man, I took that shit off you, and put it on me, man, because that motherfucker was out of pocket with that shit! Twenty years above his fucking head. He flip, man,

they got you and me and fucking Briana! No fucking way, man. Hell no! Now, I know you're family. You loved that nigga. But you want to talk that "blood is thicker than water" bullshit take that shit somewhere else, nigga! That motherfucker would have taken down the whole fucking show starting with you, killer! He was fucking everything and everybody! [Episode 33].

Revenge takes center stage in another dominant storyline that involves the Barksdale gang and rival Marlo. Season three begins with the demolition of the Towers, housing projects that once brought a lot of business to the Barksdale gang. The gang is now looking to get more territory on the corners, which includes some of Marlo's corners. Stringer Bell thinks that all of the drug dealers can benefit from joining a drug co-op, but Marlo refuses to even talk about the possibility of this with any of Stringer's soldiers. On Stringer's orders, Bodie sets up shop on the corner opposite of Marlo (Episode 27). Marlo tells Bodie to "walk back up there and pack up your people. I'm being a gentleman about it for the moment." In Episode 28, after Barksdale's corner boys are holding strong on what Marlo sees as his corners, Marlo says to Fruit, "I just want them moved. Take the young'uns with you. Give them a workout." Fruit, along with seven other soldiers, take out Barksdale's corner boys using baseball bats. The scene ends with seven of Barksdale's boys lying in the streets, immobilized. This fuels Avon's insistence on getting revenge on Marlo, an insistence that he carries throughout the season.

Women are also used in the pursuit of revenge. In Episode 33, Avon uses a woman to seduce Marlo in an effort to set him up. The woman plans a date with Marlo at the Lake Trout restaurant with no intention of meeting him there. Instead, the Barksdale gang members, including Avon, stake out the restaurant. But one of Marlo's soldiers, Snoop, discovers their car and alerts Marlo, which gives him the advantage. Marlo then opens fire on the car, injuring Avon in the process. Now Avon is even more determined to get revenge, but again, Stringer Bell tries to talk him out of it.

> Stringer says to Avon, "War, man, we past this bullshit. Man, you don't give this shit up you're gonna turn everything we built to shit." Avon replies, "You know what the difference is between me and you? I bleed red, you bleed green. What you been building for us? Huh? You know what, I look at you these days, you know what I see? I see a man without a country. Not hard enough for this, right here. And maybe, just maybe not smart enough for them out there.

Masculinity is tied with being "hard," which includes seeing violence and revenge as a legitimate form of justice. In many ways, Marlo and Avon share in their adherence to this code in a way that Stringer Bell tries to transcend. To further prove this, Marlo exacts revenge on the woman used by Avon as bait by shooting her twice in the chest and then once in the mouth (Episode 35).

Like Marlo, Avon is also inflexible when it comes to adhering to the code of revenge. In Episode 36, hitman Brother Mouzone returns to Baltimore. He goes to Avon to let him know that he is in town to seek revenge on Stringer

Bell, who attempted to have him killed in the previous season. Although Avon and Stringer Bell have a close relationship built on mutual loyalty, Avon still harbors resentment about Stringer's order to have his nephew D'Angelo murdered. It is this loyalty that prevents him from ordering a hit on or killing Stringer Bell himself, but Brother Mouzone's return provides him an opportunity to get justice. In this instance, the "code of the street" that legitimizes revenge becomes more important the code of loyalty. Therefore, Avon does nothing to stop the murder of his long-time partner Stringer Bell.

There are some challenges to the "code" of revenge, although most are rather fleeting. "Proposition Joe" tries to moderate some kind of peace agreement between Marlo and Avon (Episode 34), by trying to convince Marlo to join his co-op of drug dealers, but Marlo declines. After partner Tosha's death, Omar seriously considered walking away from "the game" rather than seeking revenge on her murderer. It was not until Barksdale's gang shot at his grandmother on a Sunday church morning that he abandoned this decision and reverted back to the code of the street.

Conclusion

Oliver (2006) argues that "street socialization" is about both the physical location and the social function of the street that creates a particular worldview (ideology, values, norms) about manhood roles and in particular, black masculinity. In *The Wire*, this particular image of black masculinity is indoctrinated early, with images of young African American boys emulating the soldiers, whether it is kids in the streets "playing Omar" (one of the gang leaders), or one of the young boys being proud of his first attempt at using a gun. "A particular type of black masculinity—one defined mainly by an urban aesthetic, a nihilistic attitude and aggressive posturing—has made its way into the cultural mainstream in the last two decades" (Henry 2004, 119). The commercial success of these images used to be limited to gangsta rap in the late 1980s and early 1990s, which worked to promote and sustain moral panics about crime and violence, fueling surveillance and policing, containment and punishment of Black men (Gray 1995, 402). According to Watkins (1998), these images have moved beyond just the world of gangsta rap, in part due to the incorporation of rap music into films, especially commercially successful films such as *New Jack City* (1991), *Boyz N the Hood* (1991), and *Menace II Society* (1993). Similar representations of black masculinity are depicted in *The Wire* and may be given more credence due to the program's claims to authenticity.

The use of violence as a way of proving ones manhood is most certainly not limited to black masculinity in *The Wire*. Throughout the season, both black and white police officers use physical force to control the bodies of the corner boys, seek revenge for a fallen officer in the same way gang members seek revenge of their fallen soldiers, and use aggression to instill respect. In this regard, we argue that the "code of the street" (Anderson 1999) is something that is not limited to poor inner city Black males. The code of the street constructs a particular type of masculinity that is tied to respect, loyalty, sexual conquest, aggression, violence, revenge and competition for scarce resources that on *The Wire* is performed by both "the street" and "the law." The difference is that representations of Black males invoking the "codes of the street" are constructed as violent whereas the police officers enactment of the "codes of the street" is too often constructed as legitimate police procedure. We argue that both in fact need to be understood as forms of violence, which work to sustain very narrow representations of masculinity.

This research is not without limitations. Future research could analyze *The Wire* in its entirety, rather than just season three, and certainly focus on the representations of women more specifically. In general, more analysis is needed of gender, race and masculinity in other TV portrayals. For example, to what extent might the "code of the street" be present in medical or family dramas, or even sitcoms? Additionally, this research focuses on the social construction of race and masculinity, which does not help us understand the dynamic and complex interpretation of these images by the public. Future studies could benefit by looking at how audiences interpret these mediated messages and how these messages help facilitate a particular understanding of social groups, communities and individual identity.

NOTES

1. In 2009, the overall poverty rate for Baltimore fell to 20.98 percent, but African Americans continued to make up 70 percent of those residents who lived in poverty. Additionally, although the violent crime rate also fell to 1513 per 100,000, Baltimore still has more than three times the violent crime rate of the nation (429.4 per 100,000).
2. We use "the law" and "the street" because these are the categories that HBO assigned to the characters on their website for the program.
3. The importance of respect as a code on the street was first articulated by Anderson in his seminal work about Black men living in Philadelphia, *Code of the Street: Decency, Violence and the Moral Life of the Inner City* (1999[0]).

REFERENCES

Altheide, David. 2004. "Consuming Terrorism." *Symbolic Interaction* 27(3): 289–308.
Anderson, Elijah. 1999. *Code of the Street: Decency, Violence and the Moral Life of the Inner City.* New York: W.W. Norton.
Berg, Bruce L. 1998. *Qualitative Research Methods for the Social Sciences,* 3d ed. Boston: Allyn & Bacon.
Connell, R.W. 1987. *Gender and Power.* Sydney: Allen and Unwin.
Connell, R.W., and James W. Messerschmidt. 2005. "Hegemonic Masculinity: Rethinking the Concept." *Gender & Society* 19(6): 829–859.
Croteau, David, and William Hoynes. 2003. *Media/Society: Industries, Images and Audiences,* 3d ed. Thousand Oaks, CA: Pine Forge Press.
Ermann, M. David, and Richard J. Lundman. 1996. "Corporate and Governmental Deviance: Origins, Patterns, and Reactions." In M. David Ermann and Richard J. Lundman (eds.), *Corporate and Governmental Deviance: Problems of Organizational Behavior in Contemporary Society,* 5th ed. 3–44. New York: Oxford University Press.

Gamson, William A., David Croteau, William Hoynes and Theodore Sasson. 1992. "Media Images and the Social Construction of Reality." *Annual Review of Sociology* 18: 373–393.

Gerschick, Thomas J. 2004. "Sisyphus in a Wheelchair: Physical Disabilities and Masculinity." In D. M. Newman and J. O'Brien (eds.), *Sociology: Exploring the Architecture of Everyday Life, 5th ed.* 114–127. Thousand Oaks, CA: Sage. (Originally published in 1998).

Glaser, Barney, and Anselm Strauss 1967. *The Discovery of Grounded Theory: Strategies for Qualitative Research.* Piscataway, NJ: Aldine Transaction.

Gray, Herman. 1995. "Black Masculinity and Visual Culture." *Callaloo* 18(2): 401–405.

Henry, Matthew. 2004. "'He is a "Bad Mother *$%@!#': 'Shaft'" and Contemporary Black Masculinity." *African American Review* 38(1): 119–126.

Henslin, James M. 1996. *Social Problems,* 4th ed. Upper Saddle River, NJ: Prentice Hall.

Jernigan, D., and Lori Dorfman. 1996. "Visualizing America's Drug Problems: An Ethnographic Content Analysis of Illegal Drug Stories on the Nightly News." *Contemporary Drug Problems* 23(2): 169–196.

Jhally, Sut, and Justin Lewis. 1992. *Enlightened Racism:* The Cosby Show, *Audiences, and the Myth of the American Dream.* San Francisco, CA: Westview Press.

Kamalakar, Anand. 2003. "HBO: Get Wired." *The World & I* 18(6): 68–73.

Katz, Jackson. 1999. Executive Producer and Director: Sut Jhally. *Tough Guise: Violence, Media & the Crisis of Masculinity.* Northampton, Massachusetts: Media Education Project. DVD.

_____. 2003. "Advertising and the Construction of Violent White Masculinity: From Eminem to Clinique for Men." In G. Dines and J.M. Humez (eds.), *Gender, Race, and Class in Media,* 2d ed: 349–358. Thousand Oaks, CA: Sage.

Kimmel, Michael. 1996. *Manhood in America: A Cultural History.* New York: The Free Press.

Kubrin, C. 2005. "Gangstas, Thugs, and Hustlas: Identity and the Code of the Street in Rap Music." *Social Problems* 52(3): 360–378.

Lanahan, Lawrence. 2008. "Secrets of the City: What *The Wire* reveals about urban journalism." *Columbia Journalism Review* January/February: 23–31.

Marshall, C.W., and Tiffany, Potter. (2009). "I am the American Dream': Modern Urban Tragedy and the Borders of Fiction." In T. Potter and C.W. Marshall (eds.), *The Wire: Urban Decay and American Television:* 1–14. New York: Continuum.

Mascaro, Thomas A. 2004. "Shades of Black on Homicide: Life on the Street: Progress in Portrayals of African American Men." *Journal of Popular Film & Television* 32(1): 10–20.

_____. 2005. "Shades of Black on Homicide: Life on the Street: Advances and Retreats in Portrayals of African American Women." *Journal of Popular Film & Television* 33(2): 56–72.

Mosher, D.L., and M. Sirkin 1984. "Measuring a Macho Personality Constellation." *Journal of Research in Personality* 18: 150–163

Oliver, William. 2006. "'The Streets': An Alternative Black Male Socialization Institution.'" *Journal of Black Studies* 36(6): 918–937.

Scharrer, Erica. 2001. "Tough Guys: The Portrayal of Hypermasculinity and Aggression in Televised Police Drama." *Journal of Broadcasting & Electronic Media* 45(4): 615–634.

Simon, David R. 2006. *Elite Deviance,* 8th ed. Boston: Pearson.

_____. 2010. "A Final Thank You to *The Wire* Fans From the Show Creator, David Simon." Retrieved from http://www.hbo.com/the-wire/index.html#/the-wire/inside/interviews/article/finale-letter-from-david-simon.html.

Soulliere, Danielle. 2006. "Wrestling with Masculinity: Messages about Manhood in the WWE." *Sex Roles* 55: 1–11.

Thompson, Robert J. 1996. *Television's Second Golden Age: From Hill Street Blues to ER.* Syracuse: Syracuse University Press.

Tyree, J.M. 2008. "*The Wire*: The Complete Fourth Season." *Film Quarterly* 61(3): 32–38.

Uniform Crime Report. 2004, 2009. Retrieved from http://www.fbi.gov/ucr/cius2006/index.html.

U.S. Census Bureau. 2004. "2004 American Community Survey" and "2009 American Community Survey." Retrieved from *http://www.census.gov/acs/www/index.html.*

Watkins, S. Craig. 1998. *Hip Hop Culture and the Production of Black Cinema.* Chicago: University of Chicago Press.

_____. 2005. *Hip Hop Matters: Politics, Pop Culture and the Struggle for the Soul of a Movement.* Boston: Beacon Press.

Zurawick, David. 2006. "David Simon has Novel Ideas about 'Wire.'" *Baltimore Sun,* September 10, 2006. *www.baltimoresun.com.*

Fictionalized Women in Trouble: An Exploration of the Television Crime Drama CSI: Miami

SARAH RIZUN

Today almost everyone in North America is exposed to some form of mass media. Television is an especially popular medium. As noted by Surette (2007, 13): "Into the 1990s television viewing ranked as the third most time-consuming activity (after sleep, work, or school) for Americans." Moreover, since its inception, television has relied on crime and violence as key audience-attracting material, and this reliance has increased dramatically in recent years (Chesney-Lind 1999, 130; Surette 2007, 13). In fact, crime and violence now receives the most widespread coverage on television (Surette 2007, 13).

Televised crime dramas appear to be especially appealing to the general public, as reflected in the recent proliferation of such programs. To name just a few, current and recent crime dramas include: *Law and Order* (1990), *Law and Order: Special Victims Unit* (1999), *Law and Order: Criminal Intent* (2001), *Law and Order: Los Angeles* (2010); *CSI: Crime Scene Investigation* (2000), *CSI: Miami* (2002), *CSI: New York* (2004), *CSI: Trilogy* (2009); *NCIS: Naval Criminal Investigative Service* (2003), *NCIS: Los Angeles* (2009); *Criminal Minds* (2005), and *Criminal Minds: Suspect Behavior* (2011). On the CBS website (2010), *CSI: Miami* is described as "a drama that follows a South Florida team of forensic investigators who use both cutting-edge scientific methods and old-fashioned police work to solve crimes." It is one of the most popular crime dramas presently on air. Actually, it was labeled by *Radio Times Magazine* as the world's most popular television series, based on a 2005 survey of 20 countries that found the program to rank in the top 10 viewing charts more frequently than any other (BBC News 2006). *CSI: Miami* thus provides a good example of the public's and entertainment media's obsession with crime.

The prevalence of crime dramas on television no doubt reflects the general public's interest in issues of crime and violence. Importantly, however, media attention does not simply reflect public perceptions and attitudes toward crime, but also helps shape them (Dye 2005, 41–42; Surette 2007, 210–12). Moreover, the mass media can have a strong influence upon the development of criminal justice and public policies (Dye 2005, 32–34, 40–42; Surette 2007, 213–21). How the creators of popular television programs such as *CSI: Miami* choose to portray crime, violence, and criminals can therefore have very "real world" consequences.

When criminalized women are the target of media attention, the potential effects can be especially disastrous. Literature that investigates the portrayal of women and their crimes in television and film indicates that they are represented in predominantly negative, erroneous, and stereotypical ways (Chesney-Lind 1999; Faith 1993a, 255–73; Faith 1993b; Faith 2005, 77–82; Humphries 2009). It is imperative to recognize that the overwhelming majority of criminalized women already face a great degree of ignorance, prejudice, and marginalization in the real world. Thus, the potential effect of egregious media representations upon public perceptions and policies is to exacerbate and reinforce the inequity that this segment of the population already experiences (Faith 1993a, 270–71; Faith 1993b, 198; Faith 2005, 82).

Despite the proliferation and popularity of crime dramas such as *CSI: Miami* and the potential consequences of how they portray criminalized women, there is a dire lack of literature on the topic. This paper seeks to address this area of neglect.[2] An audio-visual content analysis of *CSI: Miami* was conducted in order to explore how the program represents criminalized women and their crimes. This report will investigate the themes that emerged. The findings will be considered in relationship to literature that examines the portrayal of female perpetrators in television and film. In addition, the results will be compared and contrasted with the "real world" experiences and circumstances of women who violate the law, as indicated by the relevant research. Potential implications of the ways in which criminalized women are depicted in *CSI: Miami* will also be discussed. Finally, this paper will conclude with a call for a socially responsible approach to media production.

Literature Review

Physical Masculinization Versus Idealization

The literature suggests that television and film tend to produce images of criminalized women as either physically masculinized or idealized. For example, Faith (1993a, 256–58, 260–62, 270–71; 1993b) found that criminalized women are frequently presented as physically masculine and unattractive; these fictionalized female perpetrators are commonly presented as lesbians as well. On the other hand, criminalized women are sometimes portrayed in fictional accounts as "white, privileged, rail-thin, drop-dead beaut[ies]" (Chesney-Lind 1999, 120). Faith (1993a, 265) labels these female characters "super-bitch killer beauties: .... evil [women] behind the sweet and/or sexy and tantalizing demeanor."

Masculinized and idealized images of female perpetrators both reflect gendered stereotypes and demonstrate the presence of androcentricism and heterosexism in media production (Faith 1993a, 270). As stated by Reinharz (1992, 145): "Some texts may, in fact, 'reflect' conditions, but others (e.g., television and movies) are thought to 'mediate' experience, i.e., to reflect those who produced it, such as the culture industries." Surely, few criminalized women in the "real world" resemble the masculinized or idealized images produced in television and film. Like women in the general population, women in trouble with the law represent an ordinary range of physical appearances and cannot be reduced to any given type (Chesney-Lind 1999, 120; Faith 1993a, 258; Faith 1993b, 185).

Race and Class

When television and film producers decide to represent criminalized women as racial minorities or poor, they usually deploy disparaging racist and classist stereotypes (Faith 1993a, 259; Faith 1993b, 189; Faith 2005, 79). For example, these characters are typically portrayed as more dangerous than their white, middle-class counterparts (Faith 1993a, 259). For the most part, however, "virtually every minority group has been excluded ... from a significant screen presence" (Faith 2005, 79). In fact, Surette (2007, 59) has observed that "the typical criminal portrayed in the entertainment media is ... white and of high social status." The exclusion of racial minorities and the poor in television and film, and their stereotypical and unfavorable portrayals when they are included, likely reflects the dominance of white, upper/middle-class interests in media production.

The underrepresentation of socioeconomically marginalized perpetrators in entertainment media is highly inconsistent with reality. As pointed out by Owen (1999, 85), the profiles of women in American prisons

> describe a population that is poor, that is disproportionately African American and Hispanic, and that has little education and few job skills. This population is primarily composed of young women who are single heads of households; the majority of those who are imprisoned (80 percent) have at least two children.

Further, it goes without saying that these women do not resemble the derogatory stereotypes that media producers often rely on when they do portray racial minorities and the poor.

The Liberation Hypothesis

Not long after the emergence of second wave feminism, an idea arose that claimed

> as the modern women's movement has resulted in women gaining increasing equality with men in such legitimate contexts as education, occupations, family, politics, and

the economy, women have come to resemble men in the illegitimate or criminal context as well [Boritch 1997, 62].

The assumption was that "liberated" women would increasingly become like men and, therefore, would increasingly commit the serious and violent crimes traditionally perpetrated by men.

This assumption, however, is entirely unsubstantiated. According to official statistics, "most of the increase in female criminality has been in traditionally female crimes such as shoplifting, welfare fraud, and passing bad [checks]" (Boritch 1997, 65). Plus, such offenses are overwhelmingly committed by the most marginalized — not liberated — women. Indeed, the context surrounding women's crime and violence continues to reflect gendered inequities (this context will be elaborated upon later in this chapter). Nonetheless, despite the liberation thesis being "definitively refuted by subsequent research ... the popularity of this perspective, at least in the public mind, is apparently undiminished" (Chesney-Lind 1999, 116–17).

Media producers have played a central role in promoting the erroneous image of the independent, liberated woman as criminal, violent, and dangerous (Chesney-Lind 1999, 116–20; Faith 1993a, 256, 265–66; Faith 1993b, 182–84). For example, Chesney-Lind (1997, 131) has observed that "the overarching media construction of a violent woman is a woman masculinized by some form of emancipation." In a similar vein, in her discussion of "super-bitch killer beauties," Faith (1993a, 265) describes the image constructed by television and film of "the beautiful, solitary, ominous, male-identified, childless, pathologically obsessive woman, 'liberated' in anti-feminist terms, who would take what she wants at any cost," even if it involves monstrous acts of violence.

Violence

As mentioned in the introduction, violent crime has long been a central topic in the media. Mass media in general tend to focus on the unusual and sensational, since everyday matters of life would not attract much of an audience or profit (Dye 2005, 41; Faith 1993b, 187–88). Thus, it not surprising that televised entertainment programs have been found to grossly exaggerate violent and predatory crime (Surette 2007, 60–64).

Similar to media portrayals of criminalized men (Surette 2007, 60–64), criminalized women and girls are predominantly represented in television and film as exceedingly violent, predatory, and dangerous (Chesney-Lind 1999; Faith, 1993a, 255–73; Faith, 1993b). As stated by Shaw (2000, 62), it appears that "for the media, violence by women doubles the fascination." Since the 1980s especially, "architects of popular culture have subjected us to a steady stream of powerful representations of violent girls and women" (Chesney-Lind 1999, 115). The growing focus on violence committed by females suggests the popularity of the liberation hypothesis, as it reproduces the idea of escalating female crime in modern, so-called liberated times (Chesney-Lind 1999, 116–21; Faith 1993b, 182–84).

The public and media obsession with women's violent crime and dangerousness is not justified by research on women in the real world. Importantly, most criminalized women pose very little risk to society (Boritch 1997, 18; CHRC 2003, 1–2; Shaw 2000, 63). Females are responsible for a fraction of violent crime and are far more likely to be victims than perpetrators (Chesney-Lind 1999, 115, 133; Faith 1993b, 188 Shaw 2000, 61). The most common offenses that women are charged with are property- and morality-related; e.g., prostitution and drug offenses (Boritch 1997, 15–18; Comack 2006, 64–65). Moreover, contrary to what sensationalized media portrayals might suggest, the crimes that women commit tend to occur in the course of their everyday lives (Comack 1996, 27). Apparently, however, "the mundane stories of women who have committed theft or drugged themselves are not as interesting as the dramatic fictional crimes conceived by men who have traditionally feared women's powers" (Faith 2005, 80).

The Missing Context

Continuing the trend set by media portrayals of criminalized men (Surette 2007, 67–69), television and film depictions of women and their crimes tend to employ an individualized and sensationalized focus that is simplistic and devoid of contextual understanding (Chesney-Lind 1999; Faith 1993a, 255–73; Faith 1993b). For example, Faith (1993b, 189) has criticized the decontextualized representation of women's anger in film: "Whereas [in reality] anger is an appropriate response to an unjust circumstance, the anger expressed by the film characters is unfocused, displaced or depicted as an obsessive rage." For the most part, women's crime and violence is constructed in television and film to be the result of individual, typically psychological and emotional, problems (Chesney-Lind 1999, 133; Faith 1993a, 265; Faith 1993b, 177, 188–89).

The individualized problems that lead to women's fictionalized crimes tend to be gendered and reproduce traditional misogynist ideas about women's innate madness, irrationality, and emotionalism (Faith 1993a, 265; Faith 1993b, 183, 188–89; Humphries 2009). Depictions of criminalized women also tend to reproduce the myth that, when their "evil tendencies" are awakened, women "are revengeful, jealous, inclined to vengeances of a refined cruelty" (Lombrosso and Ferrero 1895, 151, quoted in Faith 1993b, 183). Humphries (2009, 72), for instance, found that depictions of female killers on *Law and Order* are "saturated with masculine stereotypes about ... sexualized women motivated by ... jealousy and sexual revenge."

The biographical and social context surrounding women's real world crime and violence is clearly missing in most television and film productions. As noted by Chesney-Lind (1999, 133), few media accounts that have represented women's [crime and] violence do adequate justice to the lack of options and desperation that characterizes the lives of the women who actually commit [criminal and] violent acts.... Instead, we witness the sporadic 'discovery' of rather heinous female offenders.

In the real world, women's crime occurs in a patriarchal, racist, and capitalist context. When considered in light of victimization (which is often long-term and perpetrated by family members), limited economic and educational opportunities, and a dire lack of social support, many women's resort to crime and violence appears to be a reasonable choice, and ideas about women's (increasing) dangerousness appear unsubstantiated (CAEFS 2010; Chesney-Lind 1999, 132–34; Comack 1996; Owen 1999, 84). For example, rather than fueled by irrationality, emotionality, jealousy, or revenge, many women's resort to crime and violence represents the need to defend or provide for themselves and/or their children (CAEFS 2010). The real world targets of women's violence, which are often abusive family members (Faith 1993b, 184; Shaw 2000, 61–62), further indicate the centrality of victimization in women's crime, the reasonableness of many women's resort to force, and the low public threat posed by criminalized women.

This study will contribute to the literature on the fictionalization of criminalized women in entertainment media by exploring how the writers and producers of *CSI: Miami* represent women and their crimes.

Method

An audio-visual content analysis of the fourth season (2005–2006) of *CSI: Miami* was conducted in order to explore how the series represents criminalized women and their criminalized actions. Season four was selected due to convenience: All 25 episodes from this season were available on DVD at a local video store. The episodes were screened for those that featured women who had committed a criminal offense and were detected by authorities. This was achieved by skipping to the final interrogation scene of each episode, which invariably revealed the criminal. Six of the 25 episodes involved portrayals of women who violate the law; in each of the six, one female perpetrator was featured. Thus, a total of six female characters and their offenses were included for analysis: Kim in "Urban Hellraisers," Valerie in "Payback," Elissa in "Silencer," Allison in "Double Jeopardy," Sienna in "Free Fall," and Mandy in "Open Water."

The duration of each episode was approximately 40 minutes, and each was viewed twice in its entirety; notes were taken while viewing episodes. The general patterns that were focused on in the viewing stage related to the characters' physical and sociodemographic characteristics, as well as the type and nature of their crimes. During the viewing of episodes, detailed notes recorded any dialogue, images, actions, interactions, and surrounding circumstances that were associated with the female characters and their crimes. After the viewing stage was complete, the transcribed dataset was manually deconstructed into common themes using the constant comparative method (Glaser and Strauss 1967; Strauss and Corbin 1990).[3] Five overlapping themes emerged from this process, categorized in the results section according to whether they related to characteristics of the women or to their crimes: supermodel women in trouble; socioeconomically privileged women in trouble; liberated women in trouble; violent crime; and unreasonable crime.

Results

Characteristics of the Women

Supermodel women in trouble[4]: Every woman portrayed as a criminal in the fourth season of *CSI: Miami* resembled a supermodel. Kim in "Urban Hell-raisers," Valerie in "Payback," Elissa in "Silencer," Allison in "Double Jeopardy," Sienna in "Free Fall," and Mandy in "Open Water" each had a symmetrical face with full lips, straight and white teeth, large eyes, manicured eyebrows, and smooth, unblemished skin. In addition, each had shoulder length or longer, shiny, well-maintained hair. The characters also maintained flawless makeup throughout each scene; however, Kim maintained a more natural appearance in terms of cosmetics.

Regarding body size and shape, all six characters were tall, thin, and had full breasts. Their outfits accentuated their physique and helped to sexualize their image. Every character wore form-fitting garments (e.g., tight pants and tops), which were often detailed with an attention-grabbing pattern or stone/jewel appliqué. In many scenes, their clothing revealed significant amounts of bare skin, such as cleavage (e.g., low-cut halter tops) and legs (e.g., miniskirts). Four of the six characters wore heels consistently, which further worked to idealize and sexualize their image. In addition, the characters were all relatively young: two were under the age of twenty-one, three were in their twenties or early thirties, and one was in her late thirties or early forties.

The physical appearance of criminalized women in *CSI: Miami* fits perfectly with the contemporary cultural ideal of the beautiful woman. This theme likely reflects white heterosexual male domination in media production more broadly (Faith 1993a, 170; Leavy 2000, ¶44). Indeed, such images of women are rampant in popular culture industries and mainstream television programs. The portrayal of women in *CSI: Miami* might reflect a general theme of the series as well; virtually all female characters in the program are presented in an idealized and sexualized manner. In their analysis of the investigators in *CSI: Crime Scene Investigation*, for instance, Bissler and Conners (this edition) found that Catherine Willows is portrayed in similar ways.

The presentation of criminalized women as supermodels in *CSI: Miami* stands in contrast with other media-produced images of criminalized women as physically masculinized and unattractive (Faith 1993a, 256–58, 260–62; Faith 1993b). The portrayal of female perpetrators in *CSI: Miami* is, however, consistent with Faith's (1993a, 265) notion of "super-bitch killer beauties." That is, all six female characters in the fourth season of *CSI: Miami* are presented as monstrous women hidden beneath incredibly attractive appearances. Certainly, media-produced images of women with flawless faces, thin bodies, and perfect breasts do not represent the ordinary diversity of women who are criminalized in the real world (Chesney-Lind 1999, 120; Faith 1993a, 258; Faith 1993b, 185). Criminalized women resemble the larger population of American women, who, for example, have a dress size that averages 14 and a bra size estimated to average 34B (Chen, LaBat, and Bye 2010, 518).[5]

Socioeconomically Privileged Women in Trouble[6]: A close second to the preceding theme is the portrayal of criminalized women as socioeconomically privileged. All six women portrayed as criminals in the fourth season of *CSI: Miami* appeared to be Caucasian, and Valerie, Elissa, Allison, and Mandy appeared to be upper or upper-middle class. Allison was the daughter of wealthy parents, Mandy was the daughter of a wealthy and newly remarried mother, Elissa was a forty-something CEO of a successful pharmaceutical company,[7] and the source of Valerie's wealth is unknown but she was a homeowner. The socioeconomic status of Kim and Sienna was more ambiguous.[8] It is also noteworthy that all six characters were well-spoken, which suggests that they have strong backgrounds in formal education. In addition, none of the characters had dependent children.

The characters' economic standing was interpreted, in part, through their clothing, which was new-looking, stylish, and often adorned with jewels or stones. Jewelry was also a standard piece of the characters' wardrobe and helped to infer their financial wealth. The characters' residences usually provided the clearest indicators of their socioeconomic status. Elissa, Valerie, and Allison each had homes that were large, architecturally unique (e.g., arched doorways, floor-to-ceiling windows), decorated with modern furniture, artwork, and sculptures, had hardwood flooring, decorative tiling, exterior landscaping, and were spotless. Elissa even made reference to her "yard people" and "pool man." Mandy's temporary residence was a first-class cruise ship, which was equipped with several pools, a theatre, modern furnishings and artwork.

The portrayal of every female criminal in *CSI: Miami* as white and of high economic status is consistent with other literature that has found racial minorities and lower economic classes to be neglected in media representations of criminalized people (Faith 2005, 79; Surette 2007, 59). This theme also appears to reflect a pattern of the *CSI* series. For example, Bissler and Conners, in thier essay in this volume, found that racial minorities and lower economic classes are greatly underrepresented among the investigators in *CSI: Crime Scene Investigation*.

The privileging of white and upper/middle-class characters likely reflects the dominance of media production in general by white, upper/middle-class interests. The presentation of criminalized women as Caucasian, wealthy, and childless in *CSI: Miami* stands in sharp contrast with the sociodemographic profile of criminalized women in America, in which racial minorities, the poor, the undereducated, and single mothers are grossly overrepresented (CAEFS 2010; Owen 1999, 85).

"Liberated" Women in Trouble[9]: A theme that is related to the previous two, but more theory-based, is that at least two of the six episodes present the modern 'liberated' woman as criminally dangerous. Elissa, the female killer in "Silencer," was a CEO of a successful pharmaceutical company — the modern career woman. Her position as a head of company provided her with the resources to hire a hit man to kill a female employee whom she believed was having an affair with her lover, also an employee. Kim in "Urban Hellraisers" was a student in university — a realm historically dominated by men. She felt compelled to fit in with the male students by participating in an underground game in which participants earn points for committing violent crimes. Her position as a university student amongst "the guys" provided her with the motivation and the means of carrying out various violent offenses, including armed robbery, kidnapping, and murder.

Elissa and Kim represent liberated women whose access to traditionally male-dominated realms, such as the economy and academia, provided them with motivations and opportunities to engage in traditionally male-dominated crimes, such as murder and robbery. These "liberated" women are selfish and dangerous. Indeed, they commit heinous acts of violence to fulfill their rather trivial desires, such as the murder of a mistress to have her lover to herself, or the murder of a bank teller to earn points in a game. This connection between women's liberation and women's crime is frequently made in media portrayals of criminalized women, despite the fact that it has absolutely no basis in reality (Boritch 1997, 65–66; Chesney-Lind 1999, 116; Faith 1993a, 64–65; Faith 1993b, 183–84).

Characteristics of the Criminal Offenses

Violent crime[10]: All six women portrayed as criminals in season four of *CSI: Miami* engaged in violent crime. As already mentioned, Kim in the episode "Urban Hellraisers" robbed a bank, kidnapped a bank manager, and murdered a bank teller using a TEC-9 assault rifle in order to earn points in an underground game. Homicides in particular were committed in every episode. In "Payback," Valerie used a stone statue to deliver a fatal blow to the head of a man who raped her six years earlier. Allison in "Double Jeopardy" used a knife to repeatedly and fatally stab the wife of her lover in the chest. In "Open Water," Mandy also used a knife to repeatedly stab and kill her stepfather in the chest.

In "Silencer," Elissa hired a professional killer to murder the women she believed was having an affair with her partner. In "Free Fall," Sienna and her lover participated in the armed robbery of a convenience store and murder of a drug lord.[11]

The focus on violent crime is by no means unique to the producers of *CSI: Miami*. As previously mentioned, crime and violence has long been key audience attracting material in the media generally and on television specifically (Surette 2007, 13). Moreover, as stated by Humphries (2009, 57): "Killers are [...] the *raison d'être* of crime dramas." *CSI* in particular relies on violent crime to provide gory crime scene material, the investigation of which is the focus of the series.

The depiction of criminalized women in *CSI: Miami* as exceptionally violent continues the trend set long ago by entertainment media, and it might also reflect the more recent popularity of the liberation hypothesis (Chesney-Lind 1999; Faith 1993a, 255–73; Faith, 1993b). The portrayal of every female perpetrator as a violent criminal in the fourth season is glaringly inconsistent with the evidence on women's crime. In reality, the commission of violent crime by women is exceptionally rare; women are typically charged with property, drug, or vice-related offenses (Boritch 1997, 15–18; Chesney-Lind 1999, 115, 133; Comack 2006, 64–65).

Unreasonable Crime[12]: In at least four of the six episodes, the female characters' motivation for their criminal and violent acts would be perceived by a "reasonable person" as illogical, abnormal, and unjustifiable.[13] In "Urban Hellraisers," for instance, Kim committed robbery, kidnapping, and murder in order to earn points in a game and fit in with her fellow classmates. Detective Horatio Caine summarized the offense while pointing out its irrational nature: "Life and death reduced to points on a board."

The unreasonableness of the female characters' use of violence is especially reflected in the role of jealousy and anger. For example, in "Open Water," Mandy killed her new stepfather because she was jealous and angry about the time her mother spent with him. In "Silencer," Elissa hired a hit man to murder a woman whom she falsely believed was having an affair with her partner. Her motivation was based on anger, jealousy, and revenge. Along similar lines, Allison in "Double Jeopardy" killed the wife of her lover so they could be together. An added motivational twist which reinforces the irrationality of Allison's violence is that she was a white-supremacist and was determined to separate her lover from his African American wife.

A partial exception to the "unreasonable" theme is an episode entitled "Payback," in which Valerie murdered her real estate agent who had raped her six years earlier. Unlike other characters, Valerie had somewhat understandable reasons for her crime. Even Detective Caine expressed sympathy for her situation: "I understand how you got there. You were in a very difficult position." By locating Valerie's offense in relation to male violence against women, the writers of this episode come closer to representing the gendered nature of women's violence (Chesney-Lind 1999, 120). In many cases, when women are charged with causing death, "their actions were defensive or otherwise reactive to violence directed at them, their children, or another third party" (CAEFS 2010). Ultimately, however, the portrayal of Valerie's use of violence does not do justice to the "real world" circumstances of women who use violence in response to abuse. Unlike many women, Valerie's resort to violence did not occur in a context of long-standing abuse, desperation, and limited options. To the contrary, she was socioeconomically privileged and had an abundance of resources and alternatives available to her. In fact, her violence appeared to be motivated more by revenge than defense and, therefore, might reflect a degree of irrationality.

The portrayal of women's crime and violence as unreasonable in *CSI: Miami* is consistent with other media portrayals in which "we witness the sporadic 'discovery' of rather heinous female offenders" (Chesney-Lind 1999, 133). The offenses committed by female characters in television and film are regularly depicted to be the result of irrationality and uncontrolled, obsessive rage — and jealousy and revenge are common motivating factors (Faith 1993a, 265; Faith 1993b, 183; Humphries 2009, 72). This portrayal of women's crime conflicts sharply with reality. Rather than fuelled by personality flaws and unreasonable motivations, women's crime is more often a rational response to intensely oppressive individual and social circumstances of systemic victimization, economic marginalization, and limited alternatives (Chesney-Lind 1999, 132–34; Comack 1996; Owen 1999, 84). For example, women's law violations are often expressions of the need to defend or provide for themselves and/or their children (CAEFS 2010). It is also worth noting that the "real world" targets of women's violence, which are frequently abusive male spouses (Faith 1993b, 184; Shaw 2000, 61–62), further illustrate the role of victimization and confirm the reasonableness of many women's criminalized actions—yet they are entirely unacknowledged by the writers and producers of *CSI: Miami* in the fourth season.

Potential Implications and Concerns

This analysis has attempted to illustrate that *CSI: Miami* presents women in trouble with the law as supermodels, socioeconomically privileged, and liberated, and their law violations as violent and unreasonable. It was also argued that such portrayals are at odds with research on criminalized women in the "real world." Consideration will now be given to the potential implications of the ways in which *CSI: Miami* represents women and their crimes, specifically in terms of public perceptions and attitudes, as well as criminal justice and public policies.

Public Perceptions and Attitudes

Any relationship between media attention and public concern is complex, but the available evidence indicates a weak to moderate correlation (Surette 2007, 210). Specifically, media effects appear to have a positive correlation with exposure and a negative correlation with direct experience and alternative sources of information (Surette 2007). *CSI: Miami* is an extremely popular television program, and the general public does not have direct experience with or alternative sources of information about crime and violence — especially women's crime and violence.[14] Therefore, the recurring themes in *CSI: Miami* may have especially strong effects on public perceptions and attitudes towards criminalized women in the 'real world.'

By fictionalizing women and their crimes to the extent it does, the writers and producers of *CSI: Miami* risk reinforcing the ignorance that has traditionally existed towards women in trouble with the law. Such fictionalization is obvious in the presentation of all six characters as supermodels; this portrayal in no way resembles criminalized women or women in general, and it may have the effect of trivializing the circumstances of women who come into conflict with the law. Moreover, the portrayal of the characters as socioeconomically privileged — perhaps even "liberated" — may send the message that women's crimes are committed in similar circumstances, and that racial, class, and gender inequities do not matter when it comes to issues of crime and justice. In fact, if the public perceives the characters to be 'liberated women,' *CSI: Miami* might send the absurd message that women's crime is a result of equality and enhanced opportunities — rather than inequality and limited opportunities — and that it essentially resembles men's crime — instead of being shaped by gendered experiences.

The writers and producers of *CSI: Miami* demonstrate a complete disregard for the real reasons that women resort to crime and violence. Instead, they construct characters and scenarios that send the message that women's crime and violence is based solely on individual personality problems (e.g., uncontrolled anger, violent propensities) and simplistic, selfish, and unreasonable motivations (e.g., to fit in with "the guys," jealousy, revenge). The portrayal of women and their offenses as expressions of personal shortcomings and unreasonable motivations might lend credence to the misogynist idea that women's crime and violence is a result of their natural irrationality and emotionality, and that "all women are potential killers and society (men) must control them" (Faith 1993a, 95). The presentation of each character as a deviant woman beneath a beautiful and sexy demeanor might work especially well to strengthen ideas about women's "hidden capacity for evil and cunning" (Faith 1993b, 183). These representations no doubt trivialize the issues that criminalized women face in the 'real world' and they represent a backlash to gains made by feminist scholars, and the women's movement in general.

The individualized and pathologized explanations of women's crime that are deployed in *CSI: Miami* are consistent with neoliberal responsibilization, as they completely overlook the context of capitalism, patriarchy, and white-hegemony that relates to the majority of women's crime and instead place blame solely upon the individual. By focusing attention away from the context in which women's law violations occur, like abuse, poverty, inadequate support, single motherhood, and limited options, and instead focusing on the role of the deviant individual, *CSI: Miami* might send the message that women's law violations in the real world are unreasonable and deserving of punishment, and that criminalized women represent a threat to the community.

The obsession that *CSI: Miami* writers and producers apparently have with sensationalized violent crime exacerbates any potential implications of the series. The persistent presentation of violent female criminals might send the message that criminalized women are much more violent than they are in reality, and it might reinforce the myth that women are increasingly engaging in "male" forms of aggression. Such presentations definitely risk reinforcing people's perceptions of criminalized women as dangerous and fearsome. In addition, the neglect of the real world context in which women resort to violence might lend further support to the idea that these women pose a risk to society, and that the community must be protected from them.

Criminal Justice and Public Policies

The literature suggests that the media have significant, but variable and multidirectional, effects on criminal justice and public policy (Surette 2007, 213). As stated by Surette (2007, 218): "The media are not the most important factor in the construction of crime and justice policy, but their influence cannot be ignored." Criminal justice officials and policy makers often look to the media for indicators of public opinion, which they then use to help inform policy decisions (Dye 2005, 34). The impact of media representations on public perceptions and attitudes might also be transferred to the policy arena through processes such as lobbying and voting (Dye, 2005, 41).

The portrayal of criminalized women in *CSI: Miami* as "spoiled" beauties who freely decide to commit heinous violent crimes for no good reason might strengthen public and political support for "crime control" measures. By presenting women's law violations as expressions of psychological and emotional issues and simplistic, selfish, and unreasonable motivations, and by completely ignoring the patriarchal, capitalist, and white-hegemonic context, responsibility for the crime problem falls solely upon the individual. Through this portrayal, existing punitive and retributive measures that are consistent with the individualization of crime might be reinforced. The series' fixation on violent crime and its construction of female perpetrators as dangerous might have particularly powerful effects in terms of legitimating law and order and community protection ideologies, practices, and policies.[1]

As pointed out by Faith (1993a, 271), media constructions of unreasonable, violent, dangerous, criminal women help

> justify the construction of new maximum security prisons for women across North America. At any given time no more than 10 percent of women confined could be accurately perceived as representing a threat to other human beings or to the social order. Media-supported notions of she-monsters have contributed to public acceptance of monetary and social costs of imprisoning women who are not dangerous.

Moreover, by disconnecting women's crime from a context of gender, economic, and racial inequity, social justice measures that address the roots of many women's troubles may be hindered (Faith 2005, 82; Surette 2007, 218). In fact, the representation of criminalized women in *CSI: Miami* may help legitimate existing social conditions that underlie women's criminalization in the first place.

Recommendations and Conclusion

The most disconcerting aspect of *CSI: Miami*'s fictionalization of women in trouble with the law is that it unfairly targets one of the most disadvantaged segments of the North American population. The potential effect of such fictionalized portrayals is to reinforce the social injustices that criminalized women already face (Faith 1993a, 270–71; Faith 1993b, 198; Faith, 2005, 82). Concerted efforts must therefore be made to produce media representations that can challenge, rather than support, the prejudice and marginalization faced by criminalized women in the real world.

It is not impossible for the media to represent criminalized women in ways that more closely reflect real world circumstances and context. Surette (2007, 219) points out, for instance, that

> sporting events are consistently placed by the media in their larger social context (the world of sports in this case) and constructed in a way that provides historical understanding and current comprehension. [By] covering justice like sports ... crime could be removed from the realm of the bizarre, grotesque, and sinister and placed in the social world.

Producers of entertainment media have great creative capacity and they could no doubt find ways of portraying women and their crimes in an entertaining, relatable, and realistic manner.

While the tendency of the media is to (re)produce erroneous, negative, and stereotypical perceptions of criminalized women, the media also has great potential to challenge such perceptions and educate the public (Faith 1993a, 270; Faith 1993b, 198; Faith 2005, 82). Therefore, creators of entertainment programs arguably have an ethical obligation to adopt a more socially responsible role, especially when representing people who are socially disadvantaged. When creating shows like *CSI: Miami*, writers and producers should devote the resources to inform themselves of the critical literature on the subject matter and allow this information to guide the content and format of the program.

The format in which stories are represented should allow for the exploration of systemic issues. Presently, the entertainment media employs the "episodic format [which] treats stories as discrete events: ... an individual committed a crime, why did he [or she] do it?" (Surette 2007, 203). A systemic format would contextualize women's criminal behaviors in terms of their individual biography and everyday lives, as well as overarching social issues, such as poverty, racism, single motherhood, and violence against women. As expressed by Faith (1993a, 97):

> Murder stories, when focused on the deed, take on the quality of monster tales, but when the deeds are contextualized and the murderers de-mystified by the details of their lives, they lose their sensational quality and much of the onus shifts to society's failures to provide relief to women trapped in intolerable situations.

Academics and well-informed others are encouraged to engage in "news-making criminology" (Barak 1988, cited in Chesney-Lind 1999, 134). That is, those who are the most knowledgeable of the 'real world' circumstances of criminalized women should work hard to infiltrate the media in order to challenge falsities and construct more realistic and responsible representations. Though it would be difficult for outsiders to connect with Hollywood producers of major television series like *CSI: Miami*, stronger connections could be made with local programs, such as news media, and the influence may eventually reach other forms. There is also a strong need for the development of programming that promotes media literacy skills among the public, so that portrayals like those in *CSI: Miami* are viewed with less legitimacy and exert less influence.

For now, much responsibility lies with the creators of entertainment programs, and much hope for the future lies with the courageous few who dare to break the mold and use their opportunity and resources in socially beneficial ways. In fact, "in the past decade, North American movies and television have introduced more honest and positive images of women ... due in part to some excellent female writers and directors" (Faith 1993b, 196). Instead of (re)producing negative and erroneous representations— such as spoiled beauties who freely commit heinous violent crimes for no good reason — the media could dispel myths, break down stereotypes, and foster consciousness-raising. Instead of demonizing individual women, the media could highlight social problems. Instead of supporting destructive crime control policies, the media could support compassion and social justice initiatives that address the roots of women's troubles with the law.

Certainly, this is an area that requires further research and activism, especially given the popularity and recent proliferation of crime dramas. The potential effects that television programs like *CSI: Miami* have on public perceptions and policy decisions are too great and too disastrous to allow such negative and erroneous representations of criminalized women to continue. Researchers are encouraged to investigate other programs, genres, and forms of media in order to build on the evidence and strengthen the demand for a socially responsible approach to media production. Criminalized women suffer too much injustice already; it is absolutely unacceptable for this to be furthered through entertainment (and other) programs.

NOTES

* This research was funded in part by the Social Sciences and Humanities Research Council of Canada.

1. Though this paper focuses exclusively on the representation of women in *CSI: Miami*, this does not imply that the representation of men is unproblematic or unimportant. Rather, a key assumption underlying this project is that social "reality" is gendered and therefore the portrayal of women in the media is inherently gendered, sends gendered messages, and has potential gendered effects. This paper is also an attempt to help compensate for the historical neglect of women's issues in academia and public policy. Nonetheless, the lack of attention to male characters is an important limitation of this project, and a comparative analysis of the representation of women and men in crime dramas such as *CSI: Miami* would be interesting for future research.

2. It is noteworthy that, upon the narrowing and solidifying of themes, as well as during the write-up stage, some scenes from some episodes were viewed for a third time in order to verify interpretations or to collect additional information.

3. The "criteria of selection" (Berg 2009, 342) used to develop this theme was any information relating to the physical image of the female characters. All visual images of the women were included for analysis, with particular attention to facial features, body shape and size, hair, clothing, and age (an appraisal of age was based on appearance and in two cases age was explicitly stated).

4. Somewhat consistent with *CSI: Miami* representations is that criminalized women in the "real world" tend to be relatively young. The average age of women in prison is 29 years (PARC 2004), whereas the average age of women in the general population is 38 (US Census Bureau 2009).

5. The criteria of selection for this theme included any information relating to the socioeconomic status of the criminalized women. Socioeconomic status was determined through an interpretation of race and class. The former was inferred through the women's physical appearances and their perceived fit with racial stereotypes (e.g., skin pigmentation). Class was determined chiefly through material possessions and physical appearance; in the case of Elissa and Kim, occupation was known and provided clues regarding economic status.

6. The success of the company was gauged, in part, by Elissa's large office decorated with a lot of modern artwork and furniture.

7. Kim was a university student and no information was given pertaining to her economic status. In reference to Sienna, Detective Frank Tripp stated: "Sonny and Cher came into this city with the clothes on their back." While this implies a lack of economic resources, Sienna's clean, new-looking, stylish clothing, jewelry, flawless makeup and well-maintained hair makes her status uncertain.

8. The criteria of selection used to develop this theme included information indicating that the woman was involved in a traditionally male-dominated arena and that this involvement was in some way connected to the commission of her offense. Only two of the six episodes included information that revealed involvement in any arena (male- or female-dominated), and both met the criteria for this theme.

9. The criteria of selection for this theme included any information (e.g., images, actions, interactions, speech) relating to the type of offense. In each case, the type of offense was explicitly stated or displayed in the data. The type of offense was classified according to general legal categories (e.g., violent, property).

10. The only reference made to Sienna's participation in the murder was made by Officer Ryan Wolf, after finding a bloody body stuffed in the trunk of the couple's stolen vehicle: "It proves Leo and Sienna were crazy, they killed the cartel boss."

11. In developing this theme, all speech, images, actions, interactions, and surrounding circumstances that indicated the reasoning and motivation for the offense were considered. In most cases, this information was chiefly revealed in the interrogation scene and the scene displaying the offense and/or the lead-up to the offense. The "unreasonableness" of the women's motivation was based on a personal conception of how a "reasonable/average person" might interpret it.

12. Valerie's offense in the episode entitled "Payback" is a possible exception, and will be discussed later. Another possible exception to the unreasonableness theme is "Free Fall," in which Sienna and her boyfriend commit armed robbery and murder. This episode involved few indicators of motivation. A comment is made that Sienna "came into [Miami] with the clothes on [her] back." While this might imply financial hardship and may add an element of 'reasonableness' to her actions and motivations, it conflicts with the physical image of Sienna (see footnote 7) and therefore lacks impact. The tone of carefree excitement that surrounds most of her crimes also diminishes the reasonableness of her law violations. In addition, despite the murder being committed in somewhat defensive circumstances (the victim was trying to kill her and her boyfriend for stealing drug money) it is still perceived as illogical by Officer Ryan Wolf, who comments: "It proves Leo and Sienna were crazy, they killed the cartel boss."

13. Surette (2007, 34) has pointed out that the general public obtains most of their information about crime and justice issues through the media, both "fact-based" and fictional forms.

14. Surette (2007, 218) has argued that media portrayals of criminals tend to enhance support for crime control initiatives, due in large part from the individualized focus employed in most media accounts.

REFERENCES

BBC News. 2006. "CSI Show Most Popular in World." Last modified July 31. *http://news.bbc.co.uk/2/hi/entertainment/5231334.stm*.

Berg, Bruce. 2009. *Qualitative Research Methods for the Social Sciences*, 7th ed. Boston: Allyn & Bacon.

Bissler, Denise L., and Joan Conners. 2012. "Inequalities in *CSI: Crime Scene Investigation*: Stereotypes in the *CSI* Investigators." In Denise L. Bissler and Joan Conners (eds.), *The Harms of Crime Media and the Perpetuation of Racism, Sexism and Class Stereotypes*: **PAGES**. Jefferson, NC: McFarland.

Boritch, Helen. 1997. *Fallen Women: Female Crime and Criminal Justice in Canada*. Scarborough, ON: ITP Nelson.

Canadian Association of Elizabeth Fry Societies (CAEFS). 2010. "Criminalized and Imprisoned Women." Accessed November 8. *http://www.elizabethfry.ca/eweek06/pdf/crmwomen.pdf*.

Canadian Human Rights Commission (CHRC). 2003. *Protecting Their Rights: A Systemic Review of Human Rights in Correctional Services for Federally Sentenced Women*. *http://www.chrc-ccdp.ca/pdf/reports/fswen.pdf*.

CBS Entertainment. 2010. "About *CSI: Miami*." Accessed March 24. *http://www.cbs.com/primetime/csi_miami/about/*.

Chen, Chin-Man, Karen LaBat, and Elizabeth Bye. 2010. "Physical Characteristics Related to Bra Fit." *Ergonomics* 53(4): 514–524. *http://pdfserve.informaworld.com.proxy.lib.sfu.ca/760958_770885140_920106553.pdf*.

Chesney-Lind, Meda. 1999. "Media Misogyny: Demonizing 'Violent' Girls and Women." In Jeff Ferrell and Neil Websdale (eds.), *Making Trouble: Cultural Constructions of Crime, Deviance, and Control*: 115–140. Hawthorne, NY: Aldine de Gruyter.

Comack, Elizabeth. 1996. *Women in Trouble: Connecting Women's Law Violations to their Histories of Abuse*. Halifax: Fernwood.

_____. 2006. "Making Connections: Class/Race/Gender Intersections—Introduction." In Gillian Balfour and Elizabeth Comack (eds.), *Criminalizing Women: Gender and (In)justice in Neo-liberal Times*: 58–78. Halifax: Fernwood.

Dye, Thomas R. 2005. *Understanding Public Policy*, 11th ed. Upper Saddle River, NJ: Pearson Education.

Faith, Karlene. 1993a. *Unruly Women: The Politics of Confinement and Resistance*. Vancouver: Press Gang.

_____. 1993b. "Media, Myths and Masculinization: Images of Women in Prison." In Ellen Adelberg and Claudia Currie (eds.), *In Conflict with the Law: Women and the Canadian Justice System*: 174–211. Vancouver: Press Gang.

_____. 2005. *Introduction to Women and Criminal Justice: Criminology 213–3 Study Guide*. Burnaby, BC: Simon Fraser University.

Glaser, Barney G., and Anselm L. Strauss. 1967. *The Discovery of Grounded Theory: Strategies for Qualitative Research*. Chicago: Aldine de Gruyter.

Humphries, Drew. 2009. "Constructing Murderers: Female Killers of *Law and Order*." In Drew Humphries (ed.), *Women, Violence, and the Media: Readings in Feminist Criminology*: 57–74. Hanover, NH: Northeastern University Press.

Leavy, Patricia. 2000. "Feminist Content Analysis and Representative Characters." *The Qualitative Report* 5, n0.1/2: (May), *http://www.nova.edu/ssss/QR/QR5–1/leavy.html*.

Lombrosso, Cesare, and William Ferrero. 1895. *The Female Offender*. New York: Appleton.

Owen, Barbara. 1999. "Women and Imprisonment in the United States: The Gendered Consequences of the US Imprisonment Binge." In Sandy Cook and Susanne Davies (eds.), *Harsh Punishment: International Experiences of Women's Imprisonment*: 81–98. Boston: Northeastern University Press.

Prison Activist Resource Center (PARC). 2004. "Women in Prison." *http://www.prisonactivist.org/articles/women-prison*.

Reinharz, Shulamit. 1992. *Feminist Methods in Social Research*. New York: Oxford University Press.

Shaw, Margaret. 2000. "Women, Violence and Disorder in Prisons." In Kelly Hannah-Moffat and Margaret Shaw (eds.), *An Ideal Prison? Critical Essays on Women's Imprisonment in Canada*: 61–70. Halifax: Fernwood.

Strauss, Anselm, and Juliet M. Corbin. 1990. *Basics of Qualitative Research: Grounded Theory Procedures and Techniques*. Newbury Park, CA: Sage.

Surette, Ray. 2007. *Media, Crime, and Criminal Justice: Images, Realities, and Policies*. 3d ed. Belmont, CA: Thomson Wadsworth.

U.S. Census Bureau. 2009. *American Community Survey*. *http://factfinder.census.gov/servlet/STTable?_bm=y&-qr_name=ACS_2009_1YR_G00_S0101&-geo_id=01000US&-ds_name=ACS_2009_1YR_G00_&-_lang=en&-redoLog=true&-format=&-CONTEXT=st*.

Ripped from the Headlines: The Depiction of Sexual Orientation–Based Hate Crimes in Television Crime Dramas

NICHOLAS GUITTAR

Americans have a strong, lasting relationship with television as a form of entertainment. Over the past fifty years, there has been a steady increase in the number of televisions per household and the overall quantity of digital media consumption per person. In fact, according to the Motion Picture Association of America, the average American consumed 1,962 hours of media entertainment in one form or another in 2007. That amounts to nearly forty hours per week for all forms of media (TV, internet, theatrical movies, etc). It has been estimated that Americans, on average, spent 32.4 hours per week watching television in 2007 (MPAA 2007). Obviously, this constitutes a major leisure activity for families in the United States. Another interesting facet of U.S. media consumption is the nation's obsession with television crime dramas. Over the past 20 years, television shows such as *Law & Order*, *CSI*, and *NCIS* have become mainstays of popular programming, and are frequently listed among the highest rated primetime television shows. In addition, many others have joined the ranks such as *Criminal Minds*, *Numbers*, *Law & Order: SVU*, *Law & Order: CI*, *CSI: Miami*, *CSI: New York*, *NCIS: Los Angeles*, *The Good Wife*, and the list goes on.

One might contemplate how the depiction of life in television contributes to our perception of the world around us. After all, only a portion of our worldview is based on first-hand experience. The rest is derived from second-hand knowledge such as news media, television and film, books, or even anecdotes shared by friends and family. Social scientists have concluded that media helps shape people's very idea of themselves and the world around them (Berger 2006). Exposure to these secondary forms of information varies from person to person; however, there are certain types of media that are more equally experienced by Americans. Television, for example, is viewed by people from all walks of life regardless of age, gender, race, ethnicity, social class, or sexual orientation. It is therefore conceivable that many of us are influenced by the depictions or portrayal of phenomena in television shows. According to

Cultivation Theory (Gerbner et al. 2002), the attitudes and beliefs of television viewers are influenced through a process in which the world, as portrayed through the media, comes to be perceived as an accurate reflection of reality (Fisher et al. 2007).

Over the past few decades, a fair amount of research has gone into deciphering how people construct their social realities from various secondary sources (Altheide and Snow 1979; Adoni and Mane 1984; Altheide 1997). The blurring of the lines between news and entertainment communication has changed our daily lives and challenged our sense of control over our lives (Altheide 1995). In this sense, one can become lost in what is "real" versus what is fictional and/or simply sensationalized. Incidentally, very little attention has been afforded to the representation of topics involving groups that are socially marginalized in entertainment media. The purpose of this chapter is to begin filling this void through the analysis of sexual orientation-based hate crimes in television crime dramas.

Social Constructionism and the Media

According to C. Wright Mills, "The first rule for understanding the human condition is that [people] live in second-hand worlds. They are aware of much more than they have personally experienced" (Mills 1963, 405). As such, the fact that an individual has not personally experienced a given phenomenon does not mean that she fails to construct a perception of it. People make assumptions about the world around them based on the different forms of media they come into contact with. In fact, other than personal experience, our social reality is constructed from three sources: significant others, groups and institutions, and the mass media (Surette 1992). These three sources comprise an individual's symbolic reality, which consists of everything that we believe to be true, yet have not witnessed firsthand. The combination of our symbolic reality with our first-hand lived experiences has come to be known as the *social construction of reality* (Berger and Luckmann 1966).

When we have little personal experience with a topic, entertainment media, such as television, provides an alternate base of knowledge upon which we draw in order to shape our perceptions. Unfortunately, few studies have looked into the depiction of marginalized groups in television media, such as the portrayal of sexual orientation-based hate crimes in any forms of media. Since different forms of media do affect our consciousness, we need to form a better understanding of how certain phenomena (i.e., sexual orientation-based hate crimes) are portrayed on television in order to better understand whether or not we are being inundated with valid representations of the actual phenomenon.

Unless we have a sincere interest in learning about a given topic or population, we are likely to learn passively through the forms of media we already ingest on a daily basis. In this sense, we must consider not only how lesbian, gay, and bisexual (LGB) persons are characterized on television, but also how frequently and where. Television content that includes positive portrayals of non-heterosexual populations and topics, although increasing in frequency, is still relatively infrequent. According to Gross (1994) the assumptions that we make about members of marginalized groups are influenced by television primarily because many people have limited awareness of, or contact with individuals different from themselves in their own lived experiences. In an ideal world, those who have limited experiences with LGB[1] persons would base their assumptions on more valid, fact-checked forms of information. However, television permeates American life, especially for adolescents (Brown and Witherspoon 2002).

Sexual minorities and the issues they face are often ignored by the media and treated as if they are an invisible population (Fisher et al. 2007). Gross (1991) described this process of exclusion as "symbolic annihilation." This sense of low visibility and power can be seen in a study by Fisher et al. (2007), which is perhaps the most comprehensive content analysis of LGB content on television. In their analysis of two seasons of television programming (six commercial broadcast and five cable networks), they looked at the content of over 2,700 program episodes. They found that non-heterosexual topics were included in about 15 percent of the programming, and that rates were lower among broadcast network programming versus cable programming.

Researchers have suggested that the lack of LGB topics and persons on television can influence viewers to perceive LGB persons and their unique issues as both rare and abnormal (Fisher et al. 2007). Although their study did not look exclusively at crime dramas, Fisher et al. (2007) concluded that, outside of movies and variety/comedy shows, shows characterized as "drama" contained more references to LGB issues than other types of programming. Presumably then, there is a fair chance of locating and analyzing a good number of references or storylines based around hate crimes committed against members of the LGB communities. The focus of this study is to take a closer look at how television crime dramas depict sexual orientation-based hate crimes. This includes reflecting on how these depictions relate to actual statistics on these crimes as well as findings from prior studies on hate crimes, and scrutinizing the details involved in the depiction of these heinous acts. This research is particularly important because people use information from television programs as "priming"—providing small pieces of information that viewers may draw on in order to help interpret various topics or events (Altheide 1997).

LGB on TV

The 1990s really paved the way for issues surrounding the lesbian, gay, and bisexual (LGB) communities to enter mainstream television. Ellen Morgan, the title character of the TV show *Ellen* (played by Ellen DeGeneres), came out as a lesbian over the course of two episodes in 1997. Although *Ellen* suffered in decreased viewership over its remaining run, it opened the door for future shows that include LGB characters and topics (Becker 2006). Since 1997, television programming has been slowly becoming more progressive in terms of the development of LGB characters and the inclusion of issues facing the LGB community. Television shows like *Will and Grace, Gray's Anatomy*, and most recently *Modern Family* have been lauded for their inclusion of gay and lesbian characters as central to the show. *Will and Grace* is still credited as the first show to truly break through the sexuality barrier by maintaining wide success with a cast that included two gay men among the four lead characters. The success of *Will and Grace* also paved the way for popular cable shows with gay and lesbian leads such as Showtime's *The L Word*, and *Queer as Folk*. According to the GLAAD (Gay and Lesbian Alliance Against Defamation) report "Where Are We on TV" (GLAAD 2010), nine different dramatic series included LGBT lead or supporting characters. Unfortunately, with LGBT characters representing only three percent of all scripted series regular characters, these shows are still the exceptions to the rule. However, the number of lead and supporting LGBT characters has nearly doubled since 2007, which is a promising trend for future coverage of LGBT issues in television entertainment (GLAAD 2010).

The inclusion of LGB characters on television is only part of the equation. Once LGB characters are written into shows the attention quickly shifts to discerning how these characters are depicted. Although there exists a few prominent LGB characters, television shows still typically marginalize or trivialize gay and lesbian issues. Gay and lesbian characters in TV shows are often tied into a storyline purely on the basis of what their sexuality adds to the story. In other words, gay and lesbian characters are rarely included as, for example, a successful professional who also happens to be gay (Becker 2006). In the case of the legal drama *Ally McBeal*, lesbian and bisexual characters were introduced, but the purpose of their inclusion was primarily as a means of allowing the title character to explore her sexuality. An understanding of the role LGB characters play in television crime dramas is important to consider in terms of how LGB issues are framed, and further how they are received by an audience.

Method

One of the major obstacles to studying television content is that there are few ways to systematically sample television episodes. One exception to this is TV news, which can be systematically sampled by using the Vanderbilt University Television News Index and Archive. Another exception is made-for-TV movies which may be sampled using the Internet Movie Data Base (IMDB) which allows researchers to conduct keyword searches and sift through lists based on date of production, genre, and a handful of other criteria. IMDB and other online databases do have some capabilities with helping search for television episodes in this study, but only in the case that the episode synopsis includes a mention of a hate crime. The synopses released by most television studios are very brief and generally contain information about only the central plot in the episode.

In the case of this sample, web searches were conducted in order to locate television episodes that contained a character or situation involving a sexual orientation-based hate crime. Web searches included keywords such as: television, drama, crime drama, hate, bias, crime, sexual orientation, gay, lesbian, bisexual, homosexuality, violence, victimization, offender, perpetrator, and victim. Particular attention was granted to reviewing "TV blogs" in which independent viewers frequently post more detailed information about the episodes of crime dramas. The use of these blogs helped me seek out episodes, after which I watched them in their entirety in order to analyze the details involving the crime. There appear to be very few qualifying cases, so my sample was only limited by the number of episodes I could identify and locate. One shortcoming of this sampling method is that there may be other crime dramas that have featured sexual orientation-based hate crimes that were not included in this sample. In other words, my reliance upon sampling via episode synopses means that there may be episodes that contain hate crimes not listed in the synopses.

The purpose of this content analysis is to serve as an preliminary look at the depiction of sexual orientation-based hate crimes in crime dramas. One element of this analysis is to compare fictional accounts with actual hate crime statistics. Hate crimes are reported in raw numbers based on the number of victims and/or incidents, so this data will allow for some comparison to the depiction of hate crimes in television. The analysis will therefore be based in comparing fictional portrayals of sexual orientation-based hate crimes to themes and patterns documented in research on real-world hate crimes as well as data on actual hate crimes.

Each episode was viewed in its entirety three times. The initial viewing was solely for the purpose of ensuring that the episode did, in fact, contain a storyline surrounding a sexual orientation-based hate crime. The second viewing was used to identify general themes, take note of some basic demographic traits of the perpetrator and victim(s) in the episode, and look for the relationships between characters and the motivations for committing the hate crime. The final viewing served as a way to confirm that no details were missed. Beyond identifying themes, no formal system of coding was used (i.e., open coding, axial coding, etc.). Were there a larger quantity of episodes, other analysis techniques would have been employed in order to identify and track themes across episodes. However, due to the limited sample size, the qualitative methods employed were fairly basic in design.

Themes and trends were identified such as the race, gender, age, and sexual orientation of both the perpetrators and the victims. Attention was also afforded to the motive of the perpetrators and the relationship (if any) between the perpetrators and their victims. Another very important aspect of this analysis was to discern the context of the crime itself and its overall depiction in the television episode. Attention was paid to the framing of the incident, and additional web searches were conducted to determine if the crime being depicted mirrored any incidents covered in the news media.

This sample includes only television content because people in the U.S. spend substantially more time with television entertainment than any other form of media (Weimann 2000). One trend is certain: there are very few characters or storylines in crime dramas that include hate crimes directed at LGB persons. This trend is consistent with other types of television programming whereby themes related to lesbian, gay, and bisexual (LGB) persons are largely ignored (Fisher et al. 2007). One might also point out that although they are increasing in prevalence, hate crimes still account for only a minor fraction of all violent crimes. Although hate crimes are relatively rare in comparison to other violent crimes, they typically garner considerable public attention due to the construction of hate crimes as attacks on an entire community of people as opposed to an individual victim.

The quantity of actual, reported sexual orientation-based hate crimes is growing, so it seems natural that television material involving such incidents would be growing as well. As seen in Figure 1, sexual orientation is now the second largest category for all hate crimes committed (trailing only those committed on the basis of race). In 2008, there were 1,617 single-bias incidents, which account for 17.7 percent of all hate crimes. These hate crimes are newsworthy events, and considering how crime drama storylines are often "ripped from the headlines," it is no surprise that sexual orientation-based hate crimes do appear in television crime dramas.

Findings: Hate Crimes in Crime Dramas

Television programming contains very few references to or examples of hate crimes directed at members of the LGB community. Hate crimes are most frequently seen in television crime dramas in which the characters of "victim" and "perpetrator" rarely carry over into subsequent storylines. Recurrent, lead characters also rarely play into the incidents themselves, except in dealing with the victims or perpetrators during the course of legal proceedings or criminal investigations. Storylines involving hate crimes are typically episodic events that are introduced and resolved (or not) within a single episode. A focus on episodic topics that are restricted to a single episode is typical of crime dramas in general. As such, there is very little time to develop characters, and this time constraint frequently leads to a barrage of stereotypical representations (Perse

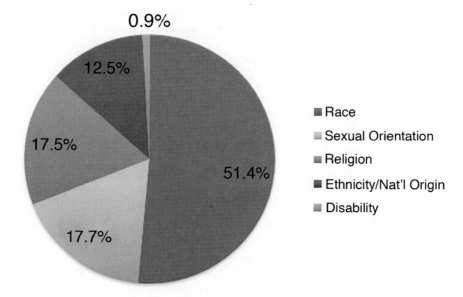

0.9%

12.5%

17.5%

51.4%

17.7%

- Race
- Sexual Orientation
- Religion
- Ethnicity/Nat'l Origin
- Disability

Figure 1. Hate Crimes Broken Down by Motivation (2008). Source: 2008 FBI/UCR http://www.fbi.gov/ucr/hc2008/incidents.html.

2001). Television still includes many stereotypical portrayals of LGB persons, from angry man-hating lesbians to hyper-feminine gay males, as well as LGB persons whose sexuality is the sole purpose of their character's inclusion in a storyline.

The relatively recent inclusion of sexual orientation as a protected group under federal hate crime legislation also makes it difficult to determine which television episodes include a true hate crime. Hate crimes have only been officially tracked in the United States since 1995, following the passing of the Hate Crime Statistics Act of 1990 (Jenness 1995), and only following the 1998 murder of Matthew Shepard have they become recognized as a social problem of significance in the United States. Simply put, the official term "hate crime" is not always used. The term "bias crime," although synonymous with "hate crime," is more often used since it is not directly associated with federal definitions. This may seem like simple semantics, but language is important because many television episodes may not categorize a crime as a hate crime. However, regardless of the terminology, the depiction of a crime may still be consistent with our current conception of hate crimes. In fact, some episodes analyzed in this study were produced and aired before the term "hate crime" was even used outside of academic circles.

In reviewing television shows and their inclusion of lesbian, gay, and bisexual issues, a few prominent themes emerge. Aside from the handful of shows that include a gay or lesbian lead character, most episodes containing LGB issues fall under the following categories: coming out stories, integrating a short-term LGB character, and discussing HIV/AIDS (Becker 2006). Based on my current analysis, another category could be: the intersection of crime and sexual orientation. Our interest here is in exploring sexual orientation-based hate crimes, but television content related to both crime and sexual orientation includes more than just hate crimes. One particularly troubling theme I observed in this analysis is the frequency with which television crime dramas actually frame lesbian, gay, bisexual, and transgender (LGBT) characters as villains. This finding is explored in greater detail below.

My initial sample included 25 episodes from television crime dramas containing characters or storylines centered on LGB issues. Only twenty percent of the sample, or five episodes, contained a crime that could be categorized as a hate or bias crime. The remainder of the episodes contained storylines about the origins of sexual orientation, use of the "gay panic" defense in courtrooms (see Lee 2003 for more on this), the interaction between religion and sexual orientation, and the bullying of children with lesbian parents, among other topics. The episodes containing hate crimes were equally diverse ranging from a serial killer bent on raping and killing lesbians to the aggravated assault of a gay teenager by another teen.

As shown in Table 1, two of the hate crimes were featured in *Law and Order*, another two in *Law and Order: SVU*, and a final one in the short-lived drama *Conviction*. The original air dates of these episodes range in time from 1995 to 2010, so social context is going to be vastly different between episodes as well.

Table 1. Summary of Episodes in the Sample

Television Series	Season	Episode	Title	Air Date
Law and Order	5	23	"Pride"	5/24/1995
Law and Order	20	16	"Innocence"	3/15/2010
Law and Order: SVU	1	11	"Bad Blood"	1/14/2000
Law and Order: SVU	11	13	"P.C."	3/3/2010
Conviction	1	2	"Denial"	3/10/2006

The framing of the incident is important in terms of how viewers perceive the perpetrators and victims of hate crimes. In typical *Law and Order* fashion, a few of the crimes were "ripped from the headlines." They included obvious references to popular cases found in the news media. A 1995 *Law and Order* episode ("Pride," Season 5, Episode 23, aired on May 24, 1995) serves as the best example of this trend. The episode covered the murder of a gay city council member by a conservative rival council member who harbored conflicted attitudes toward homosexuality. This incident drew many parallels to the 1978 murder of Harvey Milk by fellow city council member Dan White. The perpetrator in this case exacted his violence on the victim as an expression of anger over progressive trends in gay activism at the time. Many federal and state agencies were just beginning to collect hate crime data during 1995, so this may explain why a case mirroring Harvey Milk's murder was revisited at this time. Although the relation to a popular news story was evident in this episode, the connections between actual news and the storylines in the other television episodes analyzed were not so obvious.

An interesting and unforeseeable trend across the episodes analyzed was that the hate crimes in these five episodes were not all prototypical anti-gay hate crimes in which a heterosexual person victimizes a gay or lesbian victim. In three of the five episodes, the perpetrators were depicted as harboring repressed sexualities, or being closeted gay persons. In other words, they were depicted as people who exact pain on lesbians or gay men as a way of casting off an LGB identity and affirming a heterosexual identity regardless of their true sexuality. In one such episode of the television show *Conviction* ("Denial," Season 1, Episode 2, aired on March 10, 2006), a high school basketball player beats up a gay teenager while calling him names like "faggot" and "bitch." It soon comes to light that the athlete is actually gay himself, but refuses to openly admit it because he doesn't want others to "see him as a faggot." In the end, he maintains his silence in order to pass as heterosexual and therefore allows himself to be tried as a heterosexual who beat up a gay peer out of hate.

In an episode of *Law and Order: SVU* ("Bad Blood," Season 1, Episode 11, aired on January 14, 2000), a gay male is murdered by a man whose own sexuality is repressed. Again, the crime is framed as being caused by the killer's failure to accept himself as a gay male. Finally, the *Law and Order* episode which mirrored the Harvey Milk murder ("Pride," Season 5, Episode 23, aired on May 24, 1995) alludes to the conservative killer as having repressed sexual urges as well. Of course, the perpetrators in all three of the aforementioned episodes knew the victims on a personal level. This trend lies in sharp contrast to the majority of federally reported crimes, which are typically reported as "stranger crimes" (Garofalo and Martin 1993). According to data from the FBI's Uniform Crime Reporting (2008), the victims of hate crimes typically do not know their attacker. However, research on anti-gay behaviors in *non*criminal populations supports the notion that perpetrators of hate crimes often have close ties with their victims (Franklin 2000). This discrepancy might be explained by the stigma associated with reporting victimization on the basis of sexual orientation, especially when the victim knows the attacker (Lyons 2006; Herek 2009). As a result of this stigma, stranger crimes may simply appear more frequently in federal data.

Conventional television crime dramas are based on investigating the actions leading up to the crime (Sumser 1996), and stranger crimes do not offer the same sort of richness and intrigue as those crimes perpetrated by someone familiar to the victim. In other words, stranger crimes may not lend themselves to good storytelling on television. So, the disconnect between television portrayals and federal data may simply be a result of the need for story development. Another noteworthy point is that the news media (i.e., TV news, newspapers, etc.) often depict hate crimes as street attacks in which the perpetrator is a young male, or group of young males who have no prior relationship to the victim (Herek, Cogan, and Gillis 2002). The work of Herek et al. (2002) is based on actual hate crime incidents, so one might expect the hate crimes in crime dramas to be similarly depicted as street attacks between strangers. However, in all five of the television episodes included in this analysis, the perpetrators and victims knew one another. This trend is consistent with the finding from Franklin (2000) that victims of hate crimes do typically know their attackers. So, depending on whether you view representations of hate crimes via news media (strangers) or television crime dramas (acquaintances), you may end up with a different perception of whether or not the parties involved in hate crimes actually know one another.

Storylines in television crime dramas are typically episodic events that are contained within a single episode. Most of the character development is focused on the recurrent characters. As such, there is very little time to develop the episode-specific characters of offender and victim. The cases covered in television crime dramas sometimes serve as an opportunity to discuss a hot topic found in the media. Other times, the cases are merely a backdrop for helping shed further light on the lives of the lead characters. A perfect example of the latter can be found in the second *Law and Order* episode analyzed ("Innocence," Season 20, Episode 16, aired on March 15, 2010). The episode opens with the arrest and subsequent conviction of a young white male who is charged with the murder of a gay male. Elements of the violent incident are peppered throughout the episode, but with limited detail. Most of the screen time is dedicated to advancing the relationships between the show's lead characters. One positive element of this episode, which received praise in the GLAAD "Network Responsibility Index" (GLAAD 2009), is the incorporation of the victim's husband into the storyline. His portrayal added a sense of empathy and realness to both the situation and the victim; however, it was still largely overshadowed by other interactions between the lead characters of the show. The only real references to the offender's motive came in the form of reactions by the offender and his mother to allegations by the defense team that the offender himself is gay. Otherwise, the circumstances and details of the crime are left quite vague.

The victims in four of the five episodes were gay men, which is consistent with both federal data and social science research on sexual orientation-based hate crimes. For example, in 2008, 57.5 percent of all federally-reported sexual orientation-based hate crimes were "anti-gay male attacks" compared to only 11.6 percent which were "anti-gay female attacks" (Uniform Crime Report 2008). Another 27.3 percent of attacks were simply reported as "anti-gay attacks" with the sex of the victim unspecified. Herek (2009) also found that a heightened degree of victimization existed for gay males as opposed to lesbians. Using a national probability sample of 662 lesbian, gay, and bisexual adults, Herek (2009) found that approximately 20 percent of survey respondents were the victim of a person or property crime based on their sexual orientation. The self-reported victimization of gay males (37.6 percent) was substantially higher than the rate for lesbians (12.5 percent). In terms of the gender of victims then, television crime dramas appear to provide a representation consistent with the patterns found in both hate crimes and violent crime in general. Men, in general, are victimized much more frequently than women, and this pattern holds true in sexual-orientation based hate crimes.

In reality, the overwhelming majority of anti-gay hate crimes occur at the hands of delinquent youth populations, most of whom are white males (Herek and Berrill 1992). Four of the five hate crimes analyzed in this study included white perpetrators; however, they were not particularly young. Of the four white perpetrators, only one appeared to be under the age of 25, which lies in stark contrast to research on sexual orientation-based hate crimes. Most studies purport that assailants of actual anti-gay hate crimes are typically between 14 and 22 years of age (Garofalo and Martin 1993). In terms of race, the perpetrators in the five episodes analyzed were somewhat representative of federal data on offender. While four of the five episodes contained white offenders, the offender in the episode from *Conviction* ("Denial," Season 1, Episode 2, aired on March 10, 2006) represented the only black perpetrator analyzed. According to federal data in 2008 16.7 percent of the offenders of sexual orientation-based hate crimes were black (Uniform Crime Report 2008). Therefore, race was reasonably represented in the sample.

Table 2. Summary of Findings

	TV	*Reality*
Relationship between Victim(s) and Perpetrator	Familiar with one another	Strangers
Perpetrator's Gender	Male	Male
Perpetrator's Race	White	White
Victim	Gay male	Gay male
Age of Perpetrator	25–older	14–22
Motivation	Repressed Sexuality	Disapproval over orientation/ proving masculinity

Offender motivation provides fertile ground for analysis. As mentioned above, three of the five episodes in this analysis centered on offenders who exacted their vengeance on gay and lesbian victims as a result of struggling with their own, repressed, sexuality. Whether or not the perpetrators of actual hate crimes may be sexually repressed is a topic open for discussion since such information is difficult to come across. Hate crime statistics are victimological in nature. That is, most documented motivations are the result of what was said or conveyed during an attack, and such motivations are typically expressions of or disapproval over non-heterosexual orientations. Based on actual attacks, the generally accepted explanation for anti-gay hate crimes is that they serve to provide proof of masculinity or manhood (Franklin 2000; Perry 2001). For men, masculinity is intimately tied to sexuality, so the hate crimes in this analysis hold true to this research finding. Negative attitudes toward homosexuality, belief in homosexuality as a moral choice, and heterosexism are all significant predictors of hate crime victimization (Alden and Parker 2005). These three factors are well reflected in the five dramatic depictions of hate crimes analyzed in this study.

Two other prevalent motivations, belief in homosexuality as a moral choice and heterosexism, were found in three episodes analyzed (*Conviction*— "Denial"; *Law and Order*—"Innocence"; *Law and Order: SVU*—"P.C."). These two particular factors were well characterized in the final *Law and Order: SVU* episode analyzed ("P.C.," Season 11, Episode 13, aired on March 3, 2010). The perpetrator in this episode, a middle-aged white male, was upset over the increased presence of the lesbian community in his neighborhood. Little was known about the offender until the final frames of the episode, but what was apparent was his insistence that any lesbian just needed "the right man." He exacted sexual violence as a means of expressing this opinion, and he believed that the lesbians in his neighborhood simply made a moral choice to be gay, and that this choice was reversible through force. The episode contained some of the most stereotypical depictions of issues surrounding the LGBT community, and garnered some sharp criticism from GLAAD over stereotypical man-hating lesbians, unoriginal victims, and the editing out of a much-hyped kiss involving two popular female actors/celebrities (GLAAD 2010). These sorts of stereotypical depictions and studio decisions have become the focus of LGBT depictions on television. Now that lead and supporting LGBT characters are increasing in numbers, the attention of equal rights organizations as well as social scientists must focus on the quality of the content and the representation of LGBT characters on television. Further research in this area is the only way to ensure that viewers are being supplied valid representations of LGBT persons and issues related to the LGBT community.

Discussion and Conclusion

Television influences the assumptions people have about sexual minorities such as lesbian, gay, bisexual, and transgendered persons because viewers (many of whom are heterosexual) may have limited constructive interaction with such individuals (Gross 1994). It is well documented that people often live and learn vicariously through television content. Recent research on vicariousness includes the vicarious masculinity experienced by men watching televised sports

(Crawley, Foley, and Shehan 2008), and vicarious sexuality experienced by viewers of all television programming (Fisher et al. 2007). People use the experiences of others through which to model their attitudes, beliefs, and behavior, particularly in situations where their own personal experience is very limited (Bandura 2001). A quintessential example of this is the avid male football fan that has never been an athlete himself, but on Sunday afternoons believes and behaves as if he is "part of the team" (Crawley et al. 2008).

Of particular relevance to the current study is the notion that vicarious learning is especially high among youth who are still forming their sexual identities (Chapin 2000). This is a peculiar finding considering how most hate crimes committed against lesbians and gay men are perpetrated by delinquent male youth (Herek and Berrill 1992). The fact is, the way people and issues are framed via television programming has a major impact on how we perceive our social worlds. This is especially true of topics that are not frequently experienced on a personal basis.

One particularly promising trend in television is the overall increase in the coverage of LGBT issues in television entertainment. LGBT characters now account for 3.0 percent of all characters on television up from 1.7 percent just two years ago (GLAAD 2010). As more and more television audiences are being exposed to LGBT persons and issues, our attention naturally shifts away from the quantity of content and toward the quality of content. We must discern the ways in which LGBT persons and issues are depicted. In the case of this study, the focus was on analyzing the depiction of sexual orientation-based hate crimes in television crime dramas. The depiction of these crimes on television likely has a substantial influence on the viewers' own reality construction, since relatively few people have experience with such phenomena.

The majority of this analysis centered on identifying themes and trends such as the race, gender, age, and sexual orientation of the offenders and victims of each hate crime depicted. Close attention was paid to the motive behind each crime and the relationship between the offenders and victims. A final intention was to analyze the context surrounding each hate crime itself and the framing of each incident.

As is the case with so much qualitative research, unanticipated themes and trends emerged as well. The typical offender of actual hate crimes is in their teens and early twenties, while the offenders in the episodes analyzed were mostly middle-aged. This finding is not surprising considering that the average age of television viewership for the major U.S. broadcast stations recently eclipsed 50 years of age (Bauder 2010) and television viewers typically prefer to view characters of their own age (Harwood 1997). Although this trend is not surprising it still casts a skewed perception of the typical age of offenders of these violent crimes. The race and gender of victims and perpetrators was quite representative of data on actual hate crimes. Of course, the sample is far too small to make any broad generalizations.

Analysis of the episodes in this study also led to some interesting themes with regard to the sexual orientation of offenders. Three of the five episodes contained an offender who was motivated to commit their crimes on the basis of having repressed sexualities. All three of these offenders were framed as individuals who were fighting same-sex urges while trying to maintain a heterosexual visage. Unfortunately, current data on hate crimes offers little indication of whether or not actual offenders commit crimes as a result of having repressed sexualities. From a sociological perspective, it is troubling that perpetrators are being depicted as having purely inward motivations. The failure to recognize the role of societal norms and social formations of gender and sexuality virtually ignores the macro-level interactions that contribute to hate. However, engaging in a lengthy discussion of the social explanations for hate crimes is not part of the equation for good television. After all, storylines in crime dramas must be, well, dramatic. Perpetrators have to be flawed individuals and troubled souls, right?

What we do know about the motivations of hate crime offenders is that, in general, they often feel justified in their actions. Offenders feel that they are defending the moral turf of society and ridding the world of inferior groups (McDevitt, Levin, and Bennett 2002). Unfortunately, we know relatively little about any motivations that might be unique to those who commit sexual orientation-based hate crimes. It is evident, though, that the depiction of offenders as repressed is something many viewers are being inundated with. Aside from this trend and the *Law and Order: SVU* episode involving the man who was upset with the growing presence of the lesbian community in his neighborhood ("P.C.," Season 11, Episode 13, aired on March 3, 2010) there was really very little development in terms of motive in the episodes analyzed.

The frequency with which television crime dramas frame lesbian, gay, bisexual, and transgender (LGBT) characters as villains is a troubling theme observed in this analysis. This trend was particularly evident in the *CSI* franchise. While these episodes were not all included in this analysis, eight different episodes were identified that included one or more gay, lesbian, or bisexual killers. What is more troubling is that these killers are depicted as carrying out vengeance killings against prior lovers. This framing could lead viewers to wrongfully perceive of LGBT persons' relationships as particularly problematic and violent. Also identified were two episodes of *Law and Order* and *Criminal Minds* that included storylines with LGBT killers. In total, from the original sample of 25 episodes of television crime dramas, 12 episodes containing LGBT killers were identified compared to only 5 episodes in which an LGB person was the victim of a violent hate crime. Ironically then, in television entertainment, LGB persons appear to be framed as the *perpetrators* of violent crimes more frequently than the victims. Unfortunately, crime data rarely includes information on the sexual orientation of perpetrators, but such data would make for an interesting study. Such a trend could have dire influences on television audiences, particularly those who have little meaningful personal interaction with LGB persons.

If there is one thing that crime dramas should be applauded for, it is their empathetic portrayal of the victims of hate crimes. In four of the five episodes, the victims were framed as truly on the losing end of a hateful act of violence. The victims were never shown to be deserving of the harm inflicted upon them. Additionally, the victims were never blamed for their circumstances or hardships. "Blaming the victim" is a legitimate concern when looking at depictions of phenomena in television programming. News and entertainment media in the U.S. both have a history of blaming victims for contributing to or inciting the crimes committed against them, particularly in the case of violence against women (Meyers 1997) and violence against members of the LGB community (Lyons 2006). Overall, the depiction of sexual orientation-based hate crimes in crime dramas appears to provide a sensible, albeit stereotypical portrayal of these violent acts. If anything, the story development found in these episodes does at least cast sexual orientation-based hate crimes as a legitimate social problem.

NOTES

1. The acronym "LGB" is used in place of the more common "LGBT" simply because research and data on sexual orientation-based hate crimes is typically limited to lesbian, gay, and bisexual persons. The acronym "LGBT" is used only when referencing research that includes a focus on the transgender community as well.

REFERENCES

Adoni, Hanna, and Sherrill Mane. 1984. "Media and the Social Construction of Reality: Toward an Integration of Theory and Research." *Communication Research* 11: 323–340.

Alden, Helena L., and Karen F. Parker. 2005. "Gender Role Ideology, Homophobia and Hate Crime: Linking Attitudes to Macro-level Anti-gay and Lesbian Hate Crimes." *Deviant Behavior* 26: 321–343.

Altheide, David L. 1995. *An Ecology of Communication: Cultural Formats of Control*. Hawthorne, NY: Aldine de Gruyter.

_____. 1997. "The News Media, the Problem Frame, and the Production of Fear." *The Sociological Quarterly* 38: 647–688.

Altheide, David L., and Robert P. Snow. 1979. *Media Logic*. Beverly Hills: Sage.

Bandura, Albert. 2001. "Social Cognitive Theory of Mass Communication." *Media Psychology* 3: 265–299.

Bauder, David. 2010. "Broadcast TV Audience Aging FASTER Than U.S. Population." The Huffington Post, August 16, 2010. Accessed August 29, 2010. *http://www.huffingtonpost.com/2010/08/16/broadcast-tv-audience-agi_n_683009.html*.

Becker, Ron. 2006. *Gay TV and straight America*. New Brunswick, NJ: Rutgers University Press.

Berger, Arthur Asa. 2006. *Media Analysis Techniques*. Thousand Oaks, CA: Sage.

Berger, Peter L., and Thomas Luckmann. 1966. *The Social Construction of Reality: A Treatise in the Sociology of Knowledge*. Garden City, NY: Doubleday.

Brown, Jane D., and Elizabeth M. Witherspoon. 2002. "The Mass Media and American Adolescents' Health." *Journal of Adolescent Health* 31: 153–170.

Chapin, John R. 2000. "Adolescent Sex and Mass Media: A Developmental Approach." *Adolescence* 35: 799–811.

Crawley, Sara L., Lara J. Foley, and Constance L. Shehan. 2008. *Gendering Bodies*. Lanham: Rowman and Littlefield.

Fisher, Deborah A., Douglas L. Hill, Joel W. Grube, and Enid L. Gruber. 2007. "Gay, Lesbian, and

Bisexual Content on Television: A Quantitative Analysis Across Two Seasons." *Journal of Homosexuality* 52: 167–188.

Franklin, Karen. 2000. "Antigay Behaviors among Young Adults: Prevalence, Patterns, and Motivators in a Noncriminal Population." *Journal of Interpersonal Violence* 15: 339–362.

Garofalo, James, and Susan E. Martin. 1993. "Bias-motivated Crimes: Their Characteristics and the Law Enforcement Response." Final report to the National Institute of Justice. Carbondale: Southern Illinois University, Center for the Study of Crime, Delinquency, and Correction.

Gerbner, George, Larry Gross, Michael Morgan, Nancy Signorielli, and James Shanahan. 2002. "Growing Up with Television: Cultivation Processes." In Jennings Bryant and Dolf Zillmann (eds.), *Media Effects: Advances in Theory and Research, 2d ed.*: 43–67. Mahwah, NJ: Lawrence Erlbaum.

GLAAD, 2009. "2009–2010 Network Responsibility Index." Accessed September 1, 2010. *http://www. glaad.org/document.doc?id=127.*

_____. "Where We Are on TV: GLAAD's 14th Annual Diversity Study Previews the 2009–2010 Primetime Television Season." Accessed September 1, 2010. *http://www.glaad.org/document.doc?id=92.*

Gross, Larry 1991. "Out of the Mainstream: Sexual Minorities and the Mass Media." *Journal of Homosexuality,* 21: 19–46.

_____. 1994. "What Is Wrong With This Picture? Lesbian Women and Gay Men on Television." In RJ Ringer (ed.), *Queer Words, Queer Images: Communication and Construction of Homosexuality*: 143–156. New York: New York University Press.

Harwood, Jake. 1997. "Viewing Age: Lifespan Identity and Television Viewing Choices." *Journal of Broadcasting & Electronic Media* 41: 203–213.

Herek, Gregory M. 2009. "Hate Crimes and Stigma-Related Experiences Among Sexual Minority Adults in the United States." *Journal of Interpersonal Violence* 24: 54–74.

Herek, Gregory M. and Kevin T. Berrill. 1992. *Hate Crimes: Confronting Violence Against Lesbians and Gay Men.* Newbury Park, CA: Sage.

Herek, Gregory M., Jeanine C. Cogan, and J. Roy Gillis. 2002. "Victim Experiences in Hate Crimes Based on Sexual Orientation." *Journal of Social Issues* 58: 319–339.

Jenness, Valerie. 1995. "Social Movements Growth, Domain Expansion, and Framing Processes: The Gay/Lesbian Movement and Violence against Gays and Lesbians as a Social Problem." *Social Problems* 42: 145–170.

Lee, Cynthia. 2003 *Murder and the Reasonable Man: Passion and Fear in the Criminal Courtroom.* New York: New York University Press.

Lyons, Christopher J. 2006. "Stigma or Sympathy? Attributions of Fault to Hate Crime Victims and Offenders." *Social Psychology Quarterly* 69: 39–59.

McDevitt, Jack, Jack Levin, and Susan Bennett. 2002. "Hate Crimes Offenders: An Expanded Typology." *Journal of Social Issues* 58: 303–317.

Meyers, Marian. 1997. *News coverage of violence against women: engendering blame.* Thousand Oaks, CA: Sage.

Mills, C. Wright. 1963. *Power, Politics, and People: The Collected Essays of C. Wright Mills.* New York: Oxford University Press.

Motion Picture Association of America. 2007. "2007 Market Statistics." Accessed December 8, 2008. *http://www.perfspot.com/docs/doc.asp?id=815.*

Perry, Barbara. 2001. *In the Name of Hate.* New York: Routledge.

Perse, Elizabeth M. 2001. *Media Effects and Society.* LEA's Communication Series. Mahwah, NJ: L. Lawrence Erlbaum.

Sumser, John. 1996. *Morality and Social Order in Television Crime Drama.* Jefferson, NC: McFarland.

Surette, Ray. 1992. *Media, Crime, and Criminal Justice: Images and Realities.* Pacific Grove, CA: Brooks/Cole.

Uniform Crime Report. 2008. "Hate Crime Statistics, 2008." accessed November 20, 2009. *http:/www. fbi.gov/ucr/hc2008/incidents.html.*

Weimann, Gabriel. 2000. *Communicating Unreality: Modern Media and the Reconstruction of Reality.* Thousand Oaks, CA: Sage.

Crime News Sources and Crime Views: The Relationship Between News Media Exposure Patterns and Whites' Opinions About Criminal Justice Issues

Alicia D. Simmons

While antipathy toward crime is present in every society, such sentiments have become a particularly potent social and political force in the United States, whereby public opinion has partially motivated current criminal justice policies and practices (e.g., Norrander 2000; Jacobs and Kent 2007; Stults and Baumer 2007). This relationship has been described as a broken thermostat; when public opinion is punitive, the political apparatus responds by enacting like-minded policies, but rather than adjusting accordingly, public opinion remains punitive, clamoring for ever harsher responses to crime (Sharp 1999).

Scholars from a variety of disciplines have sought purchase on the sources of punitive attitudes. Since most individuals do not have direct experience with crime, it is unsurprising that the primary source of information about these matters, the news media, has been demonstrated to be consequential for public opinion on criminal justice issues (e.g., Roberts and Doob 1990; Iyengar 1991; Beckett 1997; Peffley, Shields and Williams 1996; Gilliam and Iyengar 2000; Gilliam, Valentino and Beckmann 2002; Dixon 2008). Yet our knowledge about the relationship between media exposure and criminal justice opinions is incomplete. Previous research has predominantly focused on local television newscasts (for example, Gilliam, Valentino and Beckmann 2002) while neglecting other news genres such as network television news and print newspapers. While local television news is the most widely used news media source, nontrivial portions of the public also engage with other news media (see Table 1 for information about the demographic characteristics of those who regularly engage with the news genres). Furthermore, the few studies that have examined non-local television news sources have largely examined the impact of a single genre on crime news as opposed to investigating the influence of several genres in tandem. This is a methodological deficiency, as few individuals exclusively engage with one news genre, instead sampling from many.

Table 1 Percentage of Groups Regularly Engaging with News Media Sources

	Local television	Network television	Daily newspapers
General public	52%	29	34
Male	48	27	36
Female	52	31	32
Whites	52	29	37
Blacks	61	32	24
Latinos	44	29	23
Less than high school	47	25	20
High school	58	33	30
Some college	52	28	34
College degree	47	28	45

Source: The Pew Research Center for the People and the Press (2008).

This chapter contributes to research on the link between news media exposure and opinions about criminal justice issues by using nationally representative survey data collected from 2000 to 2008 to investigate how exposure to several different news genres influences opinions on a variety of crime issues. The results indicate that, net of other factors, viewing greater amounts of local television news is positively associated with the belief that crime is on the rise, preferences for increased federal spending on crime and strong support for the death penalty. In contrast, viewing greater amounts of network television news is negatively associated with the belief that crime is rising and positively associated with preferences for decreased spending on crime. Finally, reading greater amounts of daily print newspapers is positively associated with the belief that crime is on the decline or rise as opposed to believing that the crime rate has stayed the same.

Background

News Media Coverage of Crime

Local Television News: The vast majority of research linking news media exposure and opinions about criminal justice issues has concerned local television. This genre focuses on *soft news* content, meaning topics such as the weather, sports, human interest stories and crime. Crime accounts for the largest portion of local television newscasts, and these segments are prominently featured (Klite, Bardwell and Salzman 1997; Project for Excellence in Journalism 2006). News agencies tend to emphasize rare, serious, violent, and sensational crimes (Reiner 2002), with murder accounting for approximately one-third of the coverage (Chermak 1994). Inter-reality comparisons between crime news and crime statistics reveal that violent crime is overrepresented in local news coverage (Klite et al. 1997) while property crime is underrepresented (Chermak 1994).

Beyond the *content* of news reports, *how* news segments are presented is also consequential for viewers' opinions. Local television news segments are quite short; 60 percent are less than 30 seconds long, and 80 percent conclude in less than one minute (Project for Excellence in Journalism 2006). Partly as a function of these time constraints, local television news tends to use an *episodic reporting* style, meaning that the narrative limits itself to the event at hand and neglects to provide contextual details about the story or to situate it in a broader historical context. Episodic reporting often reduces stories to their bare essentials, rehashes cultural stereotypes in order to quickly convey a message (Gilliam and Iyengar 2000), and frequently only presents one point of view in stories involving controversy (Project for Excellence in Journalism 2004).

The sum of local news media practices (i.e., an emphasis on violent crime and a reliance on episodic reporting techniques) has demonstrable impacts on viewers' opinions. For example, Gilliam and Iyengar (2000) found that frequent viewers of local news are more likely to support punitive crime responses than those who tune in less often, while Dixon (2008) found that attention to crime news was positively related to concern about crime.

Network Television News: Network television news content is dramatically different from that of local television news. Network newscasts focus on *hard news*, encompassing stories on topics such as politics, economics, and science. Network newscasts air half of the crime content provided by local television news (Project for Excellence in Journalism 2006).

As hard news content tends to be more complicated than soft news content, network television news necessarily has to devote more time to explaining the issues that it reports; 45 percent of segments are longer than one minute (Project for Excellence in Journalism 2006). In comparison to local newscasts, network newscasts employ more *thematic reporting*, which provides a rich narrative of events and their surrounding context, including information such as background details, future implications, separation of fact from conjecture, potential actions that audience members may take, and sources of additional information (Project for Excellence in Journalism 2006). On the whole, thematic reporting inhibits the use of stereotypes in news coverage.

Unfortunately, previous research has not examined the sole impact of network television news on viewers' criminal justice attitudes. However, one study that aggregates local and network news into a comprehensive news measure indicated that television news viewership is negatively related to support for capital punishment (Holbert, Shah and Kwak 2004). As previous research indicates that local television news viewership is associated with greater support for punitive criminal justice policies (Gilliam and Iyengar 2000), the above finding suggests that the influence of network television news on audience attitudes is quite different than that of its local counterpart.

Daily Newspapers: Daily newspapers tend to have substantial overlap with the stories covered by local and network television news sources, covering a mix of soft and hard news stories (Entman and Rojecki 2000). While daily newspapers cover more crime stories than the network television, they give less attention to crime than local television (Project for Excellence in Journalism 2006). Print and television news genres emphasize different types of crime; stories that are prominent in local newscasts often play a secondary role in newspapers (Entman and Rojecki 2000). For example, daily newspapers are more likely than other news genres to address white collar offenses and detail all of the crimes that a suspect is accused of (Chermak 1994).

Despite the topical overlap with other news sources, there are important differences between print and television news. First, individuals have greater control over the information they receive when reading newspapers, exposing themselves only to stories of interest and in whatever order they choose, while television displays its content in a predetermined order and does not allow for selection of stories (Eveland, Seo and Marton 2002). Second, newspapers employ a more thematic approach to reporting than television sources (Reiner 2002), a difference attributable to both the complexity of hard news stories and the greater density of information that can be provided in newsprint. This density advantage is rather significant; on average, the entire transcript of a network newscast can fit on the front page of a newspaper from a large city (Furnham, Gunter and Green 1990).

As is the case with network television newscasts, the relationship between daily newspaper readership and views on criminal justice issues has been underspecified. However, one study indicated that when compared to individuals who read court documents, newspaper readers were more likely to believe that criminal sentences are too lenient (Roberts and Doob 1990).

Public Opinion on Criminal Justice Issues

The first criminal justice issue considered is beliefs about changes in the crime rate. There are signs that the public has an erroneous view of how often crimes occur. Gallup Poll results indicated that 44 percent of Americans believe there is more crime in their area than a year ago, and 67 percent believed that crime in the U.S. has increased over the same period. When asked to describe the seriousness of the nation's crime problem, 51 percent labeled it as extremely or very serious (Saad 2007). These results are particularly troubling, as they emerge in a context in which crime rates are actually declining (Bureau of Justice Statistics 2009).

The hypotheses regarding news media exposure and perceptions of the crime rate are informed by research on *agenda setting*. This tradition asserts that the amount of coverage that the news media gives to a particular topic determines which topics the public perceives as more socially important and which are believed to be less socially important (Iyengar and Kinder 1987). In essence, agenda setting effects dictate what the news audience thinks about. As local television news zealously covers crime, it is anticipated that heavy viewers will be more likely than light viewers to perceive that crime is a serious social issue, and thus will be more likely to believe that there have been increases in the rate of criminal offending. In contrast, since network newscasts tend to deemphasize crime coverage, it is anticipated that the relationship between the amount of network news viewed and perceptions of increasing crime rates will be negative. Finally, as daily newspapers provide a wealth of crime coverage, it is hypothesized that frequent readers will be more likely to perceive an increased crime rate than infrequent readers.

Second, this chapter examines public preferences about adjustments in federal spending on crime. Scholars interested in public opinion on government spending fall into two camps. One side of the debate posits that the public views government spending as a holistic issue and does not differentiate between spending areas, meaning that those who support increased spending on defense also support increased spending on welfare. The opposing view argues that public opinion is segmented, such that opinion about welfare spending is different from that about defense spending, and so on. Within the latter perspective, there have been few studies that examine crime spending specifically. This limited body of work reveals that racial attitudes play an important role in determining these attitudes such that racially conservative individuals tend to be supportive of increased spending on crime (Barkan and Cohn 2005; Hurwitz and Peffley 2005).

The hypotheses concerning news media exposure and support for federal spending on crime draw also draws on the agenda setting literature. As crime is both prevalently and prominently featured in local television newscasts, its salience as a serious social problem should be heightened among heavy viewers as compared to lighter viewers. This increased salience should ultimately result in support for increased spending to deal with crime in order to alleviate this important social issue. In contrast to local television news, network newscasts focus their programming on hard news topics such as defense and the economy, prompting viewers to consider these topics as more important than crime. Thus frequent network news viewers will be less likely than infrequent viewers to support increased federal spending on the crime problem. Similar to network newscasts, daily papers tend to give a wide variety of news stories prominent coverage, many of which are unrelated to crime, and as such, heavy readers should be less likely than light readers to support increased federal spending on crime.

The final criminal justice opinion this article examines is support for the death penalty. The majority of Americans, 64 percent, support the death penalty for persons convicted of murder, and nearly half believe that it is not imposed often enough (Saad 2008). Opinion on the death penalty tends to be more inflexible than opinions about punishment for other types of crime (Bobo and Johnson 2004).

The hypotheses concerning the relationship between news media exposure and opinions about the death penalty draw on research indicating that aspects of news coverage influence audience members' attributions for the source of criminal offending (Iyengar 1991). *Internal attributions* place the locus of blame on the individual, holding that something within her is responsible for criminal offending. *External attributions* place the locus of blame on societal forces, holding that factors outside of her control are responsible for her criminality. Attributions have been linked to media exposure in that episodic reporting techniques are more likely to promote internal attributions as opposed to external attributions (Iyengar 1991). Research further indicates that attributions influence opinions about punishment, such that internal attributions promote more punitive policy orientations than external attributions (Cochran, Paquette Boots and Heide 2003; Sims 2003). As local television news tends to rely on episodic reporting techniques, it is anticipated that heavy viewers will be more likely than light viewers to make internal attributions about criminal offending, and thus support harsher punishments such as the death penalty. Network television news also employs episodic techniques, albeit to a slightly lesser extent than its local counterpart, and as such, frequent viewers of this genre should be more favorable toward the death penalty than infrequent viewers. Newspapers tend to employ the most thematic news reporting style, therefore, it is expected that those who are habitual newspaper readers should be more disposed toward external attributions for criminality, and thus less favorable toward the death penalty than those who read less often. See Table 2 for a summary of the hypotheses.

Table 2. Summary of Hypotheses

Compared to lighter viewers, heavier viewers of local television news will be
- more likely to believe that the crime rate has increased
- more likely to support increased federal spending on crime control
- more likely to support the death penalty

Compared to lighter viewers, heavier viewers of network television news will be
- less likely to believe that the crime rate has increased
- less likely to support increased federal spending on crime control
- more likely to support the death penalty

Compared to lighter readers, heavier readers of daily newspapers will be
- more likely to believe that the crime rate has increased
- less likely to support increased federal spending on crime control
- less likely to support the death penalty

Data and Methods

This chapter uses data from the 2000–2008 American National Election Study (ANES) to examine the relationship between news media exposure patterns and whites' attitudes about criminal justice issues. The ANES uses a multistage area probability sample from the contiguous United States, encompassing citizens who were at least eighteen years old at the time of interview. Analyses are restricted to whites because the number of non-whites in the sample is too small to generate reliable estimates.

While this research assumes that causal direction moves from news exposure to criminal justice attitudes, the cross-sectional data analyzed here cannot confirm or refute the reverse proposition, that criminal justice attitudes compel various patterns of news exposure. Yet there are sound reasons to believe that the latter is unlikely to occur. First, experiments demonstrate that audience opinion shifts occur *after* exposure to news media messages (Gilliam et al. 1996; Peffley et al. 1996; Gilliam and Iyengar 2000). Second, while a self-selection argument might posit that the news audience is primarily made up of people with a punitive criminal justice orientation, 95 percent of individuals in this sample report exposure to at least some news, with each genre being watched or read by a minimum of 72 percent of the sample; not all of these individuals are punitive. Third, while a self-selection argument might anticipate that people select news sources that confirm their beliefs and avoid news sources that contradict them, 86 percent of individuals in this study were not exclusive viewers or readers of any one medium, instead, they sampled from a variety of genres. Finally, research on exposure to political views in opposition to one's own indicates that contradictory exposure is more likely to stem from news media sources than from interpersonal communication (Mutz and Martin 2001). Thus, although this study cannot definitively state the direction of the causal arrow, it is reasonable to assume that it flows from news consumption to criminal justice opinions and not vice versa.

Dependent Variables

This study considers three crime views: beliefs about changes in the U.S. crime rate, preferences about the level of federal spending on crime, and opinions about the death penalty. Beliefs about changes in the crime rate were assessed with a measure asking respondents to what extent the crime rate in the U.S. has gotten "better," "stayed about the same," or "gotten worse." Preferences about the level of federal spending on crime were assessed with an item asking if spending should be "increased," "stay about the same" or "decreased." Finally, support for the death penalty was assessed with a measure asking respondents if they favor or oppose the death penalty for persons convicted of murder. The item originally fell along a four-point scale ranging from "strongly favor" to "strongly oppose," and was recoded into three categories, "strongly oppose," "slightly oppose/favor," and "strongly favor."

Independent Variables

To tap news media exposure, respondents were asked how many days in the past week they (a) read daily newspapers, (b) watched network television news, (c) watched local television news in the late afternoon or early evening, and (d) watched local television news in the late evening. Each item ranged from 0–7 days per week. The early and late local news categories were summed to create a comprehensive local news viewership variable ranging from 0–14.

Control Variables

This research also accounts for two groups of social psychological variables that are related to attitudes on criminal justice issues, racial attitudes and political orientations. First, research consistently indicates that racial attitudes are an important determinant of opinions about criminal justice matters (e.g., Soss, Langbein and Metelko 2003; Hurwitz and Peffley 2005; Buckler, Wilson and Ross Salinas 2009). This study controls for three types of racial attitudes toward blacks: endorsement of negative stereotypes, affective feelings and racial resentment. Beyond links to racial attitudes, past research has repeatedly demonstrated a connection between criminal justice attitudes and broader political orientations (e.g., Edsall and Edsall 1991; Beckett 1997; Jacobs and Kent 2007). Two variables are used to measure political orientation, ideology and party identification.

Finally, demographic factors have been implicated in criminal justice attitude variation. This research controls for respondents' gender, region of residence, religious affiliation, age, years of education, and household income.

Results

Table 3 details respondents' scores on the dependent and independent variables. A plurality (41 percent) of respondents thought that the crime rate had stayed about the same, while roughly a third thought it had gotten worse and a quarter believed it had gotten better. Over half of respondents (60 percent) preferred increasing federal spending on crime, while roughly a third believed it should be kept about the same. In response to questions about their support for the death penalty, the majority (56 percent) strongly favored capital punishment, while 30 percent were slightly in favor or opposed, and only 15 percent were strongly opposed. In regards to their media exposure habits, individuals who watched local television news averaged 5.6 broadcasts in the past week, those who watched network news viewed an average of 3.4 broadcasts, and those who were exposed to a daily newspaper read an average of 3.3 issues.

Table 3. Sample Characteristics

Dependent variables		News exposure variables	
Perception of crime rate		Local television news	5.6
Better	24.5%	(0–7 episodes)	
About the same	41.4	Network television news	3.4
Worse	34.1	(0–14 episodes)	
Preference for federal			
spending on crime		Print newspapers	3.3
Decrease	7.9%	(0–7 issues)	
About the same	32.3		
Increase	59.8		
Death penalty preferences			
Strongly oppose	14.7%		
Slightly oppose or favor	29.5		
Strongly favor	55.8		

Source: American National Election Study (2000–2008)

The hypotheses are tested using multinomial logistic regression. This technique is used when the dependent variable has three or more categories, and allows researchers to predict category membership based on independent variable values. These predictions are relative to one of the dependent variable's categories (known as a reference category). For example, imagine a study where the dependent variable is people's choice of ice cream flavor, with the values of chocolate, vanilla or strawberry, and where the independent variable is sex. A multinomial logistic regression using vanilla as the reference category would tell researchers whether men or women are more likely to choose chocolate instead of vanilla, and whether men or women are more likely to choose strawberry instead of vanilla. In addition to telling researchers who is more likely to prefer which flavor, regressions also tell researchers whether or not the relationships are statistically significant, meaning that the association between the two variables has not occurred by chance. For the purposes of this study, the regressions will tell us if greater amounts of exposure to the news sources is positively or negatively associated with beliefs about the crime rate, preferences for crime spending and opinions about the death penalty. Only statistically significant results will be discussed.

The first set of models presented in Table 4 addresses the relationship between news media exposure and whites' beliefs about changes in the U.S. crime rate. These models compare those who believe the crime rate has gotten "better" or "worse" to those who believe that it had "stayed about the same" (the reference category). Greater daily print newspaper readership is positively associated with asserting that the crime rate has gotten better as opposed to staying the same, although this relationship is marginally significant. Greater local television news or daily print newspaper exposure is positively associated with indicating that the crime rate has gotten worse as opposed to staying the same. In contrast, watching greater amounts of network television news is negatively associated with believing that the crime rate has gotten worse as opposed to staying the same.

The second set of models compare those who believe that federal spending on crime should be "increased" or "decreased" to those who believe it should "stay about the same" (the reference category). Viewing greater amounts of network television news is positively associated with preferring that spending be decreased as opposed to keeping it at the current level. In contrast, viewing greater amounts of local television news is positively associated with preferring increased spending as opposed to maintaining the current level.

The third set of models asses the relationship between news exposure and death penalty preferences. These models compare those who "strongly oppose" or "strongly favor" the death penalty to those who hold the more moderate views of "slightly oppose" and "slightly favor" (the reference category). Viewing greater amounts of local television news is positively associated with strongly favoring the death penalty as opposed to slightly favoring or opposing it, although this relationship is marginally significant.

Table 4 Multinomial Logistic Regression Analyses of Whites' Views on Criminal Justice Issues

	Crime rate		Crime spending		Death penalty	
					Strongly	Strongly
	Better	Worse	Decreased	Increased	oppose	favor
Local television news	0.40	0.64*	-0.41	0.68‡	-0.46	0.40†
	(0.29)	(0.27)	(0.43)	(0.21)	(0.32)	(0.23)
Network television news	0.25	-0.73†	0.68†	-0.20	0.41	0.22
	(0.25)	(0.23)	(0.36)	(0.18)	(0.28)	(0.20)
Print newspapers	0.42†	0.56†	0.01	-0.22	-0.18	-0.10
	(0.22)	(0.20)	(0.32)	(0.16)	(0.24)	(0.17)
LR _²	2460‡		2556‡		2860‡	
Nagelkerke R²	0.25		0.13		0.25	
% correct	52.4		62.1		61.7	
N	1125		1526		1484	

Source: American National Election Study (2000–2008)

Note: The reference categories for the dependent variables are as follows: crime rate-about the same; crime spending-stay about the same; death penalty-slightly oppose/favor. The models also control for respondents' age, education, sex, region, religion, political ideology, political party, racial attitudes toward blacks (i.e., stereotypes, affect, and resentment) and year of survey.

‡ p ≤ 0.001, † p ≤ 0.01, * p ≤ 0.0.5, † p ≤ 0.10

Discussion

It was hypothesized that viewing greater amounts of local television news would be positively related to beliefs that the U.S. crime rate has gotten worse, preferences for increased federal spending on crime and strong support for the death penalty. Overall, these hypotheses are supported. These findings are likely attributable to the amount of crime covered and the reporting style used in the coverage. By covering large amounts of crime, local television newscasts help set crime high on the public's agenda, prompting them to believe that a great deal of crime occurs, and thus altering perceptions of the crime rate. Further-more, by setting crime high on the agenda, local news coverage prompts viewers to prefer that increasing amounts of funds be allocated to combat the serious crime problem. Finally, the episodic reporting style of local television crime news promotes internal attributions of news makers' behavior as opposed to external attributions. If crime is inherently a problem of individual rather than societal failings, then it is clear that the proper recourse is punishment of the individual, thus promoting support for the death penalty.

In regards to network television news, it was anticipated that viewing greater amounts would be negatively related to beliefs that the crime rate is ris-ing, preferences for increased federal spending on crime and strongly support the death penalty. Overall, the results offer mixed support for the hypotheses; while the anticipated relationship between network news and perceptions of the crime rate and preferences for spending are supported, no relationship was found between viewership and opinions about the death penalty. These results likely reflect the content choices made by network news directors. As network newscasts do not cover large amounts of crime news, it is unsurprising that heavy viewers of this genre are disinclined to believe that rates of crime are on the rise because the issue is not high on their agenda of social issues. Inattention to crime news may also be related to network news viewers' preferences for crime spending. Since network newscasts tend focus on other hard news topics, issues besides crime should be ranked higher on viewers' agendas, and as such, they should be deemed more worthy of federal funds. Finally, network newscasts' inattention to crime news may also be responsible for the lack of a relationship between greater viewership and preferences on the death penalty. As crime is rarely discussed on network newscasts, it is unlikely that this type of news con-tributes to either internal or external attributions for criminal offending, and as such, has no discernable impact on viewers' punishment preferences.

Considering daily newspapers, it was hypothesized that greater amounts of readership would be positively associated with the perception that the crime rate has gotten worse and negatively associated with preferences for increased spending on crime and strong support for the death penalty. The results provide limited support for the hypotheses. Newspaper readership is unrelated to preferences for crime spending and support for the death penalty; however, it exhibits a curvilinear relationship with beliefs about changes in the crime rate. The finding that reading greater amounts of daily newspapers is positively related to beliefs that the crime rate is either improving and worsening may be a product of opposing forces canceling one another out. First, while daily newspapers do rely on crime news as a staple of their coverage, they also present a variety of hard news stories, potentially altering their ability to set certain topics high on the agenda of readers. A second factor is the greater amount of flexibility that newspaper readers have in selecting their content as opposed to television news viewers. It is conceivable that some newspaper readers are quite attentive to crime news. These readers are exposed to crime frequently, and as such, they are more likely to place crime high on their agendas, thus prompting them to perceive an increase in the crime rate and to support increased spending in order to address crime. In contrast, other readers may largely ignore crime news in favor of other topics. For these readers, crime news is rarely encountered and thus is low on their agenda; therefore they believe that the crime rate is improving and are unwilling to allocate more funding to crime control. Third, recall that daily print newspapers employ the most thematic reporting style. It may be the case that turning away from episodic reporting techniques ameliorates the impact of heavy doses of crime news. Finally, the contradictory results may also be due to a methodological artifact. The ANES does not allow for differentiation between what types of daily newspaper individuals are reading. Some daily papers, such as *USA Today*, The *New York Times*, and *The Wall Street Journal* attract national readership, while other newspapers have more geographically constrained audiences. These different types of papers undoubtedly offer differing mixes of coverage, and as such, offer differing opportunities to set crime high on readers' agendas and influence their attributions for criminal offending.

Conclusion

This research has sought to contribute to the literature on the relationship between news and public opinion on criminal justice issues. Its contributions have been couched in the fact that studies examining news genres beyond the local television news have been lacking, as have studies that compare different news genres simultaneously. This chapter demonstrates that although the amount of local television news viewership is related to news gatherer's views on criminal justice issues, other genres such as network television and daily newspapers also are associated with public opinion.

Yet this study has limitations of its own that must be addressed in future work. First, it cannot speak to the specific news content to which individuals have been exposed to. Future scholars should take note of work that couples content analyses with survey results (Jerit and Barbas 2006; Barbas and Jerit

2009) and employ this methodological technique. Second, there are additional news genres that should be explored, such as cable television news and internet newspapers and blogs. Furthermore, research indicates that non-traditional sources of news, including programs such as *The Daily Show with Jon Stewart*, *The Tonight Show*, and *Access Hollywood* have discernable impacts on viewers' on viewers' opinions about political issues (Baum 2003). Third, this study has been unable to address other important aspects of the media environment that may influence criminal justice opinions such as reality crime programs like *COPS* and *World's Wildest Police Videos*, and fictional crime programs such as *Law and Order* and *CSI*.

Despite these limitations, this research indicates that mediated messages continue to matter in the modern era. The results suggest that the content news outlets focus on and how this content is presented is related to how audience members think about the world. Perhaps if local television news sources devoted less airtime to crime and more coverage to other news topics, as network television news does, then public opinion on criminal justice issues would become less punitive. A similar effect may emerge if local television newscasts presented their stories in a more thematic reporting style, as daily newspapers do. Either way, it is clear that the news media plays a role in the public's taste for punishment. Whetting this appetite is of the utmost importance, as scholars are now in agreement that the current crime control policies in the United States are doing far more to harm this nation than they are to help it (e.g., Uggen and Manza 2006; Western 2006; Clear 2007). In particular, our criminal justice policies are having a disproportionately negative impact on minority and lower class communities, further exacerbating existing social inequalities (e.g., Western 2006; Clear 2007).

In addition to stoking a general sense of punitiveness among audience members, the news media may play a role in stoking punitiveness directed toward these particular groups. Research indicates that white and black criminals are depicted differently in local television newscasts, with blacks being more likely to be shown in handcuffs, in a mugshot, and under physical restraint than whites (Entman and Rojecki 2000), and minority group members are more likely to be featured in news programming as criminals than as positive role models (Chiricos and Eschholz (2004). Furthermore, crimes such as robbery, which are typically committed by lower class individuals, are more likely to be featured in newscasts than crimes that are typical of the middle and upper classes, such as embezzlement (Randall, Lee-Sammons and Hagner 1988). As intergroup animosity is a key component in determining punitiveness (e.g., Barkan and Cohn 1994; Soss et al. 2003; Barkan and Cohn 2005; Hurwitz and Peffley 2005; Unnever and Cullen 2007; Buckler et al. 2009), racial and social class bias in the news media plays a particularly important role in shaping audience reactions to the news and thus the policies that disproportionately impact these communities.

REFERENCES

Barabas, Jason, and Jennifer Jerit. 2009. "Estimating the Causal Effects of Media Coverage on Policy-Specific Knowledge." *American Journal of Political Science* 53(1): 73–89.

Barkan, Steven E., and Steven F. Cohn. 1994. "Racial Prejudice and Support for the Death Penalty by Whites." *Journal of Research in Crime and Delinquency* 31(2): 202–209.

_____. 2005. "On Reducing White Support for the Death Penalty: A Pessimistic Appraisal." *Criminology and Public Policy* 4(1): 39–44.

Baum, Matthew A. 2003. *Soft News Goes to War: Public Opinion and American Foreign Policy in the New Media Age.* Princeton, NJ: Princeton University Press.

Beckett, Katherine. 1997. *Making Crime Pay: Law and Order in Contemporary American Politics.* New York: Oxford University Press.

Bobo, Lawrence D., and Devon Johnson. 2004. "A Taste for Punishment: Black and White Americans' Views on the Death Penalty and the War on Drugs." *Du Bois Review* 1(1): 151–180.

Buckler, Kevin, Steve Wilson, and Patti Ross Salinas. 2009. "Public Support for Punishment and Progressive Criminal Justice Policy Preferences: The Role of Symbolic Racism and Negative Racial Stereotype." *American Journal of Criminal Justice* 34: 238–252.

Bureau of Justice Statistics. 2009. "Key Crime and Justice Facts at a Glance." Retrieved August 8, 2009. http://www.ojp.usdoj.gov/bjs/glance.htm.

Chermak, Steven M. 1994. "Body Count News: How Crime is Presented in the News Media." *Justice Quarterly* 11(4): 561–582.

Chiricos, Ted, and Sarah Eschholz. 2002. "The Racial and Ethnic Typification of Crime and the Criminal Typification of Race and Ethnicity in Local Television News." *Journal of Research in Crime and Delinquency* 39(4): 400–420.

Clear, Todd R. 2007. *Imprisoning Communities: How Mass Incarceration Makes Disadvantaged Neighborhoods Worse.* New York: Oxford University Press.

Cochran, John K., Denise Paquette Boots, and Kathleen M. Heide. 2003. "Attribution Styles and Attitudes toward Capital Punishment for Juveniles, the Mentally Incompetent, and the Mentally Retarded." *Justice Quarterly* 20(1): 65–93.

Dixon, Travis L. 2008. "Crime News and Racialized Beliefs: Understanding the Relationship between Local News Viewing and Perceptions of African Americans and Crime." *Journal of Communication* 58(1): 106–125.

Edsall, Thomas B., and Mary D. Edsall. 1991. *Chain Reaction: The Impact of Race, Rights, and Taxes on American Politics.* New York: W. W. Norton.

Entman, Robert M., and Andrew Rojecki. 2000. *The Black Image in the White Mind: Media and Race in America.* Chicago: University of Chicago Press.

Eveland, William P., Mihye Seo, and Krisztina Marton. 2002. "Learning From the News in Campaign 2000: An Experimental Comparison of TV News, Newspapers, and Online News." *Media Psychology* 4(4): 355–380.

Furnham, Adrian, Barrie Gunter, and Andrew Green. 1990. "Remembering Science: The Recall of Factual Information as a Function of the Presentation Mode." *Applied Cognitive Psychology* 4(3): 203–212.

Gilliam, Franklin D., and Shanto Iyengar. 2000. "Prime Suspects: The Influence of Local Television News on the Viewing Public." *American Journal of Political Science* 44(3): 560–573.

Gilliam, Franklin D., Shanto Iyengar, Adam Simon, and Oliver Wright. 1996. "Crime in Black and White: The Violent, Scary World of Local News." *Harvard International Journal of Press/Politics* 1(3): 6–23.

Gilliam, Franklin D., Nicholas A. Valentino, and Matthew N. Beckmann. 2002. "Where You Live and What You Watch: The Impact of Racial Proximity and Local Television News on Attitudes about Race and Crime." *Political Research Quarterly* 55(4): 755–780.

Holbert, R. Lance, Dhavan V. Shah, and Nojin Kwak. 2004. "Fear, Authority, and Justice: Crime-Related TV Viewing and Endorsements of Capital Punishment and Gun Ownership." *Journalism and Mass Communication Quarterly* 81(2): 343–363.

Hurwitz, Jon, and Mark Peffley. 2005. "Playing the Race Card in the Post-Willie Horton Era: The Impact of Racialized Code Words on Support for Punitive Crime Policy." *Public Opinion Quarterly* 69(1): 99–112.

Iyengar, Shanto. 1991. *Is Anyone Responsible? How Television Frames Political Issues.* Chicago: The University of Chicago Press.

Iyengar, Shanto, and Donald R. Kinder. 1987. *News That Matters: Television and American Opinion.* Chicago: The University of Chicago Press.

Jacobs, David, and Stephanie L. Kent. 2007. "The Determinants of Executions since 1951: How

Politics, Protests, Public Opinion, and Social Divisions Shape Capital Punishment." *Social Problems* 54(3): 297–318.

Jerit, Jennifer and Jason Barabas. 2006. "Bankrupt Rhetoric: How Misleading Information Affects Knowledge about Social Security." *Public Opinion Quarterly* 70(3): 278–303.

Klite, Paul, Robert A. Bardwell, and Jason Salzman. 1997. "Local TV News: Getting away with Murder." *The Harvard International Journal of Press/Politics*: 57402–424.

Manza, Jeff, and Christopher Uggen. 2006. *Locked Out: Felon Disenfranchisement and American Democracy*. New York: Oxford University Press.

Mutz, Diana C., and Paul S. Martin. 2001. "Facilitating Communication across Lines of Political Difference: The Role of Mass Media." *American Political Science Review* 95(1): 97–114.

Norrander, Barbara. 2000. "The Multi-Layered Impact of Public Opinion on Capital Punishment Implementation in the American States." *Political Research Quarterly* 53(4): 771–793.

Peffley, Mark, Todd G. Shields, and Bruce Williams. 1996. "The Intersection of Race and Crime in Television News Stories: An Experimental Study." *Political Communication* 13(3): 309–327.

Pew Research Center for the People and the Press. 2008. "Audience Segments in a Changing News Environment, Key News Audiences Now Blend Online and Traditional Sources." Washington, DC: The Pew Research Center for the People and the Press. Retrieved August 8, 2009. http://people-press.org/reports/pdf/444.pdf.

Project for Excellence in Journalism. 2004. "State of the News Media 2004." Washington, D.C.: Pew Research Centers. Retrieved August 8, 2009 (http://www.stateofthemedia.org/2004/)

_____. 2006. "State of the News Media 2006." Washington, DC: Pew Research Center. Retrieved August 8, 2009. http://www.stateofthemedia.org/2006/.

Reiner, Robert. 2002. "Media Made Criminality: The Representations of Crime in the Mass Media." in M. Maguire, R. Morgan, and R. Reiner (eds.), *Oxford Handbook of Criminality*: 376–416. New York: Oxford University Press.

Roberts, Julian V., and Anthony N. Doob. 1990. "News Media Influences on Public Views of Sentencing." *Law and Human Behavior* 14(5): 451–468.

Saad, Lydia. 2007. "Perceptions of Crime Problem Remain Curiously Negative." Gallup Inc. Retrieved August 8, 2009. http://www.gallup.com/poll/102262/Perceptions-Crime-Problem-Remain-Curiously-Negative.aspx.

_____. 2008. "Americans Hold Firm to Support for Death Penalty: Only 21 percent Say it is Applied too Often." Gallup Inc. Retrieved August 8, 2009. http://www.gallup.com/poll/111931/Americans-Hold-Firm-Support-Death-Penalty.aspx.

Sharp, Elaine B. 1999. *The Sometime Connection: Public Opinion and Social Policy*. Albany: State University of New York.

Sims, Barbara. 2003. "The Impact of Causal Attribution on Correctional Ideology: A National Study." *Criminal Justice Review* 28(1): 1–25.

Soss, Joe, Laura Langbein, and Alan R. Metelko. 2003. "Why Do White Americans Support the Death Penalty." *Journal of Politics* 65(2): 397–421.

Stults, Brian J., and Eric P. Baumer. 2007. "Racial Context and Police Force Size: Evaluating the Empirical Validity of the Minority Threat Perspective." *American Journal of Sociology* 113(2): 507–546.

Unnever, James D., and Francis T. Cullen. 2007. "The Racial Divide in Support for the Death Penalty: Does White Racism Matter?" *Social Forces* 85(3): 1281–1301.

Western, Bruce. 2006. *Punishment and Inequality in America*. New York: Russell Sage Foundation.

Conclusion: Cultivating
Bias in the Media

JACK LEVIN AND ERIC MADFIS

According to the Bureau of Labor Statistics (2010), watching television currently occupies a greater portion of Americans' leisure time than any other activity including socializing with friends or attending social events. Americans watch an average of 35 hours and 34 minutes of television per week, a number which typically increases with each passing year (Nielsen 2010; Gandossy 2009).

Additionally, more people get their news from local and national television than any other source, though the Internet is quickly gaining ground. Some 78 percent of Americans say they get news from a local TV station, and 73 percent say from a national network or cable TV station (Purcell et al. 2010). Newspaper readership has gradually lost ground to digital technology. In 2010, 31 percent of Americans reported receiving most of their news from a print newspaper — a figure that fell from 34 percent in 2007. Over the same period, newspaper websites grew in popularity as a main source of news from 24 percent in 2007 to 41 percent in 2010 (Pew Research 2011).

For juveniles, television is more often regarded as a source of entertainment rather than news. Nearly three-quarters of the children in the United States live in a home that possesses at least three TV sets. It is no wonder then that children consume television more than any other form of mass entertainment. On a daily basis, they watch television on average for some 2 hours and 46 minutes, but spend only 20 minutes playing video games and 21 minutes using a computer for fun. Even listening to music, which occupies 1 hour and 27 minutes of a typical child's time daily, is in second place to watching television (Roberts, Foehr, and Rideout 2005). Parental controls on their children's television viewing behavior tend to be weak — almost 50 percent of all parents fail to impose any restrictions on their youngsters' viewing behavior. In fact, some 53 percent of all parents permit a set in their child's bedroom; only 5 percent of all parents watch TV with their children aged 8 and older (Roberts et al. 2005).

For both adults and children, the entertainment context of television news and dramatic programming gives the medium tremendous potential for subtle influence and peripheral learning. By reducing awareness of manipulative intent on the part of the producers, dramatic series eliminate the defensive posture of audience members who might otherwise be put off by a message obviously intended to change their attitudes or behavior (Brehm and Brehm 1981). For decades, media critics have attributed real world violence and crime to the copious amount of violence viewed by people, particularly children, on television screens and computer monitors across the nation. The winter 2011 massacre in Tucson, Arizona, illustrated a new wrinkle in this manner of thought wherein the angry political rhetoric shown on television news was cast in the blameworthy role formerly reserved for dramatic film and television violence. Support for this particular proposition is inconsistent (Potter 1999), but the media certainly alter our perceptions of reality in myriad ways (Dill 2009). As our society becomes increasingly reliant on technological communication and mediated images, traditional distinctions meld together as never before. Baudrillard (1994) famously argued that today's media consumers are constantly beholden to simulations of reality (which he referred to as hyper-reality) wherein it is increasingly difficult to discern fantasy from reality. In the "infotainment" era where television news programs and cable networks compete for profits in exactly the same manner as dramatic fictional programming, the lines between fact and opinion, which formerly demarcated news from theater, have been similarly blurred.

This is not to say that all media consumers passively accept what they view on television or read in print and online news. However, people gain a great deal of their understanding of the world through various forms of storytelling rather than directly from experience. Such stories "socialize us into roles of gender, age, class, vocation, and lifestyle, and ... weave the seamless web of the cultural environment that cultivates most of what we think, what we do, and how we conduct our affairs" (Gerbner 2002, 485). Nowhere is this more the case than with crime stories. When the vast majority of the American populace has not had any direct experience with crime and will never become crime victims (Kappeler and Potter 2005; Muraskin and Domash 2007), media accounts do constitute "the principal vehicle by which the average person comes to know crime and justice" (Barak 1994, 3–4). Thus, stories about crime, and the manner in which perpetrators and victims are portrayed, are some of our most potent and influential renderings.

The Cultivation Hypothesis and Mean World Syndrome

Early on, George Gerbner and his associates articulated the cultivation hypothesis, according to which heavy exposure to media images functions in a powerful socializing capacity (Gerbner 1970; Gerbner et al. 1994). Therefore, the dramatized depictions on television and in the movies shape viewers' understanding of reality. Prolonged exposure to the mass media creates and cultivates attitudes which are less based in reality and more consistent with a false, media-conjured version of the world. One of the chief concerns of cultivation research was the impact of violent media imagery. Empirical research finds with relative consistency that while media violence may not directly correspond to real world violence, it often leads to increased aggression in the short term and desensitization and fear in the long term (Potter 1999).

The latter of these findings, often referred to as "the mean world syndrome" argues that a correlation exists between viewing lots of violent television and the increased fear of becoming a victim of violence (Gerbner 1970; Gerbner et al. 1994). Such viewers are unrealistically concerned about their own personal safety and about the prevalence of violent crime in society more generally.

Cultivating Bias in the Media

The mean world syndrome has become one of the main thrusts of cultivation analysis. However, the manner in which racial, gender, and class stereotypes are similarly cultivated by the media and how the promulgation of these stereotypes depicts a world that is not universally scary and mean, but rather frightening for some groups particularly fearful of the members of other groups, warrants further analysis and research. For example, because whites, females, children, and the elderly are disproportionately represented as victims in news stories (Beckett and Sasson 2000; Chermak 1995; Garofalo 1981; Mawby and Brown 1983), these groups may be particularly fearful about their personal safety (Glassner 1999). Likewise, the news media's depiction of African American males as criminals while ignoring their over-representation as the victims of crime and violence reinforces anti–Black stereotypes (Glassner 1999). Even the relative absence of certain groups in the mass media may have an impact as the relatively small number of female characters appearing in TV dramatic series may act as a symbolic indicator about their perceived lack of importance in society (Gerbner 1998).

Gerbner and Gross (1980) argued that the mass media have largely taken the place of religion and formal education in terms of influencing trends in our mores and folkways. As it has for decades, television remains the major source of our shared images of gender, race, ethnicity, age, and sexual orientation. Today, corporate media conglomerates consolidate national newspapers, wire services, cable news outlets, and Internet news aggregators to produce a convergence of opinion so that many of the same stereotypes are presented en masse to millions of Americans. Though the Internet provides potential for more critical perspectives to emerge from the new media environment, the global hegemony of the corporate media is hardly threatened by the alternative news bloggers and independent dramatists who may strive for less stereotypical and simplistic presentations of minority peoples and opinions.

Problematic Presentations

This volume presents the problem of mainstreaming negative group images in a manner which hopefully will direct more attention to the problematic media representations of gender, race, sexual orientation, and age. Based on the research conducted by the authors in this volume, we have categorized the findings as (1) presenting stereotypical and simplistic portrayals, (2) assigning vulnerable individuals to villainous roles, (3) blaming the victim, (4) encouraging punitive attitudes towards minorities, and (5) discouraging achievement.

Presenting Stereotypical and Simplistic Portrayals

The mass media often frame their messages with images that are recognizable to heterogeneous mass audiences. Such images can have harmful effects on the groups they characterize in oversimplified ways. Gender stereotypes abound. Bissler and Conners found that *CSI* episodes consistently depict male and female characters in traditional gender roles. Whiteley showcased the manner in which female homicide offenders were simplistically cast as purely evil by the media and ignored the multifaceted causes of female homicidal violence. Hepner-Williamson's research found that the largest portion of female sex offenders in her sample consisted of single women who preyed on their own female children or acquaintances. In stark contrast, newspaper accounts most typically depicted female sex offenders as married teachers who have consensual sexual relationships with their male students. Knop examined whether newspaper articles and TV and radio reports used gender-specific or gender-neutral words in describing school shooters. This research revealed that a gender-neutral discourse is generally used rather than one which recognizes the fact that the vast majority of school shootings are committed by boys. Waldron and Chambers concluded that HBO's police drama *The Wire*, which features a predominantly African American cast of characters, reinforces "hegemonic masculine" stereotypes including the tough white police officer and the violent black criminal. Roach found that methamphetamine and its users were discussed by newspaper reporters with sensational rhetoric which exaggerated the extent and danger of the problem. In particular, news accounts often framed their discussions of methamphetamine as a harm towards children, as a threat associated with other activities already popularly demonized, and as a social problem akin to an epidemic or a plague. The methamphetamine users themselves were portrayed as uncontrollable and violent.

Assigning Vulnerable Individuals to Villainous Roles

Not only do simplistic stereotypes pervade the media, but media villainy is distributed unevenly across lines of race, gender and sexual orientation. Whiteley showcased the manner in which the media describe female homicide offenders as evil, though many of them suffer from mental illness or were themselves victims of crime. Guittar similarly reported that television crime dramas frequently depict LGBT characters as villains—frequently as killers who murder former lovers in acts of vengeance.

Blaming the Victim

Vulnerable groups are too frequently depicted by the mass media as responsible for their victimization. Eliasson-Nannini and Sommerlad-Rogers found that older, male, and minority victims of serial murder are less likely to receive sympathetic newspaper coverage. Garcia concluded that *The New York Times* perpetuates numerous rape myths in their coverage of female sexual assault victims. Specifically, women who do not conform to various gender norms are more frequently deemed complicit in their victimization. In her analysis, Foss suggested that victims depicted in episodes of *CSI*, by virtue of their characteristics and lifestyle, share responsibility for their own misfortune. Such characterizations in which victims are depicted as experiencing risky lifestyles might serve to deter individuals in society from taking unnecessary risks, causing them less frequently to be in harm's way. Yet the same characterizations also give the idea that victims who are underrepresented in society — e.g., gays, women, people of color, and people with disabilities— deserve their fate and therefore are unworthy of the sympathy or support that members of the dominant group can expect to receive.

Encouraging Punitive Attitudes towards Minorities

While victim blaming may be one way to diminish sympathy for underrepresented groups, the media may encourage punitive attitudes towards minorities in numerous ways. Simmons' analysis of crime dramas suggested that the pejorative characterizations of vulnerable populations such as African Americans may encourage the tendency of audience members to support punitive measures against an entire group of people based on race. Similarly, Rizun pointed out that television could support and encourage a compassionate portrayal that addresses the actual basis for women's unlawful behavior. Instead, TV crime dramas such as *CSI: Miami* present women in trouble with the law as either supermodels or as economically privileged members of the community whose crimes are violent and irrational. Based on their media portrayal, women are either mentally ill, evil, or both. The overall impression that results from such characterizations is to treat all women who break the law and engage in criminal activity as deserving of harsh treatment.

Discouraging Achievement

Media images may inadvertently contribute to discriminatory behavior and discourage the achievement of minority groups. Bissler and Conners argued that crime dramas such as *CSI* give the unmistakable impression that working women are judged by their looks rather than their competence on the job. This portrayal may have the effect of discouraging women from using their intellectual ability in order to secure a raise, a promotion, or even a skilled position within a company. Similarly, employers may come to focus so much on attractiveness that they fail to recognize the competence of their female workers.

Promising Findings for Challenging Stereotypes through the Media

Not all of the results presented in this book should be regarded as supportive of stereotypic portrayals. In some cases, investigators reported the presence of both stereotypic as well as anti-stereotypic findings.

Guittar's study of television crime dramas, for example, indicated a recent increase overall in the coverage of LGBT issues and a strong tendency to avoid blaming gay and lesbian hate crime victims for the violence perpetrated against them. Waldron and Chambers found certain episodes of *The Wire*, in which race, sexuality, and masculinity are depicted not stereotypically but in a wide-ranging and complex manner. According to Rizun, certain motion pictures and television programs have recently introduced more positive and accurate images of women, in part because of the presence of some fair-minded and competent female directors and writers.

The potential for positive media influence can also be seen in newspaper reporting. Eliasson-Nannini and Sommerlad-Rogers found that a serial killer victim's sexual orientation, arrest history, drug use history and socioeconomic status have no impact on the type of newspaper coverage given them. Kontos found that media coverage that depicted New York City gang members as potentially violent but peaceful by choice actually served to empower progressive elements within the group at the expense of their reactionary and more dangerous counterparts.

Conclusion

Women, Asians, Latinos, and other disadvantaged groups continue to be under-represented and stereotyped when it comes to their media depictions.

These groups might take a lesson from the experience of African Americans who, with the exception of a few highly stereotypic roles such as *Amos and Andy*, were almost non-existent as characters in television programs and commercials of the 1950s. As African Americans became regarded more and more as a viable consumer market for goods and services (not to mention their effective lobbying), however, they assumed an increasingly more prominent and positive position in the corporate-based mass media (Gerbner, 1998).

Since the 1990s, African Americans have actually been over-represented in prime-time TV programs relative to their representation (12 percent) in the population of the United States (Gerbner, 1998). Numerous prime-time dramatic series, talk shows, and situation comedies now feature African Americans. On highly rated crime dramas, for example, one can view LL Cool J and Rocky Carroll on *NCIS* and Laurence Fishburne on *CSI*, not to mention Oprah Winfrey hosting two shows on her own network, Randy Jackson on *American Idol*, Lester Holt on the *Weekend Today Show*, Juan Williams on *Fox News Sunday*, Wendy Williams on the *Wendy Williams Show*, Robin Roberts on *Good Morning America*, Al Roker on *Today*, Steve Harvey on *Family Feud*, and Whoopi Goldberg and Sherri Shepherd on *The View*. As indicated by several authors in this volume, stereotypic portrayals of African Americans can still be found, but even more promising are the large numbers of black men and women who serve as experts in psychology, politics, meteorology, medicine, finance, legal matters, and the like for national talk shows and cable news networks.

Overall, African American television experts may still be under-represented, but their presence on so many programs and on such a wide range of topics would have been unthinkable a few decades earlier. Now, it is a reality — one that hopefully will continue to improve both quantitatively and qualitatively and be repeated for the many groups in our society whose members continue to be vastly under-represented or characterized pejoratively in popular culture. The ubiquitous presence of cable TV channels as well as the Internet has made possible a trend toward not-so-mass media characterizations that emphasize heterogeneity as much as uniformity. High-tech alternatives may, in the future, hold promise for more accurate, less stereotypical, characterizations of vulnerable groups in our society.

In a capitalist society, the boycott has tremendous potential for persuading commercial media interests to enhance their depiction of under-represented groups. For decades, Don Imus was a talk show host who could be counted on to espouse racial, gender, and homophobic stereotypes daily on his popular radio and television program. In April 2007, however, the so-called "I Man" went too far. He referred to the players on the Rutgers University women's basketball team, which consisted of eight African Americans and two whites, as "nappy headed hos." Days later, bowing to pressure from black leaders and employees as well as numerous important advertisers who withdrew their support, Imus was fired on both radio (WFAN) and television (MSNBC). By

November 2007, however, he was back on the air — this time, with WABC in New York City and RFD-TV. In September of 2008, the television version of "Imus in the Morning" moved from a relatively obscure cable TV outlet to the Fox Business Channel and was a fixture on some 100 radio stations around the country. Don Imus had come all the way back.

At the same time, Imus had become quite different in his approach to race and gender. For the first time, a black comedian became a regular on his show. For the first time, he interviewed activist black leaders like Dick Gregory and Jesse Jackson. For the first time, he (and his on-air staff) eliminated racist remarks or jokes from the script or their spontaneous remarks (Faber 2007).

According to Kappeler and Potter (2005), it is far easier to generate problematic crime myths than it is to debunk them. The same might be said for responding to stereotypic group images generally, whether or not crime is involved. From this perspective, a more representative media would not necessarily lead to a more just and equal world. For example, black middle-class situation comedies from the 1980s like the *Cosby Show* may have been helpful in fighting racist stereotypes, and more recent series like *The Wire* may allow for a more complex understanding of minorities. Yet, it may be a stretch to suggest that more accurate or positive representations in crime media would necessarily translate into a more just and equitable world. Many structural impediments remain even when cultural biases and misconceptions are diminished. We should work to change media images, but we should also work hard to change society.

References

Barak, Greg. 1994. *Media, Process, and the Social Construction of Crime: Studies in Newsmaking Criminology*. New York: Garland.

Baudrillard, Jean. 1994 [1981]. *Simulacra and Simulation*. Trans. Sheila Faria Glaser. Ann Arbor: University of Michigan Press.

Beckett, Katherine, and Theodore Sasson. 2000. *The Politics of Injustice*. Thousand Oaks, CA: Pine Forge Press.

Brehm, Sharon. S., and Jack W. Brehm. 1981. *Psychological Reactance: A Theory of Freedom and Control*. New York: Academic Press.

Bureau of Labor Statistics. 2010. "American Time Use Survey Summary." Accessed Feb. 6, 2011. *http://www.bls.gov/news.release/atus.nr0.htm*.

Chermak, Steven M. 1995. *Victims in the News: Crime in American News Media*. Boulder, CO: Westview.

Dill, Karen E. 2009. *How Fantasy Becomes Reality: Seeing Through Media Influence*. New York: Oxford University Press.

Faber, Judy. 2007, April 12. "CBS Fires Don Imus Over Racial Slur." CBS News. Accessed February 25, 2011. *http://www.cbsnews.com/stories/2007/04/12/national/main2675273.shtml*.

Gandossy, Taylor. 2009, Feb. 24. "TV Viewing At 'All-Time High,' Nielsen Says." *www.cnn.com* Accessed Feb 6, 2011. *http://articles.cnn.com/2009-02-24/entertainment/us.video.nielsen_1_nielsen-company-nielsen-spokesman-gary-holmes-watching?_s=PM:SHOWBIZ*.

Garafalo, James. 1981. "Crime and the Mass Media: A Selective Review of Research." *Journal of Research in Crime and Delinquency* 18(2): 319–50.

Gerbner, George. 1970. "Cultural Indicators: The Case of Violence in Television Drama." *The Annals of the American Academy of Political and Social Science* 388: 69–81.

_____. 1998. "Casting the American Scene: A look at the Characters on Prime Time and Daytime Television from 1994–1997." *Screen Actors Guild Report*.

_____. 2002. *Against the Mainstream: The Selected Works of George Gerbner*. Edited by Michael Morgan. New York: Peter Lang.

Gerbner, George, and Larry Gross. 1980. "The Violent Face of Television and Its Lessons." In Edward L. Palmer and Aimee Dorr (eds.), *Children and the Faces of Television: Teaching, Violence, Selling*: 149–162. New York: Academic Press.

Gerbner, George, Larry Gross, Michael Morgan, and Nancy Signorielli. 1994. "Growing Up with Television: The Cultivation Perspective." In J. Bryant and D. Zillman (eds.), *Media Effects: Advances in Theory and Research*: 17–42. Hillsdale, NJ: Lawrence Erlbaum.

Glassner, Barry. 1999. *The Culture of Fear*. New York: Basic Books.

Kappeler, Victor E., and Gary W. Potter. 2005. *The Mythology of Crime and Criminal Justice, Fourth Edition*. Long Grove, IL: Waveland Press.

Mawby, R. I., and J. Brown. 1983. "Newspaper Images of the Victim." *Victimology* 9(1): 82–94.

Muraskin, Roslyn, and Shelly Feuer Domash. 2007. *Crime and the Media: Headlines vs. Reality*. Upper Saddle River, NJ: Prentice Hall.

Nielsen, Inc. 2010. "Snapshot of Television Us in the U.S." Accessed Feb. 6, 2011. *http://blog.nielsen.com/nielsenwire/wp-content/uploads/2010/09/Nielsen-State-of-TV-09232010.pdf*.

Pew Research Center for People and the Press. 2011. "Internet Gains on Television as Public's Main News Source," Accessed Feb 17, 2011. *http://pewresearch.org/pubs/1844/poll-main-source-national-international-news-internet-tel*.

Potter, James W. 1999. *On Media Violence*. Thousand Oaks, CA: Sage Publications.

Purcell, Kristin, Lee Rainie, Amy Mitchell, Tom Rosenstiel, and Kenny Olmstead. 2010. "Understanding the Participatory News Consumer: How Internet and Cell Phone Users Have Turned News into a Social Experience." Pew Internet and American Life Project. Accessed Feb 6, 2011. *http://pewinternet.org/~/media//Files/Reports/2010/PIP_Understanding_the_Participatory_News_Consumer.pdf*.

Roberts, Donald F., Ulla G. Foehr, and Victoria Rideout. 2005. "Generation M: Media in the lives of 8–18-year olds." Henry J. Kaiser Family Foundation. Menlo Park, CA.

About the Contributors

Denise L. **Bissler** is an associate professor at Randolph-Macon College. She received her Ph.D. in sociology from North Carolina State University with specializations in criminology and inequality. Her research interests are incarcerated juveniles, crime and the media and the scholarship of teaching and learning; some of this work is published in *Teaching Sociology*; *Innovative Techniques for Teaching Sociological Concepts* and *Free Inquiry of Creative Sociology*.

Cheryl **Chambers** is an assistant professor at Christopher Newport University. She received her Ph.D. in sociology from North Carolina State University with specializations in inequality and crime and social control and an MCJ from the College of Criminal Justice at the University of South Carolina. She is the author of *Drug Laws and Institutional Racism* and she has published in *Police Practice & Research* and *Contemporary Sociology*.

Joan L. **Conners** is an associate professor of communication studies at Randolph-Macon College. Her research involves representations in reality television, campaign communication of U.S. Senate elections, and portrayals in political cartoons. Her work has been published in *American Behavioral Scientist*, *PS: Political Science and Politics*, and *Harvard International Journal of Press and Politics*. She received her Ph.D. in mass communication from the University of Minnesota.

Katherine **Foss** is an assistant professor in the School of Journalism at Middle Tennessee State University, where she teaches courses on media and culture, television, and health communication. Her research interests include representations of victimization, disability, and health responsibility, with publications in *Book History, Communication Quarterly, Women & Health*, and *Disability Studies Quarterly*, among others. She earned her Ph.D. in mass communication from the University of Minnesota in 2008.

Bridget A. **Hepner-Williamson** is completing her Ph.D. in criminal justice at Sam Houston State University. She has collaborated on research dealing with characteristics of female sex offenders, intelligence-led policing, and training on the use of discretion with apprehended youth. Her work has been published in *The Journal of the Institute of Justice & International Studies* and has been presented at conferences of the American Society of Criminology and the Academy of Criminal Justice Sciences.

Venessa **Garcia** is an assistant professor of criminal justice at Kean University. She has over 20 academic and professional publications in the areas of gender and policing, violence against women, and media images of female victims. In 2005, she won the New Scholar of the Year award from the Division of Women and Crime of American Society of Criminology.

Nicholas **Guittar** is an assistant professor of sociology at the University of South Carolina–Lancaster. He earned his Ph.D. in sociology from the University of Central Florida with a specialization in social inequalities. His research interests include LGBT studies, sexual identities, hate crimes, and the intersection of gender and sexuality.

Victor E. **Kappeler** is a foundation professor and chair of the Department of Criminal Justice at Eastern Kentucky University. His textbooks are commonly used by leading universities worldwide and he is recognized as a leading scholar in policing, media and the social construction of crime, and police civil liability, among other topics.

Brian **Knop** recently obtained his M.A. in sociology from the University of Mississippi. His master's thesis was a qualitative analysis of gender and sexuality at sorority and fraternity parties and in the broader Greek system in order to better understand hooking up and rape culture. He is a graduate student in the Department of Sociology at Florida State University. His research interests include masculinities, sexualities, work and organizations, media, and social problems.

Louis **Kontos** teaches at John Jay College of Criminal Justice. He has written extensively on the topic of gangs, as well as media and public opinion. His current projects include gang research, prison research, a book on violence and another dealing with the politics of social control.

Jack **Levin** is the Irving and Betty Brudnick Professor of Sociology and Criminology and co-director of the Brudnick Center on Violence and Conflict at Northeastern University. He has published 30 books and numerous journal articles and newspaper columns, primarily on hate crimes, prejudice, serial and mass murder, and school violence.

Eric **Madfis** is a doctoral candidate in the Sociology and Anthropology Department at Northeastern University, where he has been a research associate at the Brudnick Center on Violence and Conflict and teaches courses in juvenile delinquency and the sociology of violence. His research interests are in critical criminology, youth subculture and counterculture, juvenile delinquency, interpersonal violence, and crime and popular culture. In fall of 2012 he will be an Assistant Proofessor of Criminal Justice at the University of Washington, Tacoma.

Janelle M. **Eliasson-Nannini** is a sociology graduate student at Bowling Green State University where she is specializing in the areas of criminology and demography. Her research interests include the social construction of serial homicide victims through print media, delinquency, and schools.

Gary W. **Potter** is a professor of criminal justice at Eastern Kentucky University. His primary areas of scholarship are the social construction of crime and the organization of illicit markets. He has authored or co-authored several books as well as numerous articles published in scholarly journals.

Sarah **Rizun** is a graduate student in criminology at Simon Fraser University, conducting an original research project on the reintegration experiences of federally-sentenced women. Her main research interests are the criminalization of women and social justice issues. She also works as a with women in prison as an advocate for human rights.

Teresa **Roach**, M.S., is a doctoral student in sociology at Florida State University. Her academic and research interests include understanding the reproduction of inequality in society with specific attention to gender, sexuality, and substance use and misuse through the use of qualitative methods.

Alicia D. **Simmons** is an assistant professor of sociology at Colgate University. Her primary research interests focus on the relationship between the American news media and public opinion. Her work explores how exposure to crime news influences audience members' racial attitudes and criminal justice policy preferences.

Deirdre **Sommerlad-Rogers** is an assistant professor of Sociology and Criminal Justice at Greensboro College. Her areas of research include victimization, social inequalities, corrections, and corporate power.

Linda **Waldron** is an associate professor of sociology at Christopher Newport University. She completed her Ph.D. at Syracuse University with the support of an American Fellowship from the American Association of University Women. She is a qualitative researcher, specializing in youth, education and school violence, race-class-gender inequalities and the media. Her research has been published in several scholarly journals.

Kate **Whiteley** is an assistant professor in the criminal justice program at York College of Pennsylvania. She is examining the records and database of female sex offenders within Pennsylvania, which will initially generate a descriptive study of female sex offenders and later develop screening instruments that predict risks of reoffending that are gender-specific to females.

Index

acquaintance rape 18–19, 23–24, 27, 29, 34; *see also* date rape
agent of social control 74
Almighty Latin King and Queen Nation (ALKQN) 111–116, 119–125
anti-drug crusades 74
Associated Press 49, 69, 85
at risk 151, 162–164, 167

Boston Globe 56, 65, 67–69, 71
broken windows 116–117
bullying 55, 57–58, 215
Bureau of Justice Statistics 78, 92, 97, 151, 227
Bureau of Labor Statistics 239

Central Park Jogger 24, 32–34
character development 129, 148, 217
code of the street 182, 185, 187–188
Columbine 55–56
Condom Rape Case 24, 32
constructed 33, 40, 46–48, 54, 67, 72, 75, 87, 124, 135, 175, 178–179, 181, 184–185, 188, 193–194, 196, 203, 209
content analysis 41–43, 56, 67–68, 81, 98, 129, 176, 191, 195, 210, 212
corner boys 171, 173, 175, 177–181, 183, 185–187
corroboration 18, 22, 24, 26, 33, 35
crime control 202, 204, 206, 229, 235–236
crime dramas 156, 158, 168, 171, 190–191, 199, 204–205, 208–213, 215–218, 220–222, 243–245
criminal justice 18–20, 26, 32, 36, 39, 78, 81, 87, 99, 116, 191, 200, 202, 224–228, 230–231, 233, 235–236, 249–251
CSI 127, 129–130, 132–137, 139–148, 151–152, 156–166, 168, 173, 190–191, 195–205, 208, 221, 236, 242–245
cultivation 240–241; effect 155; hypothesis 240; perspective 167; theory 154, 209
culture 18–19, 23, 25–27, 29, 34, 47, 65, 100–101, 130, 137, 140, 143–144, 146–148, 167, 177, 187, 196, 226, 240, 246

Daily News 34, 56, 117, 119, 225, 227–229, 231–232, 234–236
date rape 18–19, 23, 28–30; *see also* acquaintance rape

death penalty 225, 228–234
dehumanization 160, 167
demographics 43, 45–46, 79, 81, 83, 98, 154, 195, 198, 212, 224, 231
disabilities 151–152, 154–155, 159–160, 164, 167–168, 243, 249
discrimination 40, 49, 155, 172; discriminatory 86, 148, 244
diversity 130, 143–144, 146–148, 160, 197, 215
doing gender 20, 31, 33
dominant group 155–156, 167, 174, 243
Drug Abuse Warning Network 66

emotional reaction 70, 74, 135, 145
entertainment 23, 35, 38, 175, 190, 192–193, 195, 199, 203–205, 208–209, 211, 213, 220–222, 239–240
episodic reporting 226, 229, 234–235
ethnographics 112, 176

fear 38, 41, 48, 54, 67, 72–73, 88, 98, 115, 118–119, 127, 138, 155, 160, 164, 167–168, 181, 185, 194, 241
federal spending 225, 228–234
female offenders 86, 92, 94, 98–100, 191–192, 195, 197, 200, 202
femininity 91, 94–95, 97, 100–104, 106, 134, 136
feminism 21–22, 24, 49, 91–94, 96, 101, 134, 136, 153, 201
filicide 91, 93, 97, 100
forensic journalism 29, 30, 34
framing 27, 39–41, 46–47, 53, 54, 55, 57–62, 68, 71–72, 74, 97, 100, 102, 153, 165, 166, 172, 211, 213, 215, 216, 219–221, 242

gang 32, 71, 111, 113–117, 120–123, 125, 161, 171–172, 175–177, 182–187, 244, 250; gang violence 121, 123
gender 56–60, 62, 94, 98, 130, 176, 192–194, 200–201, 205
gender-neutral 53–55, 57–61, 242
gender roles 18, 21, 87, 94, 127–128, 130, 146, 242
gender-specific frame 53–55, 57–62, 242, 251
gendered language 59
generalizability 75, 80, 88
grounded theory 69, 176

gun control 54

harm 26, 69–70, 72, 74–75, 79, 85–87, 99, 179, 184, 222, 236, 242–243
hate crime 151, 208–210, 212–222, 250
Hate Crime Statistics Act of 1990 214
headlines 27–28, 64, 70, 72, 78, 87, 95–96, 103, 111, 118, 125, 208, 213, 215
hegemony 128, 131, 133, 139, 155, 177–178, 180–182, 202, 242
hierarchy 177, 179, 183
homophobia 55
hypermasculinity 128, 174, 175; *see also* masculine
hypotheses 227–229, 232, 234

ideal male 131
ideal victim 20, 24, 32–33, 49
implications 56, 166, 180, 191, 200, 202, 226
incarceration 33, 79, 81–85, 87–88, 94–95, 100, 103, 249
inequality 101, 127, 129, 146–147, 152, 164, 174, 201, 236, 249–251
infanticide 93–94, 100, 106
infotainment 240
insanity 101–102
institutionalization 47, 65, 178
intercoder reliability 43, 176

Jack the Ripper 39, 41
jury 22, 26, 28–29, 32, 48, 78, 88, 153

King Blood 113–115, 121, 124–125
King Tone 113–115, 118–122, 124–125
Kingism 113–114, 120, 122
Kobe Bryant case 23, 34, 155, 159

law enforcement 40, 48, 64, 67, 69, 79, 114, 134, 138, 148
LexisNexis 42, 56, 82
LGBT 210–211, 213–216, 219–222, 243–244, 250
liberation hypothesis 192, 193, 199; theology 115
logistic regression 43, 45, 49–50, 232–233
Los Angeles Times 64–65, 67–73

macro 154–155, 167, 221
mainstream media 53–54, 58, 61–62, 96, 113, 116–117, 122–123, 125
male domination 130, 132–134, 138, 144, 196, 198, 205
male privilege 55
marginalization 67, 99, 101–103, 105, 156, 161, 167, 174, 177, 191–193, 200, 203, 209–210
masculinity 55, 61, 96–97, 100, 105, 131–133, 139–141, 144, 145, 171–172, 174–178, 180–182, 185–188, 191, 194, 218–219, 242, 244; *see also* hypermasculinity
mass media 40, 66, 74, 190–191, 193, 209, 241–243, 245

media coverage 18–19, 21–28, 32, 38–40, 46, 49, 53–56, 58, 61–62, 64, 67, 70, 72–75, 78–80, 82–85, 87–88, 96–98, 100, 103, 105, 111–112, 114–117, 120–122, 125, 153–155, 191–194, 196–198, 200–203, 205–206, 224–225, 227–232, 240, 242, 244
mediated messages 188, 236, 240
mental health 31, 34, 54, 55, 59, 80–81, 83–84, 88, 93–94, 96, 99, 101, 104–105, 152, 243
methamphetamine 64–75, 242
miniseries 19, 23–24, 27–34
misogyny 137, 194, 201
misrepresentations 95, 103
moral panic 39–41, 46–49, 54, 187

narrative 48, 91, 95, 98–102, 104–105, 114, 117, 125, 146, 156
National Crime Victimization 78
National Incident Based Reporting System 78
National Institute on Drug Abuse 66
National Survey on Drug Use and Health 66
neutral coverage 47
New Bedford Rape Case 24
New York Times 19, 22, 24–25, 27–34, 56, 98, 112, 117, 119, 235, 243
news media 23, 29, 38, 40–41, 53–54, 58, 64–65, 70, 72–75, 91, 95–96, 98, 152, 204, 208, 213, 215, 217, 224–232, 236, 241, 242, 251; *see also* newspaper coverage
newspaper coverage 72–73, 82, 87, 242; *see also* news media

objectification 128, 136, 144
Operation Crown 124–125

pathology 91, 93, 97, 104, 193
patriarchy 195, 202
perjury 29, 118
perpetuation 26, 127–128, 130, 132–134, 136–138, 140, 142, 144–145, 147–148, 155, 157, 163–164, 167–168, 243
police brutality 117–119, 179
police harassment 111, 116
policy 48, 64, 67, 79, 116, 202, 204–205, 229, 251
politics 18, 21, 23, 26, 40, 64, 111–113, 116–118, 121–122, 125, 153, 168, 171, 174, 181, 202, 224, 230, 231, 233, 236, 240, 249
popular culture 38, 47, 154, 193, 196, 245
poverty 75, 173–174, 188, 202, 204
power 18, 21, 25, 33, 81, 121, 128, 132, 138, 145, 151, 152, 164, 168, 174, 177–179, 181, 184, 193, 202, 210, 241, 251
prejudice 18, 32, 146, 148, 155, 191, 203, 250
primetime television 208
public opinion 18, 38, 67, 112, 118, 129, 154–155, 190–191, 200–204, 224, 227–228, 235–236, 250–251
public relations 112, 121, 123

racism 32–33, 40, 72, 98–99, 143, 146, 172, 174, 182, 204, 249
rampage school shootings 53, 56, 61
rape law reform 18–19, 21–27, 33–35
rape myths 19–22, 25–26, 28–31, 33–34, 243
recidivism 81, 86
Rideout Rape 23
Routine Activity Theory 153–154, 158, 167

sample 40–41, 43–44, 46, 56, 68–71, 73, 75, 80–84, 87–88, 98, 175, 211–213, 215, 218, 220–221, 225, 230–232, 242
school violence 53–63, 242, 250–251
self defense 96, 104, 173
sensational 24, 38–41, 47, 49, 69–75, 87, 96–97, 102–103, 105, 111, 127, 193, 194, 202, 204, 209, 225, 242
sentencing 22, 33–34, 86, 103
serial murder 38–49, 91, 243, 250
sex offenses 19, 78–88, 242, 249, 251
sexual abuse 78, 80, 83, 85
sexual assault 18–22, 30, 33, 35, 78, 81, 83, 85–86, 88, 155, 157, 159, 164–165, 167, 243
sexual harassment 134–136, 138, 144
sexual orientation 46, 208–210, 212–222, 241–244
shared responsibility 34, 151–153, 157, 167
social constructs 19, 20, 23, 25, 27, 38–40, 46–47, 64, 66–67, 73–75, 91, 97, 100–101, 105, 172, 188, 209, 250
social justice 203–204, 250
social problem 47, 55, 69, 71–75, 145, 173–174, 204, 214, 222, 228, 242, 250
socialization 94, 98, 127, 187
socioeconomic status 46, 197, 205, 244

soldiers 171, 177, 182–183, 185–188
stereotyping 24, 29, 40, 87, 94, 98–99, 125, 127–137, 139–141, 144–148, 155–156, 160–161, 164, 168, 174, 181, 182, 191–192, 194, 204–205, 213–214, 219, 222, 226, 231, 233, 241–246
stigmatization 67, 72
stranger rape 18, 19, 23, 24, 30, 32
subordination 128–129, 132–133, 140, 155, 177
sympathetic coverage 39–40, 43, 44–47, 49, 243

tabloidization 38
thematic reporting 226, 235–236
theory 39–40, 46, 47, 69, 87, 93–94, 116, 152–154, 158, 167, 176–177, 198, 209
typologies 80, 128, 152–153

Uniform Crime Report 78, 173, 216–218

victim blaming 19–20, 23–24, 27, 32, 34, 153, 243
victim facilitation 19, 154, 158–159
victimology 40, 84, 152, 154, 166
Virginia Tech 53–54, 56P
visual imagery 163
vulnerability 29, 70, 87, 116, 124, 152, 154, 158–164, 166, 242–243, 245

Washington Post 56
The Wire 171–177, 179, 183, 185, 187–188, 242, 244, 246
women's movement 18, 24, 174, 192, 198, 201